Speculation, Hedging and Commodity Price Forecasts

Speculation, Hedging and Commodity Price Forecasts

Walter C. Labys
Geneva

C. W. J. Granger
University of Nottingham

Heath Lexington Books
D. C. Heath and Company
Lexington, Massachusetts

Third printing November, 1973.

Published simultaneously in Canada.

Printed in the United States of America.

International Standard Book Number: 0-669-61051-8

Library of Congress Catalog Card Number: 72-121406

To Our Parents

Table of Contents

List of Tables

List of Figures

Figure

Preface

We feel that no apology is necessary for an empirical study of commodity prices at this time. Commodity price fluctuations are currently of great concern to economists and politicians of national and international agencies throughout the world. There have also been developed in recent years a number of powerful methods for analyzing and forecasting time series, examples being spectral analysis, stepwise regression procedures, and exponentially weighted moving averages. The present work is based on the recognition that it should be valuable to apply this battery of techniques to the study of the important problems, both practical and theoretical, associated with cash and future commodity prices.

Work commenced on the study at the University of Nottingham in early 1966, with the investigation of the basic patterns underlying a substantial number of commodity price series. We had no sooner begun, than Unilever became interested in our work. This resulted in a mutual research project into possible determinants and models of price behavior which lasted well into the summer of 1967. Other groups also became interested, particularly in the application of such models to forecasting. Consequently, we conducted a survey of forecasting techniques in a number of (UK) commodity firms including brokerage houses such as Bache and Co. and Gill and Duffus as well as commodity purchasers such as Cadbury's Ltd. and Associated British Foods.

Immersing ourselves in these practical research problems provided a degree of realism with which to attack the more theoretical statistical and econometric problems of analysis. Although the spectral and cross-spectral techniques applied here are now commonplace to the econometrician, the more advanced of these techniques, including partial and multiple cross-spectra, undergo the test of empirical application for the first time. An attempt was also made to advance the interpretation of stepwise regression methods. Many of the results reported here indicate the failure of classical regression criteria for fitting stepwise equations, and we offer suggestions for evaluating the consequent specification error.

Thus, the present study can be considered a joining of statistical and econometric theory with commodity price theory and forecasting. The book integrates this material chapter by chapter, moving from theory to practice and from price explanation to price forecasting. In the early chapters, the basic economics of commodity price theory is presented, along with the theoretical development of spectral and stepwise methods. The middle chapters concentrate on the development of a model suitable for explaining price fluctuations. This required both identifying the generating processes underlying the price fluctuations and discovering which determinants serve best to explain these fluctuations. In the final chapters, we analyze the forecast performance of the model by comparing its forecasts to those of other forecast methods. The conclusion evaluates the usefulness of our research, and chapter appendixes have been added to evaluate the statistical developments not previously tested.

We hope that the study will be of interest to a wide audience including econometricians, price theoreticians, graduate students, commodity economists, and commodity enthusiasts. *Econometricians* and *statisticians* may find something of value in the testing and evaluation of the newer spectral methods as well as the suggestions offered for fitting stepwise regression models. *Price theoreticians* should appreciate the empirical comparisons of the different price models, most of which have never been compared directly in a single study. *Commodity economists* also might make immediate use of the price models, including particularly the substantive results with respect to fats and oils. It is not known whether *commodity enthusiasts* will want to trade on the basis of our forecast findings, but at least they might want to reexamine their trading techniques in view of the findings regarding random walk. Lastly, it is hoped that *graduate students* and other *research workers* will find new results and techniques to employ in their own efforts.

To acknowledge all of the help given to us is, as always, a difficult task. Perhaps we can begin by offering a setting for the study. The Economics Department at the University of Nottingham contained a number of graduate students and junior and senior faculty members, all of whom were interested in time series analysis, forecasting or basic price research. Because of this we were able to draw on our colleagues for specialized help. Brian Tew helped with some of the theoretical economic problems. André Gabor and John Bates contributed to our understanding of more practical problems; Tony Hughes and Hedley Rees constructed for us the simple, partial, and multiple cross-spectral programs. John Payne and David Reid both developed specialized time series analysis programs for use in their Ph.D. research, and these were placed at our disposal. The first program represented an application of the stepwise algorithm strictly to time series data while the second tested the predictability of exponential smoothing and Box-Jenkins forecast methods. All of these individuals have also helped either in discussion or in reading various drafts of the chapters.

Many others also contributed their time and efforts. We thank Brian Tew for his putting the facilities and support of the Economics Department to our use. Members of the Unilever staff to whom we are indebted include Sidney Gould, Arthur Lysons, and Practip Chatterjee. Ronald Callander of the Commodity Exchange Authority (U.S.D.A.) and Walter Borg of the Consumer and Marketing Service (U.S.D.A.) kindly supplied many of the data series. Several other persons helped to give our findings a public hearing: Professor J. D. Sargan at the London School of Economics, Professor Britten for the Home Grown Cereals Authority (UK), and Professor J. C. Gilbert for the Northern Economists Association (UK). Since a substantial portion of the study was developed as a Ph.D. thesis, Professor R. G. Lipsey is to be thanked for reading that portion and offering corrections. Professor Paul Cootner and others were kind enough to read and offer comments on the book. Our wives, Jane and Patricia, also helped greatly in the effort, offering encouragement, helping with details, and typing. Lastly, if environment can be thanked for its stimulation of ideas, this book was worked on in Nottingham, England; Cambridge, Massachusetts; Princeton, New Jersey; Tuebingen, Germany; Ravello, Italy; Mykonos, Greece; Paris, France; and was finally completed in Geneva, Switzerland and San Diego, California.

We would like to emphasize that the views and opinions expressed in the book are ours alone and that we take full responsibility for what is recorded here.

The study was supported largely through the help of the Department of Economics at the University of Nottingham. Unilever Ltd. also helped considerably, giving particular support to the joint research venture. All computations were performed by the Cripps Computer Center, Nottingham University, and the Atlas Computing Service, Manchester University.

Miss Yvonne Rogers and Miss Martha Reardon are to be thanked for help in typing the manuscript and Mrs. Anne Widdowson for drawing many of the graphs.

W. C. Labys
C. W. J. Granger

Speculation, Hedging and Commodity Price Forecasts

1 Introduction

The Problem Defined

It is well known that commodity prices fluctuate widely, frequently, and in a manner altogether unstable when compared to the more regular price movements of manufactured goods. Consider the experience of sugar. The New York price was 3.2 cents per pound in May 1961, 2.0 cents in January 1962, 4.5 cents in December 1962, 12 cents in May 1963, 6.0 cents in August 1963, 7 cents in May 1964, and 3.6 cents in October 1964.[1] Similarly, the price of Ghana cocoa was 28.1 cents per pound in November 1960, 20.6 cents in March 1961, 26.2 cents in December 1961, and 20.1 cents by February 1962. Cottonseed oil rose abruptly from 12.9 cents per pound in February 1966 to 16.6 cents in August 1966, and then returned to 12.8 cents by December of that year. The fluctuations in metal prices have been just as extreme, if not more so. The London price of copper wirebars was £417.0 per ton in June 1965. It then nearly doubled to £708.7 per ton in March 1966, returning to £406.5 by August of that year. Prices subsequently have varied from £460.5 in January 1967 and £353.2 in June 1967 to £590.5 in December 1967.

Economic consequences of these difficulties are just as dramatic. Lewis attributes the severity and prolongation of the Great Depression to the cyclical contraction of primary product prices.[2] Extreme price fluctuations just before 1929 as well as a long downward trend after 1929 have been cited as a principal reason for the shattered business confidence which prevented recovery until 1936. More recently, developing countries with an export income dependent on the productions of mainly one commodity have encountered difficulties. For these countries, fluctuations in the prices of the principal commodity cause variations in export earnings, the impact of which is curtailment of necessary economic growth. Local producers in these countries also suffer from price uncertainty. Mellor explains, for example, that farmers store crops only on the basis of the previous year's patterns of price fluctuations, largely because of their inability to understand causes of these fluctuations.[3] Reliance on such a naive storage policy causes fluctuations in their own income and, ironically, can induce even greater instability in the respective price series. More extensive evidence of these and other producer difficulties can be found in documents concerned with international commodity agreements.

One can also examine the economic consequences of price fluctuations from the viewpoint of commodity consumers. Here the difficult burden falls on more developed countries, where commodities are processed and used in manufacturing. The most noticeable effect of price fluctuations is in the upward swings where manufacturers cannot adjust final prices on their product line and are forced to absorb the higher costs of the commodity inputs. This problem was stressed by Lord Cole in his remarks to the 1966 General Meeting of Unilever, where he described the possible reaction of a manufacturer to a sudden rise in the price of commodity inputs.[4] While in most cases a manufacturer would maintain profits by raising the prices of his products, it frequently happens that such a decision would result in his customers' transferring to a competitor's product. The accompanying profit squeeze would most often lead to a reduction in the manufacturer's opportunities for capital renewal and expansion.

If some means could be devised for explaining and predicting these fluctuations, some of the unfavorable consequences might then be reduced or eliminated. Considerable time and effort have been devoted to this problem, but the difficulties encountered have made results sparse. The received-price theories tend to emphasize either the random or the regular aspect of price behavior. Those of the first group generally employ tests of the distribution or variance of price changes to show that prices follow a random walk. Theories in the latter group emphasize the presence of either price trends or cycles, mainly by observing the profit patterns which result from applying simple trading rules. Also to be included in this group are theories which conform to the conventional notion that price fluctuations adjust to changes in stocks or simultaneous changes in supply and demand. Although most of these theories are adequately structured, they remain insufficient; either they have not been tested empirically or they have been tested with different commodities and over different time periods.

The purpose of this study, therefore, is to test these various explanations of price behavior, using the recently developed methods of time series analysis. This should permit a more comprehensive theory to emerge, one which can explain and predict both random and systematic price fluctuations. The very magnitude of the problem, however, limits our efforts to provide an explanation only for the short-run. As an important preliminary to reaching this goal, the market conditions and practices which have produced the price fluctuations of concern are first reviewed. The remainder of this chapter thus contains a discussion of the development and characteristics of commodity markets as well as problems that are encountered in explaining market price fluctuations. The commodity economist or econometrician not interested in this background information can immediately proceed to Chapter 2, which contains a mathematical formulation of the methods of spectral analysis and stepwise regression. The less mathematically inclined reader can advance directly to Chapter 3, where the first empirical results are presented.

Commodity Market Development

The historical growth of commodity markets has featured the development of a number of institutions contributing to the increased volume and complexity of commodity trade. The more important of these institutions have been the contracts which facilitate actual commodity trade – in particular the forward and the futures contract. Only a brief history of commodity markets is presented here, principally as they have emerged in Europe, England, and the United States. The oversimplification reduces the scope of the presentation, but it does provide a background for explaining the appearance of these more important institutions.

Europe: Early Development

The trading of commodities has accompanied the growth of civilization since its earliest periods. Although the trading history of Greece and Rome is interesting, the development of modern trading practices is best traced to medieval Europe. By the tenth century, trading activity on a relatively large scale could be found in most parts of Europe, but it tended to emanate from the Levant with Venice as the center. Trade in Venice dealt mostly in luxury goods, including spices and cloths, while trade in Western Europe comprised mostly necessities, including furs, timber, and honey. Trade between the Levant and Western Europe in this period, therefore, could be likened to the situation presently found between more developed and less developed nations.

From the eleventh to the fourteenth centuries, the number as well as the quantity of commodities traded increased rapidly. This multiplication in trade can be linked to the medieval fair. Although the history and appearance of these fairs cannot be traced with great accuracy, evidence does exist to substantiate their presence in Champagne and Flanders.[5] The character of these fairs is of considerable importance. Contrary to the popular conception that fairs occurred once yearly and at the intersections of the principal travelling routes across Western Europe, many fairs were organized to function on a regular basis and were situated in existing market towns. The fair of Champagne, for example, consisted of six fairs spread throughout the year and rotated among four market towns. The fairs lasted from one to two months beginning with January-February; accordingly, their location was cycled through the towns of Lagny, Bar, Provins, Troyes, and again, Provins and Troyes.[6]

Because these fairs were so well established, it was relatively easy for certain trading institutions and practices to become standardized. Merchant associations were formed in which foreign and domestic merchants cooperated with various government authorities to establish the actual dates and places of the fairs.[7] Similarly, the ethics of trading became incorporated into the "law merchant." This code represented a practical guide for the ethical conduct of all business at the fair and governed both domestic and foreign participants. Enforcement was made possible through "courts of the fair" or courts of the "dusty feet" (*pieds poudrés*) which received their authority from local governments. Such a code made possible on an international scale practices such as written contracts of exchange, letters of credit, agreements to grading of merchandise, and even forward trading. While most trading at the fairs was for merchandise on the "spot" or ready for delivery, a document from a fair at Ypres suggests that a form of forward trading was already in limited practice. Registered obligations (*lettres de faire*) were offered which constituted a promise to fulfill payment at the next fair.[8] Payment could be made with commodities but equally with cash, service, or merchandise. Even more significantly, the liability of the obligations could be transferred to a third party.

The range of commodities traded at these fairs greatly exceeded those of earlier periods. Goods reaching the fairs from southern Europe were the more exotic, ranging from spices to oranges, apricots, cotton or even silk. Goods travelling from northern Europe and the German Hansa were more substantial, including timber, grain, wool, cloth, potash, silver, and iron. The commodity which came to dominate the trade, however, was wool cloth. Trade in wool cloth became so important that the center of its production, Bruges, also became the major commodity trading center of western Europe. While the rise of cloth trade in Bruges contributed to the decline of the local fairs as major trading centers by the fifteenth century, the industrialization of Italy, political difficulties within France, and several lesser factors can also be cited as causes. Particularly, urban life had developed to such an extent that cities could provide permanent trade in most commodities. Bruges retained its predominance until late in the fifteenth century, when a number of factors, political and otherwise, led to the ascendency of Antwerp as the major cloth center. Antwerp held this position for over a century, its position declining gradually with the onset of the wars of the Reformation. Major European trading activity then shifted to Amsterdam. It is to the history of trading in England, however, that we turn for further institutional developments.

England: The Forward Contract

As cities began to grow in size and commercial importance, commodity trading began to take place in special markets known as "bourses" in Europe and "exchanges" in England.[9] The early exchanges were essentially meeting places where buyers and sellers could trade commodities as well as merchandise throughout the entire year. The exchanges also generated sufficient financial activity to become recognized as reliable sources of credit. It was for this reason that Sir Thomas Gresham advised Elizabeth I to open the Royal Exchange in London.[10] The Exchange flourished from its inception in 1570; by the end of the seventeenth century, London had become the commercial and financial center of the world. Although the exchange accommodated trade in a variety of commodities, it never formally supported the buying or selling of negotiable securities. The first appearance of any form of exchange in stock certificates or rights to ownership occurred in approximately 1585 in Amsterdam. It was only later that a similar exchange began in London.

As economic conditions improved and the volume of trading on the London exchanges increased, dealers began to specialize in the trade of individual commodities. These dealers who engaged in spot and, more importantly, in forward transactions provided the market with the useful service of risk coverage.[11] Some form of risk had always confronted merchants both in making purchases and in taking delivery, and the magnitude of the risk had increased as markets became more distant and sellers more anonymous. While insurance could be obtained against the risks of shipment of delivery, no protection was offered against the prices which one might have to pay or charge for commodities purchased or sold. The dealers absorbed this risk in forward trading by acting as middlemen, buying and selling commodities for the opportunity of profit. In return, they faced (1) the risk of nonshipment and the necessity to replace the commodity at higher than contract price as well as (2) the risk of cancellation and the necessity to sell the commodity at lower than contract price. The ultimate effects of their activity was that the seller was assured of a buyer at a reasonable price while the purchaser was assured not only of a favorable price but also of acceptable quality.

In London, dealer specialization coincided with the dispersion of the commodity exchanges from the Royal Exchange. The new exchanges tended to concentrate about Mincing Lane, a location within easy reach of the Pool, where ships deposited their commodity cargoes.[12] These individual exchanges, taken together, became known as the London Commodity Exchange. Trade took place in a number of commodities including cocoa, coffee, hides, skins, rubber, sugar, tea, wool, shellac, copra, drugs, spices, gum, jute, sisal, and essential oils. Several of the commodity exchanges accommodating specialized trade moved from Mincing Lane and were separately housed. The Baltic exchange, for example, was organized to facilitate shipments to the Baltic as well as to foster special trade in grains, oilseeds, and tallow. Similarly, the Corn Exchange moved to a separate location and gradually extended its list of grains. The Metal Exchange separated itself at a much later date and moved to its own premises in 1881. The only major market located outside of London was the Liverpool Cotton Exchange, also organized in 1881.

United States: The Futures Contract

The various commodity exchanges which emerged in London, Amsterdam, and other cities also began to appear in cities spread across the United States. The nineteenth century saw the development of a country capable of producing a wide range of commodities. While these commodities were traded in thousands of small markets, larger central markets sprang up in the larger cities, including Chicago, New York, New Orleans, St. Louis, and Savannah. Of these, New York was the first to emerge as a major trading center, with exchange principally in cotton. The latter commodity was particularly important because of the city's location on the shipping route between the plantations of the South and the mills of the North. Trade in other commodities increased as the port of New York assumed greater importance in international trade. A formal domestic commodity exchange could be found on Broad Street and an international commodity exchange on Wall Street.[13] Although Chicago did not have an important position with respect to overseas trade, both the new railroads and canal networks soon made the city a major center for internal trade. Agricultural and other primary commodities moved into Chicago from the West and these exchanged for manufactured goods and other agricultural commodities from the East. A formal commodity exchange could be found in Chicago at the beginning of the nineteenth century, although it was not officially organized as the Chicago Board of Trade until 1848.[14]

The appearance of the futures contract can be related to the phenomenal expansion of trade in Chicago at that time.[15] As stated above, the many commodities moving into the city required a continual enlargement of market and storage facilities. Manufactured goods, especially in the form of farm implements, were purchased in large quantities as soon as commodities could be converted into cash. To provide the liquidity necessary for capital expansion and to compensate for the long distances of transporting goods, increased use was made of the forward or "to arrive" contract. Major risks were incurred not only because of fluctuations in prices and uncertainty of shipment but also because of the intense competition encountered in producer markets. Although some risk could be absorbed by specialized dealers, as was the case of London markets, the volume of trade at Chicago had expanded so greatly that a sufficient number of dealers was not available to cover all of the risk requirements.

Price risks could be covered, therefore, only if the risk could be transferred to a third party. This would require a speculator who would own the contracts from the time the commodity was produced until the time when the commodity was consumed. This arrangement would be possible only if the forward contract could be made sufficiently appealing to attract speculators. Such a transformation was brought about by the futures contract, which extended the liability of the forward contract, permitting the latter to be more easily traded before delivery. The exchange of futures contracts also required several other essential modifications.[16] First of all, it necessitated that the commodity selected be easily graded and that the grading be maintained by regular government inspection. Second, payment had to be set at the time of delivery. Third, prices had to be reported openly and everyone given an opportunity to trade at a desired price. Fourth, buyers and sellers were accepted only if they could satisfy the accompanying financial responsibility. Last of all, the number of buyers and sellers had to be sufficiently large to provide continuous opportunities for trade.

The futures contract was first used in the exchange of wheat, a commodity whose grade could be easily standardized. Wheat futures contracts were first negotiated at the Chicago Board of Trade in 1865, only a few years after the Board's inception. Futures contracts were soon established for other commodities at Chicago and speculators rapidly entered the market. The popularity of this institution soon moved eastward. At the New York Produce Exchange, futures trading commenced in most of its commodities by the 1870s. About the same time, futures trading began at the newly organized New Orleans and New York Cotton Exchanges. The New York Coffee Exchange opened in 1885 with futures trading, as did its successor, the Coffee and Sugar Exchange. By 1930, the futures markets for rubber, silk, tin, copper, silver, and hides were organized into the Commodity Exchange, Inc. of New York. As shown in Table 1-1, futures trading has expanded to include beef cattle, beef carcasses, coffee, corn, cottonseed meal, cottonseed oil, cotton, eggs, flaxseed, lead, oats, platinum, pork bellies, potatoes, rye, soybeans, soybean meal, soybean oil, turkeys, grease wool, grease tops, and zinc. Futures exchanges for all commodities were closed during World War II, but resumed shortly thereafter. The most recently added futures markets accommodate trade in mercury, frozen orange juice, propane, and broilers.

Commodity Market Characteristics

Equally important to the understanding of commodity price behavior is a review of some of the basic facts which relate to trading on these markets. These facts or characteristics are presented in considerable detail elsewhere and we shall review only those which seem relevant to the present study.[17] The section begins with a description of the commodities most frequently traded on cash as well as futures markets. Background information is provided as to the purposes of futures trading, functions of the futures market, and the composition of traders on that market. Also related to market composition is a discussion of the manner in which the Commodity Exchange Authority reports hedging and speculative positions.

Commodities Traded

As explained in the historical summary, commodities are traded on a large number of markets in Europe, England, and the United States; major commodity markets, in fact, can be found in almost every country of the world. Our present concern is with the more specialized of these markets known as *futures markets.* Even here, as many as 60 or 70 international markets exists, although trading is limited to 40 or 50 commodities.[18] Table 1-1 summarizes the more active futures markets, ranging for example, from barley and cocoa to yams and zinc.

Of greater importance are the characteristics of the contracts used in the exchange of these commodities. Table 1-2 summarizes these characteristics for a number of commodities traded on American futures markets. Briefly reviewing that table, all contracts are quoted in a per-unit price which may be adjusted upwards or downwards depending on whether the delivery grade of the commodity is superior or inferior to the specified or basic grade. Furthermore, the contract must describe a prespecified volume or weight of the commodity, and price variations due to bidding cannot fall below a suggested minimum.

The "most actively traded futures months" refer to the date when the volume

Table 1-1

Locations of Major Commodity Futures Markets

	Barley	Broilers Iced	Cattle (Live)	Citrus	Cocoa	Coffee	Copper	Corn	Cotton	Cottonseed Oil	Eggs (& Frozen)	Fishmeal	Flaxseed	Grain Sorghums	Hides
Chicago Board of Trade		•	•					•							
Chicago Mercantile Exchange			•								•				
Citrus Assoc. of N.Y. Cotton Exch.				•											
Commodity Exchange Inc., N.Y.							•								•
Kansas City Board of Trade								•						•	
London Cocoa Terminal Market Assoc.					•										
London Coffee Terminal Market						•									
London Commodity Exchange															
London Corn Trade Assn.	•							•							
London Metal Exchange						•									
London Sugar Terminal Market Ass'n.															
London Wool Terminal Market Ass'n.															
Minneapolis Grain Exchange														•	
N.Y. Cocoa Exchange					•										
N.Y. Coffee & Sugar Exchange						•									
N.Y. Cotton Exchange									•						
N.Y. Mercantile Exchange															
N.Y. Produce Exchange										•		•			
Paris Commodity Exchange															
Rubber Trade Ass'n. London															
Sydney Greasy Wool Futures Market															
Winnipeg Grain Exchange	•		•										•		
Wool Assoc. of the N.Y. Cotton Exchange															

Hogs (Live)		●																					
Lead				●						●													
Lumber		●																					
Mercury				●																			
Molasses															●								
Oats	●																					●	
Palladium and Platinum																	●						
Plywood	●																●						
Pork Bellies (Frozen)		●																					
Potatoes		●															●						
Propane				●																			
Rapeseed																						●	
Rubber				●																●			
Rye	●																					●	
Silver	●			●						●													
Soybeans	●																						
Soybean Oil	●							●															
Soybean Meal	●																		●				
Sugar											●				●				●				
Tin				●						●													
Wheat	●				●								●										
Wool & Tops												●									●		●
Zinc				●						●													

Source: *How to Buy and Sell Commodities* (New York: Merrill Lynch, Pierce, Fenner & Smith, January 1970), p.55.

Table 1-2

Contract Characteristics for a Group of Commodities Traded on American Futures Markets

Commodity	*Prices Are Quoted*	*Contract Size Minimum Price Variation (1¢ or $1 moves)*	*Most Actively Traded Futures Months*
Broilers (Iced)	Dollars per Cwt.	25,000 lbs. 2-1/2 points=$6.25 $1.00/cwt.=$250	Jan., Mar., May, July, Sept., Nov.
Cattle, Live (Chicago Merc. Ex.)	Dollars per Cwt.	40,000 lbs. 2=1/2 points=$10.00 ($1.00/cwt.=$400)	Feb., April, June, Aug., Oct., Dec.
Choice Steers (Chgo Bd of Tde)	Dollars per Cwt.	27,600 lbs. 2-1/2 points=$6.90 ($1.00/cwt.=$276)	Jan., Feb., April, June, Aug., Oct., Dec.
Citrus (Frozen Concentrated)	Cents per Pound	15,000 lbs. 5 points=$7.50 (1 cent=$150)	Jan., Mar., May, July, Sept., Nov., Dec.
Cocoa	Cents per Pound	30,000 lbs. 1 point=$3.00 (1 cent=$300)	Mar., May, July, Sept., Dec.
Copper	Cents per Pound	50,000 lbs. 1 point=$5.00 (1 cent=$500)	Jan., Mar., May, July, Sept., Oct., Dec.
Corn	Dollars per Bushel	5,000 bu. 1/8¢=$6.25 (1 cent=$50)	Mar., May, July, Sept., Dec.
Cotton No. 2	Cents per Pound	50,000 lbs. 1 point=$5.00 (1 cent=$500)	Mar., May, July Oct., Dec.
Eggs (Fresh Shell)	Cents per Dozen	18,000 doz. 5 points=$9.00 (1 cent=$180)	Sept., Oct., Nov. Dec., Jan.
Flaxseed-Rapeseed (Winnipeg)	Dollars per Bushel	1,000 bushels 1/8¢=$1.25 (1 cent=$10)	May, July, Oct., Dec.

Crop Year (marketing year)	Normal Seasonal Price Pattern *High*	*Low*	*Important Economic Factors Affecting Prices*
None	Feb., Mar., July	Nov. Dec.	Size of breeding flock, egg set, chicks placed.
None	Spring and Fall	Summer and Winter	Cattle on feed reports, inventory of cattle and calves on farms and ranches, calf crop, shipment of stocker and feeder cattle into the corn belt, cattle slaughter and beef production.
Dec. 1 to Nov. 30	Winter	Summer	Weather, crop estimates, weekly FCOJ movement.
Oct. 1 to Sept. 30	Aug.	May	World crop reports, political conditions, rate of imports, data on imports, stocks, grindings, producer measures.
None	None	None	Production and consumption figures from the Copper Institute, governmental export controls and stockpiling policy.
Oct. 1 to Sept. 30	Aug.	Nov. Dec.	Crop estimates, surplus disposal, carryover deliverable stocks, disappearance, loan tie up, other feed supplies, weather.
Aug. 1 to July 31	Aug. to Sept.	Jan. to Feb.	U. S. Government program, world and U. S. crop estimates, carryover, consumption, and textile industry activity.
None	Nov.	April	Number of layers on farms, storage stocks, production, consumption, weather.
Aug. 1 to July 31	Summer	Winter	Crop reports: Canada, U. S. and World, weather and exports

(*continued*)

Table 1-2 (*continued*)

Commodity	*Prices Are Quoted*	*Contract Size Minimum Price Variation (1¢ or $1 moves)*	*Most Actively Traded Futures Months*
Hogs, Live	Dollars per Cwt.	20,000 lbs. 2-1/2 points=$5.00 ($1.00/cwt.=$200)	July, Aug., Sept., Oct., Nov., Dec.
Lumber	Dollars per 1,000 Board Feet	40,000 board feet 25¢=$10 ($1.00=$40)	Mar., May, July (initially)
Mercury	Dollars per Flask	10 flasks of 76 lbs. each 1 dollar=$10	Mar., May, July, Sept., Dec.
Oats	Dollars per Bushel	5,000 bu. 1/8¢=$6.25 (1 cent=$50)	Mar., May, July, Sept., Dec.
Platinum	Dollars per Ounce	100 troy ozs. 5 cents=$5.00 ($1/oz.=$100)	Mar., June, Sept., Dec.,
Plywood	Dollars per Ounce	50 troy ozs. 10 cents=$5.00 ($1/oz.=$50)	Jan., April July. Oct.
Plywood (Chicago)	Dollars per 1,000 Square Feet	69,120 sq. feet 10¢=$6.91 ($1.00=$69.12)	Jan., Mar., May, July, Sept., Dec.
Plywood (New York)		70,000 sq. feet 10¢=$7.00 ($1.00=$70)	every calendar month
Pork Bellies (Frozen)	Cents per Pound	30,000 lbs. 2-1/2 points=$7.50	Feb., Mar., May, July, Aug.
Potatoes Idaho (Chi.) (100 lb. bags)	Dollars per Cwt.	50,000 lbs. (1 cent/cwt.=$5.00)	Nov., Mar., Apr., May
Potatoes, Maine (NY) (50 lb. bags)			
Propane (LPG)	Cents per Gallon	100,000 gals. 1 point=$10 (1 cent=$1000)	Jan., Feb., May, Sept., Dec.

Crop Year (marketing year)	Normal Seasonal Price Pattern *High*	*Low*	*Important Economic Factors Affecting Prices*
Oct. 1 to Sept. 30	June to Aug.	Nov. to Jan.	Cold storage stocks, hog slaughter, sliced bacon production, live hog prices, pig crop reports-sow farrowings, breeding intentions, inventory numbers.
None	Winter	Summer	Economic conditions construction activity (housing starts), weather.
None	None	None	Production general economic conditions, stocks
July 1 to June 30	May	Aug.	Crop estimates, deliverable stocks, imports, carryover, loan entries, other feed supplies.
None	None	None	Production, general economic conditions, stocks.
None	None	None	Production, general economic conditions, stocks.
None	Winter	Summer	Economic conditions construction activity (housing starts), weather.
Oct. 1 to Sept. 30	June to Aug.	Nov. Dec.	Cold storage stocks, hog slaughter, sliced bacon production, live hog prices, pig crop reports-sow farrowings, breeding intentions, inventory numbers.
July thru June, bulk Oct. thru May	April Spring	Dec. Summer	Crop estimates, total U. S. Fall stocks, carlot shipments, truck holdings 16 cities, Maine & Idaho situations, weather.
None	Winter	Summer	Production, consumption, general economic conditions, weather.

(*continued*)

Table 1-2 (*continued*)

<table>
<tr><th>Commodity</th><th>Prices Are Quoted</th><th>Contract Size Minimum Price Variation (1¢ or $1 moves)</th><th>Most Actively Traded Futures Months</th></tr>
<tr><td>Rye</td><td>Dollars per Bushel</td><td>5,000 bu.
1/8¢-$6.25
(1 cent=$50)</td><td>Mar., May, July, Sept., Dec.</td></tr>
<tr><td>Silver (New York)</td><td rowspan="2">Dollars per Troy Ounce</td><td>10,000 troy ozs.
10 points=$10
(1 cent=$70)</td><td>Jan., Mar., May, July, Sept., Dec.</td></tr>
<tr><td>Silver (Chicago)</td><td>5,000 troy ozs.
10 points=$5.00
(1 cent=$50)</td><td>Feb., April, June, Aug., Oct., Dec.</td></tr>
<tr><td>Soybeans</td><td>Dollars per Bushel</td><td>5,000 bu.
1/8¢=$6.25
(1 cent=$50)</td><td>Jan., Mar., May, July, Aug., Sept. Nov.</td></tr>
<tr><td>Soybean Meal</td><td>Dollars per Ton</td><td>100 tons
5 points=$5.00
($1.00/ton=$100)</td><td>Jan., Mar., May, July, Aug., Sept. Oct., Dec.</td></tr>
<tr><td>Soybean Oil</td><td>Cents per Pound</td><td>60,000 lbs.
1 point=$6.00
(1 cent=$600)</td><td>Jan., Mar., May, July, Aug., Sept. Oct., Dec.</td></tr>
<tr><td>Sugar No. 10 (Domestic)</td><td rowspan="2">Cents per Pound</td><td rowspan="2">112,000 lbs.
1 point=$11.20
(1 cent=$1120)</td><td rowspan="2">Jan., Mar., May, July, Sept., Nov.</td></tr>
<tr><td>Sugar No. 8 (World)</td></tr>
<tr><td>Wool Grease</td><td>Cents per Pound</td><td>6,000 lbs.
1 point=$6.00
(1 cent=$60)</td><td>Mar., May, July, Oct., Dec.</td></tr>
</table>

Crop Year (marketing year)	Normal Seasonal Price Pattern *High*	*Low*	*Important Economic Factors Affecting Prices*
July 1 to June 30	Aug.	Jan.	Crop estimates, deliverable stocks, Canadian situation, exports, loan entries, price U. S. wheat, feeds.
None	None	None	Production, consumption, government policy on silver sales.
Sept. 1 to Aug. 1	May	Oct.	Crop estimates, deliverable stocks, crush, exports, loan entries, vegetable oil consumption, weather, meal price, cotton crop.
Oct. 1 to Sept. 30	July	Oct.	Total supply; Production of commercial formula feeds; exports, prices received by farmers for meat animals and products.
Oct. 1 to Sept. 30	May	Nov.	Soybean and cotton crop estimates, crush, exports, visible supplies, other fats & oils supply and demand.
Quota— Calendar Year			U. S. Sugar Act, national income, consumption, quotas, supplies in Northeast.
Oct. 1 to Sept. 30	Aug. to Sept.	Mar. April	Economic conditions, world crop estimates, especially Cuba, world demand vs. free world supplies.
Domestic— April 1 to March 30	Dec.	May June	Production, general conditions in wool textile business, imports, world production, sheep population trends, military use, gov't support program.

Source: *How to Buy and Sell Commodities* (New York: Merrill Lynch, Pierce, Fenner & Smith, January 1970), pp. 36, 37.

of a commodity secured in a contract is available for delivery. The month of delivery normally depends on a commodity's natural characteristics. Wheat, for example, is delivered in July, September, December, March, and May. Correspondingly, July is the principal harvest month for winter wheat; September is the same for spring wheat; December is the last month of navigation on the Great Lakes; March is the first month of navigation; and May is the final month before the new crop harvest begins.

The "crop" or "marketing year," while important to the specification of the delivery months, also helps to identify the seasonal pattern in prices. When the new crop is first marketed, related prices will normally be lowest for the year; similarly, when the stocks of the crop will be lowest just before harvest, prices will be the highest. For commodities which do not have a regular harvest or extraction period, price seasonals do not normally appear. Also related to price movements are the many factors describing consumption and production as well as general economic conditions. Examples of the former are changes in existing livestock numbers which might use the commodity as feed, or fertilizer and weather conditions which might affect its supply. Economic conditions might include changes in industrial activity or government loan programs.

Two-Fold Trading

It should be noted that for each of the commodities discussed so far trading takes place on physical markets as well as on futures markets. As mentioned in the historical summary, commodities may be traded according to (1) contracts which specify delivery on the spot, (2) contracts which specify delivery at some time forward, and (3) contracts which specify forward delivery but also permit frequent transfer of liability.[19] The first two forms of contracts exchange on the market known as the physical market; this market exists solely to handle the physical exchange of a commodity, regardless of whether the commodity is also traded on the futures exchange. The physical market has two other names as well. It is called the *spot market* since it transfers contracts which call for immediate delivery of the physical commodity on the spot. It is also termed the *cash market* because it requires that most contracts be paid for in cash on the spot. Even though the payment of some of these contracts can be deferred, "cash market" is a convenient term and has been adopted for this study.

Most of the trading on the cash market actually takes place in the contracts for forward delivery. In addition to specifying commodity characteristics such as price, quantity and quality, which would be included in a cash contract, the futures contract could be considered similar to a forward contract except that, as mentioned above, the former possess special characteristics which facilitate the transfer of liability.[20] Some question exists as to whether the market for futures contracts is truly separate from the market for cash and forward contracts. Because a transaction on the futures market can be matched by a similar but opposite transaction on the cash market, some have insisted that the markets are not truly independent. It does appear, nevertheless, that the markets can be considered separate. Each market (1) performs distinct operations, (2) occupies a physically distinct location, and (3) has its transactions described by a separate set of price and quantity variables.

Also essential to a discussion of these two markets is the relative degree to which trading takes place in these markets, especially if one wants to compare the relative effect of physical and futures trading on price behaviour. Differences in trading activity between these markets can be measured by two different sets of statistics. The first set compares total levels of futures trading for various commodities to the respective levels of futures contracts tendered or settled for delivery. The percentage of contracts tendered, accordingly, reflects the proportion of total futures contracts that actually end in delivery, a rough measure of physical exchange in the cash market. Corresponding data have been summarized in Table 1-3 for a number of commodities. The percentage of contracts tendered, as averaged over the years 1950-1969, ranges from 0.44% for cotton to 1.87% for oats, indicating that the volume of trade in the physical commodity is only a small percentage of the total volume of futures trading.

The second set of statistics compares total levels of futures trading for various commodities to the actual volumes of production. Data for wheat, corn, and soybeans is summarized in Table 1-4 over the same span of years. While the production of corn exceeds the volume of futures trading for a number of years, similar comparisons for the other two commodities confirm the results suggested above. Production of wheat is about one-fourth the volume of futures trading; and, for soybeans, the ratio varies from one-tenth to one-twentieth. Although the evidence presented in Table 1-4 is less comprehensive than that of Table 1-3, futures trading can be considered to be the dominant activity in the exchange of a number of commodities.

Why Futures Trading?

Futures trading has been justified historically according to its ability to cover that portion of market risk not met by forward trading. The principal mechanism through which risk coverage occurs is hedging. Yet, hedging takes place for a number of reasons other than risk coverage. Since the analysis of these reasons is complex and can be found elsewhere, we review only the more elementary factors which give rise to hedging, particularly those associated with uncertainty. Houthakker has hypothesized that uncertainty occurs in commodity markets because of the lag in time arising between the production and consumption of a commodity.[21] This gap is most often attributed to factors such as seasonality in agricultural production, periodicity in extraction processes, lengthy shipping periods, or any other factor which generally defers consumption. The effect of this lag is that inaccurate expectations regarding future levels of production and consumption cause unplanned fluctuations in price, giving rise to two different forms of uncertainty: social and individual.

Table 1-3 Volume of Futures Contracts Tendered and Total Volume of Futures Traded, Including Average Percentages of Tendering

Year	*Wheat*[a] *(bu.)*	*Corn*[a] *(bu.)*	*Oats*[a] *(bu.)*	*Rye*[a] *(bu.)*	*Soybeans*[a] *(bu.)*	*Potatoes* *(c.l.)*	*Eggs* *(c.l.)*	*Cotton*[a] *(bales)*	*Cottonseed Oil*[a] *(lb.)*	*Soybean Oil*[a] *(lb.)*	*Soybean Meal* *(tons)*
1950-1951	38,016[b]	21,238	16,060	17,983	17,276	63	2,364	125.2	28,020	12,600	16,700
	4,675,715	2,236,588	1,617,253	576,216	2,952,610	2,627	148,811	79,067	7,531,700	3,532,620	2,292,000
1951-1952	34,578	12,205	38,535	7,864	8,848	263	767	162.1	95,160	33,960	7,300
	4,341,700	2,639,606	2,239,200	426,600	2,953,200	18,181	90,005	94,887	7,989,700	2,155,600	1,972,500
1952-1953	39,597	29,942	48,091	9,896	7,903	998	1,287	357.3	69,180	85,260	24,300
	3,780,534	2,811,204	2,421,172	703,044	3,346,329	123,449	145,588	91,335	3,050,280	3,048,720	1,837,900
1953-1954	31,364	9,374	13,036	13,548	21,738	1,256	601	385.0	34,560	75,020	53,400
	4,763,276	2,343,979	1,232,496	724,630	5,147,957	67,525	149,163	44,886	871,680	4,711,260	4,054,000
1954-1955	16,910	19,752	8,329	11,236	16,659	1,349	2,480	328.6	32,040	34,380	63,600
	3,969,062	2,213,472	757,619	815,407	4,952,249	197,186	258,507	50,395	825,180	4,318,500	5,741,300
1955-1956	16,008	32,310	17,910	6,168	38,837	390	2,449	98.6	61,200	75,300	114,700
	4,180,556	2,762,007	687,325	574,098	5,541,841	126,339	425,900	39,954	3,451,860	8,185,200	6,663,000
1956-1957	21,486	34,663	16,681	7,704	40,807	816	1,309	22.9	75,600	129,300	132,600
	4,885,821	2,275,888	643,368	913,312	4,479,827	137,178	368,816	22,306	4,551,840	12,583,200	6,254,600
1957-1958	41,737	27,055	9,699	3,877	47,560	2,516	3,192	46.8	35,880	185,760	154,100
	5,202,953	2,011,322	453,635	998,266	3,943,177	188,169	371,701	25,202	3,570,780	8,954,580	6,684,900
1958-1959	47,472	10,335	14,853	1,867	50,655	1,343	1,257	138.5	65,340	77,820	191,200
	4,359,288	2,008,074	533,266	780,942	2,794,406	95,741	374,302	19,709	3,425,166	9,414,060	19,325,000
1959-1960	57,880	27,509	9,434	8,538	48,212	507	3,998	17.0	71,580	200,220	125,400
	2,577,091	1,680,553	577,346	713,171	5,612,517	284,894	412,207	4,903	3,212,280	8,123,820	17,499,000

1960-1961	31,539	16,424	25,924	12,293	72,054	835	1,832	69.9	51,060	93,900	715,400
	2,488,972	2,125,812	839,713	426,337	12,593,240	189,275	489,756	2,878	5,339,640	23,401,980	25,388,900
1961-1962	43,242	67,282	25,736	12,083	69,960	1,557	294	156.5	51,840	545,340	683,200
	4,140,753	4,902,772	1,605,155	1,356,684	4,851,734	237,691	268,857	3,493	3,476,580	16,312,740	27,276,500
1962-1963	73,449	47,590	12,705	8,338	21,954	329	1,394	46.5	196,020	971,460	183,000
	5,151,500	3,521,000	883,500	747,700	8,371,700	152,103	296,975	3,037	4,733,100	23,591,940	33,288,500
1963-1964	46,710	18,006	21,635	9,655	75,574	2,414	2,789	7.1	171,240	1,457,920	1,088,500
	5,354,900	3,760,400	610,700	671,100	13,701,700	178,680	134,590	946	5,492,580	25,733,760	27,065,300
1964-1965	43,641	52,820	13,210	3,485	73,626	1,803	1,519	17.8	126,540	233,880	800,800
	2,825,900	3,701,600	483,200	260,300	19,533,500	602,521	63,261	205	1,676,460	33,979,920	30,187,600
1965-1966	46,002	32,092	4,765	6,281	73,961	558	2,584	3.6	17,460	87,780	231,800
	6,000,100	5,375,800	398,500	399,400	16,277,000	412,970	96,224	66	5,235,000	35,238,300	37,732,900
1966-1967	80,616	99,490	19,730	8,584	26,670	655	498	2.6	4,920	307,800	202,200
	10,425,400	13,068,000	569,200	276,400	9,500,700	702,460	71,138	86	2,213,400	25,784,760	42,317,800
1967-1968	107,147	54,635	2,205	7,120	54,680	1,571	633	123.4	4,020	414,540	485,300
	9,259,500	7,559,500	413,700	192,800	4,805,400	411,771	40,928	19,742	10,500	16,039,680	33,284,600
1968-1969	90,427	53,865	8,075	2,185	67,520	591	1,872	158.7	60	73,680	649,200
	6,930,200	8,585,500	693,000	135,900	4,713,800	566,936	257,256	15,419	2,280	25,584,960	40,564,400
Av. %[c]	0.95	0.88	1.87	1.36	0.61	0.42	0.74	0.44	1.79	1.75	1.60

[a]Units of 1000 omitted from volume figures.

[b]Upper figure is volume tendered and lower figure is total volume traded, both according to crop year.

[c]Percentages represent *volume tendered* X 100% averaged over all years.

Source: Commodity Exchange Authority, *Commodity Futures Statistics*, various issues 1951-1969 (Washington: U. S. Department of Agriculture).

Table 1-4

Annual Volume of Futures Trading and Volume of Crop (Billions of Bushels)

1950-1969	Wheat		Corn		Soybeans	
	Crop	*Trading*	*Crop*	*Trading*	*Crop*	*Trading*
1950-1951	1.02	4.68	3.06	2.24	0.30	2.95
1951-1952	0.98	4.34	2.90	2.64	0.28	2.95
1952-1953	1.30	3.78	3.28	2.81	0.30	3.35
1953-1954	1.17	4.76	3.19	2.34	0.27	5.15
1954-1955	0.98	3.97	3.01	2.21	0.34	4.95
1955-1956	0.94	4.18	3.18	2.76	0.37	5.54
1956-1957	1.00	4.88	3.46	2.28	0.45	4.48
1957-1958	0.96	5.20	3.42	2.01	0.48	3.94
1958-1959	1.45	4.36	3.80	2.01	0.58	2.79
1959-1960	1.13	2.58	4.28	1.68	0.53	5.61
1960-1961	1.36	2.49	4.35	2.12	0.56	12.59
1961-1962	1.23	4.14	3.60	4.90	0.68	4.85
1962-1963	1.09	5.15	3.61	3.52	0.67	8.37
1963-1964	1.14	5.35	4.02	3.76	0.70	13.70
1964-1965	1.28	2.82	3.48	3.70	0.70	19.53
1965-1966	1.32	6.00	4.08	5.38	0.84	16.28
1966-1967	1.31	10.42	4.12	13.07	0.93	9.50
1967-1968	1.52	9.26	4.76	7.56	0.98	4.80
1968-1969	1.57	6.93	4.38	8.58	1.08	4.71

Source: *Grain Trade Statistical Annual*, 1955, 1960, 1966, and 1969 (Chicago: Chicago Board of Trade).

Social uncertainty is apt to occur in more elemental forms of markets. Individuals trading in these markets are reasonably certain as to what decisions have to be made regarding their own production and consumption. They are not certain, however, as to what decisions other individuals will make in the market, and, accordingly, as to what prices will transpire in the market. For example, producers are likely to be aware of their future output and consumers of their future needs, but neither is certain of the effects of each other's decisions on future market prices. To remove the uncertainty of having to complete a transaction in the future, both producer and consumer engage in forward trading.

Individual uncertainty, on the other hand, is slightly more complex and normally occurs in markets more sophisticated in nature. Individuals in these markets are not only uncertain as to the nature of prices in the future, they are also uncertain as to their own production and consumption. This latter form of uncertainty is normally a result of the indefiniteness of future economic conditions. An individual who has sold forward, for example, may now realize that he would have obtained a higher price had he sold his crop on the cash market at harvest time. While price uncertainty can be somewhat reduced by forward trading, the uncertainty as to what market conditions may be at the time of harvest can only be reduced by futures trading or hedging. The hedger takes an opposite position in the futures market from that in the cash market. If price changes in both markets move roughly together, the profits in one market will be offset by losses in another. At the same time, the trader will have sold or procured desired amounts of the commodity.

That the principal purpose of futures trading is to remove individual uncertainty through hedging, however, has been questioned by a number of economists.[22] Working, in particular, discounts this purpose since prices rarely move together in both markets and, as a result, hedges are seldom perfect.[23] Rather, traders in the market consider cash and futures transactions together and act to take advantages of differences between prices in the two markets. Hedging between these markets is thus a form of arbitrage in which traders depend on their ability to forecast irregular rather than regular price movements.

One instance in which Working attests to a simple risk-reducing property of hedging is when he proposes that hedging can help to reduce the costs of holding inventory. Both Working's and Houthakker's arguments have been taken up and explored by other economists. Most recently, Cootner has rephrased the arguments, giving a wider explanation for the practice of hedging and supporting his explanation with analogies from financial markets.[24] His results add to the realization that hedging is practiced for a variety of reasons; these include the reduction of individual uncertainty as well as intermarket spreading, other forms of arbitrage, and inventory cost minimization.

How the Futures Market Works

Futures trading takes place on an organized exchange and through the medium of a broker. The liability of the futures contract accepted is not covered by a particular person, but by the clearing house subordinate to the exchange. As a result, contract positions can be readily taken or cancelled without the presence of a particular buyer or seller. Contract positions are normally classified as being held by a hedger or speculator, either of whom can be long or short. A hedger is one who holds a position in the futures market opposite to that he holds in the cash market whereas a speculator normally holds a "net long or net short position for gain and not as a normal incident to operating a producing, merchandising, or processing business."[25] A hedger can instigate a futures transaction by taking a short or long position in the market. A short hedge may involve the selling of futures contracts to protect inventories against a price fall. A long hedge may consist of an acquisition of futures contracts to protect against a price increase where a dealer has committed himself to sell a commodity not yet produced. Of course, hedging normally takes place for reasons more than simple risk coverage.

At the risk of oversimplifying these reasons, an elementary example has been introduced to illustrate the placing and cancelling of a hedge. Consider the case of a grain elevator operator in Chicago who buys 10,000 bushels of wheat on August 1st. Since present conditions prevent a forward sale of his purchase, the operator hedges by selling an equal amount of May futures contract against it. The transaction by which he hedges his wheat and, subsequently, sells it to a miller is summarized in Table 1-5.

Table 1-5

Example of a Short Hedge

	Cash Market		Futures Market
		Initiating the Hedge	
Aug. 1:	Buys 10,000 bu. at $1.75	Aug. 1:	Sells 10,000 bu. May futures at $2.00
		Cancelling the Hedge	
Nov. 31:	Sells 10,000 bu. at $1.65	Nov. 31:	Buys 10,000 bu. May futures at $1.90
		Net Gain or Loss	
Loss:	$0.10/bu.	Gain:	$0.10/bu.

As shown in the table, the operator buys the wheat at $1.75 on the cash market and sells it for $2.00 in futures contracts; both operations occur on August 1st. The operator then finds a miller who is interested in buying his wheat and, consequently, sells the 10,000 bushels on November 31st. The sale is for $1.65 per bushel and the operator must cancel his futures position by purchasing 10,000 bushels in futures contracts at $1.90. Without the presence of a hedge, the operator would have lost $0.10 per bushel in actual wheat. Because of an equal decline in the futures price, he has purchased an equal amount of futures contracts with a net gain of $0.10/bu. The selling hedge, therefore, has protected the operator from a loss resulting from a price fall. Of course, the operator has profited from this transaction since the original price paid to the farmer contained a discount for storage charges.

The zero net gain in this hedge has depended on a perfect correlation between cash and futures prices, a phenomenon not often found in reality. More typical gain and loss situations have been depicted in Table 1-6. As can be seen in that table, differences in price movements between the cash or spot market and the futures market result in differences in gains or losses. These gains and losses also vary as the purpose of one's hedge varies, i.e., long or short. The same results can also be shown to vary with arbitrage or hedging between markets as well as with spreading between futures contracts of different maturity. A description of hedging operations which reflect the more complex trading purposes described above can be found in the sources cited in this section.

Who Trades: Hedgers vs. Speculators

One method for assessing the role of hedging in futures operations is to compare relative levels of hedging and speculative activity in the market. It is true that the total short position in the market must equal the total long position, but the level of short hedging need not call forth an equal amount of long speculating. Data describing the relative numbers of hedgers and speculators trading in the various futures markets is not readily available except for the group of commodities which come under the jurisdiction of the Commodity Exchange Authority. The Authority, in acting as the major regulatory body for commodity exchanges in the United States, has several distinct functions. These include (1) licensing futures exchanges, (2) licensing brokers and commission futures merchants, (3) auditing the records of brokerage firms, (4) governing trading activities, (5) investigating complaints, (6) regulating the total positions that may be held by one individual and the volume of trading permitted in one day, and (7) making and publicizing market surveys and analyses.[26]

In fulfilling the last of these functions, the Commodity Exchange Authority publishes open interest, corresponding commitment of reporting traders, volume of trading, volume of contracts tendered or settled by delivery, and futures prices. The open interest and commitment figures are the ones describing the levels of trading by hedgers and speculators as well as their respective positions. This information is obtained through the requirement that each trader whose position exceeds a given level of contracts must report the nature of his position. Actual positions are measured in terms of open interest or the number of futures contracts which have been "entered into and not yet liquidated by an offsetting contract nor fulfilled by delivery."[27]

Table 1-6

Variations in Gains or Losses Resulting from Differences in Cash and Future Price Movements

Price Movements		Results			
		to one who is "long" in the spot market		to one who is "short" in the spot market	
Spot Price	*Future Price*	*Unhedged*	*Hedged*	*Unhedged*	*Hedged*
Falls	Falls by same amount as spot	Loss	Neither profit nor loss	Profit	Neither profit nor loss
Falls	Falls by greater amount than spot	Loss	Profit	Profit	Loss
Falls	Falls by smaller amount than spot	Loss	Loss, but smaller than unhedged loss	Profit	Profit, but smaller than unhedged profit
Falls	Rises	Loss	Loss, but greater than unhedged loss	Profit	Profit, but greater than unhedged profit
Rises	Rises by same amount as spot	Profit	Neither profit nor loss	Loss	Neither profit nor loss
Rises	Rises by greater amount than spot	Profit	Loss	Loss	Profit
Rises	Rises by smaller amount than spot	Profit	Profit, but smaller than unhedged profit	Loss	Loss, but smaller than unhedged loss
Rises	Falls	Profit	Profit, but greater than unhedged profit	Loss	Loss, but greater than unhedged loss

Source: B. S. Yamey, "An Investigation of Hedging on an Organized Produce Exchange," *Manchester School* 19 (1951): 308.

An example of the open interest data as reported in *Commodity Futures Statistics* is shown in Table 1-7. Total open interest or open contracts is divided according to (1) reporting hedgers, (2) reporting speculators, and (3) nonreporting traders. The last is a residual category and represents primarily small speculators. Each of these major categories is further divided into long and short positions. That this data can be used to assess relative levels of hedging and speculating activity can be seen from a tabulation of net long and net short positions made by Hieronymus.[28] Table 1-8 lists monthly net positions in soybeans, beginning July 1958 and ending August 1961. The reported hedging position generally equals the sum of the reported and nonreported speculating position, although it exceeds the reported speculating position alone. Since the nonreported position frequently is not entirely speculative, one can observe that the normal condition for the market is to be slightly unbalanced, i.e., corresponding hedging and speculative positions are unequal. As will be shown later, this has important implications for the type of price behavior which one can anticipate in the market.

Commodity Price Fluctuations

A major problem of present theories of commodity price behavior, as specified in the introduction, is that they have not been tested over a wide range of commodities nor have they been unified to be capable of explaining both random and systematic price movements. This problem stems chiefly from the difficulties of explaining time series which possess generating processes as complex as those underlying commodity price changes. In this section, some of the information provided above regarding commodity markets is utilized to explain why commodity price fluctuations are more erratic than those found on more conventional markets. The problem of explaining these fluctuations is then reviewed, with emphasis placed on the major theories of commodity price behavior found today. Finally, spectral methods of time series analysis are offered as a useful statistical approach for improving and unifying these theories.

Irregularity of Price Fluctuations

Commodity prices can be seen to fluctuate irregularly to a greater or lesser degree, depending on whether they are compared with price fluctuations in manufactured-goods markets or speculative markets. When compared to the price fluctuations of manufactured goods, commodity prices fluctuate more frequently and more widely. As explained in the discussion of market uncertainty, this appears to be a result of differences in inventory levels or the gap between production and consumption. Manufacturing inventories rarely represent more than two months' consumption while agricultural inventories sometimes account for more than twelve months' consumption. When commodi-

Table 1-7

Example of Reported Futures Commitments

Long and short commitments of reporting and nonreporting traders, principal markets, semimonthly, July 1965 to June 1966

Date		Total open contracts	Nonreporting (small) traders' speculative and hedging commitments		Reporting (large) traders' commitments classified by them as speculative or hedging — Speculative			
					Long or short only		Long and short (spreading)	
			Long	Short	Long	Short	Long	Short
		SOYBEANS, Chicago Board of Trade (In thousands of bushels)						
July	15	259,159	93,426	117,630	11,920	29,469	74,995	74,995
	31	233,423	70,880	113,319	11,811	19,385	71,389	71,629
August	15	242,570	71,347	116,243	10,610	24,607	75,670	75,925
	31	235,551	60,579	112,564	7,420	23,941	80,289	80,574
September	15	252,782	56,305	120,370	9,852	26,223	82,317	82,582
	30	254,489	56,621	118,555	9,383	20,435	82,837	82,852
October	15	260,045	69,887	111,517	10,245	25,046	85,355	85,355
	31	254,957	88,496	99,923	17,507	19,858	92,106	92,106
November	15	260,573	100,226	85,230	16,241	13,775	102,391	102,391
	30	256,427	95,895	75,659	15,418	11,587	102,559	102,219
December	15	278,218	107,947	72,222	19,986	15,136	102,770	102,770
	31	279,625	105,818	77,944	28,371	12,845	102,006	102,006
January	15	241,663	101,613	67,994	31,686	11,918	71,204	71,204
	31	234,753	111,482	70,275	27,622	8,399	61,529	61,529
February	15	244,076	122,815	76,877	34,462	6,950	57,844	57,844
	28	223,999	116,706	69,528	22,512	6,285	55,806	55,806
March	15	204,667	102,753	66,401	17,195	7,927	51,024	51,024
	31	202,694	101,836	68,346	17,445	10,590	50,343	50,343
April	15	215,728	97,549	70,090	28,972	7,650	57,187	57,187
	30	236,541	99,274	73,169	35,717	4,616	74,430	74,540
May	15	222,090	94,749	74,070	31,917	8,840	62,914	62,684
	31	220,315	91,315	76,765	29,418	8,053	61,892	61,662
June	15	233,653	89,340	87,746	23,334	10,510	73,947	73,947
	30	224,012	75,247	79,422	21,494	8,462	75,294	75,294
Average		240,500	90,921	87,577	20,439	14,271	75,337	75,353

Long and short commitments of reporting and nonreporting traders, principal markets, semimonthly, July 1965 to June 1966 (cont.)

Reporting (large) traders' commitments classified by them as speculative or hedging (cont.)						
Speculative (cont.)		*Hedging*		*Total*		
Total						
Long	*Short*	*Long*	*Short*	*Long*	*Short*	
SOYBEANS, Chicago Board of Trade (In thousands of bushels, *cont.*)						Date
86,915	104,464	78,818	37,065	165,733	141,529	15 July
83,200	91,014	79,343	29,090	162,543	120,104	31
86,280	100,532	84,943	25,795	171,223	126,327	15 August
87,709	104,515	87,263	18,472	174,972	122,987	31
92,169	108,805	104,308	23,607	196,477	132,412	15 September
92,220	103,287	105,648	32,647	197,868	135,934	30
95,600	110,401	94,558	38,127	190,158	148,528	15 October
109,613	111,964	56,848	43,070	166,461	155,034	31
118,632	116,166	41,715	59,177	160,347	175,343	15 November
117,977	113,806	42,555	66,962	160,532	180,768	30
122,756	117,906	47,515	88,090	170,271	205,996	15 December
130,377	114,851	43,430	86,830	173,807	201,681	31
102,890	83,122	37,160	90,547	140,050	173,669	15 January
89,151	69,928	34,120	94,550	123,271	164,478	31
92,306	64,794	28,955	102,405	121,261	167,199	15 February
78,318	62,091	28,975	92,380	107,293	154,471	28
68,219	58,951	33,695	79,315	101,914	138,266	15 March
67,788	60,933	33,070	73,415	100,853	134,348	31
86,159	64,837	32,020	80,801	118,179	145,638	15 April
110,147	79,156	27,120	84,216	137,267	163,372	30
94,831	71,524	32,510	76,496	127,341	148,020	15 May
91,310	69,715	37,690	73,835	129,000	143,550	31
97,281	84,457	47,032	61,450	144,313	145,907	15 June
96,788	83,756	51,977	60,834	148,765	144,590	30
95,776	89,624	53,803	63,299	149,579	152,923	*Average*

Source: Commodity Exchange Authority, *Commodity Futures Statistics,* no. 382 (Washington: U.S. Department of Agriculture, 1966), p. 51.

Table 1-8

Month-End Net Position of Reporting Hedgers, Reporting Speculators, and Nonreporting Traders, All Soybean Futures (July 1958-August 1961)

Month	*Nonreporting traders*	*Reporting speculators*	*Reporting hedgers*
	(thousands of bushels; + = Long; − = Short)		
1958			
July	+740	+5,810	-6,550
August	-289	+6,145	-5,856
September	+2,954	+9,314	-9,314
October	+36,914	+15,438	-52,352
November	+40,431	+15,378	-55,809
December	+32,956	+13,599	-46,555
1959			
January	+30,699	+11,507	-42,206
February	+22,828	+11,329	-34,157
March	+17,664	+8,331	-25,995
April	+14,192	+5,232	-19,424
May	+9,403	+432	-8,971
June	-537	+3,102	-2,565
July	+10,651	+6,025	-16,676
August	+1,636	+3,815	-5,451
September	+3,595	+1,072	-4,667
October	+30,576	+12,603	-43,179
November	+67,840	+8,101	-75,941
December	+60,195	+11,127	-71,322
1960			
January	+63,906	+7,677	-71,583
February	+57,219	+1,621	-58,840
March	+44,436	-1,627	-43,836
April	+29,083	-2,271	-26,812
May	+26,061	-7,826	-18,235
June	+13,577	-5,069	-8,508
July	+6,190	+3,640	-9,830
August	+8,187	+2,570	-10,757
September	+21,704	+5,181	-26,885
October	+61,104	+29,308	-90,412
November	+68,857	+21,833	-90,690
December	+62,357	+37,130	-99,487
1961			
January	+83,052	+34,940	-177,992
February	+81,173	+41,721	-122,894
March	+71,776	+38,709	-110,485
April	+50,605	+33,797	-84,402
May	+36,243	+20,793	-57,036
June	+12,849	+16,907	-29,766
July	+7,868	+4,395	-12,263
August	-88	-970	+1,058

Source: T. A. Hieronymus, *Uses of Grain Futures Markets in the Farm Business,* Bulletin no. 696 (Urbana: University of Illinois Experiment Station, 1963), p. 17.

ty price fluctuations are compared to price fluctuations found in purely speculative markets such as the stock market, one would not expect the former to fluctuate quite as irregularly. Commodity prices are similarly subject to speculation, but they also correspond to more regular market forces such as supply and demand. The fact that commodity price fluctuations might resemble stock price fluctuations is of some importance, since the latter have been found to exhibit a known pattern, that of random walk.[29]

A useful way of comparing these various price series can be found in Figures 1-1 and 1-2. Both figures contain four price series, all related to the production of margarine: (1) margarine prices representing the prices of a producer's good, (2) cottonseed oil cash prices describing a margarine input, (3) cottonseed oil futures prices implicitly describing a margarine input, and (4) Swift & Co. common stock prices referring to a typical margarine producer. Figure 1-1 illustrates the relatively irregular behavior of the cottonseed oil cash and futures prices as compared to the margarine price series. The same figure also demonstrates the extent to which the cottonseed oil cash and futures series behave as irregularly as the Swift & Co. common stock series. While the behavior of the last three series may not seem random, as is commonly alleged for speculative price series, this doubt can be removed by examining the changes or first differences of the price series in Figure 1-2. Very little fluctuation can be found in the manufactured-good price differences, but both the commodity and stock price differences fluctuate extensively and in a manner which can be clearly termed random.

Sources of Price Irregularity

Sources of commodity price irregularity can be identified generally, although it is difficult to isolate them particularly. Sometimes price irregularity is ascribed to so-called "unpredictable" events such as devaluation of currency, changes in the prospects of war or changes in government policy. At other times, the irregularity is related to "predictable" factors such as the inelasticity of demand relative to fluctuating supply or the excess of speculation relative to hedging. In either situation, the degree of influence varies, depending on whether the short run or the long run is being considered. Only the short run is considered here, both because of immediate goals and because the short run represents the better starting point for analyzing longer-run price behavior.

Beginning with the demand-supply explanation for price irregularity, classical price theory tells us that market prices will be stable so long as demand and supply remain in equilibrium; once this equilibrium condition changes, prices will accordingly vary. Recent experience confirms that the demand for commodities remains relatively constant over short periods.[30] This is particularly true in developed economies, where consumers' habits change slowly and food consumption is not likely to be reduced with rising prices. Industrial demand in developed countries also tends to remain constant, with manufacturers responding only slowly to price variations. It is changes in supply, therefore, that must be responsible for price irregularity. Starting with agricultural commodities, one finds that weather or changes in technique often

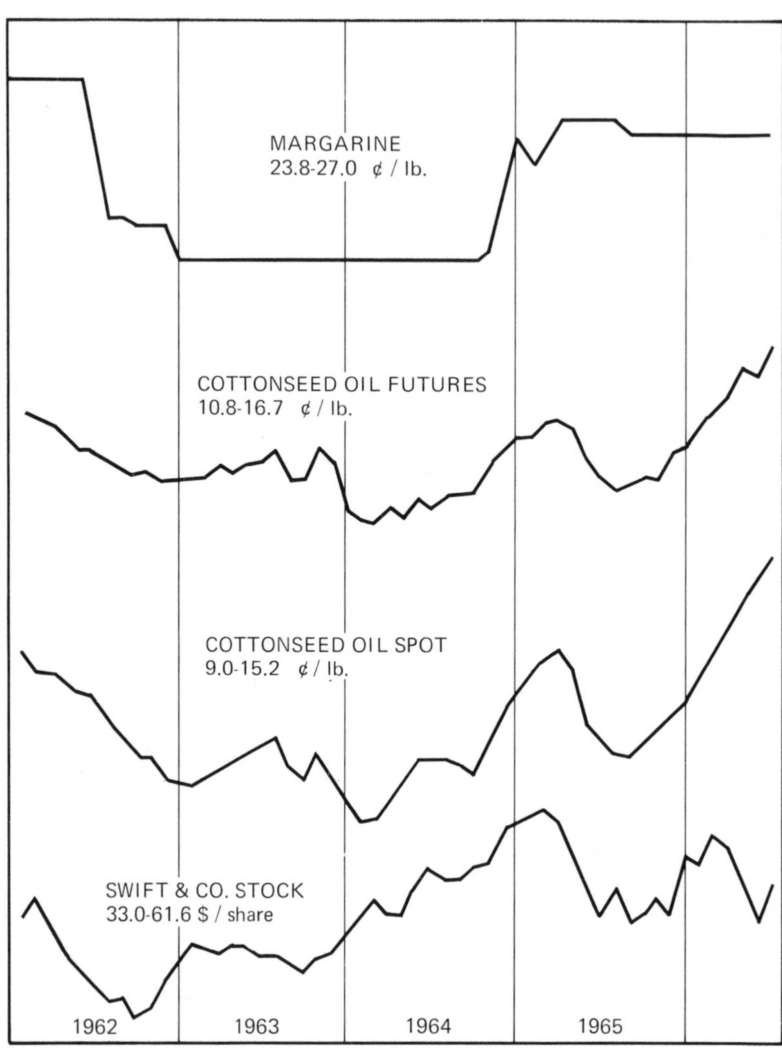

Figure 1-1 Relative Behavior of Commodity and Stock Market Prices. Source: U.S. Department of Commerce, Economic Research Service, Commodity Exchange Authority; and Investment Statistics Laboratory Inc.

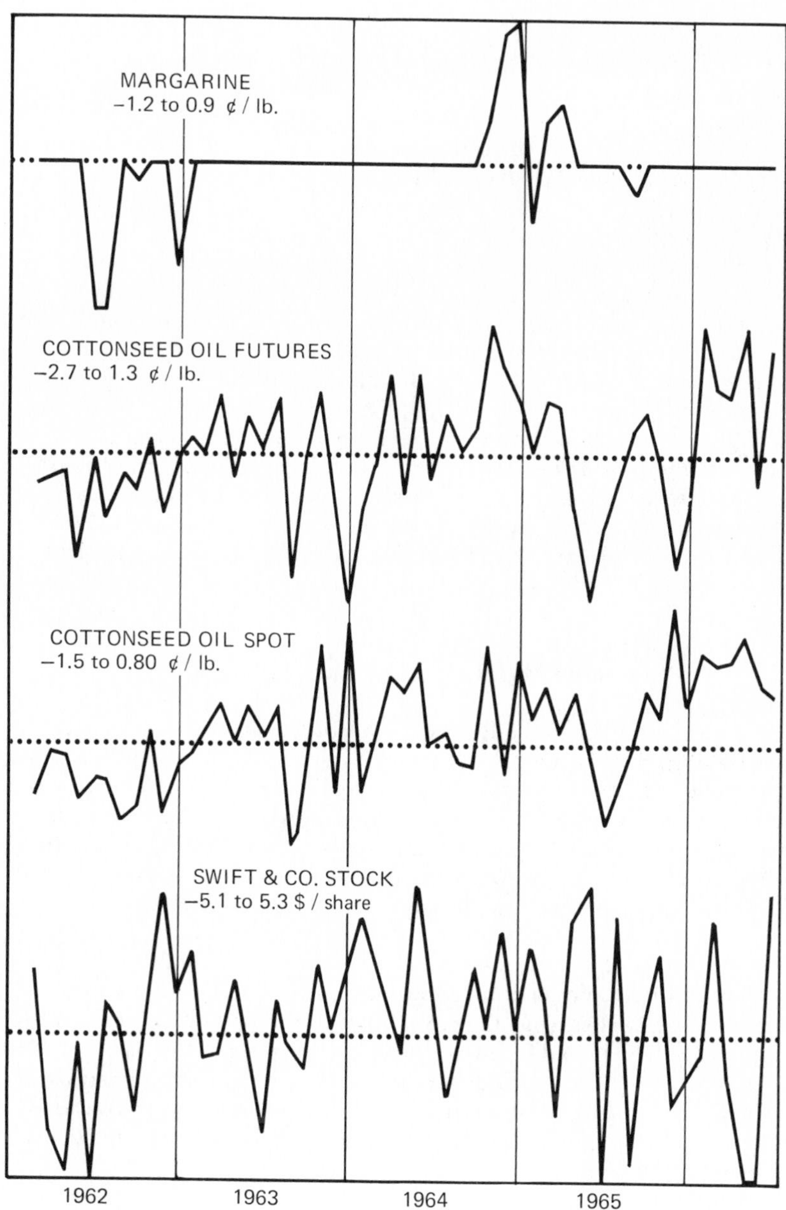

Figure 1-2 Relative Behavior of Commodity and Stock Price Differences. Source: Same as Figure 1-1.

produce unexpected changes in supply; for extracted commodities, unusual geological conditions or unexpected labor problems are likely to change supply. In developing countries, where crop disease and political turmoil are common, these circumstances are likely to be even more severe. Since demand remains relatively inelastic and supply changes frequently, market equilibrium becomes unstable and prices subsequently behave irregularly.

The effects of speculation and hedging on price behavior cannot be stated so explicitly. When speculation and hedging are compared relatively, the normal condition for market balance is that they equal one another. Frequently, however, speculators will enter the market in proportionately greater numbers. That excess speculation makes prices even more irregular is demonstrated by the example of a speculator who is also a stockholder.[31] Normally, such a speculator will reduce price fluctuations, since he purchases when prices are low and sells when prices are high. His actions, however, do not always follow this pattern. If prices are falling because of declining demand and the stockholder anticipates that they will fall further, he is likely to refrain from further buying. Similarly, if prices are rising because of increasing demand, he will refrain from selling, expecting the price to rise further. Either reaction causes price to deviate further from its equilibrium value; when this condition is added to an already unstable demand-supply situation, prices are bound to exhibit erratic behavior.

Explaining Price Fluctuations

As stated earlier, a number of different theories or concepts have emerged to explain the nature of commodity trading and commodity price behavior; the more important of these theories have been conveniently summarized by Working and appear in Table 1-9. Receiving most attention in recent discussions of commodity price behavior has been the concept of reliably anticipatory prices. That is, changes in commodity prices represent an appropriate response to available information regarding future demand and supply. Working first proposed this theory, emphasizing that the absence of positive or negative correlations between any two successive price changes represents an appropriate response to randomly appearing information.[32] While attempts to verify this theory will be explained in Chapter 3, it is worth noting that it has been tested and confirmed in published studies by Larson and Brinegar.[33] Even Larson, however, found some evidence of positive or negative correlation in price changes. The presence of systematic price behavior has also been confirmed to some extent by Smidt and Houthakker through observing the profits that result from different trading rules.[34]

Other attempts to explain commodity price behavior have also suggested the presence of systematic behavior in price changes; these studies have either identified a trend in prices corresponding to Keynes's notion of "risk premium" or have been able to relate price movements to forces in the market or in the economy. Most of the latter explanations have followed the conventional supply-demand model and have employed longer-run data than that used in the above tests. Among the earlier of these explanations were those offered by Taussig, Schultz, Wold, and Jureen.[35] Explanations since then have been based on models embodying market forces in the form of simultaneous equations. Most recently, Weymar has presented strong evidence which relates short-term price movements to changes in inventories.[36] His explanation, however, is more closely related to price spread as defined in the price-of-storage concept in Table 1-9.

One final attempt to explain price behavior should be included here. It relates the instability in commodity prices to profits and speculation.[37] This theory is only indirectly causal since price instability can be judged only after speculation is linked to profits. One must first decide whether speculation is profitable and then whether this speculation increases or reduces the amplitude of price fluctuations. Concerning the first part of this theory, the evidence linking profits and speculation is conflicting. Other tests which couple the speculative activity of the stock holder to price amplitudes have also proven indecisive. In sum, this argument seems to have reached an impasse. An effective test has yet to be devised which will determine whether speculation, either profitable or unprofitable, produces instability in commodity prices.

New Statistical Methods as an Aid to Explanation

This cursory discussion of the various price explanations or theories suggests the predicament of commodity price theory today. While considerable effort would be necessary to develop a theory applicable to short-, medium-, and long-term price fluctuations, at least the short-term explanation can be improved, providing a unified explanation of random and systematic movements in the same price series. These movements should also be linked to explanatory forces such as supply demand, hedging, and speculation. What is needed, therefore, is an investigation of commodity price behavior which utilizes modern statistical methods capable of analyzing prices both independently and in relation to other influences, and which encompasses a wide range of commodity experience.

Econometricians presently have available a number of powerful methods for analyzing such time series, namely spectral analysis, stepwise regression procedures, and exponentially weighted moving averages. The first of these methods, which provides the basis for most of the present study, was initially applied in the physical sciences to detect faint cyclical patterns buried in predominantly random data. Its most well-known application in Economics has been with stock market price behavior.[38] While spectral methods have been applied to stock prices to detect the presence of alleged trading cycles, the methods can be correspondingly applied to commodity prices not only to discern trading cycles but also to achieve a more uniform explanation of regular and irregular price behavior. The same methods can also test the correlation

Table 1-9

New Concepts Concerning Futures Markets and Prices

New Concepts[a]	Displaced Concepts
1. *Open-Contract Concept:* Futures markets serve primarily to facilitate contract holding (1922).	Futures markets serve primarily to facilitate buying and selling. (Disproved.)
2. *Hedging-Market Concept:* Futures markets depend for their existence primarily on hedging (1935; 1946).	Futures markets depend for their existence primarily on speculation. (Disproved.)
3. *Multipurpose Concept of Hedging:* Hedging is done for a variety of different puposes and must be defined as the use of futures contracts as a temporary substitute for a merchandising contract, without specifying the purpose (1953).	Hedging is done solely to avoid or reduce risk. (Disproved.)
4. *Price-of-Storage Concept:* Storage of a commodity is a service supplied often at a price that is reflected in intertemporal price spreads, and because the holding of commodity stocks can afford also a "convenience yield," the price for storing small stocks is often negative (1933; 1949).	Storage of a commodity is a service that is supplied only in response to an assured or expected financial return equal to or greater than the cost, the latter calculable ordinarily without regard to the quantity of stocks to be stored. (Disproved.)
5. *Concept of Reliably Anticipatory Prices:* Futures prices tend to be highly reliable estimates of what should be expected on the basis of *contemporarily available information* concerning present and probable future demand and supply; price changes are mainly appropriate market responses to changes in information on supply and demand prospects (1934; 1949).	Futures prices are highly unreliable estimates of what should be expected on the basis of existing information; their changes are largely unwarranted. (A wholly unproved inference; accumulating evidence mainly supports the new concept.)
6. *Market-Balance Concept:* A significant tendency for futures prices to rise during the life of each future is not uniformly present in futures markets, and when it exists is to be attributed chiefly to lack of balance in the market (1960).	Aversion to risk-taking, leading to risk premiums, produces a general tendency toward "normal backwardation" in futures markets, statistically measurable as a tendency for the price of any future to be higher in the delivery month than several months earlier.

[a]Dates shown in parentheses are years in which the concepts may be said to have emerged. Where two dates are shown, the earlier one is the date of publication of evidence recognized as challenging the older concept; the later date, that of first-known publication of at least the substance of the new concept.

Source: Holbrook Working, "New Concepts Concerning Futures Markets and Prices," *American Economic Review*, 52 (June 1962): 432.

between fluctuations in prices and their corresponding determinants. Tests between prices and supply, demand, hedging, or speculation can be formulated in the traditional manner of correlation analysis. Spectral methods, however, in addition to supplying a statistic similar to the correlation coefficient, simultaneously determine the nature of the lead-lag between the corresponding series.

Furthermore, spectral methods offer advantages over multiple correlation or regression techniques. The latter techniques have often attempted to use determinants observed monthly or quarterly to explain simultaneously the trend, cyclical, seasonal, and error components of a price series. Spectral methods, in contrast, convert observations measured over time to a frequency configuration so that the relationship between determinants and price can be specified according to the short-, middle- or long-run frequency range of influence. This property of spectral decomposition has not only made possible the structuring of the general price model presented in the following chapters, it has also proven an effective device for selecting alternative forecast models.

Plan for this Study

The present study attempts to advance commodity price theory by developing a model of short-term price behavior capable of both explanation and prediction. The latter is emphasized because, of the many studies directed towards price behavior, few have been interested in the practical problems of price forecasting. A necessary preliminary to the plan for this study is the qualification of the actual commodity price series under investigation. Price series have been selected for commodities traded on domestic American markets, and, in particular, on those markets featuring both physical and futures exchanges. Although many of the internationally produced commodities occupy important positions in world trade, it is only the domestically produced commodities which possess records of hedging and speculation. For the first part of the study, the commodities selected represent almost one-half of the commodities traded on American futures markets; for the later part, the list is more restrictive. As mentioned above, the short-run record of these various price series provides a good background for analyzing short-, medium- and long-run price movements; short-run analysis is also of practical value to the processor or manufacturer who must forecast price fluctuations to optimize his return per unit of inventory. The price fluctuations dealt with, therefore, will be principally monthly, covering the period 1950 to 1966 with forecasts through 1967. Inclusion of these years not only isolates a period when the economy was relatively free of unusual shocks but also limits the study to the more important post-World War II period.

The approach taken in this attempt to formulate a more uniform theory of price behavior has been:

1. to analyze patterns of price fluctuations inherent to both cash and futures price series;

2. to investigate the influence of expectations as expressed between futures prices and cash prices;
3. to determine the relationship to prices of simply quantity influences including volume, open interest, hedging, speculating, demand, and supply;
4. to extend this investigation to more general influences arising from fluctuations in the economy;
5. to establish a hierarchy of these influences, so as to formulate a general model of commodity price behavior;
6. to compare price forecasts obtained from the general model to those produced by other methods; and
7. to draw conclusions concerning the quality of the general model, the effectiveness of various forecast methods, and the usefulness of the results for policy making.

The various topics listed above determine the subject matter of the subsequent chapters with the exception of Chapter 2, which provides an introduction to the methods of spectral analysis. The study formally begins in Chapter 3 with an investigation of the underlying nature of price fluctuations for a large group of commodities. The estimated power spectra suggest that these fluctuations have a strong random component, but some regularity has been discovered in the fluctuations of seasonal or longer duration. Before an explanation of these longer-run components is presented, the price analysis in Chapter 4 turns to the influence of market expectations. In particular, futures prices are considered as expected values of the cash price, and cross-spectra are estimated to test correlations as well as lead-lags between the respective price series.

The simple price-quantity theory of demand is investigated in Chapter 5 to help determine possible causes of the longer-run price regularities. When physical influences such as supply or demand fail to provide an adequate price explanation, the study turns to the evaluation of speculative influences. Both hedging and speculating are found to play a greater role in price formation than was previously recognized. In Chapter 6, the range of possible influences is extended to other factors such as commodity substitution, economic fluctuations, and market pressures, all of which are presented within the context of a general hypothesis of price behavior.

The results of these investigations are brought together in Chapter 7, where stepwise regression models have been constructed for soybean oil, cottonseed oil, soybean meal, soybeans, rye, and wheat. The various influences which offer at least a marginal explanation of commodity price behavior serve as inputs to the stepwise regressions, and the outcome allows a ranking of the more important influences in terms of their relative significance. Price fluctuations are linked to prices of substitutable commodities, levels of hedging and speculating, the pressures of demand on supply, and business-cycle indicators, in that order.

These various results become transformed into a general model of price behavior in Chapter 8. While the general explanation of price fluctuations varies slightly from commodity to commodity and the level of multiple correlation is only low to moderate, the uniformity obtained in the results suggests a potential for forecasting.

Alternative forecast methods considered appropriate for forecasting commodity prices are presented at the outset of Chapter 9. Results from forecasts produced by the general model are then compared to forecasts prepared from several of the alternative methods. Many of the forecast results substantiate the earlier findings concerning the random walk hypothesis. Conclusions for the various aspects of the study are drawn together in Chapter 10, where the objectives pursued at the beginning of the study are compared to the results achieved. Particular attention is given to the implications of the results for policy making; the closing remarks point to the areas which the study has opened for further research.

2 Statistical Background

Introduction

With this chapter, we briefly introduce the statistical techniques used in our empirical investigations in different parts of the study. As the data we shall be using are invariably in the form of time series, the techniques we shall present are those particularly designed for such data. These include principally the methods of spectral analysis and secondarily the methods of stepwise regression. Since many of the variations of these methods are examined here for the first time, our hope is also to evaluate the usefulness of the new techniques, employing the material of the later chapters. This appraisal is subsequently reported in Appendixes to Chapters 7 and 9 and in Chapter 10.

The Analysis of a Single Time Series

Description of a Time Series

Consider a variable whose value can be recorded at specified moments of time. If the variable can be recorded at every moment of time, it can be denoted by $x(t)$ and is called a continuous time series or stochastic process. An example would be temperature measured at some specific location. If the variable can only be recorded at equally spaced moments of time, such as weekly car production, it can be denoted by x_t and is called a discrete time series. Note that any continuous series can be recorded as a discrete series but not vice versa. Thus, for instance, temperature could be recorded every hour; but car production could not be measured at every moment of time, as it represents an accumulation over a set period of time. We shall discuss only discrete series as the theory is easier and because most data is actually of this form. It is important to distinguish between the theoretical series X_t $(t = \ldots, -1, 0, 1, \ldots)$ of values that might have been obtained, which will be called the generating process, and the actual observed data, x_t $(t = 1, \ldots, n)$. The distinction is similar to that between population and sample in classical statistics. The analysis of a series will be taken to mean the estimation or discovery of important properties of the generating process by investigation of the data.

It is generally considered to be too ambitious to attempt to make statements about the distribution of the generating process or subsets of it and so attention is usually fixed on the first and second moments of the process, i.e., the mean $m_t = E(X_t)$, variance $\sigma^2{}_t = E[(X_t - m_t)^2]$, and covariances $\mu(t, s) =$

$E\{[X_t - m_t]\ [X_s - m_s]\}$. If one had available a number of realizations of the process, that is several observed series, than it might be possible to attempt to estimate all of these quantities. It is, unfortunately, usually the case that only a single sample or observed series is available and so it is not possible to estimate even the first and second moments for all t and s or even the values at times for which observations are available. Consequently, restrictions on the variability over time of these moments have to be assumed to exist before any worthwhile estimation can take place. The basic assumption on which virtually all time series analysis is founded is that of stationarity. A process is said to be (second-order) stationary if its mean and variance are constant over time and $\mu(t, s) = \mu(t - s)$, that is, the covariance between any two terms depends solely on the difference in time and not the absolute time at which they are recorded. The assumption of stationarity essentially says that the law that generates the data is constant over time. Given the assumption of stationarity, one can now obtain estimates of the covariances of the form.

$$\hat{\mu}(k) = \frac{1}{n - k} \sum_{t=k+1}^{n} (x_t - \bar{x})(x_{t-k} - \bar{x}) \qquad (2.1)$$

where

$$\bar{x} = \frac{1}{n} \sum_{t=1}^{n} x_t$$

although more sophisticated estimates are sometimes used.

Time Series Models

The estimated covariances generally contain all of the relevant information about the series that will be used but various transformations of the sequence $\hat{\mu}(k)$ $(k = 0, 1, \ldots)$ have been found to be more useful in that they are easier to interpret. Most of the earlier interpretations occur in connection with various plausible models that have been suggested for the underlying generating process. It will be found useful if we list some of these models:

Purely random or white noise series. A series is said to be purely random series (or a white noise) if $\mu(k) = 0$, $k \neq 0$, i.e., X_t and X_s are uncorrelated for all $t \neq s$. X_t will then be a set of uncorrelated random variables, each from the same distribution, as one might find, for instance, in a table of random numbers. One point about such a sequence that might be noted is that X_t cannot be predicted by any linear sum of past values of the series.

Linear cyclic model. This model assumes that the series is made up of a number of purely cyclical terms, i.e.,

$$X_t = \sum_{j=1}^{m} c_j \cos(\omega_j t + \theta_j) + \epsilon_t \tag{2.2}$$

where ϵ_t is a white noise series. The point about this model is that it consists of a sum of purely cyclical components with amplitudes c_j, frequencies ω_j (i.e., periods $2\pi/\omega_j$) and phases θ_j together with a white noise residual. This model has now been largely abandoned in economics, although not entirely, but is still important in meteorological, geological; and technological series. The problem of how to estimate the parameters of the model was solved at the turn of the century by Schuster [1900] who pointed out that the function

$$I_n(\omega) = \frac{1}{n}\left[\left(\sum_{j=1}^{n} x_j \cos 2\pi j\omega\right)^2 + \left(\sum_{j=1}^{n} x_j \sin 2\pi j\omega\right)^2\right] \tag{2.3}$$

has sharp peaks at $\omega = \omega_j$ and that the heights of the peaks were proportional to c_j^2, the squares of the unknown amplitudes. This function is known as the periodogram.

Autoregressive model. This model is one in which the variable is a linear sum of its past values, i.e.,

$$X_t = \sum_{j=1}^{m} a_j X_{t-j} + \epsilon_t \tag{2.4}$$

so that X_t is formed by a linear sum of earlier X's plus a white noise residual. Such a model will be found to contain no strictly cyclical components and so, if the periodogram is formed from data generated in this fashion, the resulting diagram takes on a form that is of little direct use, partly due to the unfortunate statistical properties of the periodogram. The coefficients $\hat{a}_j$ in the autoregressive model can be found by least squares, i.e., the $\hat{a}_j$'s are chosen so as to minimize

$$J = \sum_{t=m+1}^{n}\left(x_t - \sum_{j=1}^{m} a_j x_{t-j}\right)^2 \tag{2.5}$$

The solution involves the inversion of a matrix of covariances.

Moving average model. This model is one where X_t is formed by a linear sum of past and present terms of the white noise series, ϵ_t, i.e.,

$$X_t = \sum_{j=0}^{k} b_j \epsilon_{t-j} \tag{2.6}$$

Such a model produces a series with no purely cyclical terms although a given finite length of data could appear to contain near cycles. It can be shown that any moving average model can be closely approximated by an autoregressive model, and vice versa. This fact is used in one of the methods of estimation for moving average models, although the details of this method need not be discussed here.

Other models can also be suggested, such as a mixture of the autoregressive and linear cyclic models. In economics, such a mixed model has frequently been proposed, in that it has been suggested that an economic variable can be usefully decomposed into the components: trend + business cycles + seasonal + (autoregressive) residual. The object of the analysis was, then, to determine the properties of each component.

Spectral Analysis of Time Series

In the 1940s, some work by Wiener, Kolmogoroff, and others suggested a new approach which both generalized earlier methods and also enabled considerable advances to be made in interpretations of the analysis. However, this new method, known as spectral analysis, involves more complicated mathematics and so is more difficult to explain. A detailed account has been given elsewhere.[a] All that we shall do here is to provide the basic concepts in mathematical terms and then attempt to explain them in terms of analogies.

The two formulae which provide the basis of the whole method are the so-called spectral representation of the covariance sequence

$$\mu(\tau) = E(X_t \overline{X}_{t-\tau}) = \int_{-\pi}^{\pi} e^{i\tau\omega} dF(\omega) \tag{2.7}$$

and the spectral representation of the series, called for convenience the Cramer representation

$$X_t = \int_{-\pi}^{\pi} e^{it\omega} dz(\omega) \tag{2.8}$$

where $z(\omega)$ is a complex random function having the properties

$$\begin{aligned} E[dz(\omega)\,\overline{dz(\lambda)}] &= 0 & \omega &\neq \lambda \\ &= dF(\omega) & \omega &= \lambda \end{aligned}$$

[a]The interested reader should consult the references cited at the end of the chapter.

and where $F(\omega)$ is a distribution function times a positive constant, so that $F(\omega_1) \geqslant F(\omega_2)$ for all $\omega_1 \geqslant \omega_2$ and $F(-\pi) = 0$.

Anyone unfamiliar with Fourier transforms or complex random functions is likely to find these formulae awesome. It is possible, however, to explain the basic ideas underlying the formulae fairly simply. Consider a time series made up of a number of purely cyclical components with amplitudes a_j, frequencies ω_j ("frequency" ω corresponds to "period" $p = 2\pi/\omega$), and phases θ_j, i.e.,

$$X_t = \sum_{j=1}^{m} a_j \cos(t\omega_j + \theta_j) \tag{2.9}$$

and suppose that for any particular realization of the process (i.e., any observed sample), the a_j and θ_j's are selected at random from some given distributions. One might consider for instance, all the a_j's coming from normal distributions with zero means, so that $a_j \sim N\ (o,\sigma_j^2)$ and all the θ_j's from rectangular distributions on $(-\pi,\ \pi)$. Further, suppose that all the a_j's and θ_j's are independent of one another. For any particular realization the a_j's and θ_j's will be fixed at the start and will remain constant, but in terms of the underlying generating process X_t they will be random variables. Thus, X_t in the finite sum of independent components, each of which has associated with it a different frequency. By direct evaluation, one finds that

$$\text{var}(X_t) = \frac{1}{2}\sum_{j=1}^{m} \sigma_j^2$$

and (2.10)

$$\mu(\tau) = \text{cov}(X_t, X_{t-\tau}) = \frac{1}{2}\sum_{j=1}^{m} \sigma_j^2 \cos \tau\omega_j$$

so that the importance of each component can be measured in terms of the contribution it makes $(1/2\ \sigma_j{}^2)$ to the total variance of X_t. Similarly, one can represent the sequence $\mu(\tau)$, $\tau = 0, 1, 2, \ldots$ by

$$\mu(\tau) = \int_{-\pi}^{\pi} \cos \tau\omega \, dF(\omega) \tag{2.11}$$

where $F(\omega)$ is a step function, with steps of size $1/2\sigma_j{}^2$ at ω_j and flat everywhere else. This latter equation is a real version of equation (2.7).

Suppose now that we consider a generalization of this model so that the *number* of components becomes extremely large and the contribution made to the variance of X_t by any one component becomes small. We could then talk about the contribution made to var X_t by all components with frequencies in some given band of frequencies. If we add up the contributions to var X_t made by all components with frequencies less than or equal to ω_0, this is then equal to the function $F(\omega_0)$ introduced above. It is seen that as all frequencies must lie in the region $(-\pi, \pi)$, that $F(-\pi) = 0$ and $F(\pi) = \text{var } X_t$.

A simpler version of equation (2.7) is:

$$\mu(\tau) = \int_{-\pi}^{\pi} \cos \tau\omega \, f(\omega) \, d\omega \qquad (2.12)$$

Here $f(\omega)$ is the derivative of $F(\omega)$ and is called the power spectral density function or power spectrum. It arises in the limit considered above when no one component makes a finite contribution to var X_t but the sum of components with frequencies in any small band do make a finite contribution. The distinction is similar to that made in statistics between the frequency function for a continuous random variable as compared to a discrete random variable where no such frequency function exists.

To summarize, the model considered has the following properties:

1. The series X_t is decomposed into a large (uncountable) number of independent components, each of which is associated with a different frequency.

2. The relative importance of any group of components is measured by their contribution to var X_t. In particular, if no one component makes a finite contribution, then the contribution of all components with frequencies in the band $(\omega, \omega + d\omega)$ is $f(\omega) \, d\omega$, $f(\omega)$ being the power spectrum.

The idea of decomposing an economic variable is not a new one. The decomposition into trend + "business cycles" + seasonal + residual has already been mentioned. A trend, being a very smooth, slow-moving component, can be thought of as having a very long, possibly infinite period, and so corresponds to extremely low frequencies, i.e., near zero. The "business cycles" would correspond to the next lowest frequency band, possibly corresponding to periods of between 20 and 100 months, say. The seasonal component is found at frequencies $2\pi j/12$ $(j = 1, 2, \ldots, 6)$ when using monthly data, i.e., a twelve-month period and its harmonics. The "residual" term corresponds to the sum of all the other frequency components. An alternative decomposition used in economics is long-run (long periods, low frequencies), middle-run, and short-run (short periods, high frequencies).

Interpreting the Spectral Representation

As the spectral concept is not a particularly easy one, this section is devoted to giving an analogy that has been found useful in the past. (Readers who feel that they already fully understand the concept should pass on to the next section.)

Consider the total amount of sound (or noise) coming over a very wide radio band. If we had a very crude instrument which transformed all the noise into sounds that the human ear can hear, the resulting cacophony would resemble the type of (stationary) time series that we are usually trying to analyze; that is, it is built up of many components, each of which we would like to know more about. Just as the ear can filter out sounds and concentrate on a particular one, so can a radio concentrate on a particular wave band. It is certain that everyone has at some time swung the dial of a radio set across a wave band, and the experience there gained can be used in an explanation of the spectrum. Suppose that we have a simple radio set that does not emit the actual words or sounds found at any frequency but only indicates the total power (or amount) of sound. By this we mean in effect that our simple radio set has the ability to look at one wave length (frequency) at a time without being distracted by what is to be found at other frequencies. If we used our set in England at 3 A.M. (i.e., when no stations are broadcasting), the set would not register zero amount of sound at every point but rather a small, constant amount. This is due to all the "atmospherics" and internally produced noise of the set and thus corresponds to receiving a purely random signal. If, however, some stations are broadcasting at that time, theoretically each will be sending signals at one frequency only. The radio will now show the small, constant (background) noise at all frequencies except at a finite number (corresponding to the number of stations) where it will record the power put out by each station. The radio will thus find the position of the frequencies at which the stations are broadcasting together with the strength of signal being received at these frequencies.

In practice, as everyone knows, the sound from a particular station is not to be found only at a single point but rather is spread around the point, although with decreasing power. (Incidentally, if the sound were literally at only one point of the line it would be impossible to find with a perfect radio.) Figure 2 - 1 illustrates the three types of signals discussed above.

We now define a spectrum as a diagram showing the size of the amplitude of each frequency to be found in a particular time series. It should not be surprising to learn that it may be proved that perfect knowledge of a spectrum will determine the properties of a time series, but not its actual values, due to the probabilistic elements involved. In any case, the spectrum will certainly show which are the important components of the series. This can be seen in Figure 2-1 where diagrams (i) to (iii) illustrate spectra of different time series: (i) is, of course, the spectrum of a purely random, independent series (white noise); (ii) is the theoretical spectrum of the linear cyclic model; whereas (iii) represents the perfect estimate (should such a thing exist) of the spectrum of a time series of finite length generated by the linear cyclic model. (Diagram (iii) corresponds to the shape that Schuster was hoping his periodogram would take.)

It might be noted that even if the stations were broadcasting as in diagram (ii), a real radio is unable to concentrate on a single wavelength, but rather gives the output over a small wave band, centered on this wavelength, possibly with weights decreasing from the center of the band outward. Thus, even if the stations were broadcasting as in (ii), the radio's output would resemble diagram (iii). This is the identical situation to that when we attempt to estimate the

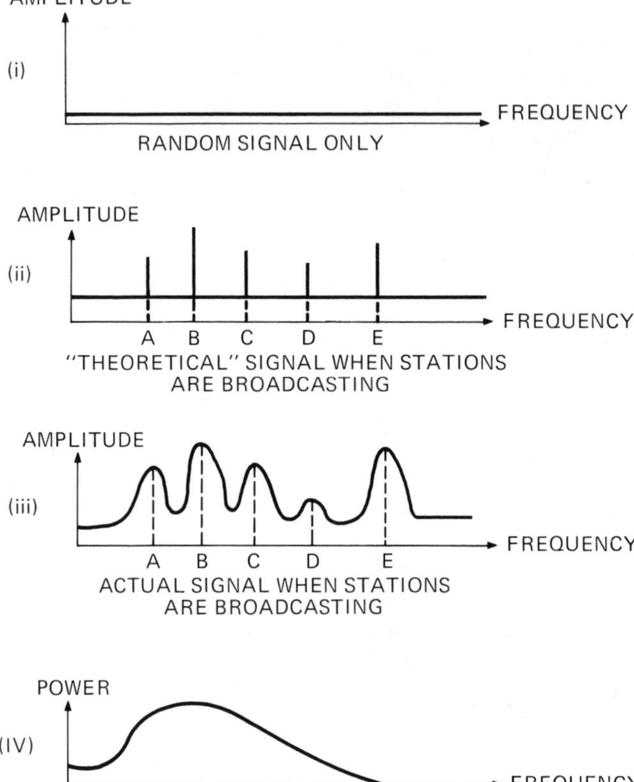

Figure 2-1 Hypothetical Spectral Shapes

spectrum; having only a finite amount of data available, we are forced to estimate the spectrum over a finite number of frequency bands.

Suppose that our simplified radio was now attached to a radio telescope which is directed toward some point in the Milky Way. It is possible that the resulting plot of power against frequency looks like diagrams (i) or (iii), but it is also plausible to expect a more complicated diagram as in (iv) and (v). It is clear that such "spectra," as we may now think of them, cannot arise from series which are derived from a linear cyclic model. On the other hand, it is perfectly possible for a series from a linear regressive model to produce such a smooth spectrum, although a smooth spectrum does not necessarily indicate that a linear regressive model is the correct one. Many more-complicated systems could also produce a similar shape.

By examining a spectrum, the important bands of frequencies may be seen; although little can be said about the underlying generating process (except, perhaps, that it is doubtful that it is linear cyclic).

It must be emphasized that the above analogy has been presented only to help understand the ideas involved in the concept of a spectrum and, like all analogies, it must not be taken too far or examined too deeply.

Spectra and Filtering

One other use of the spectrum is to specify the effect of a linear filter on the data. Suppose one has a series X_t with spectrum $f(\omega)$ and that a second series Y_t is formed by

$$Y_t = \sum_{j=1}^{m} c_j X_{t-j} \tag{2.13}$$

then Y_t is said to be a filtered version of X_t and it can be shown that the spectrum of Y_t is given by $f_y(\omega) = c(\omega)\, f(\omega)$ where

$$c(\omega) = \left| \sum_{j=1}^{m} c_j e^{-ij\omega} \right|^2 \tag{2.14}$$

It is seen that by choosing the c_j's properly, one can make the spectrum of Y_t have approximately any desired shape. In particular, one can reduce in importance or completely remove any purely cyclical component. Thus, suppose X_t is measured monthly and has a seasonal component. Then if

$$Y_t = \frac{1}{12} \sum_{j=1}^{12} X_{t-j} \tag{2.15}$$

it can be shown that Y_t will have no seasonal component but, of course, the effect of such a filter will have other consequences also, which can be determined by equation (2.14).

This idea is also useful in dealing with trends. There is no generally accepted and satisfactory definition of what is meant, in practice, by a trend. It is generally taken to be a very smooth component, either continually increasing or continually decreasing; and is usually taken to be well represented by some simple function of time, such as a linear or exponential or polynomial function. One point about such functions is that they never repeat themselves, so that they can be said to have an infinite period and hence a zero frequency. It is seen that trend terms, in theory at least, only affect the spectrum at zero frequency. Thus, if one devises a filter which cuts out low frequencies, to a large extent this filter will effectively remove trend. One way of doing this, for instance, is to form a moving average of the series X_t, i.e.,

$$Z_t = \frac{1}{2m + 1} \sum_{j=-m}^{m} X_{t-j} \tag{2.16}$$

and then forming $X_t - Z_t$. It is also possible to remove trends by regression techniques, that is by estimating a postulated trend curve from the data and then subtracting it. However, the side effects of this procedure are less easily characterized.

Examples of Spectra

It is seen then, that the spectrum will suggest the type of model that might be fitted to the data. A very flat spectrum suggests a white noise (purely random); a smooth spectrum would suggest an autoregressive model but any sharp spikes would indicate the possible presence of purely cyclical components.

As an example of spectra, we show two estimated spectra using interest data.[1] Figure 2-2 shows the spectrum of the one-year bond rate using quarterly data over the period 1924 to 1962. It is seen that low frequencies are very much more important than high frequencies, as is often found for economic time series.

Figure 2-3 shows the spectrum of the first differences of Consols together with 95% confidence bands. The spectrum is seen to be generally flat, as for a white noise series, but with extra power at frequency components corresponding to periods of two and four years. A tentative explanation for the appearance of these "cycles," given in the original paper, is that, on most occasions, the UK monetary crises happen to have fallen in odd-numbered years in the period 1939 to 1961.

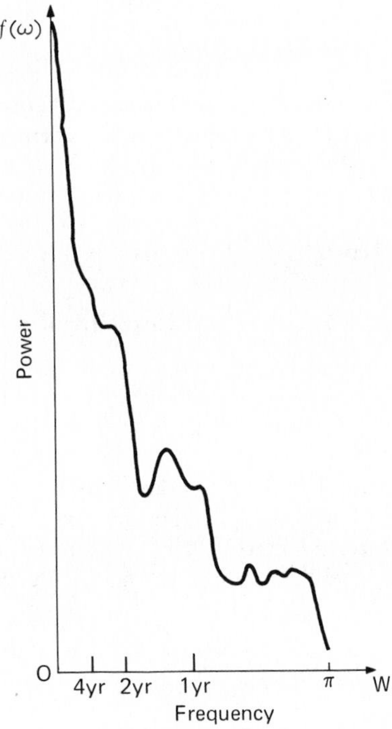

Figure 2-2 Spectrum of One-Year Bond Rate.

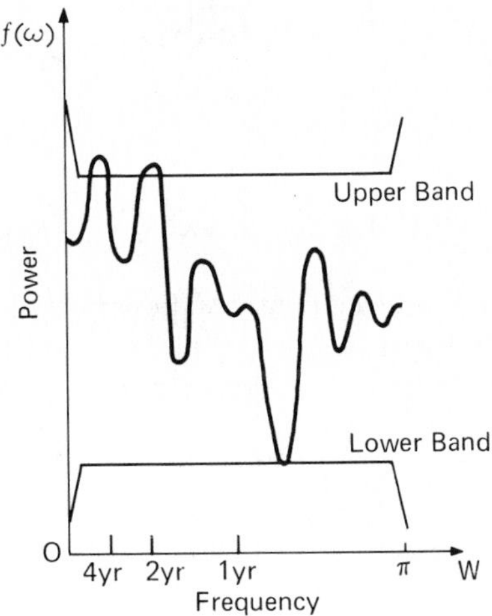

Figure 2-3 Spectrum of Consols First Differences with 95% Confidence Bands.

The Analysis of Two Time Series

Cross-Spectral Analysis

Now consider two stationary series X_t, Y_t with spectra $f_x(\omega)$, $f_y(\omega)$. They are said to be jointly stationary if the relationship between them is time-invariant, at least as far as second order moments is concerned. Thus the cross-lagged covariances.

$$\operatorname{cov}(X_t, Y_{t-\tau}) = \mu_{xy}(\tau) \tag{2.17}$$

depend only on the lag τ and not on time t. These covariances also have a spectral representation

$$\mu_{xy}(\tau) = \int_{-\pi}^{\pi} e^{i\tau\omega}\, dcr(\omega) \tag{2.18}$$

and, if the series contain no purely periodic components, $dcr(\omega)$ can be replaced by $cr(\omega)d\omega$. $cr(\omega)$ is called the cross-spectrum and is, in general, a complex function of ω. It is usual to consider two other functions derived from $cr(\omega)$, as they are easier to interpret. These functions are the coherence $c(\omega)$ defined by

$$C(\omega) = \frac{|cr(\omega)|^2}{f_x(\omega)f_y(\omega)} \tag{2.19}$$

and the phase $\phi(\omega)$ given by

$$\phi(\omega) = \tan^{-1}\left[\frac{\text{Imag. part of } cr(\omega)}{\text{Real part of } cr(\omega)}\right] \tag{2.20}$$

If the Cramer representations of X_t, Y_t are

$$X_t = \int_{-\pi}^{\pi} e^{it\omega} dz_x(\omega), \qquad Y_t = \int_{-\pi}^{\pi} e^{it\omega}\, dz_y(\omega) \tag{2.21}$$

then a consequence of the series being jointly stationary is

$$\begin{aligned} E[dz_x(\omega)\overline{dz_y(\lambda)}] &= 0, & \omega &\neq \lambda \\ &= cr(\omega)d\omega & \omega &= \lambda \end{aligned} \tag{2.22}$$

Coherence and Decomposition

It is possible to understand the interpretation of these cross-spectral functions by returning to the basic concept of decomposition introduced in the previous section. Each series can be decomposed into many uncorrelated components each associated with a frequency ω. The random amplitude of the ω-frequency component of X_t is $dz_x(\omega)$. The variance of $dz_x(\omega)$ is $f_x(\omega)d\omega$ and the covariance between $dz_x(\omega)$ and $dz_y(\omega)$ is $cr(\omega)d\omega$. It thus follows that the coherence $C(\omega)$ represents the square of the correlation between the amplitudes of the ω-frequency components of the two series. Thus, the spectral approach does not give one a single measure of the degree to which two series are related but measures the degree of relatedness in terms of the coherence for each frequency component in the decomposed series. From its definition, $C(\omega)$ must lie in the range 0 to 1 and so, as stated before, is interpreted as the square of a correlation coefficient. A low value of coherence indicates that the series are little correlated at that frequency, a value near one suggests that these series are highly related at that frequency. It is seen that the coherence diagram gives one a much more sophisticated way of measuring the extent to which series are related.

Lag Structure and Decomposition

The second aspect of investigating the way series are related is to look for a lag structure. In spectral analysis this is done by using the phase diagram. In the decomposition of the series each component is associated with a frequency. To fully characterize each component, one needs its amplitude (i.e., the variance of $dz(\omega)$) and also the phase, i.e.,

$$\tan^{-1} \frac{\text{Imag. part of } dz(\omega)}{\text{Real part of } dz(\omega)} .$$

The differences in the phases of $dz_x(\omega)$ and $dz_y(\omega)$ is given by the phase function $\phi(\omega)$. If there is no lag between the series then $\phi(\omega)$ will be zero for all ω. If there is a simple time lag, i.e., $Y_t = aX_{t-k} + Z_t$ where Z_t is some series uncorrelated to X_t then $\phi(\omega) = k\omega$, so by examining the slope of $\phi(\omega)$ the lag k can be estimated. Note that k need not be an integer, so that if monthly data is used it is possible to observe a lag of a fraction of a month. More complicated lag structures can, in theory, be observed, i.e, the lag over low frequencies could be longer than the lag between between the series over high frequencies. A particular case of this is when the phase diagram lies about some constant, i.e., $\phi(\omega) = a$. This case, known as a fixed-angle lag, can be interpreted as being a time lag of a/ω at frequency ω, so that for low frequencies (long periods) the lag is great but it decreases as frequency increases (period decreases). The exception for this case is when $a = \pm\pi$ as if $X_t = -Y_t$ the phase diagram will be $\phi(\omega) = \pm\pi$. (The cases are the same; as from its definition, the phase diagram is periodic outside the range $(-\pi,\pi)$).

There are two important considerations concerning the interpretation of the phase diagram. There is clearly no point in looking for a lag structure between two unrelated series, so that one must first look at the coherence diagram to see that the series are related before attempting to interpret the phase diagram. When the coherence is low the phase estimate becomes extremely erratic and is hence difficult to interpret in any case. Secondly, the interpretations of phase mentioned above have all been in terms of one series lagging the other. However, if there is feedback present between the two series, the theoretical shape of the phase diagram is usually very complicated and interpretation in terms of lags is no longer possible. Unfortunately, a satisfactory statistical technique for investigating feedback relations is not yet available.

Interpreting the Cross-Spectrum

To summarize the use of the cross-spectral functions discussed here, consider X_t and Y_t each decomposed into k components

$$X_t = X_{1t} + X_{2t} + \ldots + X_{kt}$$

$$Y_t = Y_{1t} + Y_{2t} + \ldots + Y_{kt}$$

X_{1t}, Y_{1t} might represent very low frequencies; X_{2t}, Y_{2t} the next lowest frequency band, and so forth. As X_t is stationary, we know that X_{it}, X_{jt} are uncorrelated, all $i \neq j$. Similarly for Y_{it} and Y_{jt}. If the series are jointly stationary then it follows that X_{it} and Y_{jt} will be uncorrelated, all $i \neq j$. Thus, the extent to which two series are interrelated can be fully characterized by considering the extent to which corresponding frequency components are related. The coherence diagram $C(\omega)$ measures the square of the correlation between X_{it} and Y_{it} at the frequency ω_i associated with these components. Similarly, $\phi(\omega_i)/\omega_i$ can be interpreted as measuring the time lag between these components, unless $C(\omega_i)$ is very small or unless feedback is suspected.

In the previous section, the idea of a filter was introduced. If $F(X_t)$ is a filtered version of X_t then the effect on the spectrum was discussed above. As far as the cross-spectrum is concerned, if $F(X_t) = \Sigma\, d_j X_{t-j}$ and if the cross-spectrum between X_t and Y_t is $cr(\omega)$, then the cross-spectrum between $F(X_t)$ and Y_t is $d(\omega)\ cr(\omega)$, where $d(\omega) = \Sigma\, d_j e^{-ij\omega}$. It follows that the coherence between $F(X_t)$ and Y_t is the same as that between X_t and Y_t, but the phase diagram is altered by filtering one of the series.

Examples of Estimated Cross-Spectra

As an example of the use of cross-spectral functions we return again to the interest rate data used in the previous section. Figures 2-4 and 2-5 show the coherence and phase diagrams between the one-year bond rate and the four-year bond rate.

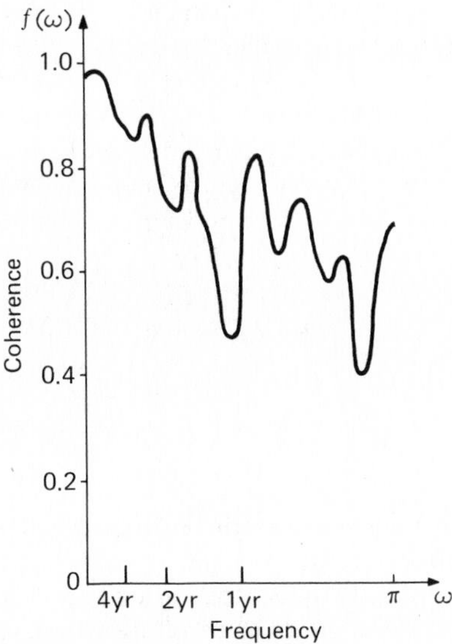

Figure 2-4 Coherence Between One-Year Bond Rate and Four-Year Bond Rate.

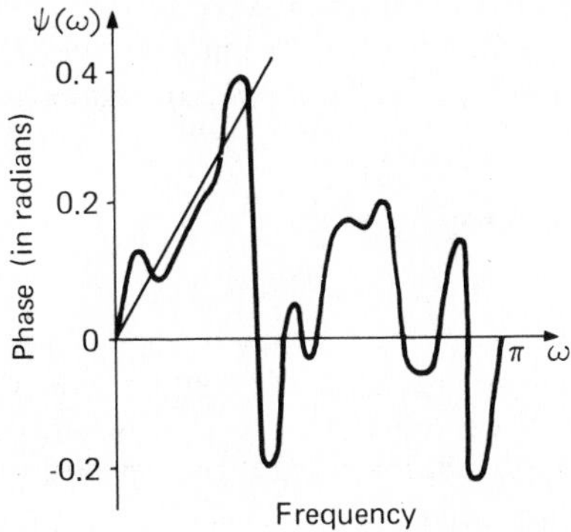

Figure 2-5 Phase Difference Between One-Year Bond Rate and Four-Year Bond Rate.

The coherence is seen to be falling as frequency increases, suggesting that the low frequency components move together more than do higher frequency components. The phase diagram is particularly interesting. For the low frequencies, which had the highest coherence values, the one-year rate seems to be leading the four-year rate as the phase diagram is seen to be linear. The slope of the phase diagram suggests a lead of approximately nine weeks. However, higher frequency components seem to have no lead or lag structure, as the phase diagram lies about zero.

The Analysis of Several Time Series

Partial Cross-Spectrum

One frequently would like to investigate the relationship between two series after having removed the effect of one or more other series. To do this we use the concept of partial spectral analysis. Just as the cross-spectrum, via the coherence, enables us to measure the (square of the) correlation between the amplitudes $dz_x(\omega)$, $dz_y(\omega)$ of the ω-frequency components of two series, the partial cross-spectrum, via the partial coherence, enables us to measure the (square of the) partial correlation between $dz_x(\omega)$ and $dz_y(\omega)$, having taken out the effect of say $dz_z(\omega)$.

For our purpose, it is convenient to regard spectral analysis as a form of analysis of variance, the components of variance being associated with various frequencies instead of the conventional rows and columns. Extending this idea to multiple time series $(X_{1t}, X_{2t}, \ldots, X_{mt})$, we can regard the $m \times m$ matrix of (auto) spectra and cross-spectra

$$\Sigma(\omega) = [S_{ij}(\omega)] \tag{2.23}$$

as estimating the covariance matrix of the time series of frequency ω (when one uses estimated spectra it will be seen that we should use the expression "around frequency ω" rather than "at frequency ω"). In this matrix $S_{ii}(\omega)$ represents the spectrum of X_{it}, and $S_{ij}(\omega)$ represents the cross-spectrum between the series X_{it} and X_{jt}. Fixing frequency temporally (at ω), we may proceed to form from the matrix Σ such (complex-valued) quantities as correlations between frequency ω components and partial correlations.

Denote the component of the ith time series around frequency ω by $X_i(\omega)$. Consider the computation of $P_{1\cdot 2}(\omega)$, the partial correlation of $X_1(\omega)$, $X_2(\omega)$ given $X_j(\omega), j > 2$. First partition Σ into submatrices as follows:

$$\Sigma = \left(\begin{array}{c|c} \Sigma_{11} & \Sigma_{12} \\ \hline \Sigma_{21} & \Sigma_{22} \end{array}\right) \tag{2.24}$$

The partitioning lines are between the second and third rows, and second and third columns. Next form the 2 x 2 matrix

$$\Sigma_{12 \cdot k} = \Sigma_{11} - \Sigma_{12}\, \Sigma_{22}^{-1}\, \Sigma_{21} \tag{2.25}$$

then

$$\Sigma_{12 \cdot k} = \begin{pmatrix} S_{11 \cdot k}(\omega) & S_{12 \cdot k}(\omega) \\ S_{21 \cdot k}(\omega) & S_{22 \cdot k}(\omega) \end{pmatrix} \tag{2.26}$$

is the partial auto and cross-spectral matrix for the series X_{1t} and X_{2t} with k denoting the set 3, 4, . . ., m.

The partial coherence is given by

$$C_{12 \cdot k} = \frac{|S_{12 \cdot k}(\omega)|^2}{S_{11 \cdot k}(\omega) S_{22 \cdot k}(\omega)} \tag{2.27}$$

and similarly a partial phase can be defined.

Multiple Cross Spectrum

It is also of interest to consider the generalization of the multiple correlation coefficient. Suppose that an optimum linear combination of the series X_{3t}, $X_{4t}, \ldots, X_{mt}$ has been subtracted from X_{1t} leaving $\tilde{X}_{1t}$, and similarly for $\tilde{X}_{2t}$ leaving $\tilde{X}_{2t}$ then the above functions can be interpreted as being the spectra, coherence, and phase for the two series $\tilde{X}_{1t}$, $\tilde{X}_{2t}$.

It is also possible to measure the extent to which one series is related to an optimum combination of a whole set of other series. The matrix $\Sigma(\omega)$ is now partioned into submatrices

$$\Sigma = \left| \begin{array}{c|c} S_{11}(\omega) & \Gamma_{12}(\omega) \\ \hline \Gamma_{21}(\omega) & \Gamma_{22}(\omega) \end{array} \right| \tag{2.28}$$

where now the partioning lines are between the first and second rows and the first and second columns. The function

$$\Sigma_{1,p}(\omega) = S_{11}(\omega) - \Gamma_{12}(\omega)\Gamma_{22}^{-1}(\omega)\Gamma_{21}(\omega) \tag{2.29}$$

is the partial (auto) spectrum of the series $\overline{X}_t$, where $\overline{X}_{1t}$ is X_{1t} minus the optimum combination of X_{jt}, $j \epsilon p$, where p is the set (2, 3, . . ., m). Thus $\overline{X}_t$ is the residual process when all (linear) information about X_t contained in X_{2t}, $X_{3t}, \ldots, X_{mt}$ has been removed. The multiple coherence function $M_{1,p}(\omega)$ defined by

$$M_{1,p}(\omega) = 1 - \frac{\Sigma_{1,p}(\omega)}{S_{11}(\omega)} \tag{2.30}$$

is a direct generalization of the square of the multiple correlation coefficient (i.e., the coefficient of determination, R^2) and can be interpreted accordingly at each frequency. When $m = 2$, only two processes are involved and $M_{1,2}(\omega) = C(\omega)$, the coherence.

An alternative method of analyzing multiple series, based on regression techniques is described in the section on stepwise regression.

Estimation Procedures for Spectral Analysis

When one attempts to estimate a spectrum one is in fact attempting a very subtle analysis, which, of course, requires considerable amounts of data. A series of at least 100 terms is usually required, and is very unlikely to successfully estimate complicated spectra or cross-spectra with less than 50 pieces of data. The data will usually be assumed to be stationary, although a trend in mean can be successfully removed prior to spectral estimation either by regression or by filtering.

As the time series we use are collected at time intervals an equal distance apart, it follows that one cannot "look at" frequency components corresponding to very short periods. In fact, given monthly data, one cannot directly observe a component having period shorter than two months, corresponding to the frequency π. Further, due to symmetries in the definitions used, the only frequency range worth considering is that between 0 and π. The estimation problem using a single series is therefore to estimate $f(\omega)$ $0 \leqslant \omega \leqslant \pi$. Given a finite length of series, it is clearly not generally possible to estimate a continuous function, such as $f(\omega)$, at every point on the line. At most one can hope to get estimates of some average value of $f(\omega)$ over each of a set of small frequency bands. In practice, one estimates a function

$$\hat{f}(\omega) = \int_0^{\pi} b_\omega(\lambda) f(\lambda)\, d\lambda \tag{2.31}$$

where $b_\omega(\lambda)$ is a function which is nearly one for λ near ω and is zero or almost zero for λ not near ω, i.e., has a shape possibly of the form:

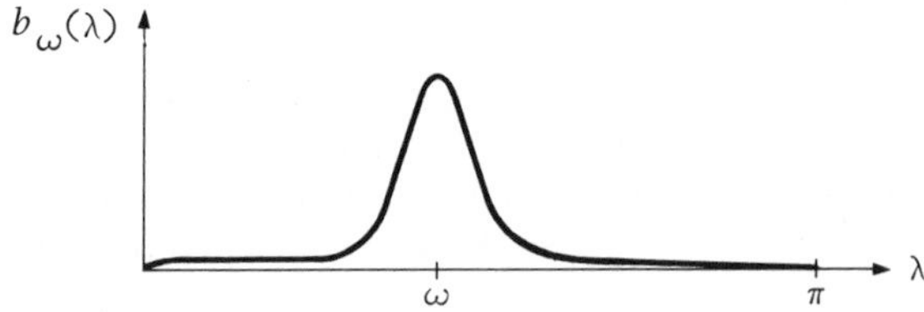

Functions such as $b_\omega(\lambda)$ are called "windows" as by their use one effectively views the spectrum $f(\omega)$ through a narrow slit or window.

The periodogram previously mentioned is an estimate of the spectrum. Although it provides an estimate that is almost unbiased it does have otherwise rather unsatisfactory statistical properties. Apart from the occasional peak, one is basically looking for a rather smooth shape for the underlying true spectrum. Unfortunately, the periodogram is invariably very unsmooth in nature, with a large variance of estimate, and so the basic spectral shape is difficult to observe. The periodogram also has the statistical property that it is not consistent, so that adding further data does not necessarily improve the estimate. However by smoothing the periodogram, by the use of a window, a more satisfactory estimate of the spectrum can be obtained, being both consistent and smoother.

Although spectral estimates can be produced by first forming a periodogram and then smoothing it, the estimates used in this book are formed in a more direct, but equivalent manner. The covariances are estimated by

$$C_k = \frac{1}{n}\sum_{t=1}^{n-k}(x_t - \bar{x})(x_{t+k} - \bar{x}) \tag{2.32}$$

where

$$\bar{x} = \frac{1}{n}\sum_{t=1}^{n} x_t \qquad \text{given data } (x_t, \quad t = 1, \ldots, n).$$

The spectrum is estimated at frequency points $\omega_j = \pi j/m$, $j = 0, \ldots, m$ by the formula

$$\hat{f}(\omega_j) = \frac{C_0}{2\pi} + \frac{1}{\pi}\sum_{k=1}^{m} C_k\lambda_k \cos\omega_j k \tag{2.33}$$

where

$$\begin{aligned}\lambda_k &= 1 - \frac{6k^2}{m^2}\left(1 - \frac{k}{m}\right) & 0 \leqslant k \leqslant \frac{m}{2} \\ &= 2\left(1 - \frac{k}{m}\right)^3 & \frac{m}{2} \leqslant k \leqslant m\end{aligned} \tag{2.34}$$

The weights λ_k used here are those for the Parzen window and the resulting estimate has the useful property that $\hat{f}(\omega_j)$ cannot take a negative value. In the formula given, the spectrum is estimated at $m + 1$ frequency points and the estimate uses only the first $m + 1$ values of the sample autocovariances. These numbers need not, in fact, be equal but were for the calculations presented here. One normally refers to m as the cutoff point or number of lags used. The higher m, in general, the less smooth will be the resulting spectral estimate, i.e., variance increases, but bias becomes less important. The bias is usually not of great importance unless the spectrum has a great slope. However, bias is of importance when one is estimating the value of the spectrum near a large peak corresponding to a strictly periodic component. As the window will not usually be zero at a neighboring frequency, one will get "leakage" from this peak into estimates at nearby frequencies. It is due to this that trend and seasonal terms are usually removed, or reduced in importance, before analyzing a time series.

The cross-spectrum is estimated in a similar fashion. The cross-covariances are estimated by

$$C_{yx}(k) = \frac{1}{n} \sum_{t=1}^{n-k} (x_t - \bar{x})(y_{t+k} - \bar{y})$$

$$C_{xy}(k) = \frac{1}{n} \sum_{t=1}^{n-k} (y_t - \bar{y})(x_{t+k} - \bar{x}) \qquad (2.35)$$

for data $(x_t, y_t \;\; t = 1, \ldots, n)$ and the cross spectrum by

$$\text{Real part of } Cr(\omega_j) = \frac{1}{4\pi} [C_{xy}(0) + C_{yx}(0)]$$

$$+ \frac{1}{2\pi} \sum_{k=1}^{m} \lambda_k [C_{xy}(k) + C_{yx}(k)] \cos \omega_j k \qquad (2.36)$$

$$\text{Imaginary part of } Cr(\omega_j) = \frac{1}{2\pi} \sum_{k=1}^{m} \lambda_k [C_{xy}(k) - C_{yx}(k)] \sin \omega_j k \qquad (2.37)$$

and where λ_k are the Parzen weights given above. The coherence and phase estimates are formed by inserting the estimates of their components into the expressions.

The partial and multiple spectra are estimated by forming the estimate of the matrix $\Sigma(\omega)$, by replacing each element of the matrix by the spectral or cross-spectral estimates, and then by performing the matrix operations described in the previous section.

Experience has indicated that these estimates are generally satisfactory, the only possible exception being the coherence, which is frequently biased and has a large variance except for very long series. We shall not here go into details of confidence intervals or tests of hypotheses. Most of the available theoretical results in these fields are not completely satisfactory, being asymptotic results. Accounts can be found in the books by Granger and Hatanka and by Jenkins and Watts. Confidence intervals for short series based on a simulation study can be found in the paper by Granger and Hughes.

Stepwise Regression

Although spectral methods are well suited for investigating relationships between two or more time series they do not provide actual models. Models are useful for investigating causal relationships and are essential for prediction. When forecasting a stationary time series using past values of the series, forecasts can be immediately obtained once an autoregressive model has been fitted to the data, i.e.,

$$x_t = \sum_{j=1}^{k} \alpha_j x_{t-j} + \epsilon_t \tag{2.38}$$

where, for an optimum forecast ϵ_t will be a white noise (purely random) series uncorrelated to $x_{t-j}, j > 0$.

When several series are available x_{it}, $i = 1, \ldots, m$, say, then one will usually wish to explain the current value of a particular series in terms of the other series, i.e.,

$$x_{1t} = \sum_{j=0}^{k_2} \alpha_{2j} x_{2,t-j} + \sum_{j=0}^{k_3} \alpha_{3j} x_{3,t-j} + \ldots + \epsilon_t \tag{2.39}$$

If the terms a_{20}, a_{30}, etc. are included in the model then one gets simply an explanatory model, with current x_{1t} possibly being explained by past and present values of the other series. However, for a predictive model terms involving current values of $x_{2,t}$, $x_{3,t}$, etc. cannot be included in the model. In either case, the number of terms that might be used to explain x_{1t} could be very large and so, with only a fairly short time series available, one will encounter estimating problems.

It is clearly sensible to ask if a method can be used which only includes the really important variables and lags in the model. A way of doing this is to use a stepwise procedure.[5] To explain this method consider for the moment a non time series situation. Suppose that we wish to "explain" as best as possible a random variable X in terms of a set of random variables $Y_1, Y_2, \ldots, Y_m$. We first find the Y variable which is most correlated to X, Y_p say. Find a_{1p} such that $E\,[(X - a_{1p} Y_p)^2]$ is minimized. Thus, the best regression for X based on a single variable is $a_{1p} Y_p$, using a least-squares criterion of "best." This represents the first step. Now find which of the *remaining* Y's is most correlated to $X_1 = X - a_{1p}Y_p$, say Y_q. Now find a_{2p}, a_{2q} which minimize $E\,[(X - a_{2p}Y_p - a_{2q}Y_q)^2]$. Thus, the best regression for X based on a pair of variables is $a_{2p}Yp + a_{2q}Y_q$. Note that in general a_{2p} will be different from a_{1p}, i.e., the coefficient of Y_p will vary as further, dependent information is added to the regression. We are now at the second step. The remaining Y's are now correlated to the second-step residual $X_2 = X - a_{2p}Y_p - a_{2q}Y_q$ and the most correlated variable selected for inclusion in the regression equation involving three variables, together with Y_p and Y_q. It should now be clear how the rest of the third step follows together with the subsequent steps. In practice, of course, the expected sum of squares to be minimized would be replaced by the actual sum of squares of the residuals over the set of available data.

Although this stepwise, iterative method was originally designed for sets of data of the type used in the previous paragraph, there is no reason why it should not to be used with time series data. The variable to be explained is x_{1t} and the explaining variables can be $x_{k,t-j}$, $k = 2, \ldots, m, j \geqslant 0$. In practice, one will have to limit the maximum j used in order to have sufficient data upon which to apply the technique.

The one remaining problem is how many steps to use, i.e., when to stop adding further variables? This is, in fact, a very difficult and unsolved problem even in the non time series case and is vastly more difficult when using time series. For our own purposes, overfitting is slightly preferable to underfitting, but if the overfitting is excessive, that is, far too many explanatory variables are introduced, then the predictive performance of the model will be reduced. In such a case, one would be moving from slight overfitting to what has been called "data mining." If one has enough variables one must eventually find a model that seems to fit extremely well. The obvious quantity to look at is the extent to which the most recently added variable has contributed to the total variance of the variable being explained. If we are considering the pth step, the contribution made by the pth added variable is

$$\Delta R_p^2 = R_p^2 - R_{p-1}^2$$

where

$$R_p^2 = 1 - \frac{\text{variance } p\text{th step residual}}{\text{variance of } X_t}$$

is the coefficient of determination.

For ordinary regression analysis tests are available to check whether the addition to R^2 made by the new variable is significantly nonzero. However, for stepwise regression the situation is more difficult as one is not merely adding a randomly chosen variable to the explanatory set but the most correlated variable of those remaining. If all the explanatory variables were independent, an appropriate test for ΔR^2 would be akin to testing the maximum F-ratio (or, essentially, a maximum of a set of chi squares) as being significantly nonzero. This would be possible for the first step but corrections of an unknown type would be needed for later steps. When the explanatory variables are not independent, as will generally be true for time series data, it is doubtful if this procedure is acceptable even for the first step.

Nevertheless, one does need *some* criteria for stopping the step-wise process even if it is not the optimum method. In forming our models we have kept adding terms until the classical test for ordinary regression theory suggests that the most recent step did not produce a significantly better fit. This test can be found in any textbook of econometrics and consists of forming the ratio of the increase in the amount of the variance explained by adding the latest variance to the sum of squares of residuals after adding this variable and then testing this ratio by an F test with $(1, n - p - 1)$ degrees of freedom at the pth step. The same theory also provides an estimate of the standard deviation of the estimated parameter at each stage. The test described is equivalent to forming the ratio of the square of this estimated parameter to its variance and then using the F test as before. This procedure will almost certainly be optimistic, as suggested above, and will not stop the stages of the regression early enough. In an appendix to Chapter 7 we examine our results critically and suggest an alternative decision rule.

Further checks on the stopping have also been applied, including a test for serial correlation among the residuals. These are also discussed further in Chapter 7.

Further References

The above account of the statistical techniques used has only briefly introduced what are rather complicated and technical methods. A fuller account concentrating on the interpretation of results can be found in C. W. J. Granger and M. Hatanka, *Spectral Analysis of Economic Time Series* (Princeton: Princeton University Press, 1965), and a more recent and more mathematically rigorous account is G. M. Jenkins and D. G. Watts, *Spectral Analysis and its Applications* (California: Holden Day, 1968).

Alternative accounts of spectral analysis have been given in M. Nerlove, "Spectral Analysis of Seasonal Adjustment Procedures," *Econometrica* 32 (1964), pp. 241-286; and in G. S. Fishman, *Spectral Methods in Econometrics* (Cambridge: Harvard University Press, 1969).

Concerning estimation problems, a history of the topic has recently been provided by J. Tukey, "An Introduction to the Calculations of Numerical Spectrum Analysis" in *Spectral Analysis of Time Series,* edited by B. Harris (New York: John Wiley and Sons, 1967), and a very full account of the theory underlying estimation procedure is found in E. Parzen, *Time Series Analysis Papers* (California: Holden Day, 1968).

The statistical properties of the estimates are studied by simulation techniques in C. W. J. Granger and A. O. Hughes, "Spectral Analysis of Short Series – A Simulation Study," *Journal of the Royal Statistical Society* A (1968), pp. 83-99.

Full accounts of stepwise procedures have been given by F. J. Anscombe, "Topics in the Investigation of Linear Relations fitted to the Method of Least Squares," *Journal of the Royal Statistical Society* 29, Series B (1967), pp. 1-52; W. K. Smillie, *An Introduction to Regression and Correlation* (New York: Academic Press, 1966); and N. R. Draper and H. Smith, *Applied Regression Analysis* (New York: John Wiley and Sons, Inc., 1966).

3 The Random Behavior of Commodity Prices

Introducing the Random Walk

The first step in any analysis of a group of time series is to analyze each individual series in isolation from the others. Only in a later chapter will the interrelationships between series be considered. In terms of prediction, the first step consists of seeing how well the future values of some series can be predicted using present and past values of this series. For price series arising from speculative markets one particular model has been continually investigated, the so-called random walk model. For series obeying such a model, price changes are unpredictable using previous price changes; symbolically the model is expressed as:

$$P_t = P_{t-1} + \epsilon_t \tag{3.1}$$

where P_t is the price series recorded at specified moments of time. e.g., daily market close and ϵ_t is a white noise series with zero mean. That is:

$$E(\epsilon_t) = 0 \quad \text{and} \quad E(\epsilon_t \epsilon_s) = 0 \qquad t \neq s \tag{3.2}$$

Thus, price change $P_t - P_{t-1}$ is equal to ϵ_t, which – being white noise – is unpredictable from previous price changes.

If the model is prefectly correct, there are a number of obvious implications about the nature of price series. It can be shown, for instance, that the series cannot contain any cycilical or other deterministic components, such as a seasonal variation; nor can the price series be constrained to lie between barriers. The same, of course must be true for the price changes series (denoted by ΔP_t throughout this book). This further implies that so-called technical methods of investment analysis will be less likely to be useful in predicting future prices. The model does *not* say that price changes are unpredictable if one used all available information; they are only unpredictable using previous price changes.

There are, in fact, various other forms of the model that have been suggested or implied by other writers and this has led, unfortunately, to a surprising amount of misunderstanding of what is actually an extremely simple model.[1] The form we shall be using, stated above, makes no assumption as to the distribution of the ϵ_t nor does it assume that the variance of ϵ_t is constant over time, although this variance is assumed to be finite. It has been found for the stock market that the variance of ϵ_t appears to depend on the amount or volume of trading during the time interval over which the price change is taken. As this volume changes from one period to another, it follows that the variance of ϵ_t

changes also. In these circumstances it is very difficult to investigate empirically the distribution of ϵ_t. Fortunately, the methods we employ depend only on the autocorrelation or covariance structure of the series; consequently, the random walk model can be investigated in the form proposed here. If the model is correct, the spectrum of price changes will be flat over the entire frequency range. To consider ways in which the model could break down we need to discuss specific models. If the price changes contain a seasonal, the spectrum will have a peak at the seasonal frequency and be flat elsewhere. If the price changes contain a trend, the spectrum will have a peak at zero frequency and be flat at all other frequencies. If ΔP_t and ΔP_{t-1} are positively correlated, the spectrum will generally decline in value as frequency increases; but if ΔP_t and ΔP_{t-1} are negatively correlated, then the spectrum will increase in value with increasing frequency. To be yet more specific, consider the model

$$\Delta P_t = \alpha \Delta P_t + \epsilon_t \tag{3.3}$$

and let $f(\omega)$ be the spectrum of ΔP_t, which will be given by

$$f(\omega) = \frac{\sigma_\epsilon^2}{2(1 + \alpha^2 - 2\alpha \cos \omega)} \tag{3.4}$$

taking the variance of $\epsilon_t = \sigma_\epsilon^2$ to be a constant for the time being. (If it is not a constant, then σ_ϵ^2 can be approximately replaced by average variance of ϵ_t in the formula.) The ratio of the height of $f(\omega)$ at the two extremes of the frequency range is then

$$\lambda(\alpha) = \frac{f(0)}{f(\pi)} = \left(\frac{1 + \alpha}{1 - \alpha}\right)^2 \tag{3.5}$$

Some illustrative values are:

α	$\lambda(\alpha)$
0.00	1.00
0.01	1.04
0.05	1.22
0.10	1.49
0.20	2.25
-0.01	0.98
-0.05	0.82
-0.10	0.67
-0.20	0.44

It is interesting to note that for the model in (3.3), the proportion of the variance of ΔP_t explainable by ΔP_{t-1} is given by α^2, for $|\alpha| \leqslant 1$. This model will be called the simple Markov model for price changes. The random walk model corresponds to the case $\alpha = 0$.

When one estimates the spectrum of ΔP_t generated by such a simple Markov model, it is seen that if α is positive, the spectrum will generally be downward sloping; if α is negative, the spectrum will generally be upward sloping. With $\alpha = 0.10$ there will theoretically be a 50 percent difference in the values of $f(0)$ and $f(\pi)$, and such a difference should certainly be detectable given time series of 150 terms or more. This is, in fact, a model which is only slightly different from the random walk model; since with $\alpha = 0.10$, only 1 percent of the variance of ΔP_t is explainable by ΔP_{t-1}. Thus in this sense, models which differ only slightly from the random walk model should be detectable by spectral techniques. If the spectrum of ΔP_t is not flat, it is not suggested that α be estimated from (3.5) using spectral estimates, as the first autocorrelation (i.e., the correlation between ΔP_t and ΔP_{t-1}) provides a better estimate.

Previous Work on the Random Walk Model

The earliest account of the random walk model as found in speculative markets is that of a particularly brilliant Ph.D. thesis completed by Bachelier at the University of Paris in 1900.[2] Although this work was largely ignored in connection with the stock market until the late 1950s, the same model was both proposed and investigated for commodities by Working in a series of papers of consistently high quality beginning in 1934. In an early paper, he attempted to simulate a randomly behaving commodity price series by summing a series of random numbers – a reasonable procedure since summing a number of random price changes with mean zero results in a random walk series.[3] Working compared this artificial series to several futures price series and found a strong resemblance. The result was the suggestion that commodity price behavior is most appropriately described by the random walk model.

This suggestion has lead to subsequent attempts to investigate the appropriateness of the model. There is an interesting difference in the conclusions of the studies using commodity prices compared to studies of the random walk model for stock market prices. The vast majority of the work on the stock market has reached the conclusion that the random walk model is at the very least an excellent approximate model for stock market prices.[4] Most of the studies using commodity prices, however, have rejected the model although not always in a consistent manner. Working, for example, has reported a tendency for positive serial dependence (with lags of more than one day) in prices for Chicago corn, wheat, and rye futures;[5] and negative serial dependence in some intraday future prices.[6] Larson suggests the existence of some linear dependence in the future prices for corn; that is, changes in corn future prices tend to be succeeded by changes in the same direction more often than is predicted by a random walk.[7]

Both Houthakker and Smidt have investigated the use of simple trading rules and, because of the apparent profitability of these rules, suggest that the random walk model is incorrect. Houthakker believes his result to be due to the presence of seasonal patterns, whereas Smidt says that his results indicate a negative serial correlation in soybean prices.[8]

Not only are the results found by the various studies inconsistent but one can unfortunately easily find fault with the actual statistical techniques used in some cases. Larson's study, for instance, is based on ratios of certain observed ranges in price change series. The method seems to be highly dependent on an assumption that the variance of price changes is constant over time. As the variability of price changes will depend on the volume of trading and as this volume is observed to be highly variable, the assumption upon which Larson's study is based seems to be a doubtful one. It is unclear how one should interpret his results when this assumption is removed.

There are also dangers in the use of methods investigating specific and apparently simple trading rules as used by Houthakker and Smidt. This is shown by some studies by Alexander using stock market prices.[9] In his first study using a so-called filter rule, Alexander rejected the random walk model. However, following some criticism of the practicality of his rule, he subsequently withdrew most of his conclusions.[10] Finally, a very complete and careful study by Fama and Blume reaches the conclusion that the results obtained from the particular class of trading rules considered do not in any way contradict the random walk model.[11] It is not clear whether the same or similar criticisms can be applied to the work by Houthakker and Smidt. In any case, it is clear that further empirical work is required.

Empirical Investigation – Monthly Price Series I

Two sets of price series have been investigated. The first set consists of monthly futures prices for thirteen commodities, representing roughly one-half of the important commodities traded on American futures markets, together with six corresponding cash price series. Data was not readily available for the other seven cash price series. The period used was January 1950 to July 1965, representing a long stretch of postwar years having relatively stable price levels. With the total length of each monthly series at $n = 186$, spectra have been estimated for first differences of each of the respective series.

Futures Prices

In general, the spectra found for the futures series were flat and one could rarely reject a random walk model with any confidence. By this we mean that all or virtually all of the points of the estimated spectrum lie between two horizontal 95% confidence lines set about the horizontal average value for the spectrum.

See Figure 3-1, for example. More particularly, several of the spectra do seem to contain features which suggest that the random walk model is only a crude approximation to the truth. Some of the spectra peak at seasonal frequencies, exhibiting evidence of seasonal elements; other spectra are slightly higher at low frequencies than at high frequencies, suggesting some small positive correlation between adjacent price changes. These results contrast with estimates of spectra for the first differences of stock market prices, which are invariably very flat. This suggests that whereas the random walk model is an extremely good approximation to the truth for the stock market, this model is a cruder approximation to the truth for commodity prices.

For this set of data, the most noticeable nonrandom walk components were usually those associated with the seasonal (12 months) and its harmonics (6, 4, 3, 2, 4, 2 months). We can classify the spectra into four groups: Group I – pure random walk; Group II – slight suggestion of seasonal component; Group III – barely significant seasonal component, and Group IV – clearly significant seasonal component. While no seasonals occur in the flat spectra of Group I, the seasonals in the spectra of Groups II and III are only noteworthy because peaks occur at frequencies having a clear interpretation (i.e., seasonal frequencies at which peaks might be expected). These peaks rarely represent more than a few percent of the total variance of the price change series. The seasonals in the spectrum of Group IV, therefore, are the only ones which can be accepted with confidence. As a check on the reality of the seasonal peaks, the spectra of the actual price series were also estimated after the removal of a linear trend by regression. The trend removal has the same effect as a filter in removing very low frequencies and so spectra of the residuals can be estimated even if the actual series obeys a random walk model. The spectra of the price series after trend removal all take on the so-called typical spectral shape, having very high values at low frequencies and steadily falling off, apart from the occasional peak, to a low value at high frequency.[12] As can be seen in Table 3-1, the evidence about seasonals from these new spectra generally matched that from the price difference series. Confirmation for individual commodities are reported in the next section.

For now, let us examine each of the first difference spectra in greater detail, beginning with the Group I commodities. Table 3-1 lists cottonseed oil, potatoes, eggs, and cocoa as members of this group. They are all identified by relatively flat spectra since all of the estimated points lie well within the 95% confidence bands. (Confidence bands have been applied according to the theory presented earlier.)[13] The cocoa spectrum has been selected as an example for this group and appears in Figure 3-1.

The commodities in Group II have equally flat spectra, but the latter also contain frequency patterns which correspond to the annual cycle and its harmonics. The spectrum for corn prices in Figure 3-2 has several distinct but insignificant waves which correspond to periods of 12 months, 4 months, and 2.4 months respectively. The lard spectrum has a similar shape, but the waves are centered at 24, 6.4, and 4 months respectively.

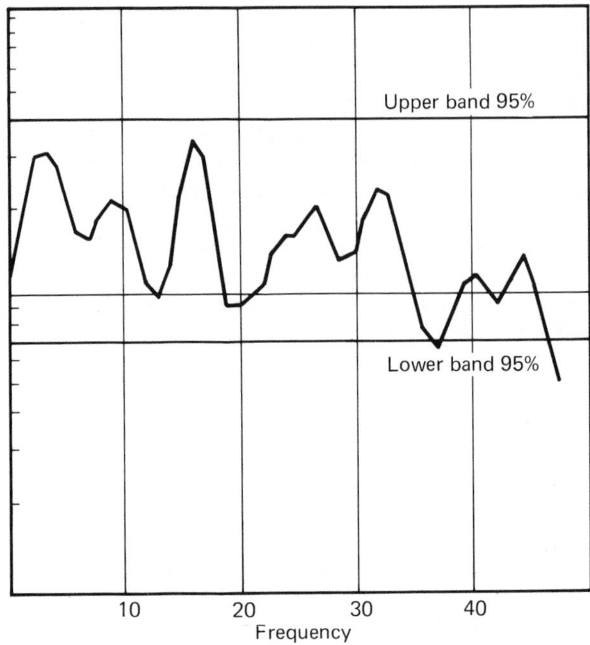

Figure 3-1 Example from Group I: Power Spectrum of First Differences Cocoa Futures Prices Monthly, 1950-1965.

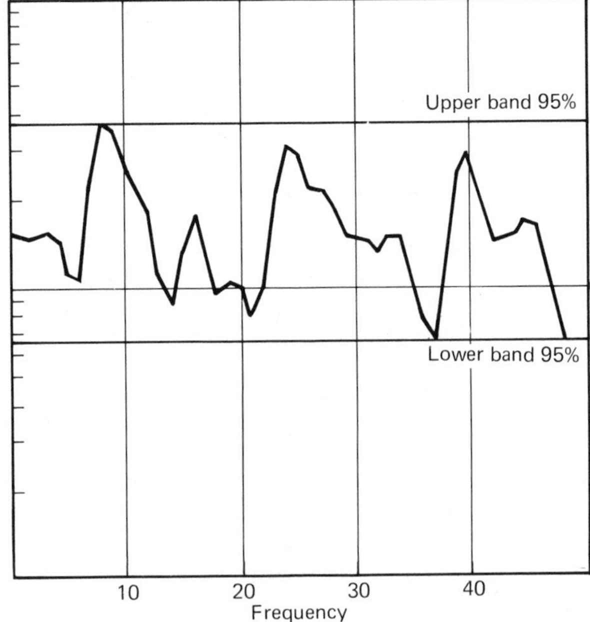

Figure 3-2 Example from Group II: Power Spectrum of First Differences Corn Futures Prices Monthly, 1950-1965.

Table 3-1

Spectral Analysis Commodity Cash and Futures Prices

Monthly: January 1950-July 1965
Observations = 186
Estimated Lags = 48

Power Spectra	*Group*	*First Difference Components*[a]	*Typical Shape Components*[b]	*Component Variance*
		Futures Prices		
Cotton Oil	I	–	(32)	
Potatoes	I	–	(40)	
Eggs	I	–	(32)	
Cocoa	I	–	(48)	
Corn	II	–	4	1.5%
Copper[c]	II	–	–	
Flax[d]	II	–	–	
Lard	II	–	(40)	
Soybeans	II	–	–	
Soybean Meal	II	–	–	
Soybean Oil	II	–	(40)	
Cotton[e]	III	8,2.4	8,2.4	1.0, 0.9%
Rye	III	12	12	1.3%
Oats	III	12	12,4	1.1, 0.8%
Oats[f]	III	12	–	
Wheat	III	12	12,6, 3	1.0, 0.8, 1.0%
		Cash Prices		
Coca	I	–	(48)	
Soybeans	I	–	–	
Oats	II	12	12	1.3%
Copper[c]	II	–		
Lard[g]	II	–	(40)	
Corn	III	4	4	1.4%
Wheat[h]	IV	S12	12,6	1.5, 1.3%

[a]Components significant at 95% level.

[b]Approximate business cycle component.

[c]LME 3-month forward and cash prices. April 1953-March 1968.

[d]Winnipeg monthly: January 1950-June 1963.

[e]The 8 month frequency is not a seasonal harmonic.

[f]Winnipeg monthly: January 1950-June 1963.

[g]Monthly: January 1948-December 1962.

[h]Grade is Red Winter No. 2.

With Group III, some of the frequency components exceed the 95% confidence bands, but only to the extent that they can be considered slightly significant. The wheat spectrum, which displays a seasonal component, is given as an example in Figure 3-3. Since the confidence limits lack exactness, these components should only be accepted on the basis of additional information. Wheat is the only commodity for which such information is readily available. Not only Cootner but also Hieronymus and Gray have found a seasonal pattern in wheat.[14] Although other commodities such as oats and rye have displayed similar peaks in frequency, little extraneous information exists to substantiate them. For cotton, the strongest frequency component corresponds to an 8-month period. This component might be explained as an 8-month harmonic of the 40-month business cycle. It is for this group that the typical shape results reported in the next section will be most helpful.

Monthly futures prices may also be considered on foreign markets, but their behavior does not appear to deviate significantly from the domestic market. Spectra have been estimated for Winnipeg flax and oats prices, as well as London copper prices, and the random walk model has been confirmed for both commodities. As shown in Table 3-1, the flax spectrum has been classified as Group II and the oats spectrum as Group III.

Cash Prices

The principal difference in the spectra for cash prices is the strength of the seasonal component. Of the cash price series tested, cocoa, corn, oats, and soybeans could be explained as simple random walk. Corn differed slightly, with a wave centered at the 4-month harmonic. Wheat showed the greatest difference with a strong seasonal in both basic grades. The spectrum for wheat, which has been reproduced in Figure 3-4, suggests a sizeable jump at the 12-month frequency. The seasonal for this group is clearly significant and it can be classified as Group IV. Since this is the only jump in a relatively flat spectrum, one can explain the price behavior of cash wheat as a 12-month shifting seasonal superimposed on a basic random walk. Although some dealers in the market have accepted the near futures prices as a forecast of the cash price, the spectra for cash and futures prices resemble each other for only two (lard and soybeans) of the six commodities tested. This appears to be sufficient justification for considering the two price series separately.

Seasonal Components Verified

When spectra are estimated from the original price series rather than the first difference series, they have been found to follow the typical spectral shape as explained above. The power tends to be concentrated at the lower frequencies and then declines almost exponentially as the frequency increases. In terms of

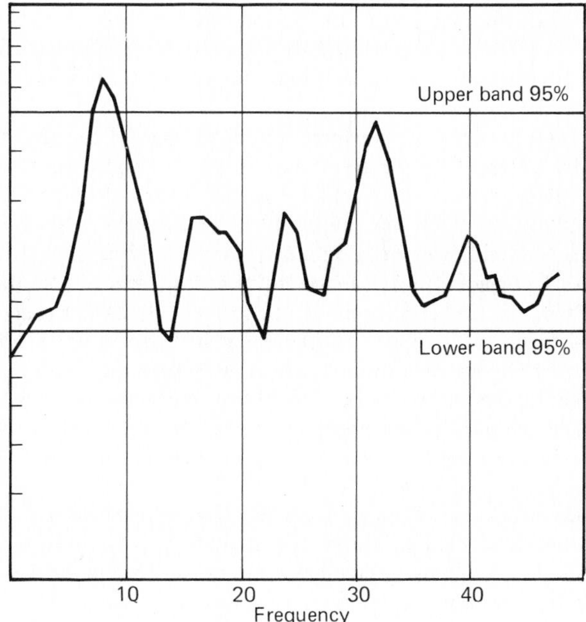

Figure 3-3 Example from Group III: Power Spectrum of First Differences Wheat Futures Prices Monthly, 1950-1965.

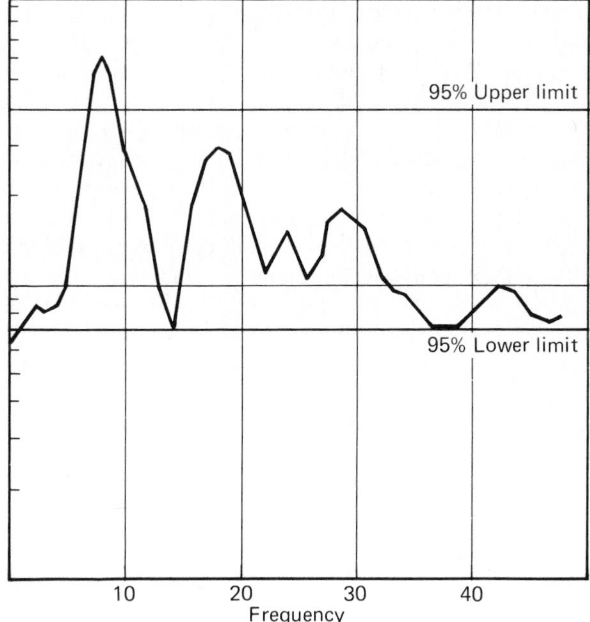

Figure 3-4 Example from Group IV: Power Spectrum of First Differences Wheat Cash Prices Monthly, 1950-1965.

the data, this implies that the longer the period of a component, the larger is its amplitude. The typical spectra generally demonstrate that the cash and futures price series possess certain seasonal and long-run components which cannot be explained by random walk alone.

The seasonal components which appeared significant in the first difference spectra (especially for the commodities in Group III) have been confirmed in the typical spectra. When an attempt is made to justify these components on the basis of actual market behavior, one might object that normal trading activity on a speculative market will remove a regular pattern in prices as soon as it is discovered. Several considerations can be advanced to relieve this doubt. The first is that the futures market as contrasted to the stock market is an imperfect market. The existence of carryover insures a seasonal rise in price. Even if this imperfection were not present, however, the activity of traders need not remove any patterns except the most obvious ones. For the commodity market, the seasonal and other components are not particularly obvious. The contribution of each component to the total variance in price as reported in Table 3-1 is in the vicinity of 1%.[a]

Figure 3-5 describes the typical spectrum for wheat futures prices. To establish 95% confidence bands about the spectrum, a "true" spectrum was superimposed on the figure using free-hand methods. The seasonal component which was found in the first difference spectrum, together with the 3-month harmonic are significant at the 95% level. An estimate has been produced for the contribution of each of the components to the total variance in price. The seasonal appears to explain approximately 1.4%, the 5-month harmonic 0.8%, and the 3-month harmonic 1.0% of the total variance. By returning to Table 3-1, one can find a similar explanation for cash wheat prices.

The typical spectrum for oats also confirms the presence of a seasonal component. As reported in Table 3-1, both the seasonal and the 4-month components, which explain 1.1 and 0.8% of the total price variance respectively, are significant at the 95% level. Only the seasonal, which represents 1.3% of the total price variance was significant for the oats cash price series. Although the seasonal component in rye accounted for 1.3% of the total price variance, the peak shifted constantly, making it barely significant at the 12-month mark.

Finally, seasonal components in cotton and corn were verified. Both the 8-month and 2.4-month components proved significant for cotton, but they do not conform to any known pattern and they account for only 1.0 and 0.9% of the total variance respectively. An even more unusual finding was the significance of the 4-month harmonic in corn futures prices, a commodity from Group II. Although this component lacks significance in the first difference spectrum, it appeared significant in the typical spectrum for the corn cash price

---

[a]This contribution can be estimated, realizing that the total spectral area is roughly equivalent to the total variance of the corresponding time series. The proportion of the spectral area occupied by a peak in the spectrum, therefore, indicates the percentage contribution of that peak in explaining the total variance of the respective time series.

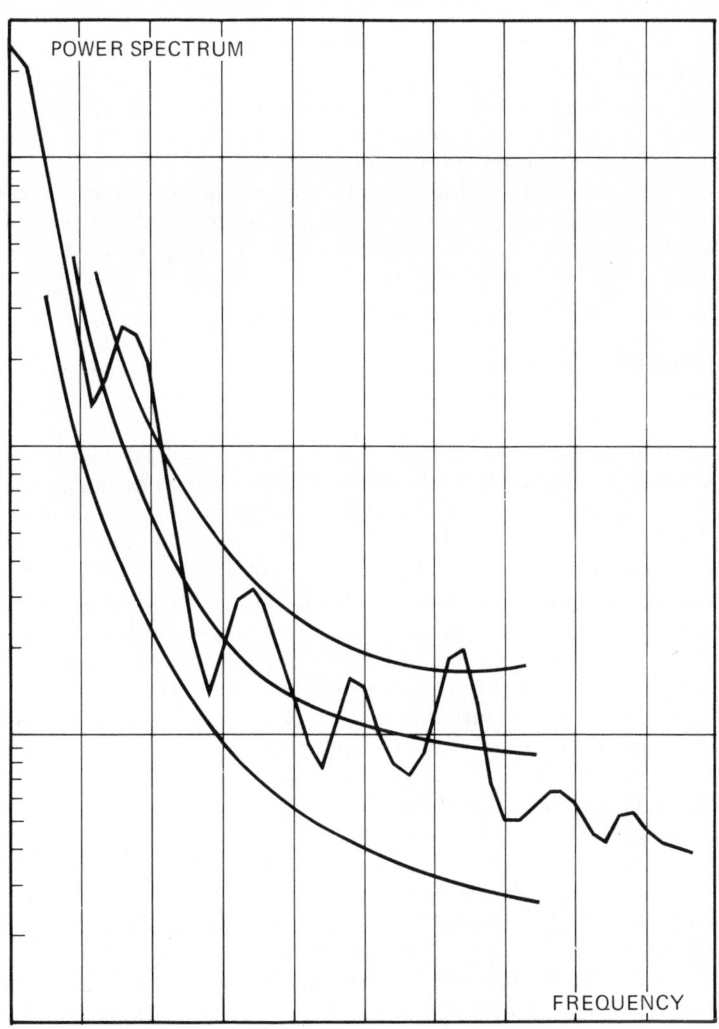

Figure 3-5 Typical Spectrum of Wheat Futures Prices Monthly, 1950-1965.

series. The existence of this component might be rationalized, given the assumption that it was insufficiently profitable to be removed, but no direct evidence could be found.

Removing the linear trend from the futures price series has suggested a minor business cycle or roughly thirty to fifty months for a large group of commodities. The presence of these components is reported in Table 3-1, and an example of such a component appears in the lard spectrum of Figure 3-6. Since these peaks are rarely significant and contribute little to the total variance of the price series, there is no evidence to suggest that these peaks describe a true characteristic of the American economy. One can only conclude that these peaks reflect the tendency for certain commodities to follow the long-run fluctuations of the American economy as a whole.[15]

Empirical Investigation – Monthly Price Series II

The random walk model is stated in terms of instantly recorded price series; that is, series recorded at specific moments of time. The data used in the previous section were all of this nature and so were relevant for studying the random walk model. Of course, if one used data which has been transformed in some way or is not recorded instantaneously, one would not expect to find similar results. Since in the later chapters prices have been related to data describing supply or demand totalled over a month, it was suggested to us in our work with several firms that better results might be obtained with average instead of closing prices. For this reason as well as certain theoretical ones, monthly average prices have been used from Chapter 6 onwards. Both cash and futures price series were investigated for a total of six commodities: soybean oil, cottonseed oil, soybean meal, soybeans, rye, and wheat. The period covered extended from August 1957 to June 1966, giving $n = 107$ observations.

For many models, the effect of monthly averaging can be a very complicated one, but if the daily series obey a random walk the effect can be completely determined. This was originally pointed out by Working, who proved that some earlier work by Cowles on stock market price data, in which Cowles rejected the random walk model, was incorrect because averaged data had been used.[16] Working's effect can be demonstrated by considering X_t to be a random walk series, formed from daily prices such that the price change per day is white noise. From this series, construct the averaged series P_t by averaging over m values of X_t. For example, if P_t is an average weekly series, m might be 5; or if P_t is an average monthly series, m might be about 20. Working observed that the effect of forming such an average was to make the correlation between successive changes in average prices, ΔP_t and ΔP_{t-1}, a constant equal to $(m^2 - 1)/(4m^2 + 2)$. Thus, for monthly averages, adjacent monthly changes would have a correlation coefficient of about ¼ even when the daily price series obeyed a

Figure 3-6 Typical Spectrum of Lard Futures Prices, Linear Trend Removed Monthly, 1950-1965.

Table 3-2

Spectral Importance of Seasonal Factors: Averaged Cash and Futures Prices

Monthly: August 1957-June 1966
Observations = 107
Estimated Lags = 24

Power Spectra	*Grouping for Cash Prices*	*Grouping for Futures Prices*
Cottonseed oil	I	I
Wheat	II	I
Rye	II	II
Soybean oil	II	II
Soybeans	II	III
Soybean meal	IV	III

random walk model. The importance of this conclusion for our results is that even though the random walk model is correct for the original prices, the spectrum of the monthly average price would be downward sloping as frequency increases. In an appendix to this chapter, the effect of averaging a random walk series is considered in some detail.

Because of the averaging effect, this new set of data is by no means ideal for investigating the random walk. The estimated spectra generally do decline with increasing frequency as predicted above for an averaged random walk. Evidence will be presented in Chapter 9, where alternative techniques are used, suggesting that the averaged random walk model fits the series well. However, some of the estimated spectra do show evidence of the presence of seasonal components. This can be seen in Table 3-2, which uses the same grouping scheme as above for classifying seasonal components, i.e., Group I (random walk) to Group IV (significant seasonal). The classification of most of the price series in groups other than Group IV is clearly sufficient evidence in favor of rejecting the possibility of a seasonal component being superimposed on the random walk model for the averaged series.

Empirical Investigation – Weekly Prices

Spectra were also estimated for a number of weekly closing price series, the results of which are summarized in Table 3-3. Basically, the spectra of weekly price changes were flat, although occasionally there was an indication of the presence of the harmonic of a seasonal component. It is generally more difficult to observe a seasonal component in weekly data than in monthly data, as the seasonal corresponds to such a low frequency. An example of the spectra obtained is shown in Figure 3-7, which was formed from the weekly price changes in cash corn prices, for the period 1950-1965. The one apparently significant peak corresponds to a 12½ week period, i.e., the 4-month harmonic of the seasonal component.

Figure 3-8, which shows the spectrum of weekly wheat cash prices over the period 1887-1916, has been included to provide a comparison with some results obtained by Kendall, who provided an early confirmation of the random walk model in his analysis of wheat and cotton prices.[17] The data used for estimating the spectrum was identical to Kendall's, although analysis was performed for a shorter period (Kendall's analysis covered two periods: 1883-1915 and 1920-1936). The spectral shape for the shorter series is again basically flat except for a peak corresponding to a period of 12½ weeks, i.e., a seasonal harmonic.

One other spectral result obtainable from weekly and not monthly series is the possibility of detecting price cycles in the range of two months to two weeks. No such cycles could be found for the wheat series or any of the other weekly series investigated. Thus, apart from the discovered seasonal harmonics, it appears that the random walk model is a good approximation to the truth for the weekly series considered.

Empirical Investigation – Daily Prices

Daily price series represents the most detailed form of price series available for most commodity markets. Both futures and cash closing prices were investigated for the period August 1964 to July 1965, giving $n = 260$ observations. One would not expect to find any seasonal components for such a length of data, but the possibility does exist to discover shorter-length trading cycles as well as random walk.

Daily price series have been drawn from the commodities included in the monthly analysis as well as from sugar, coffee, rubber, and the Dow Jones cash and futures indexes. As shown in Table 3-4, the random walk model provides a good explanation of the daily price behavior for all of the given commodities except for cotton and cocoa. For the cotton and cocoa futures price series, the spectrum took the shape given in Figure 3-9. The presence of a rising trend in that spectrum implies that the first differences in prices are negatively autocorrelated. This result can reasonably be explained by the actual price behavior experienced in the respective markets.

Table 3-3

Spectral Analysis: Commodity Cash and Futures Prices

Weekly: First differences
August 1961-July 1965
Observations = 208
Estimated Lags = 48

Power Spectra	*First Difference Interpretation*[a]	*Group*	*Annual Harmonics*
		Futures Prices	
Corn[b]	R	I	–
Lard[c]	R	I	–
Oats	R	I	–
Rye	R	I	–
Wheat	R	I	–
Soybeans	R	II	–
		Cash Prices	
Lard[c]	R	I	–
Soybeans	R	I	–
Soybean oil	R	II	–
Corn[b]	R	III	4

[a]R = random walk.

[b]Weekly: August 1950-September 1965

[c]Weekly: January 1958-December 1962

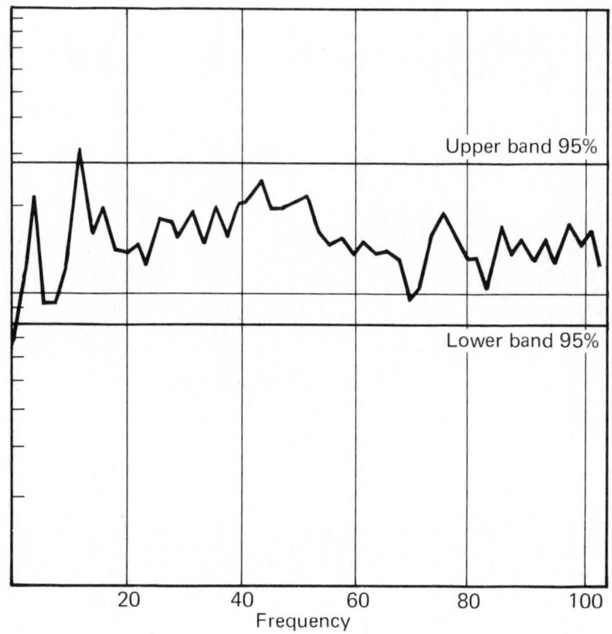

Figure 3-7 Power Spectrum of First Differences Corn Cash Prices Weekly, 1950-1965.

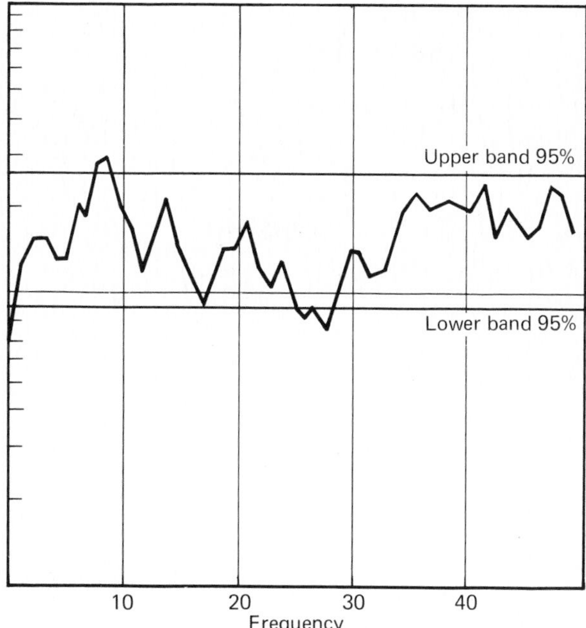

Figure 3-8 Power Spectrum of First Differences Wheat Cash Prices Weekly, 1887-1916.

Table 3-4

Spectral Analysis: Commodity Cash and Futures Prices

Daily: First differences
August 1964-July 1965
Observations = 260
Estimated lags = 48

Power Spectra	*Group*	*First Difference Interpretation*[a]
		Futures Prices
Coffee	I	R
Corn	I	R
Dow-Jones Index	I	R
Oats	I	R
Rye	I	R
Rubber	I	R
Soybeans	I	R
Sugar	I	R
Wheat	I	R
Cocoa	–	N
Cotton	–	N
		Cash Prices
Dow-Jones Index	I	R
Cocoa	I	R
Coffee	I	R
Rubber	I	R
Sugar	I	R
Cotton	–	–

[a]R = random walk; N = negative autocorrelation.

Beginning with cotton, one finds that its price experienced almost no trend over the period August 1964 to July 1965. Futures prices climbed above 32 cents per pound only three times during the entire period and never fell below 31 cents per pound. With such a narrow price spread, it is plausible that most price increases were followed by a price decrease and vice versa. This tendency for price changes to constantly reverse directions or be negatively correlated is known as "technical reaction" and it is likely to arise under certain conditions of profit seeking. Such a pattern arises also if there exist barriers around the current price, as has been found for example for within-day stock market price changes. Barriers can arise from standing buy and sell orders placed above and below the most recent price (limit orders) or, where there exists some price control mechanism, such as that placed by a government agency. The narrow range of movement of cotton prices in the period considered suggests that such barriers could well have existed.

For cocoa, however, it is more difficult to suggest a reason for finding negative autocorrelation. Prices moved steadily downward through the period from 22 cents per pound to 15 cents per pound. Taking first differences should remove most of this trend but not necessarily all of it. The upward sloping spectrum for price changes could have arisen from surges of optimism and pessism about this downward trend or from changes about the trend contained within narrow limits; but no clear reason has been found.

The only other exception that can be cited to the general confirmation of the random walk model in daily prices is the occasional appearance of a weekly cycle. For several of the examined spectra, peaks appear at 5 days and 2.5 days corresponding to a (working) weekly cycle and its first harmonic. The presence of such cycles appeared particularly strong superimposed on the spectrum for cotton cash prices and it is given as an example in Figure 3-10. Such cycles, however, are never of considerable importance and it is doubtful if they could be used profitably.

Closed Market Activity

One final aspect of market behavior that can be investigated with daily prices is the relation of market time to real time. (This test was originally formulated for use with stock price data.)[18] The purpose of testing this relationship is to determine whether the daily observations are sufficiently nonequispaced to upset any hypothesized relationship between price and other economic variables. If the market were perfect, then each day's opening price would be the same as the previous day's closing price. Since the market is not perfect, its performance should be compared during the time when it is open, closed overnight, and closed over weekends.

One method for testing this behavior is to estimate the variance for several of the opening and closing price series mentioned above. Variances have been calculated between the differences of Monday's opening and Friday's closing

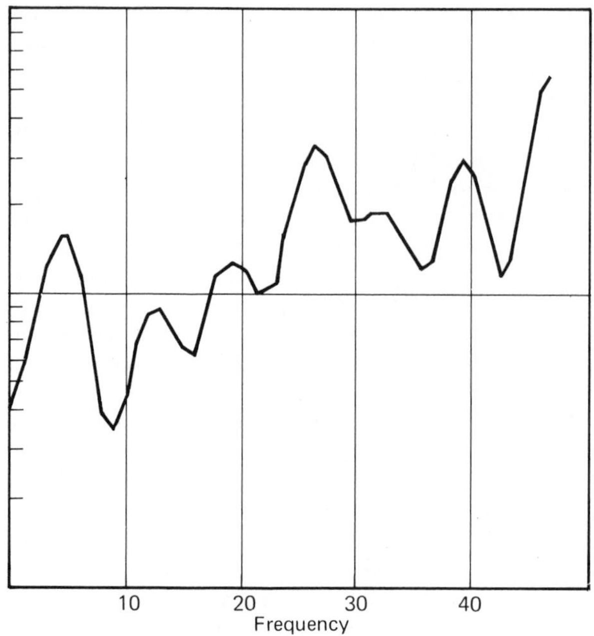

Figure 3-9 Power Spectrum of First Differences Cotton Futures Prices Daily, 1964-1965.

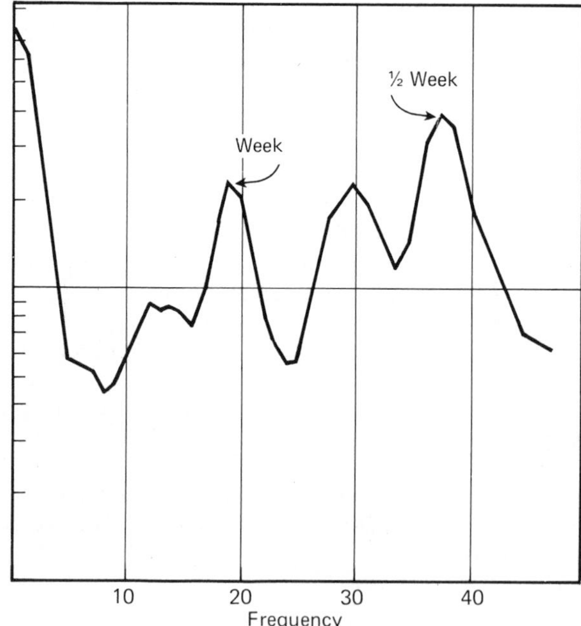

Figure 3-10 Power Spectrum of First Differences Cotton Cash Prices Daily, 1964-1965.

Table 3-5

Futures Price Variance: "Open" and "Closed" Markets (Daily: August 1964-July 1965)

Price Series	Variance *Wheat*	*Corn*	*Soybeans*
Overnight price change:[a]			
Monday-Tuesday	0.581	0.364	2.209
Tuesday-Wednesday	0.883	0.753	1.919
Wednesday-Thursday	0.117	0.875	2.004
Thursday-Friday	0.762	0.072	2.963
Average	0.586	0.516	2.274
Price change for typical day (Wednesday)	0.420	0.904	4.352
Price change over weekend	0.614	0.173	2.895

[a]Price change = closing price − opening price.

price, each weekday's opening and the previous day's closing price, and the opening minus closing prices for Wednesday. The results have been reported in Table 3-5 for wheat, corn, and soybeans. In general, they agree with those found for the stock market by Godfrey, Granger, and Morgenstern, i.e., the variance of price change overnight and over the weekend is almost as great as during the day.

The conclusion that can be drawn from these results is that the price determining activity of the futures market continues even though it is closed. Since the variance per unit time decreases over the weekend, the market operates at a slower speed than during the week. This causes the daily observations to be nonequispaced with respect to the time interval of change. In addition, the continuation of activity even after the market is closed suggests that expectations concerning the state of the market play a significant role in the determination of futures prices. This result will become more meaningful in the next chapter, where expectations are investigated further.

Conclusions

Consider the model:

$$\Delta P_t = \alpha \Delta P_{t-1} + S(t) + \epsilon_t \tag{3.6}$$

where ΔP_t is the price change series; $S(t)$ is a seasonal series with zero mean; and ϵ_t is a purely random, white noise series, again with zero mean. The results of our analysis reported above suggest that such a model fits all commodity price change series very well with α either zero or a very small, positive number. Thus, most series obey a random walk or near random walk, although on some occasions a seasonal pattern can be found. For daily price change series a weekly cycle is also occasionally found. These cyclical components vary in importance from one commodity to another.

It has been suggested before that purely speculative markets cannot produce price series having predictable components or patterns. If they did, components or patterns would be "traded" out of existence. Why then do some commodity series contain such components? There seem to be several possible reasons. Commodity markets are not pure speculative markets, as goods are actually sold in them by producers and bought by consumers or their representatives. The production of many commodities is very seasonal in nature and demand may also be seasonal. As the transaction cost is not negligible, due to storage, insurance, and commissions, one would not necessarily expect *all* of the seasonal pattern to be played out – only enough of it for the use of this pattern for determining a buying or selling policy to be barely profitable. In fact, the seasonal components are of small importance in the actual price series, in that they contribute only a small proportion of the total variance of price. It might also be argued that some commodity markets are not sufficiently sophisticated to eliminate completely every predictable component. We return to this point again in Chapter 5. It is worth noting Houthakker's comment "that commodity price developments are watched by relatively few traders, most of them quite set in their ways; even in the most active futures markets the volume of serious research by participants seems to be quite small. It is therefore possible that systematic patterns will remain largely unknown for a very long time."[19] Certainly our results agree with this statement.

Appendix to Chapter 3

The Averaging of a Random Walk Process[20]

Suppose that X_t is a random walk process, so that

$$X_t = X_{t-1} + \epsilon_t \tag{3A.1}$$

where ϵ_t is a zero-mean, white noise series, i.e., $E(\epsilon_t) = 0$ and $\text{cov}(\epsilon_t, \epsilon_s) = 0$, $t \neq s$ and variance $\epsilon_t = \sigma^2$, all t. It follows that the first differences of X_t over m periods is

$$\begin{aligned}\Delta^{(m)}X_t &= X_t - X_{t-m}\\ &= \epsilon_t + \epsilon_{t-1} + \dots + \epsilon_{t-m+1}\end{aligned} \tag{3A.2}$$

and $\Delta^{(m)}X_t$ has mean zero and variance $m\sigma^2$.

Now suppose that a series is produced by averaging m terms of X_t, averaging the following m terms and then taking the difference between the two averages, that is

$$\begin{aligned}Y_t^{(m)} &= \frac{1}{m}(X_t + X_{t+1} + \dots + X_{t+m-1})\\ &- \frac{1}{m}(X_{t-1} + X_{t-2} + \dots + X_{t-m})\end{aligned} \tag{3A.3}$$

An example of such an averaging would be to average the daily closing price of some commodity over all the days in a month. $Y^{(m)}$ is the difference between the average price in one month and the average price in the previous month. Note that any X_t only occurs once in every "month." This should not be confused with a *moving* average of length m of a series X_t, where any individual X_t will appear in every m adjacent averages. From (3A-2) it is seen that

$$\begin{aligned}Y_t^{(m)} = &\frac{1}{m}[X_t + (X_t + \epsilon_{t+1}) + \dots + (X_t + \epsilon_{t+1} + \epsilon_{t+2} + \dots + \epsilon_{t+m-1})]\\ &- \frac{1}{m}[(X_t - \epsilon_{t-1}) + (X_t - \epsilon_{t-1} - \epsilon_{t-2}) + \dots\\ &+ (X_t - \epsilon_{t-1} - \dots - \epsilon_{t-m+1})]\end{aligned}$$

which may be written

$$\begin{aligned}Y_t^{(m)} = &\frac{1}{m}[(m-1)\epsilon_{t+1} + (m-2)\epsilon_{t-2} + \dots\\ &+ \epsilon_{t+m-1} + m\epsilon_t + (m-1)\epsilon_{t-1} + \dots + \epsilon_{t-m+1}]\end{aligned} \tag{3A.4}$$

As the ϵ_i's are mutually uncorrelated, it follows that

$$\text{var } Y_t^{(m)} = \frac{\sigma^2}{m^2} [(m - 1)^2 + (m - 2)^2 + \ldots + 1^2 + m^2 + (m - 1)^2 + \ldots + 1]$$

$$= \frac{(2m^2 + 1)\sigma^2}{3m} \qquad (3A.5)$$

Now consider the *previous* averaged monthly difference $Y_{t-m}^{(m)}$. It will also contain $\epsilon_{t-1}, \epsilon_{t-2}, \ldots, \epsilon_{t-m+1}$ as seen from (3A.4) and so will be correlated to $Y_t^{(m)}$. Considering $E(Y_t^{(m)}, Y_{t-m}^{(m)})$, one finds

$$\text{cov } E(Y_t^{(m)}, Y_{t-m}^{(m)}) = \frac{1}{m^2} [1(m - 1) + 2(m - 2) + \ldots + (m - 1)1]$$

$$= \frac{(m^2 - 1)\sigma^2}{6m}$$

and so

$$\text{corr } (Y_t^{(m)}, Y_{t-m}^{(m)}) = \frac{m^2 - 1}{2(2m^2 + 1)} \qquad (3A.6)$$

and, except for very small m it is seen that this correlation is closely approximated by ¼.)

If one now inspects the term $Y_{t-2m}^{(m)}$, it is seen that it contains no ϵ_i in common with $Y_t^{(m)}$ and so it follows that

$$\text{corr } (Y_t^{(m)}, Y_{t-km}^{(m)}) = 0 \qquad \text{all } k > 1$$

Thus, if a daily price series obeys a random walk model, then a change series using monthly average prices will have autocorrelation sequence

$$\begin{aligned} \rho_k &= \text{corr } (Y_j, Y_{j-k}) \\ &= 1 \quad \text{for} \quad k = 0 \\ &= \frac{1}{4} \qquad\quad k = 1 \\ &= 0 \qquad\quad k > 1 \end{aligned} \qquad (3A.7)$$

A model having such an autocorrelation sequence is the moving average model

$$Y_j = \eta_j + \alpha\eta_{j-1} \qquad (3A.8)$$

where η_t is white noise series. Note that

$$\text{var } Y_j = \sigma_\eta^2 (1 + \alpha^2)$$

and

$$\text{cov } (Y_j, Y_{j-k}) = \sigma_\eta^2 \alpha \qquad k = 1$$

$$= 0 \qquad k > 1$$

For the particular autocorrelations in (3A.7), we must have

$$\frac{\alpha}{1 + \alpha^2} = \frac{1}{4}$$

that is

$$\alpha = 2 \pm \sqrt{3}$$

If α is restricted to obey $|\alpha| \leqslant 1$, the solution is $\alpha = 2 - \sqrt{3}$ which may be taken to be 0.3. Thus first differences of averaged daily, random walk prices will be given by the model

$$Y_j = \eta_j + 0.3\eta_{j-1} \qquad (3A.9)$$

Any moving model can be well approximated by an autoregressive model. The autoregressive model corresponding to (3A.8) is

$$Y_j + \sum_{i=1}^{\infty} (-\alpha^i) \, Y_{j-i} = \eta_t$$

and so the model (3A.9) is well approximated by

$$Y_j - 0.3 Y_{j-1} + 0.09 Y_{j-2} - 0.027 Y_{j-3} = \eta_t \qquad (3A.10)$$

where η_t is white noise. This equation (3A.10) will provide a method of predicting changes of average prices to be used in Chapter 9.

4 An Expectations Theory of Cash and Futures Prices

Introduction

The notion of expectations has often appeared in discussions of commodity price behavior. Although expectations are generally known to influence both cash or physical and futures markets, it is only by examining the expectations relationship between these markets that market similarities and differences can be clarified. The goal of this chapter is to determine whether futures prices respond to changes in market expectations and, as such, anticipate cash prices. A similar proposition is examined regarding the expectations relationship between the prices of near and more distant futures price series. Attention is also directed to the interdependency between the near futures price series of different commodities. All three of these relationships have a potential for prediction. The identification of an expectations relationship would enable near futures prices to be used as a predictor for cash prices and more distant futures prices to be used as a predictor for near futures prices. Similarly, the discovery of a lead-lag, particularly between prices of substitutable commodities, could result in the use of a "price leader" for forecasting. These possibilities are discussed in the final section, which summarizes the major findings of the empirical tests.

Expectations Theory in Perspective

That an expectations relationship should exist between cash and futures prices has been widely debated in the literature. To formulate a theory of expectations, one must review some of the relevant arguments, and, at least initially, the question of why cash and futures prices should be related at all. Houthakker has postulated that futures trading in the form of hedging is feasible only when the correlation between cash and futures prices is large enough to overcome the risk premium that is paid to speculators.[1] Recall from the hedging example presented in Chapter 1 that profits in the futures market will offset losses in the cash market only when cash and futures prices move by the same amount and in the same direction. Hedging depends on a certain amount of correlation to be effective, but many factors such as the difference in grades between cash and futures contracts serve to upset this correlation. When other arguments are examined, however, sufficient evidence exists to suggest that cash and futures prices move together, at least in the long-run fluctuations.[2]

Accepting this evidence, one can advance the notion of correlation one step further to reach the theory that futures prices represent an expected value of the cash price. Working, who was one of the first economists to investigate this theory, proposed that the "prices of commodity futures are the marked expression of consciously formed opinions on probable prices in the future.[3] He reviewed several versions of this hypothesis as presented by R. C. Hawtrey to members of the Federal Trade Commission, but could not find any empirical results to support its validity. Working's impressions were divided:

> It is not true that futures prices afford forecasts of price changes in the sense in which one speaks of the price forecast of a market analyst. Neither is it true that futures prices provide no sort of forecast of price change. Broadly, it seems that futures prices afford forecasts of changes that will probably occur in response to some classes of influences, and that they give within themselves no anticipatory indication of price changes that may develop from certain other classes of influences. But it is difficult to define these classes in general terms that are not open to misinterpretation.[4]

Working never advanced further a theory of price expectations in this form. Because of the presence of carryover stocks, he concluded that expectations of future developments tend to influence both futures and cash prices equally.[5] This theory has not received attention in more recent literature except for its appearance in a discussion of speculative price behavior presented by Samuelson.[6] While he has not developed a model which could be directly tested here, such a model can be formulated by turning to recent studies regarding the term structure of interest rates. One such study, for example, hypothesizes that the rate of interest for a two-year loan be compounded from the spot rate for loans of one-year and the forward rate for one-year loans.[7] Also of interest is the role that spectral methods have played in testing such hypotheses. A recent study has employed the cross-spectrum to test the hypothesis that forward rates are unbiased estimates of expected future rates.[8]

The relevance of such studies for formulating an expectations hypothesis of cash-futures price behavior is realized when one compares the similarity of the futures market to the bond market. Cootner has gone to some length to explain the correspondence between these markets.[9] His argument rests on two specific features. First of all, interest rates in the bond market refer to notes of varying maturity while prices in the futures market describe contracts of varying delivery date. Secondly, the supply curve of liquidity expressed in bonds can be likened to the number of futures contracts or stocks of a commodity in storage. On the basis of this comparison, the present authors feel strongly that the notion of expectations is relevant for explaining commodity price behavior.

An Expectations Hypothesis

The theory of expectations as applied to commodity prices would lead one to hypothesize that futures prices represent an expected value or unbiased estimate of cash prices. If the risk premium paid to speculators were included, it would stipulate that futures prices are biased estimates of cash prices.

The unbiased version is of interest here and can be formulated as follows. Let $X_{t-S,S}$ represent a near futures price series formed at time $t - S$ to mature S units later at delivery time t. Also let Y represent the value of the cash price series at the respective delivery date t. Thus, the hypothesis can be stated in the form

$$X_{t-S,S} = E(Y_t) \tag{4.1}$$

This expression implies that the price of a futures contract in the present will effectively be a predictor of the cash price at the time of delivery or contract expiration, t. As an example, on January 1st, the price of the March futures contract represents an unbiased estimate of the cash price anticipated on March 1st.

It is important to realize that the futures price will prove to be a predictor only if the cash price is predictable. This will follow only if the cross-spectrum reveals a high correlation between futures and cash prices and futures prices clearly lead cash prices. Since cash prices are likely to follow the random walk model implied in Chapter 3, futures prices are not likely to have a forecast value unless the random movements in both series are reasonably coordinated. For the case of randomly behaving prices, the current value of the cash price series is likely to be just as good a predictor of the cash price at the time of delivery.

The method actually selected for testing the hypothesis involves relating cash prices to three separate futures price series. Compiling as many as three series is possible since up to eight different futures contracts may exist for a particular commodity. For this study, prices have been compiled for only the three nearest futures contracts. If $X_{t,S}$ represents the near futures price series, then $X_{t,M}$ and $X_{t,L}$ represents price series of contracts due to mature at succeeding delivery dates.[a] For example, if $X_{t,S}$ represents the price of the December contract for wheat on November 1st, then $X_{t,M}$ and $X_{t,L}$ represent prices of the March and May contract on the same date. The expectations hypothesis would properly state that the futures series $X_{t-S,S}$, $X_{t-M,M}$, and $X_{t-L,L}$ must not only lead Y_t, but also that the more distant series $X_{t-M,M}$ and $X_{t-L,L}$ must lead the less distant series $X_{t-S,S}$. The hypothesis applied to all possible pairs of price series would read:

$$\left.\begin{aligned} X_{t-S,S} &= E(Y_t) \\ X_{t-M,M} &= E(Y_t) \\ X_{t-L,L} &= E(Y_t) \end{aligned}\right\} \tag{4.2}$$

$$\left.\begin{aligned} X_{t-M,M} &= E(X_{t-S,S}) \\ X_{t-L,L} &= E(X_{t-S,S}) \\ X_{t-L,L} &= E(X_{t-M,M}) \end{aligned}\right\} \tag{4.3}$$

To empirically test the hypothesis, the cross-spectrum has been estimated between three futures series and a related cash price series for a number of commodities. The estimations procedure is such that all of the above pairs of

---

[a] S is defined as the interval in time between the present near futures price and the futures expiration date. A similar meaning can be attached to M and L; only the intervals are successively greater, i.e., L (Long) $>M$ (Medium) $>S$ (Short).

relationships have been examined simultaneously. The series we use in the calculations are $X_{t,S}$, $X_{t,M}$, $X_{t,L}$, and Y_t.

Before explaining these tests further, it is worth mentioning the difference between the expectations hypothesis about to be tested and the interesting theoretical results achieved by Samuelson.[10] Consider a futures contract represented by $X_{t-T,T}$ made at time $t - T$ to be fulfilled T units ahead, i.e., at time t. Now consider the sequence of futures contracts $X_{t-T,T}$ for varying $T = n\ (n - 1, \ldots, 2, 1, 0)$ but fixed t, with $X_{t,0} = Y_t$. Samuelson proves that if every futures price in this sequence is an optimum forecast of an expectation of Y_t, then the sequence of futures prices will be a random walk. That is, the best predictor of $X_{t-k,k}$ is $X_{t-k-1,k+1}$ and the change in the futures $X_{t-k,k} - X_{t-k-1,k+1}$ is unpredictable from earlier changes in the sequence. This result, although obviously interesting, is not relevant to the futures series considered by us which consists of sequences $X_{t-T,T}$ for fixed T and varying t. An appendix to Chapter 3 of Granger and Morgenstern discussed under what conditions Samuelson's result can be used to imply that the futures sequence we consider will be random walk, but no satisfactory, acceptable conditions are found.[11]

Proceeding with the tests outlined above, one finds two particular difficulties in using futures price series in the stated form. First of all, the futures prices are not always the same distance in time from the cash prices. The near futures price series reflects contracts that may be one month forward of the cash price in May but two or three months forward in April or March. This could confuse the interpretation of a lead appearing in the phase diagram, but later results will show the absence of any such problem. The interpretation of leads had also been improved through the use of closing prices which provide a more accurate specification of the observations in time than do average values. A second difficulty is that cash prices correspond to one grade of a commodity while futures prices represent several different grades. The natural tendency is for market forces to affect prices differently, depending on the grade represented. In the present study, this effect has been minimized by selecting cash price series which correspond to the major grade traded in the futures contract.

Interpreting the Expectations Hypothesis

Cross-spectral estimates have been prepared between all pairs of cash and futures prices using first differences of monthly prices. The exact method of compiling the different futures price series, together with a list of price sources, is reported in Appendix A. The interpretation of the expectations hypothesis begins with an explanation of the coherence and phase diagrams for wheat. Coherence and phase are then interpreted for the remaining commodities including oats, soybeans, corn, cocoa, and lard. Emphasis is placed on the coherence results since the coherences tend to follow a recognizable pattern over time. The notion of expectations is then reexamined with respect to the various findings. This section closes with a consideration of two special aspects of the expectations

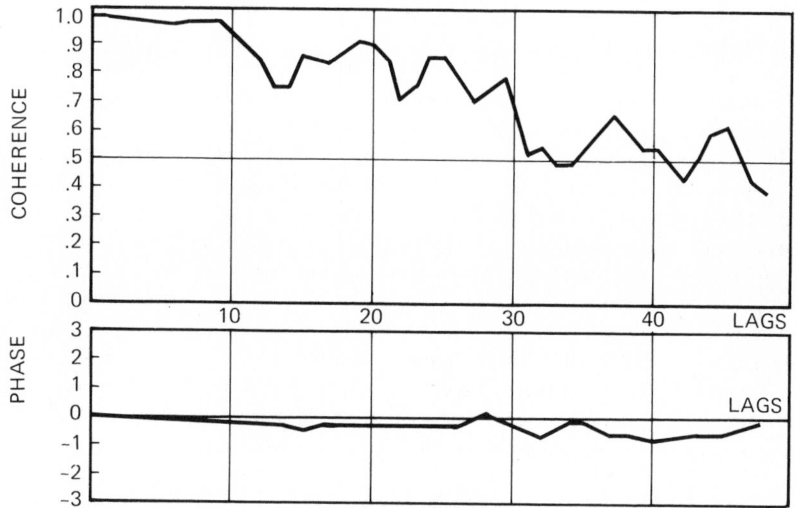

Figure 4-1 Cross-Spectrum Between Wheat Price Differences: $Y_t, X_{t,S}$ Monthly: 1950-1965.

hypothesis, the possibility of an additive explanation and the importance of contract spacing.

Cross-Spectral Results for Wheat

Many of the coherence diagrams depict a cash-futures relationship substantiating the expectations hypothesis, but the phase diagrams do not display the required lead of futures over cash prices. To provide a better understanding of the coherence and phase estimates, the following diagrams have been selected from the cross-spectra for wheat. Each describes the relationship between cash and one of the futures price series. The first such diagram, Figure 4-1, summarizes coherence and phase values between cash and near futures prices at Chicago. The basis grade that has been chosen to represent the cash prices is Red Winter No. 2. The coherence diagram can be considered typical of those found for the various commodities, but the phase diagram differs slightly in that it suggests a possible lead.

Analyzing the coherence diagram first, one finds that the coherence between the cash price Y_t and the near futures price $X_{t,S}$ remains generally high for the long-run frequencies, but fluctuates over the middle- and short-run frequencies. If any relationship exists between the cash and futures prices, then it will appear in the long-run frequency band of high coherence. In the shorter-run frequencies, the nonconstant coherence implies that any fluctuations of frequency

ω for the cash price series Y_t cannot be attributed entirely to fluctuations of a similar frequency for the futures series $X_{t,S}$.

As for the corresponding phase diagram, a lead can be detected for wheat futures prices over cash prices, but it is extremely small. In order for a lead-lag to be observed, the phase diagram should form a linear trend over some frequency range. Positive or negative phase values as well as a positive or negative trend indicate the direction of the lead; the magnitude of the lead is measured by the angle of trend m/j where m is the total number of estimated lags and j the frequency point where the trend line reaches a phase value equal to π. The phase values of Figure 4-1 imply that changes in wheat futures prices lead changes in cash prices by 30 degrees or one week. This lead could provide evidence for the expectations hypothesis.

Figures 4-2 and 4-3 feature the coherence and phase diagrams for cash prices Y_t and the more distant futures prices, $X_{t,M}$ and $X_{t,L}$. While the coherence diagrams have the general properties described above, the phase diagrams reflect a more complicated lead-lag relationship than that of Figure 4-1. The phase diagram of Figure 4-2 suggests leads at several different frequencies, but an interpretation of these leads must be questioned on the basis of a corresponding decline in coherence. This latter phenomenon is often found in the cross-spectrum; it arises from the tendency of the phase estimates to have a large variance at low values of coherence. One must limit any interpretation of the phase diagram in Figure 4-2, therefore, to the region below the band, $j/2m = 7/96$ c/m.

In this region, the change in futures prices is leading changes in cash prices, but the relationship is not that of a uniform lead. The long-run fluctuations are leading by a different amount than the short-run fluctuations. Between the lower frequency bands 0 and 5/96 c/m, the lead is m/j = 48/44 or approximately one month. For the slightly higher frequencies, from 5/96 to 7/96 c/m, the lead is approximately three months. Beyond 7/96 c/m, as mentioned above, the phase diagram becomes less decipherable. Such a lead, however, cannot be further interpreted since the phase values lack statistical significance.

Other Cross-Spectral Results

Coherence and phase results for a number of commodities including wheat are summarized in Table 4-1. Recalling the assumption made earlier, one finds that choice of the basis grade for the cash price series is not too critical for the testing of the expectations relationship. The coherence and phase values which have been found for wheat are the same regardless of the basis grade. A more significant result is that the pattern of coherence values which is found for wheat is generally followed by the other commodities. The previous section reported for wheat a high coherence between Y_t and $X_{t,S}$ but only a moderate coherence between Y_t and $X_{t,M}$ or $X_{t,L}$. Table 4-1 also suggests moderate coherence between the near futures price series $X_{t,S}$ and the more distant series $X_{t,M}$ and

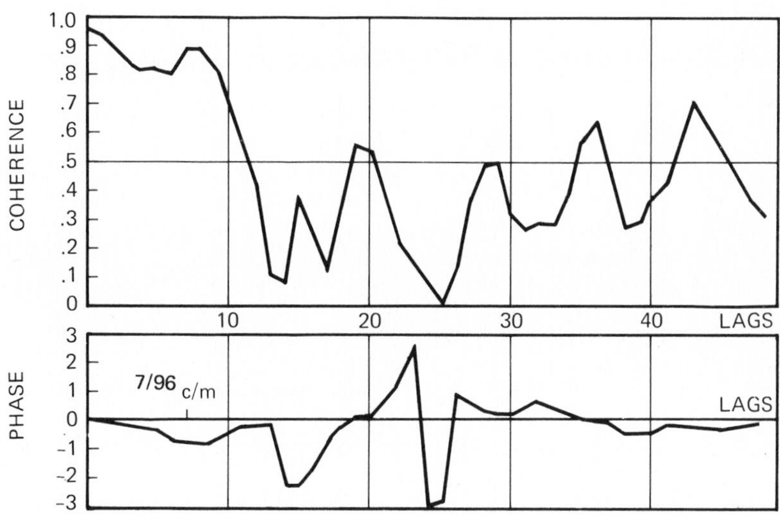

Figure 4-2 Cross-Spectrum Between Wheat Price Differences: $Y_t, X_{t,M}$

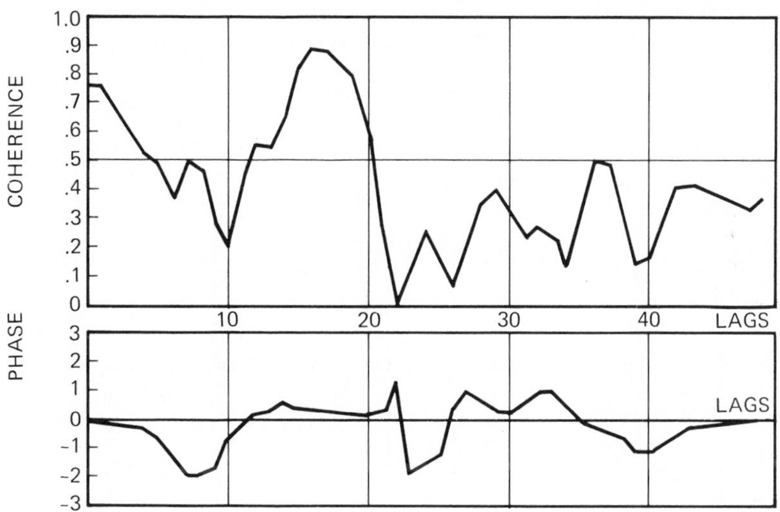

Figure 4-3 Cross-Spectrum Between Wheat Price Differences: $Y_t, X_{t,L}$

Table 4-1

Cross-Spectrum: Cash Prices and Three Consecutive Futures Prices

Monthly: First Differences
January 1950-June 1965
Observations = 186
Estimated Lags = 48

			Coherence, Lead											
			$Y_t, X_{t,S}$		$Y_t, X_{t,M}$		$Y_t, X_{t,L}$		$X_{t,S}, X_{t,M}$		$X_{t,S}, X_{t,L}$		$X_{t,M}, X_{t,L}$	
			C[a]	L[b]	C	L	C	L	C	L	C	L	C	L
Wheat	1950–1965	Red No. 2[c]	H	F	M	0	M	0	M	0	M	0	H	0
Wheat	1950–1965	Hard No. 2	H	F	M	0	M	0	M	0	M	0	H	0
Oats	1950–1965	Heavy No. 2	L	R	M	0	M	0	M	0	L	0	H	0
Soybeans	1950–1965	Yellow No. 1	H	0	H	0	M	0	H	0	M	0	M	0
Corn	1950–1965	Yellow No. 2	H	0	M	0	L	0	H	0	L	0	L	0
Cocoa	1950–1965	Ghana	H	0	M	0	H	0	H	0	H	0	H	0
Lard	1948–1962	Drums	H	0	H	0	M	0	H	0	H	0	H	0

[a]C ≡ Coherence: H = Some coherence values above 0.8, most above 0.5; M = Most coherence values between 0.6 and 0.3; L = Few coherence values above 0.4

[b]L ≡ Lead: F = Lead of futures over spot prices; R = Futures lead reversed; O = No lead.

[c]Grade of cash price series.

$X_{t,L}$. A slight increase in coherence can be found between the adjacent price series representing the most distant delivery dates, $X_{t,M}$ and $X_{t,L}$.

These same patterns with few exceptions are repeated for soybeans, corn, lard, and cocoa prices. The coherence between the cash and the more distant futures prices declines more rapidly for corn than for wheat. The adjacent futures series with the highest coherence shift from the more distant futures date for wheat to the closer delivery date for corn and soybeans. For oats, not only was the cash near-futures coherence low, but the implied lead of the futures over the cash price series was reversed. Where leads appeared for any of the other commodities, they were always in the correct direction, but of insufficient magnitude to be statistically significant. The lack of significant leads between the appropriate price series prevents a verification of the expectations hypothesis as presented at the outset of this chapter. Before this hypothesis is interpreted with respect to the obtained results, it would be useful to examine further the time patterns found among the various coherences.

Futures Relationships Over Time

The above results suggest that the correlations between the various price series vary directly with the separation of the corresponding futures contracts over time. Furthermore, the correlations appear to be higher between the long-run than the short-run movement of the price series. To explain both of these phenomena, coherence values have been averaged for each commodity, and then placed in a matrix of the following form which reflects the strength of the relationship between the various cash and futures prices over time.

$$\begin{bmatrix} \bar{C}(Y_t, X_{t,S}) & \bar{C}(Y_t, X_{t,M}) & \bar{C}(Y_t, X_{t,L}) \\ & \bar{C}(X_{t,S}, X_{t,M}) & \bar{C}(X_{t,S}, X_{t,L}) \\ & & \bar{C}(X_{t,M}, X_{t,L}) \end{bmatrix} \tag{4.4}$$

Values listed in the top row describe the average coherence between the cash and near and the cash and more-distant futures price series respectively. The remaining values reflect the coherences between the various futures price series.

The same matrix can also be used to describe the suggested differences between long and short-run coherences. Spectral decomposition can be used to divide the coherence and phase diagrams into a set of frequency ranges describing the long-, middle-, and short-run frequencies respectively. For the present analysis, average coherence values have been reported only for the long- and short-run frequencies. The long-run coherences represent an average taken over the first 16 of 48 lags and represent periods of 6 months to approximately

4 years; the short-run coherences are averaged only over the final 16 of 48 lags and cover a period of 2 to 3 months.[b]

The futures relationships over time can now be explained in terms of the coherence values presented in the matrices of Tables 4-2 and 4-3.[c,12] The differences in correlation between the cash and futures prices in the long- as compared to the short-run frequencies can be observed in the differences in coherence patterns between these two tables. The predominance of symmetry along the rows, columns, and diagonals of Table 4-2 as compared to the lack of symmetry in Table 4-3 offers sufficient evidence that the expectations hypothesis proposed in this form might be more appropriate for longer-run price movements. This result has been confirmed through a separate test of the expectations hypothesis using daily data. Table 4-4 indicates that only low to moderate coherences and no leads can be found between similar cash and futures price arrangements for daily data.[d]

Considering only the long-run coherence matrix of Table 4-2, one can explain the pattern whereby the correlation between the various price series varies over time. The general tendency is for the correlations between the price series to diminish as the time span between the futures date and cash date increases. A more specific statement as to the nature of this variation has been summarized below; it holds true for all of the above commodities except oats.

1. The average coherence between cash and futures prices declines as the distance of the contract delivery date increases from the cash date (matrix top row).
2. The average coherence between near and more distant futures prices declines as the delivery period between the contracts widens (matrix rows and columns).
3. The average coherence between coincident futures prices declines as the delivery date for each pair of contracts becomes more distant from the cash date (matrix diagonal).
4. The average coherence between the near and the more distant futures contract prices is less than that between any of the adjacent contracts both near and distant.

---

[b]Since the period is defined as the reciprocal of the frequency ($T = 1/f$), the coherence diagram at lag points 2 and 16 represents periods of $2m/j = 96/2$ and 96/16 or 48 and 6 months respectively. Similarly, the periods corresponding to 32 and 48 lags are 96/32 = 3 months and 96/48 = 2 months respectively.

[c]No confidence bands have been applied to the average coherence values of this or the succeeding chapters. The present state of spectral theory is such that confidence bands for average coherence are not known with any reasonable accuracy. The limits of this accuracy are discussed by Hughes. Cf. p. 62.

[d]The cross-spectrum for daily cash and futures prices as well as the Dow-Jones spot and futures indexes reveals only a weak relation between cash and futures prices. The coffee and sugar near and more distant futures prices are correlated a little more strongly.

Table 4-2

Time Structure Matrices: Cash Prices and Three Consecutive Futures Prices—Average Coherence at Long-Run Frequencies

Monthly: First Differences
January 1950-June 1965
Observations = 186
Estimated Lags = 48

	Wheat[a]			*Wheat*[b]			*Corn*	
.93	.68	.55	.86	.65	.50	.82	.58	.16
	.81	.57		.81	.57		.77	.24
		.68			.68			.30

	Soybeans			*Oats*			*Cocoa*	
.93	.68	.42	.27	.63	.48	.94	.80	.79
	.82	.45		.37	.32		.98	.92
		.66			.84			.96

	Lard	
.86	.76	.68
	.91	.80
		.94

[a] Spot is Soft Red Winter No. 2.

[b] Spot is Hard Winter No. 2.

Table 4-3

Time Structure Matrices: Cash Prices and Three Consecutive Futures Prices—Average Coherence at Short-Run Frequencies

Monthly: First Differences
January 1950-June 1965
Observations = 186
Estimated Lags = 48

	Wheat[a]			*Wheat*[b]			*Corn*	
.54	.46	.32	.49	.42	.29	.20	.33	.15
	.40	.30		.40	.30		.54	.20
		.43			.43			.39

	Soybeans			*Oats*			*Cocoa*	
.71	.58	.59	.24	.26	.21	.89	.79	.71
	.64	.45		.36	.34		.84	.71
		.71			.58			.82

	Lard	
.18	.18	.09
	.58	.34
		.47

[a]Spot is Soft Red Winter No. 2.

[b]Spot is Hard Winter No. 2.

Table 4-4

Cross-Spectrum: Cash Prices and Three Consecutive Futures Prices

Daily: First Differences
August 1964-July 1965
Observations = 260
Estimated Lags = 48

			Coherence, Lead											
			$Y_t, X_{t,S}$		$Y_t, X_{t,M}$		$Y_t, X_{t,L}$		$X_{t,S}, X_{t,M}$		$X_{t,S}, X_{t,L}$		$X_{t,M}, X_{t,L}$	
			C[a]	L[b]	C	L	C	L	C	L	C	L	C	L
Cocoa	1964–1965	Ghana	L	0	M	0	M	0	L	0	L	0	H	0
Coffee	1964–1965	Santos	X	0	X	0	X	0	H	0	M	0	H	0
Cotton	1964–1965	1" Middling	X	0	X	0	X	0	X	0	X	0	L	0
Rubber	1964–1965	Sm. Sheets	L	0	M	0	M	0	M	0	L	0	M	0
Sugar	1964–1965	Raw	L	0	L	0	L	0	H	0	M	0	H	0
Dow Jones Indexes	1964–1965	Index	L	0										

[a]C = Coherence: H = Some coherence values above 0.8, most above 0.5; M = Most coherence values between 0.6 and 0.3; L = Few coherence values above 0.4; X = Majority of values below 0.25.

[b]L = Lead: 0 = No lead.

Nature of Expectations

While the results express a tendency for the correlations between cash and futures and near and more distant futures prices to follow a definite time pattern over the long-run frequencies, the same results do not provide evidence that futures prices are capable of predicting cash prices. Similar time patterns have appeared in the Granger-Rees study in as far as the coherences between interest rates decline as bond maturity increases, but certain leads also appeared in the phase diagrams which lend support to a predictive or expectations hypothesis.[13] At best, the present results suggest that correlations tend to be highest between more proximate price series and perhaps this information could be used as an aid to forecasting.

Several suggestions can be offered as to why it has been difficult to confirm the expectations hypothesis in this direct form. Whether or not our results, in fact, preclude a rejection of the hypothesis is commented on in the conclusions. From a technical point of view, direct confirmation of the hypothesis in the form of observed lags is likely to have been upset by the presence of feedback in the price series, i.e., the frequent reversal of causality between price formations in the cash and futures markets. This particular problem is not likely to be solved until better methods are devised for breaking down feedback and investigating directions of causality.[14]

Of the nontechnical reasons, the most probable one is that cash and futures prices react simultaneously to market developments, and a change in prospects produces no lagged effects. Another possibility is that all of the monthly commodities tested except cocoa and lard come under the price support program of the Commodity Credit Corporation; as a result, the prices of these commodities may be less free to react to basic market forces. One final reason for the lack of expectations is that the composition of traders differs for each market. When different segments of the market trade with varying motives, it is unlikely that the prices which emerge in the cash and futures markets could be linked by a single factor, i.e., that futures prices anticipate the future.

Additivity

The expectations hypothesis defines the relationship between the near futures and cash price series as

$$X_{t-S,S} = E(Y_t) \tag{4.5}$$

Similar expressions have been written in (4.2) for the more and most distant futures price series. Having examined the cross-spectral relationships between the various pairs of price series, one can raise the question of whether the explanation of cash price series provided by one futures price series can be added to the explanation provided by another futures price series to increase the overall explanation of cash prices. This might be expressed as follows:

$$a_S X_{t-S,S} + a_M X_{t-M,M} + a_L X_{t-L,L} = E(Y_t) \tag{4.6}$$

Table 4-5

Average Partial Coherence Between Cash and Futures Prices: Long-Run Frequencies

Monthly: First Differences
January 1950-June 1965
Observations = 186
Estimated Lags = 48

	(1)	*(2)*	*(3)*
Cocoa	.54	.19	.23
Corn	.69	.26	.12
Oats	.14	.46	.33
Soybeans	.76	.22	.09
Wheat	.79	.44	.25

Column (1) shows the average partial coherence between Y_t and $X_{t,S}$ holding $X_{t,M}$ and $X_{t,L}$ constant.

Column (2) shows the average partial coherence between Y_t and $X_{t,M}$ holding $X_{t,S}$ and $X_{t,L}$ constant.

Column (3) shows the average partial coherence between Y_t and $X_{t,L}$ holding the $X_{t,S}$ and $X_{t,M}$ constant.

Thus, the expected value of the cash price is the weighted averages of prices of three successive futures price series. If Y_t is the expected value on November 1st of the cash price expected December 1st, then the expected price is determined not only by the December futures price, but also the March and May futures price, all three specified on November 1st.

Employing the partial cross-spectrum will help to test this proposition, without having to form the weighted averages. This method, a generalization of partial correlation, measures the coherence between Y_t and $X_{t,S}$ when the influence of the remaining futures price series, $X_{t,M}$ and $X_{t,L}$, are removed. More relevant to the present question, the partial coherence can tell us whether $X_{t,M}$ or $X_{t,L}$ provide further explanation of cash prices with the influence of $X_{t,S}$ and the remaining price series removed.

The partial coherence and phase results obtained from the partial cross-spectra are reported for a sample of five commodities in Table 4-5. The average partial coherences shown in the first column suggest that the near futures price series $X_{t,S}$ provides the best explanation of the cash price series for the included commodities except oats, when the effect of the remaining variables is removed. The values in the second column imply that the next-distant futures price series $X_{t,M}$ also provides an explanation of the cash price series, although not as much as the near price series. For the most-distant price series, $X_{t,L}$ as reported in column three, the explanation is only marginal, expecially for corn and soybeans. No answer has been obtained as to why the more-distant futures price series for oats should offer a better explanation of cash prices than the near futures price series. Even with partial influences, no lags have developed between the cash and futures price series; for this reason, the three futures price series have not been combined into the weighted average model given in equation 4.6.

Contract Spacing

The conclusions that have been reached so far have been based on a spacing between the month of the cash transaction and the month of contract delivery which is nonuniform. As discussed earlier, the near futures price series can reflect contracts which might be one month forward of the cash price in May but two or three months forward in April or March. To observe the effects of this spacing on the results, the futures price series must be arranged more carefully so that the spacing becomes uniform, i.e., the reported futures price is only one month, two months, or any other integral month from the cash date. This was difficult to achieve for all the commodities tested, but it has been possible to rearrange the soybean and wheat futures price series to represent delivery months equally spaced from the cash date, ranging from one to nine months.

The spectral results for uniform contract spacing are summarized in Table 4-6. For the first five months with soybeans and for the first three months with wheat, the cash-futures coherence values follow the declining time pattern explained above. The soybean coherence index remains constant for the first three months and declines for the last two. The corresponding average coherence values fall from 0.81 to 0.37. For wheat, the average coherences decline from 0.96 to 0.56, and this corresonds to a fall in the index from very high to high. Where leads could be found, they are in the correct direction, but none are significant.

Thus, commodity cash and futures prices, when uniformly spaced by delivery month, decline linearly over time in their correlation with each other, but this linearity disintegrates as soon as the delivery date becomes more than three to five months from the spot date. This disintegration, however, does not distort any of the previous results. For the nonlinear region, average coherences may vary from month to month, but the general decline in coherence is the same as that achieved with only approximate contract spacing.

Table 4-6

Cross-Spectrum: Cash and Futures Prices—Uniform Contract Spacing

Monthly: First Differences
January 1950-June 1965
Observations = 92
Estimated Lags = 24

Futures Lead	*Coherence Index*[a]	*Soybeans Average Coherence*	*Lead*[b]	*Coherence Index*	*Wheat Average Coherence*	*Lead*
1 mo.	H	.81	0	V	.96	0
2 mo.	H	.80	0	H	.75	0
3 mo.	H	.64	0	H	.56	0
4 mo.	M	.57	0	H	.63	0
5 mo.	L	.37	0	M	.56	0
6 mo.	M	.51	0	M	.51	0
7 mo.	L	.34	0	M	.53	0
8 mo.	M	.52	0	M	.46	0
9 mo.	L	.34	0	L	.39	0

[a]Coherence: V = Many coherence values above 0.95; H = Some coherence values above 0.8, most above 0.5; M = Most coherence values between 0.6 and 0.3; L = Few coherence values above 0.4.

[b]Lead: 0 = No lead.

Futures Price Behavior Between Commodities

Another form of relationship between commodity prices deserving attention is that of the relative behavior of near futures prices between commodities. Futures prices would generally be expected to move together, at least according to the influence of major business cycles. If a strong relationship exists between certain commodities, then this will be reflected in a relatively high coherence, and in some cases the prices of one commodity may lead the prices of another.

A previous comparison of several commodities offered a hint of interdependence. The cross-spectrum was estimated for corn, wheat, oats, and rye from the first differences of monthly futures prices for the period 1921-1951. Not only did corn demonstrate a moderate coherence with wheat and oats, but corn prices led wheat and oats prices by 3.4 and 3.2 months respectively. Both leads were significant at the 95% confidence level. A lead of this duration may seem exceptional, but it is partially explicable by differences in the major harvest periods. With the crop year beginning in October for corn and July for oats and wheat, it is likely that the price lows reached in corn were later reflected in the lows of oats and wheat.

To provide a general test of relative price behavior, one or more commodity price series have been selected from each of the *Wall Street Journal*'s major commodity classifications, i.e., foods, grains, and feeds, fats and oils, textiles and fibers, and metals. The final list includes most of the commodity series tested in the previous chapter. Interruptions of trading activity on the metals market prevent the compilation of a metal series which would be coincident with other prices. Table 4-7 summarizes the coherence relations among the various commodities. Coherence values in that table have been averaged only over the long-run frequencies, the range of most likely covariation.

The commodity comparisons have been made among groups and within groups. The highest coherence (0.55) that can be found among the major commodity groups occurs between soybeans from the grains and feeds group and soybean oil from the fats and oils groups. Moderate coherences emerge between cotton from the textiles and fibers groups and several oils from the fats and oils group. The coherences of cotton with cottonseed oil and cotton with soybean oil are 0.39 and 0.32 respectively. Cotton shows a surprising relation with several other commodities, particularly coherence values of 0.41 with rye and 0.34 with corn. Within the grains and feeds group, moderate coherences appear between rye and wheat (0.32), corn and soybeans (0.32) and corn and soymeal (0.33). A higher coherence can be found between soybeans and soybean meal (0.68). Within the fats and oils group, a high coherence (0.69) emerges between the only included commodities, soybean oil and cottonseed oil. None of the above relationships were accompanied by the prices of one commodity leading or lagging the prices of another.

One can explain the few interdependencies that do exist on the basis of price elasticity of substitution. The high coherence between soybean oil and cottonseed oil reflects, for example, the relationship between two oils which are often interchanged as inputs to the soap and detergent industry. The link between soybeans and soybean oil, soybeans and soybean meal, and cotton and cottonseed oil is also one of substitution, but only with respect to the decision to deal with the original commodity or its converted by-product. The moderate coherence between rye and wheat (0.32) might also be expected since rye has some relation to wheat as bread flour. Similarly, one might anticipate a moderate coherence between oats and corn, which are directly competitive as animal feed, but only a low value (0.15) is found. Another exceptionally low

Table 4-7

Average Coherence Between Commodity Futures Prices Long-Run Frequencies

Monthly: First Differences
January 1950-June 1965
Observations = 186
Estimated Lags = 48

	Wheat	Soyoil	Soymeal	Soybeans	Rye	Potatoes	Oats	Eggs	Corn	Cottonseed oil	Cotton	Cocoa
Cocoa	.08	.18	.26	.26	.14	.12	.06	.12	.20	.14	.12	–
Cotton	.20	.32	.17	.18	.41	.14	.15	.12	.34	.39		
Cottonseed oil	.12	.69	.18	.29	.18	.17	.06	.20	.21			
Corn	.24	.25	.33	.32	.29	.16	.15	.15				
Eggs	.18	.12	.18	.16	.27	.13	.13					
Oats	.18	.10	.20	.17	.11	.09						
Potatoes	.18	.15	.09	.12	.11							
Rye	.32	.13	.17	.18								
Soybeans	.22	.55	.68									
Soymeal	.16	.26										
Soyoil	.14											
Wheat	–											

coherence (0.26) is that between soybean oil and soybean meal, both of which are converted products of soybeans.

No general conclusions can be reached as to the influence of the geographical location of the market. The strong coherence between soybean oil sold at Chicago and cottonseed oil sold at New York, however, does imply that substitution characteristics are sufficiently strong to outweigh differences in location. A better test of this proposition would require futures prices for one commodity but from several markets. Since only a few relationships have been found, the structure of the futures market can generally be regarded as heterogeneous. One would expect more uniformity in price movements, given that the market is speculative and highly subject to general economic and political influences. Perhaps the only explanation is that these factors do influence prices, but that each commodity is affected in a different way.

Conclusions

The expectations hypothesis considered above stated that a futures price represented an expected value of the cash price at the time of its maturity, i.e.,

$$X_{t-T,T} = E(Y_t)$$

where $X_{t-T,T}$ represents a futures price formed at time $t - T$, to mature T units later at time t; and Y_t is the cash price at time t. If this expectations hypothesis is true, then the futures prices will effectively be predictions of later cash prices. Whether or not our results support such a hypothesis depends on the view taken of the predictability of cash prices. It was found that near futures prices $X_{t,S}$ reached at time t were highly related to the current cash price Y_t. If the best prediction of future cash price is current cash price, that is cash prices follow a random walk, then one has $E(Y_t) = Y_{t-T}$ and so $X_{t-T,T}$ and Y_{t-T} should be highly related and the expectations hypothesis would hold true. If, however, market analysts could predict cash prices, then for the expectations hypothesis to be correct, one should find futures prices leading cash prices. No strong evidence for the existence of such leads was found.

If one accepts that futures prices do represent anticipated later cash prices, then traders would combine the current cash price and their prediction as to the future movement of cash prices in reaching their anticipated or expected value. One would expect that these predictions, made on all available market information and not presumable just on past cash price movements, would be given greater weight the longer the distance to the maturity of the futures contract. That is, longer futures would place less weight on current cash price. The fact that longer futures contract prices ($X_{t,M}$, $X_{t,L}$) were found to be less related to current cash prices supports this belief. However, as no leads were found between future prices and cash prices, this indicates that the traders were in fact unable to predict cash prices.

It is thus seen that our results do not contradict the expectations hypothesis provided that it is accepted that future cash prices are not predictable. Results to be presented in later chapters, particularly Chapter 9, will support this view. Our results certainly suggest that futures prices will not be useful for predicting cash prices.

When the notion of expectations is applied to the relation between commodity price series, no lead-lags could be found and the price movements proved to be relatively independent. Higher coherences did occur between some price series, but only where the commodities were highly substitutable. Such information, nonetheless, is of value in explaining price movements in markets such as fats and oils where a large number of substitutes are readily available.

While expectations have not appeared as a strong price-making force in the respective markets, the levels of coherence achieved between the cash and futures prices suggest that other forces in the market induce this covariation. Any further explanation of prices, therefore, requires a more elaborate evaluation of market relationships, an investigation which begins in the next chapter.

5 The Nature of Demand

Introduction

To formulate a general model of price behavior, one must first study the market determinants of price. An obvious beginning for that study is the simple quantity theory of demand. Studies of other speculative markets such as the stock market have shown that demand theory fails to offer an adequate explanation of price behavior. However, with commodity futures and cash markets, a greater variety of quantity relatives are available. Price fluctuations can be related to both speculative and physical variables. The former encompass volume of trading and open interest while the latter include supply, demand, and stock levels. The chapter begins by examining the price-volume relationship and continues by refining this relationship as that of price-supply and demand. The open interest relationship is studied next; accordingly, greater detail is provided by considering its division into hedging and speculating. Partial spectral analysis has been added at this point to learn whether hedging and speculating provide a better explanation of price change than do supply and demand. Hedging and speculating are further investigated as a price influence by being combined into a ratio which reflects the excess of speculating over hedging or market imbalance. The conclusions show that demand theory is somewhat wanting in explaining speculative price movements and that hedging and speculating exert a greater influence on price fluctuations than was previously recognized.

Demand Theory and Speculative Markets

Economists have long recognized the difficulty of applying conventional demand theory to the irregular price movements prevalent in security or commodity markets. Several different approaches have been proposed to explain the response of commodity prices to demand; three major ones are summarized below. The first approach attempts to explain prices within the supply-demand framework. The second bypasses supply and demand as such, and relates the irregularity of price behavior to certain market phenomena. While the third approach is a variant of the first, its use of spectral techniques and its application to stock markets makes it particularly relevant here.

The Limits of Supply and Demand

The realization that supply and demand do not always respond to change in price or vice versa was presented in an early study by Taussig.[1] He argued that the supply of a commodity coming into the market does not always decrease when the price falls, nor does it necessarily increase when the price rises. Such disparities often occur during periods of market activity which correspond to the "bull or bear" phenomenon found on stock markets. Consider an example of price behavior during a period of bear activity. When observed from the supply side, a lowering in price may not necessarily lead to a reduction in the supply of the commodity offered. The fear of a further price fall may induce an even greater supply to be offered on the market; consequently, the price will fall even further.

Taussig continued this argument by explaining that a price run could not increase indefinitely and that supply and demand would eventually come into play. The uncertainty of the workings of supply and demand would only occur within limits which Taussig termed the "penumbra." These limits would increase as the market conditions became more precarious, but ultimately their absolute level would be related to the conditions of supply and demand. Taussig believed that such a theory could be applied to either commodity or security markets, but he regarded it as being more relevant for the former, where supply and demand represent real market forces.

Surprisingly, this theory still appears in explanations of commodity price behavior today. Bernstein, for example, uses the concept to describe a relationship between line charts and supply-demand curves.[2] He accomplishes this task by first assuming that supply and demand are best represented not by single lines intersecting to determine one price, but rather a number of lines forming various prices, which oscillate about a so-called "normal" value. This provides incentive for replacing the normal supply and demand curves with a set of bands as shown in Figure 5-1. These bands, when translated to the line charts on the right, form a trading range. The effect on prices of a shift in demand relative to supply can be seen in Parts A and B of that figure. In Part A, demand and supply are in equilibrium for the time interval under investigation, and the corresponding trading range remains constant. In Part B, demand increases relative to supply. This results in a transformation of the trading range with prices moving upwards. Unfortunately, the concept of the "penumbra" provides no basis for a rigorous quantitative model.

Response to Information

Economic research in general has criticized the inadequacy of explanations such as the above as a framework for describing shorter-run, speculative price behavior.[3] Working has suggested that the original demand framework as devised by Marshall explained price-related intentions to buy and sell rather than actual prices resulting from successive bids and offers.[4] Because he found a strong random component in futures prices, Working states that supply and demand are inoperative forces even within the broad limits of Taussig's "penumbra." In short, the theory of a market in which price and quantity are highly interrelated

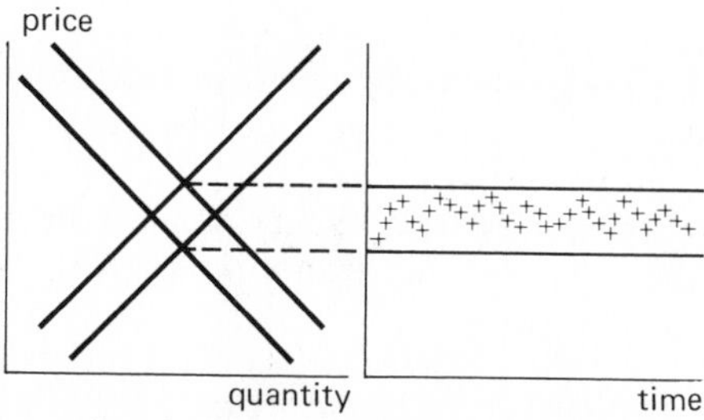

Part A: Fixed Supply-Fixed Demand

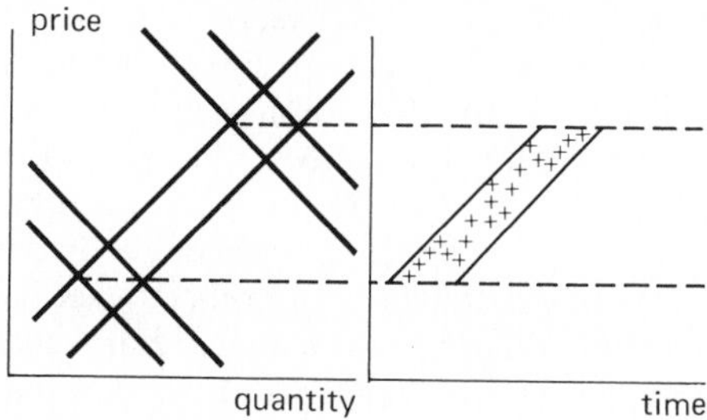

Part B: Fixed Supply-Increased Demand

Figure 5-1 Influence of Supply and Demand on Futures Price Movements. Source: Modified from Bernstein, "How Commodity Price Charts Disclose Supply-Demand Shifts," *Commodity Yearbook* (1958), pp. 35-36.

is not applicable to speculative trading. Consequently, Working offers a theory of expectations, one which rests on the premise that all price changes are formed according to anticipations of supply and demand rather than on the basis of their immediate values.[5] This theory attempts to relate changes in futures prices to the price-making activity found in the market. As such, the behavior of the trader provides the motivation for price change. Contrary to the assumptions of pure competition which underlie market exchange, traders do not have perfect knowledge of the market. As a result, they must search constantly for new information which will give them some indication of future changes in supply and demand. Yet, new information is unpredictable or emerges randomly. With this knowledge, Working establishes the final link for a model relating anticipations to price behavior. It is the random quality of new information and not changes in supply or demand which is responsible for the irregular behavior of futures prices.

As indicated in Chapter 3, Larson has provided a simple confirmation of this theory, but he has based the results on his discovery of random price behavior rather than by linking the resulting price behavior to a measure of new information. Working has related price behavior to new information, but his results are limited and feature only one commodity. In order to assess the value of this method, we have attempted to relate soybean cash and futures prices to U.S.D.A. supply forecasts. The results of this test, however, have not proven adequate; consequently, the following approach has been adopted for explaining price fluctuations. (This is not to be interpreted as a rejection of his hypothesis, only that it was too difficult to test it directly within the constraints of the present study.)[6]

The Spectral Approach

Spectral analysis itself does not furnish a new theory of demand; it only provides a more rigorous test of demand in the short-run situations where both price and quantity are changing frequently. It accomplishes this task by specifying the price-quantity relationship over short-, middle-, and long-run frequencies as well as by determining lead-lag or causality between price and quantity. For price series moving as randomly as futures prices, spectral methods can at least answer the question of whether price and quantity are related over limited frequency ranges such as those corresponding to seasonals or short-run business cycles. These methods have already received application in demand tests of stock market prices; they normally involve estimating the cross-spectrum between a variety of stock prices and their corresponding volume of trading.[7] The results of these tests, while not confirming a strong demand structure in stock prices, demonstrate that spectral methods are extremely sensitive for identifying interrelationships between variables.

When spectral methods are utilized for price-quantity tests in commodity markets, several difficulties are encountered. First of all, simple tests between price and quantity do not include other intervening forces such as excess speculation or fluctuations in the economy. These forces will be introduced at a later stage when a more general explanation of price change is developed. Secondly, the absence of statistical significance in the accompanying phase diagrams has prevented an assessment of the sign of the price-quantity relationship. Since the purpose of this section is only to measure the strength of the interrelationship between price and quantity variables, no attempt has followed to identify any of the quantity variables specifically as supply or demand.[8] Finally, the present explanation of demand has expressed price as a function of quantity. This causality limits the interpretation of the various results in as far as it is the reverse of normal demand theory, but such a reversal is necessary for constructing a model of price change.

Price-Volume Relationships

Even with the difficulties mentioned above, one can proceed to test the suggested price-quantity relationships. The first such relationship to be tested is that between price and the volume of futures trading, a speculative variable

Table 5-1

Futures Prices and Transactions Volume: Average Coherence at Long-Run Frequencies

Monthly: January 1950-June 1965
Observations = 186
Estimated Lags = 48

	$\overline{C}_{\Delta P, \Delta V}$	$\overline{C}_{(\Delta P)^2, V}$
Cotton	.30	.44
Cottonseed oil	.13	.13
Corn	.12	.16
Eggs	.18	.26
Oats	.22	.14
Potatoes	.44	.59
Rye	.16	.10
Soybean meal	.11	.05
Soybean oil	.16	.09
Soybeans	.13	.20
Wheat	.26	.29

which corresponds to the volume of trading in the stock market. Sources of monthly data here and for the following tests can be found in Appendix A. Cross-spectral estimates have been prepared between closing prices of near futures contracts and the related volume of transactions. Two different methods of estimation were used. The first tests the simple theory of demand by examining the relationship between the first differences of both series, ΔV and ΔP. The second proposes an alternative, if price and volume are not directly related, then the possiblility of a relationship exists between volume V and the extent to which price changes $(\Delta P)^2$.

The coherence values for the price and volume series are summarized in Table 5-1. Each entry represents an average for the long-run frequencies only, i.e., the first 16 of 48 estimated lags. Because coherence values are so low for the shorter-run frequencies, comparison is only feasible in the long run. The average coherences for the first difference series are low, ranging from 0.11 for soybean meal and 0.12 for corn to 0.30 for cotton, 0.44 for potatoes and 0.26 for wheat. That cotton, potatoes, and wheat display slightly higher coherences than the other commodities cannot easily be explained. A check on many different futures' characteristics such as absolute volume of trading, quantity of futures transactions, value of trading, and tendering rates produced no explanation. A remaining possibility centers about the level of speculation in these commodities, a topic which will receive more attention later. For the present, Working's explanation is sufficient: these commodities undergo heavy speculative trading and are the more prominent in their respective exchanges.[9] As such, they attract the attention of unskilled speculators who are likely to respond to any noticeable change in price by rushing to buy or sell. Small changes in price, therefore, are likely to produce large changes in the volume or trading.

The relationship between volume and the extent of the price change does not appear to be much stronger than that between the first differences of both series. The average coherence increases from the change-in-price to the price-squared method only six times and decreases four times. From the coherence diagrams, no conclusive evidence could be found with respect to the possibility of price and volume being more strongly related at seasonal frequencies. Oats, wheat, and rye display slightly higher coherences in the seasonal as compared with other frequencies, but not to a degree which can be considered significant. A phase lag fails to appear between price and volume for all the commodities tested.

These results, with the exception of a few commodities with higher price-volume coherences, correspond to those found previously for the stock market: price and volume do not display the functional relationship suggested by conventional demand theory. When compared to the forecasting techniques of traders in the futures market, this conclusion appears not at all unreasonable. Traders do not find a one-to-one relationship between changes in price and volume; in fact, an increase in volume intensifies rather than changes the direction of price movement.[10] With an increase in volume, for example, a price rise would advance upwards; similarly, a price fall would continue downwards. Concerning the lack of reasonable coherences between volume and the extent of the price changes, one finds that these results do not agree with those found on stock markets. Coherences found for the futures market, with the exception of cotton and potatoes, were generally below those found elsewhere for the stock market.[11]

Price-Demand-Supply Relationships

Explaining price movements in terms of physical supply and demand is equally difficult; the erratic nature of futures price movements leaves few changes that these forces can account for. Furthermore, as observed in Chapter 1 (pages

Table 5-2

Futures Prices and Stocks, Supply, Demand: Average Coherence at Long-Run Frequencies

Monthly: January 1950-June 1965
Observations = 186
Estimated Lags = 48

	Average Coherence[a]					
	$(\Delta P)^2$ with			ΔP with		
	S	D	St	ΔS	ΔD	ΔSt
Cottonseed oil	.10	.10	.11	.19	.30	.19
Soybean meal	.13	.20	.18	.20	.28	.12
Soybean oil	.14	.09	.10	.29	.21	.13
Soybeans	–	.14	–	–	.25	–
Rye[b]	–	.10	–	–	.13	–
Wheat	–	.28	–	–	.13	–
Cocoa[c]	.27	–	.15	.12	–	.09

[a]Coherence between price variation and supply, demand, stocks; also between price differences and differences in supply, demand, stocks.

[b]Monthly: July 1950-June 1965.

[c]Monthly: January 1951-June 1966.

17-20), most of the trading in commodities occurs on the futures rather than on the physical market. Since the volume measure of trading can hypothetically be divided into supply and demand, the present price explanation should be slightly better than that found for stock markets. The physical data has been arranged to test simple price-quantity relationships as above. Cross-spectra are estimated between first differences of prices (ΔP) and demand (ΔD), supply (ΔS) and stocks (ΔSt), as well as between demand (D), supply (S), stocks (St) and the extent of the price change $(\Delta P)^2$. Stock accumulations are measured at the beginning of the month. Since physical data is not readily available on a monthly basis for most commodities, only demand *estimates* could be obtained for soybeans, rye, and wheat.

Coherences between the various price and quantity series have been averaged over the long-run frequencies and appear in Table 5-2. Reported coherences are generally low. Soybeans, rye, and wheat display coherences of 0.25, 0.13, and 0.13 respectively between the first differences of price and demand. Corresponding values for cottonseed oil, soybean meal, and soybean oil are 0.30, 0.28, and 0.21. Coherences found between demand and the extent of the price change are even lower. For the latter three commodities, Table 5-2 exhibits coherences of 0.10, 0.20, and 0.09. The only commodities for which the price variation measure $(\Delta P)^2$ is higher than the first difference comparison are wheat and cocoa. For wheat, the coherence between price and demand rises to 0.28 and for cocoa the coherence between price and supply reaches 0.27.

The only possible result which can be gleaned from Table 5-2 involves a comparison of first difference values. For certain commodities, the coherence between price and the supply-demand series is greater than that between price and the corresponding volume series. Cottonseed oil, soybean meal, and soybean oil display demand coherences of 0.30, 0.28, and 0.21 respectively as compared to the volume coherences of 0.13, 0.11, and 0.16. The price-demand coherence for soybeans (0.25) also exceeds the price-volume coherence (0.13). The coherences between price and supply-demand are higher at the seasonal frequencies for most commodities, but the seasonal peaks lack statistical significance. No phase lags appear between any of the series. In summary, the coherence values imply that for most of the commodities tested only a very limited relationship exists between price and supply or demand. For wheat and rye, even this relationship is absent.

Price-Open Interest Relationships

Open interest is a second futures market statistic which can be tested as a possible quantity determinant of price. This variable has been defined in Chapter 1 as the number of futures contracts which have been entered into and not yet liquidated by offsetting contracts nor fulfilled by delivery. These contracts arise when a buyer or seller enters the futures market and takes a new position. When the same buyer or seller liquidates his position by an offsetting futures transaction, open interest is accordingly reduced. Similar to the previous cross-spectral tests, the price-quantity relationship is tested between differences in prices (ΔP) and open interest (ΔOI) as well as between open interest (OI) and the extent of price change $(\Delta P)^2$.

Table 5-3 summarizes coherence values averaged over the long-run frequencies for the respective price-open-interest pairs. The coherence values for the first difference comparisons are relatively low, ranging from 0.07 for soybean meal to 0.33 for cotton. Similar values appear between open interest and the extent of the price change, where coherences range from 0.05 for soybean meal to 0.32 for cotton. Some rough comparisons can be drawn between the results of this table and the price-volume response of Table 5-1. Cotton, potatoes, and wheat display moderate coherences in first difference comparisons on both tables. This is also true for open interest and the extent of the price change comparison except that oats has a slightly higher coherence than wheat. As suggested earlier, the slightly higher coherences which appear between prices and quantity

Table 5-3

Futures Prices and Open Interest: Average Coherence at Long-Run Frequencies

Monthly: January 1950-June 1965
Observations = 186
Estimated Lags = 48

	$\bar{C}_{\Delta P, \Delta OI}$	$\bar{C}_{(\Delta P)^2, OI}$
Cotton	.33	.32
Cottonseed oil	.20	.09
Corn	.08	.12
Eggs	.17	.10
Oats	.18	.25
Potatoes	.29	.28
Rye	.27	.11
Soybean meal	.07	.05
Soybean oil	.14	.07
Soybeans	.14	.10
Wheat	.30	.23

measures of transactions activity are likely to occur for commodities traded by large numbers of unskilled speculators. Generally speaking, the coherence values do not confirm the price-quantity relationship suggested by conventional demand theory. When the relation between price and open interest is compared to market practices, one finds the above result to be reasonable. Open interest rather than being directly related to price movements is used in conjunction with these movements to help explain whether a market is weak or strong.[12]

Price-Speculating-Hedging Relationships

The open-interest measure of trading activity is superior to the volume measure in as far as the former can be defined or enumerated in much greater detail.

When an open position is taken in the market, the holder must report the nature of his position: long or short, hedging or speculating. A definition of the hedging appears in Chapter 1, but it is worth adding at this point that some difficulty exists in classifying data to best represent this category of traders. Opinion is divided among four different methods of classifying hedgers; these include motivation, price forecasts, market position, and market access.[13] The official C.E.A. definition hinges on the concept of market access. That is, hedging positions are limited to futures contracts which cover not more than the volume of cash commitments for which a processor or manufacturer has fixed or anticipated sales requirements.[14] In short, the definition of a hedger can be reduced to that of a trader holding a futures position who at the same time has access to the cash market. Whether the hedge is long or short depends on the nature of the transaction. A short hedge may involve the selling of futures to protect inventories against a price fall. A long hedge may consist of an acquisition of futures to protect against a price increase where a dealer has committed himself to sell a commodity not yet purchased. Speculative positions are normally defined as being opposite or complementory to those held by the long or short hedger. As described in Chapter 1, these positions are also held for gain rather than for purposeful stockholding.

That open interest should display a greater relationship with prices when divided into hedging and speculating can be explained by recalling the open interest figures presented in Chapter 1 (pages 22-25). In fact, one can follow the reasoning of Hicks in postulating that short hedging and long speculating represent the effective supply of and demand for futures contracts respectively.[15] Practically speaking, one could attempt to define these variables as supply or demand by constructing an appropriate simultaneous equation model, but this is beyond the scope of the present study. The present results include only the cross-spectra which have been estimated between changes in the respective quantity measures, hedging and speculating.

Data was available for all commodities previously tested except for cotton and eggs. The coherence values reported for these commodities in Table 5-4 are low, ranging from 0.13 for oats to 0.36 for wheat. When these coherence values are compared to those found for demand tests of volume, open interest, supply and demand, slight differences can be found. Average coherences between the price and short hedging or long speculating pairs exceed those between the price-volume pairs for all commodities except for oats and potatoes. The same is true for the price-open-interest pairs except for potatoes and rye. When the hedging and speculating coherences are compared to those between price and supply-demand, the former display a slight superiority. The price-hedging coherence is greater than the price-supply value for cottonseed oil ($0.26 > 0.10$) but not for soybean meal ($0.15 < 0.20$) or soybean oil ($0.20 < 0.29$). The price-speculating coherences exceed those of price-demand for soybeans ($0.32 > 0.25$), soybean oil ($0.22 > 0.21$), rye ($0.21 > 0.17$), and wheat ($0.31 > 0.13$), but not for soybean meal ($0.15 < 0.28$) or cottonseed oil ($0.26 < 0.31$).

Table 5-4

Futures Prices and Short Hedging, Long Speculating: Average Coherence and Phase at Long-Run Frequencies

Monthly: First Differences
January 1950-June 1965
Observations = 186
Estimated Lags = 48

	$\bar{C}_{P, H_S}$	$\bar{\phi}_{P, H_S}$	$\bar{C}_{P, S_L}$	$\bar{\phi}_{P, S_L}$	$\bar{C}_{H_S, S_L}$
Cottonseed oil	.26	0	.26	0	.43
Corn	.19	1.0	.16	1.0	.66
Oats	.21	0	.13	1.2	.45
Potatoes	.21	0.5	.32	1.2	.73
Rye	.25	0	.21	0.5	.15
Soybean meal	.15	0	.16	1.0	.29
Soybean oil	.20	0.5	.22	1.0	.62
Soybeans	.22	1.0	.32	1.0	.66
Wheat	.36	0	.31	0	.48
			Cash Prices		
Corn[a]	.21	1.3	.11	1.0	.66
Oats	.26	0	.24	0	.45
Soybeans	.17	1.0	.27	1.0	.66
Wheat[a]	.35	1.6	.28	0	.48

[a]Long-run frequency range shifted from frequency points 0-16 to 5-21.

In addition to the cross-spectra displaying limited coherence between speculating, hedging, and prices, the phase diagrams suggest that long speculating leads futures prices for all of the included commodities except for wheat and cottonseed oil. The coherence values reported in Table 5-4 might be considered too low to justify the lead, but a runs-significance test of phase values demonstrates 90% confidence for soybean meal, corn, wheat, and oats and 95% confidence for the remaining commodities. The nature of the lead is fixed angle or one which varies proportionately with the period of a component. In short, the demand for futures contracts leads the prices of these contracts and this lead increases as the relationship is extended over the long run. The lead constant is $\pi/3$ for most commodities and $\pi/6$ for potatoes and rye. No lead appears between the short hedging and long speculating series to indicate that hedging gives rise to speculating in the market.

Yet one more interpretation can be offered for the phase diagrams by relating them to a phenomenon found in the stock market. Observers of that market often take an interest in the number of investors who go "short" in a stock. An investor goes short when he borrows stock to sell at a later date. He must then buy stock in order to return the borrowed shares. The short interest, which is the number of shares sold short on a given stock, is considered important because it is assumed to represent a latent demand for the stock. In a recent study, however, Smith found no useful predictive information about prices in short interest.[16] To investigate the presence of latent demand in commodity markets, cross-spectra have also been estimated between changes in short hedging, long speculating and *cash* prices for four commodities, as shown in Table 5-4.[a] As for futures prices, no reasonable coherences appear over short- or medium-run frequencies, but possibly significant coherences appear over the long-run frequencies. Again, in most cases the phase diagram was generally flat over low-frequency bands and suggested a fixed angle lead of both short hedging and long speculation over cash prices. The evidence available thus supports the idea that, at least for low frequencies, both of these variables measure a latent demand of some kind which subsequently affects prices.

However, it must be admitted that it is not easy to interpret fixed-angle phase-lags without making an assumption about the direction of causality between the variables. As indicated in Chapter 4, our present understanding of causality and feedback is not sufficient to help us interpret these lags. It is, nevertheless, interesting to note that a consistent shape appears for the phase diagram in so many cases.

---

[a]Up to this point, short hedging has been considered to represent the supply of speculative opportunities to the futures market, but, in another sense, it can be considered deferred demand since closing a hedge often requires purchasing the cash commodity at some point in the future.

Partial Spectral Analysis of Speculating Relative to Demand

The relative influence of hedging and speculating on price formation as compared to supply and demand can be further measured by utilizing the partial cross-spectrum. This is an interesting relationship to test since the former displayed slightly higher coherences than the latter for four out of six commodities. To begin the test, assume as above that long speculating represents speculative demand and that it can be contrasted with physical demand. Assume further that the partial coherence between futures prices (P), physical demand (D), and speculative demand (L) is similar to the partial correlation between prices and physical demand or prices and speculative demand when the influence of the third variable is removed. Partial cross-spectra have been estimated for the given commodities, and the average partial coherences, together with the average simple coherences, appear in Table 5-5. The partial coherence results confirm the predominance of speculative over physical forces. Except for soybean meal and possibly cottonseed oil, the partial coherences between price and speculative demand are greater than those between price and physical demand.

These results can be further explained by examining the relation between price, physical demand, and speculative demand in terms of their hypothetical frequency components. As shown in the following expressions, the frequency characteristics of any variable can be decomposed into a set of components, each describing a different frequency range of the spectrum:

$$L = L_1 + L_2 + L_3 \qquad (5.1)$$

$$\updownarrow$$

$$P = P_1 + P_2 + P_3 \qquad (5.2)$$

$$\updownarrow$$

$$D = D_1 + D_2 + D_3 \qquad (5.3)$$

Since the partial and simple coherence values presented in Table 5-5 are roughly similar, both physical demand D and speculative demand L act on price without a common influence and can be considered independent. Each has a separate influence on price and this can be expressed in terms of the frequency components given above. Over one segment of the frequency range, the speculative demand component L_1 influences the price component P_1. Over another segment, the physical component D_2 affects P_2. Since Table 5-5 reports low to moderate coherences between physical and speculative demand, the components L_3 and D_3 can be said to be linked to each other but not to price.

Market Composition and Market Imbalance

An alternative approach to examining the relationship between prices and levels of hedging and speculating is to consider the latter as forces which balance the

Table 5-5

Futures Prices, Physical Demand and Long Speculating: Average Simple and Partial Coherences at Long-Run Frequencies

Monthly: First Differences
January 1950-June 1965
Observations = 186
Estimated Lags = 48

	Average Coherence Between					
	P, D[a]	$P, D.S_L$[b]	P, S_L	$P, S_L.D$	D, S_L	$D, S_L.P$
Cottonseed oil	.30	.18	.26	.19	.18	.09
Soybean meal	.28	.22	.16	.16	.31	.30
Soybean oil	.21	.15	.22	.25	.26	.29
Soybeans	.25	.20	.32	.28	.29	.26
Rye	.13	.15	.21	.21	.14	.18
Wheat	.13	.12	.31	.27	.17	.14

[a]Columns headed by two variables represent the simple coherence between these variables.

[b]Columns headed by three variables represent partial coherence, e.g. $P, D. S_L$ is the coherence between P and D with the effect of S_L removed.

futures market. Depending on whether the amounts of hedging or speculating are in equilibrium a market can be said to possess excess speculation. The impact of excess speculation on price behavior will be investigated from two different points of view: (1) the possibility that excess speculation directly influences price behavior and (2) the possibility that excess speculation influences the responsiveness of price to supply or demand. The measure of excess speculation which will be used in this analysis is known as the "speculative index." This index is considered to provide a much better measure of this phenomenon than the simple ratio of long speculating to short hedging.

The Speculative Index

The speculative index was originally designed by Working to determine the role that speculation played in futures market activity.[17] Since the formulation of the index will be considered only briefly in this study, the interested reader should consult the original source for greater detail. Only one aspect of its original formulation need be emphasized at this point. That is, one must be clear as to which assumption should be made concerning the reclassification of the nonreporting traders used in estimating the index. As explained in Chapter 1, the official C.E.A. statistics divide open interest into (1) reporting hedgers, (2) reporting speculators, and (3) nonreporting traders. The nonreporting or small traders represent a residual between total and reported open interest. Since the positions of the nonreporting traders are unavailable, the total amounts of hedging and speculating in the market are not known with great accuracy. The simplest solution and that followed by Rockwell and Houthakker has been to call the nonreporting contracts speculative.[18] Working, however, has attempted to reclassify the contracts as either hedging or speculating. Nonreporting contracts, therefore, have been distributed according to the reported speculating-hedging ratio among both the long speculating and the short hedging categories.

The construction of the speculative index can best be explained by returning to the concept of market balance, which stipulates that short hedging must equal long speculation. This equilibrium can best be understood by first measuring the degree to which short hedging is balanced by long hedging and long speculation. Working has devised ratios of hedging and speculating for this purpose:

$$R_h = \frac{H_L}{H_S} \tag{5.4}$$

$$R_s = \frac{S_L}{H_S} \tag{5.5}$$

where:

H_L = Long hedging commitments

H_S = Short hedging commitments

S_L = Long speculating commitments

The first ratio describes the amount of short hedging in the market that is covered by long hedging. The second ratio is complementary to the first and explains the proportion of coverage that is attributable to long speculating. Together, the ratios express the speculating and hedging response to short hedging, the basic determinant of market balance.

The speculative index proceeds a step beyond the above. The amount of short hedging that is balanced by long hedging is subtracted from the totals of short hedging to give the quantity of short hedging ($H^{\mu}{}_S$) that must be carried by long speculation (S_L). Each commodity normally has a greater amount of long speculating than that which is needed to cover net short hedging and this excess speculation is reflected in the speculative index.

$$T = \frac{S_L}{H_S^{\mu}} \qquad (5.6)$$

where:

S_L = Long speculating commitments

H_S^{μ} = Unbalanced short hedging commitments

The degree to which the index exceeds one measures the excess speculation or the imbalance in the market. The actual index that is used in calculation differs from the conceptual index and includes the proportionate division of non-reporting contracts into long speculating and short hedging. Working has shown that short speculating is not essential to this ratio since it is the purchasing of contracts by speculators that offsets short hedging. The expression for the speculative index, therefore, is not one of pure balance and involves only the long speculating position; the short hedging position is still adjusted for long hedging.[19]

Estimating the Index

To determine the impact of excess speculation on price behavior as suggested above, one must first estimate the speculative index for the previously considered commodities. This has been possible for all of the included commodities except cotton and eggs. Estimates of the index for the included commodities are reported in Table 5-6 and conform to those found by Working

Table 5-6

A Comparison of Market Ratios, Speculative Indexes, and Seasonal Price Behavior

Monthly: January 1950-June 1965
Observations = 186

	Hedging Ratio: R_h[a]	*Speculating Ratio:* R_s[b]	*Speculative Index:* T[c]	*Seasonal Group*[d]
Potatoes	.47	1.01	1.26	I
Cottonseed oil	.57	.98	1.25	I
Soybean meal	.72	.70	1.22	II
Corn	.53	.82	1.19	II
Soybean oil	.46	.82	1.18	II
Soybeans	.90	.89	1.31	II
Rye	.41	1.05	1.16	III
Wheat	.50	.83	1.19	III
Oats	.14	1.04	1.12	III

[a] $R_h = H_L/H_s$
[b] $R_s = S_L/H_s$
[c] $T = S_L/H_s^{\mu}$

[d] Seasonal groups represent varying patterns of price behavior as determined by first-difference spectra.

(over a shorter period).[20] It is also important to determine whether the speculative index remains constant over time; accordingly, Table 5-7 has been included. In general, the index remains stable, but some of the year-to-year variations are larger than what would be expected. Most of these variations, however, can be explained by what Working terms economic influences: (1) the degree to which speculative activity is changing and (2) the ability of the speculators initiating that activity.

Using these influences to clarify extremes in the index, one can explain the change of the cottonseed oil index from 1.09 in 1958-1959 to 1.72 the

Table 5-7

Speculative Index over Time[a]

	Potatoes	*Cottonseed Oil*	*Soybean Meal*	*Corn*	*Soybean Oil*	*Rye*	*Soybeans*	*Wheat*	*Oats*
1950-1951	1.45	1.19	1.04	1.17	1.08	1.17	1.49	1.13	1.18
1951-1952	1.51	1.12	1.32	1.19	1.30	1.20	1.45	1.18	1.14
1952-1953	1.32	1.23	1.36	1.24	1.25	1.19	1.36	1.13	1.12
1953-1954	1.18	1.16	1.18	1.23	1.09	1.06	1.31	1.06	1.11
1954-1955	1.31	1.08	1.20	1.13	1.12	1.06	1.52	1.21	1.13
1955-1956	1.24	1.06	1.02	1.15	1.07	1.12	1.34	1.24	1.07
1956-1957	1.31	1.18	1.28	1.18	1.19	1.10	1.40	1.21	1.12
1957-1958	1.28	1.28	1.17	1.20	1.21	1.09	1.27	1.37	1.10
1958-1959	1.20	1.09	1.21	1.27	1.12	1.18	1.16	1.23	1.12
1959-1960	1.19	1.72	1.35	1.32	1.54	1.10	1.22	1.18	1.12
1960-1961	1.30	1.59	1.21	1.17	1.30	1.06	1.14	1.26	1.06
1961-1962	1.16	1.52	1.37	1.15	1.22	1.72	1.30	1.14	1.14
1962-1963	1.15	1.30	1.26	1.14	1.10	1.23	1.21	1.14	1.23
1963-1964	1.16	1.16	1.03	1.14	1.09	1.11	1.25	1.20	1.11
1964-1965	1.26	1.08	1.23	1.16	1.07	1.07	1.25	1.14	1.07

[a]Expressed as a twelve-month average.

following year by the numbers of nonprofessional or small traders as well as by a decline in the short hedging position. The jump in the rye index from 1.06 in 1960-1961 to 1.72 in 1961-1962 can also be discussed in terms of a sharp rise in unskilled speculation and a decline in short hedging. Smaller changes in the index for other commodities can be explained by shifts in the long or short positions. The only exception is the rise in the soybean oil index from 1.12 in 1958-1959 to 1.54 in 1950-1960 where no immediate explanation can be found. The hedging and speculating ratios presented in Table 5-6 confirm the opinions given previously concerning the composition of the market. Most of the hedging ratios are near one-half and this reflects a market in which long hedging is never sufficient to cover short hedging. The incidence of speculating ratios near one confirms the tendency of long speculating to balance short hedging. This balance can be better explained in terms of the speculative index. Since the values of the index as summarized in Table 5-6 range from 1.12 for oats to 1.31 for soybeans, the market can be described as leaning towards imbalance with speculation the dominant force.

The Impact of Imbalance

One can measure the impact of market balance on both price fluctuations and price response as suggested earlier by comparing the speculative indexes to the seasonal indexes listed in Table 5-6.[21] The seasonal indexes or groups have been shown in Chapter 3 to reflect changing patterns of price behavior. Group I represents price series which exhibit pure random walk, Group II describes a weak seasonal pattern, and Group III displays a slightly significant seasonal. The values of the speculative indexes, when compared to the above groupings, display a correspondence which is regular but not overwhelming. Potatoes and cottonseed oil, commodities which display the highest speculative indexes of 1.26 and 1.25, demonstrate almost a pure random walk (Group I) in first differences of monthly prices. Soybean meal, soybean oil, and corn show less than pure random walk in their grouping (Group II); this conforms to their having the next highest speculative indexes, 1.22, 1.18, and 1.19. Soybeans with an index of 1.31 is the exception in Group II, but this value can be reconciled since soybeans also has the highest hedging ratio, 0.90. With an abundance of long hedging, little unbalanced hedging remains, and even a small amount of speculation (the R_S ratio shows a substantial proportion of long speculation) could easily produce large values in the speculative index. The remaining commodities which suggest limited seasonality (Group III) also have lower speculative indexes. Rye, wheat, and oats display values of 1.16, 1.19, and 1.12 respectively.

From these comparisons one can proceed to evaluate the impacts of market imbalance mentioned earlier. First of all, the comparisons suggest an agreement between the speculative index and the seasonal groups. Thus, commodities with high levels of excess speculation have exhibited distinctly random patterns of price behavior. Correspondingly, commodities with lower levels of speculation have displayed more regular patterns of behavior. While this result offers no suggestions as to the relation between excess speculation and price stability, it does confirm the hypothesis that speculation does influence price patterns. Concerning the second suggested impact of market imbalance, these comparisons cannot be extended to demonstrate that prices are less responsive to supply-demand where speculation is high and more responsive to supply-demand where speculation is low. With high levels of speculation and no seasonal patterns, one would expect little or no correlation between prices and supply-demand. Conversely, lower levels of speculation should coincide with slightly higher correlations between prices and supply-demand. Only a few comparisons are possible because of limited data, and relating the index values to several of the coherence values in Table 5-2 produces no positive results. Moderate coherences such as that estimated for cottonseed oil (0.30) and low coherences such as that estimated for rye (0.13) are contrary to the values of the speculative indexes (1.25 and 1.16 respectively). Further analysis of this proposition must await better and more extensive data.

Conclusions

A review of past research suggests that no appropriate model exists for explaining the response of price to quantity in the futures market. Cross-spectral methods have been employed to test the applicability of the simple quantity theory of demand to this market, but no positive results have emerged. This result has been confirmed even with the variety of quantity determinants available for these tests. Prices have been related to volume, open interest, supply, demand, hedging, and speculating. Trading volumes and open interest display low coherences while supply and demand show only slightly higher values. When speculating and hedging are examined, nevertheless, one finds a possible quantity explanation of price.

Both simple and partial coherence tests indicate that the correlation of prices with short hedging or long speculating is marginally better than that found between price and supply or demand. When hedging and speculating are considered relatively or in terms of market balance, levels of excess speculation can be related to the price patterns which evolve in the market. That hedging and speculating should influence price is reasonable when one recalls that the total value of contract trading in the futures market is often much greater than the value of physical supply or demand. The outcome of this analysis, therefore, is that both hedging and speculating play a greater role in price formation than was previously recognized.

Even with this discovery, considerable difficulty remains in postulating a simple demand explanation for commodity prices. Because of the low coherence values accompanying hedging and speculating, it is reasonable to believe that the activity of traders represents just one of many influences which serve to explain price fluctuations. The rationalization becomes more likely when one recalls the price explanation offered by the partial coherence analyses. That is, both physical and speculative quantities influence price, but each affects price over a different range of frequencies. The relationship between price change and quantity, therefore, is extremely complex. Perhaps the best explanatory model could be constructed by isolating the influence of a complete set of variables, each over a different frequency range with respect to the dependent or price variable. While such an approach must await the further development of spectral techniques, one can begin by extending the simple demand model to other influences, a task taken up in the next chapter.

Endogenous and Exogenous Influences

Introduction

The present chapter represents a necessary step towards constructing a general model for explaining both futures and cash price fluctuations. This step essentially consists of presenting and testing a hypothesis which is sufficiently general to include a wide range of possible commodity price influences. The hypothesis attempts to explain price fluctuations, not only by rearranging the quantity determinants of the previous chapter to better reflect market forces, but also by considering other relevant factors such as commodity substitution and economic conditions. Some of the factors influencing price are endogenous, since their values are determined by a simultaneous interaction within the market. Others can be considered exogenous, since their influence arises outside of the market. The actual testing of the hypothesis requires evaluating cross-spectral estimates prepared between futures and cash prices and a number of determinants. This preliminary selection process, consequently, provides the explanatory variables necessary for constructing the individual price equations in the next chapter.

Approach

The approach taken to develop a broader theory of price explanation has been to propose a number of possible price determinants in the form of a general hypothesis. Statistical analysis then permits the selection of a smaller number of determinants as being the most relevant for specifying the cash and futures price functions. Two reasons can be offered as to why this approach is preferable to one which tests only one or several preselected determinants. First, available research regarding commodity price theory has not suggested which of a number of possible determinants are the most suitable, nor even whether a stock or flow specification is the more correct one for a price equation. Secondly, the cross-spectral methods which are being employed can efficiently handle large amounts of data, permitting us to make a better final selection of determinants. In essence, empirical results will be used to develop a structure for explaining price behavior rather than working to the reverse. The total number of determinants can be classified into four groups as (1) acting through demand, (2) acting through supply, (3) acting through economic conditions, and (4) acting through speculative influences. The peculiar characteristic of these determinants is that they represent phenomena which can be quantified. One would like to include other determinants such as those related to political phenomena, but they cannot be sufficiently quantified to be of use here.

The Hypothesis

Fluctuations in commodity prices can be said to arise from a number of measurable influences which can be arranged as follows:

1. Acting Through Demand
   a. Domestic consumption
   b. Exports
   c. Derived demand for final products
   d. Government stock piling and aid programs
   e. Demand relatives such as the prices of substitutable commodities, substitutes resulting from innovation, or consumption/stock ratios
2. Acting Through Supply
   a. Production
   b. Stocks
   c. Weather
   d. Government subsidy and crop-control programs
   e. Supply relatives such as the production of substitutable commodities, innovation induced increases in production, or production/stock ratios
3. Acting Through Economic Conditions
   a. Business conditions as reflected in industrial production, unemployment, and the general price level
   b. Credit conditions which define the availability of loans for speculation or commodity storage
4. Acting Through Market Composition
   a. Speculation
   b. Hedging

Since not all of these determinants are relevant for explaining monthly price behavior, it is necessary to restrict the above list to only those which are viable in the short run. Thus, monthly price fluctuations can be said to respond on the demand side to changes in consumption, exports, and the prices of substitutable commodities. They respond on the supply side to production and especially to stocks. Chapter 5, however, reports that only a limited association exists between prices and supply or demand as such. For this reason, prices should not only be related to the above components but also, as the experience of commodity forecasters suggests, to the relative pressure of demand on supply or stocks. The remaining supply and demand factors are of lesser importance. Weather is a factor influencing prices over the year; government policies change less frequently than what can be considered short run. Consequently, both of these factors are omitted from the evaluation.

Economic conditions or contractions and expansions of the economy are also believed to influence commodity price behavior. These factors are probably more relevant to longer-run price movements such as those found in quarterly or annual data. Because supply and demand have remained in relative equilibrium over the test period, however, it is likely that monthly prices will react to these conditions. Consequently, commodity prices are related to several indicators of general business activity as well as to a more specialized group of credit indicators. With respect to the factors classified as speculative, the previous chapter has shown that a relationship exists between price fluctuations and hedging and speculating. No need exists to reexamine this relationship until the following chapter.

Cross-Spectral Tests

To test the various influences outlined in the above hypothesis, cross-spectral estimates have been prepared between first differences of both prices and the finally selected determinants. Before explaining the results of these tests, it would be helpful to note the restrictions that have been met in performing the tests. Restrictions on the availability of physical data limit the choice of commodities to a smaller number than that examined in Chapter 5. If a greater choice were available, the more suitable commodities would be those whose price fluctuations exhibit nonrandom behavior or those classified in price Groups III and IV as specified in pages 67-72. As it was, research continued with those commodities for which data was available and interest was greatest: soybean oil, cottonseed oil, soybean meal, soybeans, rye, and wheat.

Another restriction is that the selected determinants must provide a basis for the general model of price change; consequently, regression equations must be constructed for each of the given commodities. This requires *reducing* the span of the time series to the period extending from August 1957 to June 1966. Such a period provides a time series long enough for spectral analysis, but at the same time short enough to be economically significant, i.e., devoid of data adjustments as well as of structural changes in the economy. The inclusion of data from 1965 to 1966 occurred because of the availability of later data at that stage in the study.

A final restriction (described in pages 72-76) is the use of *average* prices rather than *closing* prices. Use of average prices somewhat limits the interpretation of price movements; but, as previously explained, prices in this form are more likely to reflect monthly influences contained in the data.

Supply and Demand Response

Although Chapter 5 discloses only a weak relationship between futures prices and supply or demand, the hypothesis suggests that prices may be related to the components of supply and demand. For present analysis, supply is divided into production and stocks, demand into domestic consumption and exports. The definitions of the various components remain the same from commodity to commodity except for domestic consumption. The latter is defined for soybeans as those beans which have been crushed for oil; for rye it contains both flour millings and amounts distilled for alcohol. Lastly, for wheat, it includes only flour millings.

Cross-spectral tests have been performed between first differences in prices and the above components for the indicated commodities. The coherences shown in Tables 6-1 and 6-2 have been averaged over all frequences rather than just over the long run, since the number of estimated lags has been reduced from 48 to 24. The strength of association between the series, however, still predominates in the long-run frequences. No phase lags can be found between any of the series. This, however, is to be expected, as the coherence relationship between all price and component pairs is low.

The coherence values which appear between futures prices and the various components range from 0.05 to 0.34. The lower extremes (soybean oil exports = 0.05, cottonseed oil stocks = 0.07, rye consumption = 0.09) imply the lack of any dependence between certain series. The highest coherence value (0.34) occurs between prices and wheat stocks, a reasonable relationship since carryover in the wheat market is extensive during the period under study. Soybean meal and oil prices are not explained very well by their own levels of stocks and consumption, nor by the stocks and consumption of soybeans. A similar test has been performed using changes in stocks and prices rather than just stocks and prices. For soybean oil, cottonseed oil, and soybean meal, this test has taken the form of a comparison between the second difference in stocks and first difference in prices. The coherence values (0.17, 0.07, and 0.20) resulting from the second difference comparison are about the same or less than those found from the first difference comparison. The cash price relationships reported in Table 6-2 resemble those of the equivalent futures price series.

Pressure Index Response

Demand and supply may also be tested as a price influence when considered relative to one another. The pressure of demand on supply is often considered a more immediate influence on price than are the influences taken individually. While a typical pressure ratio measures total demand relative to total supply, the ratios of production to stocks and consumption to stocks are also important. For example, the pressure of consumption on stocks can be said to reflect a rate of domestic usage while the pressure of production on stocks can indicate a rate of supply absorption. Several other pressure ratios have been formed and appear in Tables 6-3 and 6-4. Most of them are variants of the consumption and absorption ratios. Ratios of exports to stocks are also included for soybeans, rye, and wheat.

The cross-spectrum has been estimated between first differences of cash and futures prices and the various pressure ratios. The coherence values for all of the commodities are summarized in Tables 6-3 and 6-4. A more limited number of results appear for the grains because of a lack of production and supply data.

Table 6-1

Physical Response: Average Coherence Between Futures Prices and the Components of Supply and Demand

Monthly: First Differences
August 1957-June 1966
Observations = 107
Estimated Lags = 24

	Futures Price Series					
Variables	*Soybean Oil*	*Cottonseed Oil*	*Soybean Meal*	*Soybeans*	*Rye*	*Wheat*
Supply	.15	.14	.21	–	–	–
Demand	.12	.20	.20	.26	.13	.13
Stocks	.19	.07	.20	.12	.16	.34
Production	.14	.14	.23	–	–	–
Domestic Consumption	.18	.14	.21	.20	.09	.27
Exports	.05	.12	.15	.23	.14	.16
Soybean Stocks	.18	–	.21	–	–	–
Soybean Crushings	.17	–	.20	–	–	–

The reported coherences are low, similar to the cross-spectral results found between prices and the individual components. Certain ratios, however, do offer a marginally better explanation of price. As shown in Table 6-3, the demand/stocks ratio provides the best explanation of price change for cottonseed oil, soybeans, and rye ($\overline{C}$ = 0.18, 0.24, and 0.22 respectively). The stocks/consumption ratio yields the highest coherence for soybean oil, soybean meal, and wheat ($\overline{C}$ = 0.21, 0.21, and 0.28).

The effectiveness of price response to the pressure ratios as compared to the components taken individually is reflected in the differences between the coherence values for the respective price pairs. If the stocks/consumption values are chosen, for example, then the pressure indexes are more correlated with prices than are consumption or stocks for soybean oil, soybeans, and rye. Also, no worse an explanation is provided for soybean meal. Coherence values for these and for the remaining commodities are summarized in Table 6-5.

Table 6-2

Physical Response: Average Coherence Between Cash Prices and the Components of Supply and Demand

Monthly: First Differences
August 1957-June 1966
Observations = 107
Estimated Lags = 24

Variables	Cash Price Series					
	Soybean Oil	*Cottonseed Oil*	*Soybean Meal*	*Soybeans*	*Rye*	*Wheat*
Supply	.16	.18	.13	–	–	–
Demand	.10	.20	.13	.20	.10	.13
Stocks	.15	.08	.15	.13	.24	.32
Production	.18	.17	.15	–	–	–
Domestic Consumption	.15	.16	.14	.23	.12	.24
Exports	.05	.13	.15	.19	.11	.12
Soybean Stocks	.16	–	.15	–	–	–
Soybean Crushings	.16	–	.16	–	–	–

The soybean oil ratio coherence is 0.21 as compared to 0.18 and 0.19 for consumption and stocks. For rye, the ratio coherence is 0.17, while the individual values are 0.09 and 0.16. Soybeans similarly has a ratio value of 0.21 but only 0.20 and 0.12 for the components. These figures represent only slight improvements. When cottonseed oil, soybean meal, and wheat are inspected, no increase in coherence can be found. As Table 6-4 shows, the improvement which occurs with cash prices is not noticeably better. One can conclude, therefore, that demand measured relative to supply offers at most only a marginal improvement in the explanation of price. Any further comment should await the stepwise regression analysis which will be offered in the next chapter.

Price Index Response

A final endogenous relationship to be considered in this chapter is the response of commodity prices to changes in the prices of other commodities. Sufficient

Table 6-3

Pressure Index Response: Average Coherence Between Futures Prices and Selected Pressure Indexes

Monthly: First Differences
August 1957-June 1966
Observations = 107
Estimated Lags = 24

Index	*Soybean Oil*	*Cottonseed Oil*	*Soybean Meal*	*Soybeans*	*Rye*	*Wheat*
Demand/Supply	.14	.11	.17	–	–	–
Demand/Stocks	.15	.18	.20	.24	.22	.23
Consumption/Supply	.14	.10	.09	–	–	–
Consumption/Stocks	.12	.17	.20	.21	.18	.24
Stocks/Consumption	.21	.08	.21	.21	.17	.28
Production/Stocks	.15	.14	.20	–	–	–
Exports/Stocks	–	–	–	.21	.19	.19

evidence exists to argue that the prices of certain commodities are highly interrelated. The cross-spectral analysis of the general futures market at the end of Chapter 4 has uncovered, for example, a close association between commodity prices within the substitutable oils group and the grains and feeds group respectively. What underlies this relationship of one price to another is a complex set of adjustments, some of which arise from the cross-elasticity of demand. This might be explained in two ways. First, the price of one commodity might change along with the prices of other commodity substitutes in response to an overall change in demand or supply. Second, the price of the same commodity might change in response to alterations in the demand or supply of the substitutes. These separate influences can be further complicated by the interactions between the demand or supply of the commodity to be explained and of the other commodities.

Table 6-4

Pressure Index Response: Average Coherence Between Cash Prices and Selected Pressure Indexes

Monthly: First Differences
August 1957-June 1966
Observations = 107
Estimated Lags = 24

Index	*Soybean Oil*	*Cottonseed Oil*	*Soybean Meal*	*Soybeans*	*Rye*	*Wheat*
Demand/Supply	.11	.08	.10	–	–	–
Demand/Stocks	.15	.16	.14	.19	.19	.21
Consumption/Supply	.13	.10	.06	–	–	–
Consumption/Stocks	.12	.14	.14	.25	.27	.28
Stocks/Consumption	.15	.09	.16	.23	.24	.31
Production/Stocks	.15	.18	.14	–	–	–
Exports/Stocks	–	–	–	.17	.14	.16

Since the purpose of this analysis is to obtain only a general understanding of how the prices of one commodity vary with the prices or supply and demand of other commodities, all of the likely cross-effects are grouped into a single price index. Although a naive approach to a complex problem, this is the simplest alternative to constructing a more formidable relationship which would define switching between the prices of various commodities. Given a group of similar or substitutable commodities, therefore, one can determine the relationship between the prices of the various commodities by comparing the prices of one commodity to an index composed of the remaining commodity prices. The commodity relationships which appear in the market are such that several indexes can easily be composed. One can relate the prices of a commodity to the prices of domestic commodity substitutes, foreign commodity substitutes, or to the prices of its converted products. Once again, cross-spectral methods will be used for testing these relationships.

Table 6-5

Futures Coherence Comparisons

	Stocks/Consumption	*Consumption*	*Stocks*
Soybean oil	.21	.18	.19
Cottonseed oil	.08	.14	.07
Soybean meal	.21	.21	.20
Soybeans	.21	.20	.12
Rye	.17	.09	.16
Wheat	.28	.27	.34

Price Index Composition

The various price indexes selected to explain the given commodity price series are presented below. For most commodities, prices could simply be related to the prices of competing commodities. Where this has proven ineffective, more complex indexes are composed; the soybean index, for example, is based on the converted value of soybean oil and soybean meal. Wheat is the most difficult price series to explain, and neither of the proposed indexes produces adequate results. Weights for the various indexes have been selected on the basis of 1962 being a typical crop year and according to the relative value of a commodity in domestic consumption. Sources of the newly introduced data may be found in Appendix A.

Oils Index. The oils market, which consists principally of soybean oil, cottonseed oil, and lard, is one in which the commodities are highly substitutable. A price index has been prepared in which the index for each of the oils is the weighted sum of lard and the remaining oil prices. The indexes for soybean oil and cottonseed oil are:

$$I_{11} = (0.52)P_2 + (0.48)P_3 \tag{6.1}$$

$$I_{12} = (0.69)P_1 + (0.31)P_3 \tag{6.2}$$

where

P_1 = Soybean oil prices

P_2 = Cottonseed oil prices

P_3 = Lard prices

Meal Index. Soybean meal and cottonseed meal are close substitutes; but to relate soybean meal to a price series other than that of cottonseed meal itself, the soybean-cottonseed-lard complex has been chosen to demonstrate the influence of generally competitive commodities.

$$I_2 = (0.44)P_1 + (0.21)P_2 + (0.20)P_3 + (0.15)P_5 \tag{6.3}$$

where

P_4 = Soybean meal prices

P_5 = Cottonseed meal prices

Rye Index. The price index of commodities substitutable with rye is based on the weighted price of oats and corn. While rye does not receive major competition through substitution with these commodities, all three are generally related for their use in feed.

$$I_3 = (0.86)P_6 + (0.14)P_7 \tag{6.4}$$

where

P_6 = Corn prices

P_7 = Oats prices

Soybean Index. The price of soybeans has been postulated to depend on the prices of soybean meal and oil. A first index has been constructed which expresses bean prices as the weighted sum of meal and oil prices.

$$I_{41} = (0.43)P_1 + c(0.57)P_4 \tag{6.5}$$

where c is the conversion factor from cents-per-pound to dollars-per-ton. A second index weights the prices according to the yield (which changes monthly) of meal or oil that is obtained from a bushel of soybeans. The formulation of this index follows the standard definition for converting meal and oil prices to bean prices where the residual is the crushing margin.

$$I_{42} = W_1P_1 + W_4P_4 \tag{6.6}$$

where

W_1 = Soybean oil yield (lb./bu.)

W_4 = Soybean meal yield (lb./bu.) which includes conversion to prices measured in \$/ton.

Foreign Index. This has been devised to determine the influence of foreign oils on the domestic oil market. It consists of a weighted average of those foreign oils which serve as reasonably close substitutes to soybean oil, cottonseed oil, and lard.

$$I_5 = (0.37)P_8 + (0.16)P_9 + (0.34)P_{10} + (0.08)P_{11} + (0.05)P_{12} \qquad (6.7)$$

where

P_8 = Groundnut oil prices

P_9 = Palm oil prices

P_{10} = Coconut oil prices

P_{11} = Whale oil prices

P_{12} = Fish oil prices

Grain Index. To investigate further the market interactions among grain prices and to provide an acceptable price index for wheat, the following indexes have been constructed based on the weighted sum of major grain prices. The list of commodities to be included follows the U.S.D.A. classification of grains; only grain sorghums has been removed from that list because of its relatively low value in consumption. The indexes for soybeans, rye, and wheat are:

$$I_{61} = (0.50)P_6 + (0.09)P_7 + (0.28)P_{13} + (0.05)P_{14} + (0.07)P_{15} \qquad (6.8)$$

$$I_{62} = (0.46)P_6 + (0.08)P_7 + (0.24)P_{13} + (0.06)P_{15} + (0.15)P_{16} \qquad (6.9)$$

$$I_{63} = (0.61)P_6 + (0.10)P_7 + (0.01)P_{14} + (0.08)P_{15} + (0.20)P_{16} \qquad (6.10)$$

where

P_{13} = Wheat prices

P_{14} = Rye prices

P_{15} = Barley prices

P_{16} = Soybeans prices

Wheat Relative Index. Since the wheat substitute index has displayed almost no correlation with wheat prices, an alternative price index has been constructed. This index is based on the principal that the relative strength of a commodity price as measured against an average market price can be utilized as an indicator of price movements.[1] While such an index represents nothing more than a deflated price series, it does provide some indication of how prices are moving in response to the market. Both futures and cash indexes can be constructed from

$$I_7 = \frac{P_{17}}{P_{18}} \tag{6.11}$$

where

P_{17} = Wheat cash (futures) prices

P_{18} = Dow Jones Commodity cash (futures) price index

Coherence Results

Table 6-6 summarizes the coherence relationship between futures prices, prices of commodity substitutes, and the related price indexes. The highest coherence (0.85) occurs between wheat futures prices and the wheat relative index. This value, however, cannot be considered highly meaningful since the relative index represents little more than a deflated futures price series. The next highest and more meaningful coherence is found in the substitutable oils index with values of 0.51 for soybean oil and 0.36 for cottonseed oil. These coherences follow from the highly substitutable properties of oils and lard as inputs to firms using edible oil inputs. For soybean futures prices, the index of converted commodities weighted by yields displays a slightly higher coherence (0.44) than that obtained from simple consumption weights (0.35). A coherence of this magnitude suggests that soybean prices are partially determined by the prices of its converted products. When considering the relationship between soybean meal prices and the meal index, one finds a coherence of only 0.26; this appears to result from including commodities in the index which are not direct substitutes for meal.

For the remaining price indexes, coherence values are considerably lower. The coherence between soybean oil, soybean meal, cottonseed oil prices and the index of competitive foreign oils never rises above 0.17. The rye index, based on oats and corn prices, demonstrates a coherence of only 0.20 with rye prices, mainly because oats and corn are not direct substitutes for rye. Quite similarly, the weak substitutability of soybeans, rye, and wheat results in the grain index displaying coherences of only 0.12, 0.16 and 0.12 with soybeans, rye, and wheat respectively. The price response of the cash price series in Table 6-7 does not differ significantly from that reported for the above prices.

Economic Conditions Response

Although no formal theory exists which relates commodity price changes to the expansion and contraction of the economy, the experience of futures traders

Table 6-6

Price Index Response: Average Coherence Between Futures Prices and Weighted Price Indexes

Monthly: First Differences
August 1957-June 1966
Observations = 107
Estimated Lags = 24

Index	*Soybean Oil*	*Cottonseed Oil*	*Soybean Meal*	*Soybeans*	*Rye*	*Wheat*
Oils	.51	.36	–	–	–	–
Meal	–	–	.26	–	–	–
Rye	–	–	–	–	.20	–
Soybeans[a]	–	–	–	.35	–	–
Soybeans[b]	–	–	–	.44	–	–
Foreign	.17	.17	.10	–	–	–
Grain	–	–	–	.12	.16	.12
Relative	–	–	–	–	–	.85

[a]Weights based on value of consumption.

[b]Weights based on changing yields of soybean meal and oil.

suggests that economic fluctuations strongly influence commodity price formation.[2] This point has been emphasized in one particular study where the pressures of cyclical change have been related to the interaction between the prices of commodities and their corresponding supply or demand.[3] When considering the response of cash and futures prices to economic fluctuations frequent enough to be of interest here such as shorter-term business cycles, one encounters several difficulties in measuring this response. First of all, most futures contracts mature in several months, a time span representing only a fraction of the period of the shortest cycles. Secondly, the shortness of the period under investigation in the present study poses a limitation. The nine years from 1957 to 1966 can include at most the experience of only two or three of the shorter cycles.

In spite of such difficulties, however, it should be possible to detect the

Table 6-7

Price Index Response: Average Coherence Between Cash Prices and Weighted Price Indexes

Monthly: First Differences
August 1957-June 1966
Observations = 107
Estimated Lags = 24

Index	*Soybean Oil*	*Cottonseed Oil*	*Soybean Meal*	*Soybeans*	*Rye*	*Wheat*
Oils	.51	.27	–	–	–	–
Meal	–	–	.19	–	–	–
Rye	–	–	–	–	.20	–
Soybeans[a]	–	–	–	.43	–	–
Soybeans[b]	–	–	–	.52	–	–
Foreign	.19	.12	.11	–	–	–
Grain	–	–	–	.11	.24	.16
Relative	–	–	–	–	–	.74

[a]Weights based on value of consumption.

[b]Weights based on changing yields of soybean meal and oils.

influence of these shorter-run fluctuations on the various price series for several reasons. For many commodities, supply and demand are relatively in equilibrium (no substantial trend in prices) over the period of interest. In addition, economic conditions are reflected through more than one cyclical phenomenon including general business conditions, credit conditions, and, to a lesser extent, stock market prices. Finally, the possibility of finding cyclical interrelationships is further helped by the use of cross-spectral methods. These methods possess the advantage of measuring cyclical relationships over all time points and not just at peaks and troughs.[4] This is particularly important here since swings of any frequency in the economy seldom display the periodicity commonly associated with peaks and troughs. A further advantage of the spectral approach is that it enables us to measure cyclical response over all frequencies. Thus, the possibility exists of measuring the influence on prices of long swings as well as shorter-run fluctuations in the economy.

Business Conditions

The most general cyclical influences which can be related to the various commodity price series are those normally identified as indicators of business conditions: industrial production, unemployment, and price levels. While definitions for the different indicators can be found in Table 6-8, the relation of these indicators to price behavior might be described as follows. Given a stable set of supply and demand conditions, cyclical expansions or improvements in business conditions can generally be associated with rising production, falling unemployment, and stable or slightly inflationary prices. Under these circumstances, commodity price changes tend to follow the general price movement upwards. Conversely, cyclical contractions are accompanied by declining production, increasing unemployment, and a possible decline in the general price level. Thus, commodity prices would also drift downwards.

The cross-spectral results reported in Tables 6-9 and 6-10, however, suggest only a limited response of prices to the three indicators. Beginning with the futures comparisons in Table 6-9, one finds the weakest dependence between prices and the index of industrial production. Coherence values range from only 0.03 for cottonseed oil to 0.14 for wheat. Futures prices tend to respond a little better to the layoff rate; the coherence value for cottonseed oil prices is 0.12 but wheat reaches a value of 0.21. The Dow Jones Futures Price Index, the price index most closely related with commodity behavior, has been chosen to reflect the general price level. Prices respond to this indicator about the same as to the layoff rate, with rye and wheat having coherence values of 0.24 and 0.26 respectively. Since the same levels of coherence are reported for the cash price series, the conclusion must be that only a limited relationship exists between commodity prices and the more general indicators of business conditions.

Credit Conditions

Moving to more specific cyclical influences, one finds a distinct possibility for relating price behavior to changes in the availability of credit. With respect to the futures market, it is obvious that purchasers of futures contracts borrow to cover their holdings much in the same way that buyers of stocks make frequent use of credit. This is particularly noticeable in stock markets where margin requirements, the maximum amount of credit that any broker can provide for a customer, are a necessary feature of the market. Both bank loans and diversions from working capital are the major sources of credit for the stock market, but the former is the more likely source for the futures market.[5]

Table 6-8

Definitions of Selected Economic Indicators[a]

Business Conditions

Federal Reserve Board Index of Industrial Production: This index measures changes in the physical volume or quantity of output of manufactures, minerals, and of electric and gas utilities. *Source:* Board of Governors of the Federal Reserve System (208).

Layoff Rate in Manufacturing Establishments: Layoffs are suspensions without pay initiated by the employer during the calendar month. *Source:* Department of Labor Statistics (241).

Dow Jones Spot and Futures Indexes: Both indexes consist of an average of daily closing prices from a group of selected commodities. *Source:* Dow Jones & Co.

Credit Conditions

Consumer Installment Credit Extended: Extensions include all consumer credit held by financial institutions and retail outlets which is scheduled to be repaid in two or more installments. *Source:* Board of Governors of the Federal Reserve System (249).

Consumer Installment Credit Repaid: Above credit series repaid (249).

Net Consumer Installment Credit: Net credit is credit extended minus credit repaid.

Excess Reserves of All Member Banks of the Federal Reserve System: Excess reserves are the difference between reserves actually held and required reserves. They indicate the extent to which member banks may legally expand their loans and investments without having recourse to the Federal Reserve Banks. *Source:* Board of Governors of the Federal Reserve System (246).

Borrowings from Federal Reserve Banks: The borrowings of member banks from the Federal Reserve (246).

Free Reserves: The difference between the excess reserves of member banks and member-bank borrowings at Federal Reserve banks.

Open Market Interest Rate of (prime 4-6 months) Commercial Paper: *Source:* Federal Reserve Bank of New York (248).

Open Market Interest Rate of (prime 90 days) Bankers Acceptances: *Source:* Federal Reserve Bank of New York (248).

Open Market Yield on 3-Month Treasury Bills (note on new issues – U.S. Government Securities): *Source:* Board of Governors of the Federal Reserve System (248).

Table 6-8 (*continued*)

Stock Market Conditions

Dow Jones Stock Price Index: The index is an average of daily closing prices from a group of representative stocks listed on the New York Stock Exchange *Source:* Dow Jones & Co. (259).

Standard & Poor's Combined Stock Price Index: This index of 500 stocks computed relative to the base period (1941-1943) approximates the average price level of all stocks listed on the New York Stock Exchange. *Source:* Standard & Poor's Corporation (259).

[a]All definitions except those for the Dow Jones Spot and Futures Indexes have been taken in whole or in part from *Business Statistics 1963 Biennial Edition,* Office of Business Economics, U.S. Department of Commerce (Washington: U.S. Government Printing Office, 1963). The numbers shown in parenthesis describe the page location in that issue.

Several different measures or indicators can be fruitfully employed to relate the availability of bank loans to futures price changes. The first such indicator is the rate of interest. The rates which have been found to most effectively describe short-term availability are the three-month treasury-bill rate, the rate on commercial paper, and the rate on bankers' acceptances. Another indicator describing the availability of credit is the reserve position of the Federal Reserve to its member banks. The proper measures of this position are borrowed reserves; excess reserves; and their difference, net free reserves. A final credit indicator which is more related to the consumer sector is the level of consumer installment credit. This is measured by credit extended, credit repaid, and the net change between these positions. All three indicators – interest rates, reserves, and installment credit – also have been related to both futures and cash prices. The arguments for the relation of cash prices to credit are not as direct as those for futures prices, except that the availability of credit probably influences the decision to move commodities into storage.

The coherence results of relating the indicators to prices are presented in Tables 6-9 and 6-10. The credit indicators displaying the highest relationship with futures prices are consumer installment credit extended and the net change in consumer installment credit, but even here the coherence values are low. Most coherences for credit extended are about 0.15 except for a coherence of 0.30 with wheat. Values for the net change indicator reach 0.21 for soybean oil and 0.32 for wheat. The relation of the Federal Reserve position to futures prices is lower. The coherence of prices with excess reserves ranges from 0.11 for cottonseed oil to 0.18 for soybean oil. For the net free reserve position, found to be a good indicator of recessions and expansions, the higher coherences are

Table 6-9

Economic Conditions Response: Average Coherence Between Futures Prices and Selected Economic Indicators

Monthly: First Differences
August 1957-June 1966
Observations = 107
Estimated Lags = 24

Index	Futures Price Series					
	Soybean Oil	*Cotton-seed Oil*	*Soybean Meal*	*Soybeans*	*Rye*	*Wheat*
Business Conditions						
Industrial Production	.08	.03	.13	.09	.12	.14
Layoff Rate	.15	.12	.14	.12	.16	.21
Futures Index	.15	.18	.12	.12	.24	.26
Credit Conditions						
Consumer Installment Credit:						
Extended	.16	.11	.15	.15	.15	.30
Repaid	.11	.11	.15	.15	.11	.16
Net Credit	.21	.13	.14	.16	.14	.32
Federal Reserve:						
Borrowed	.11	.12	.11	.08	.11	.12
Excess	.18	.11	.12	.13	.11	.14
Net Reserves	.13	.11	.10	.09	.15	.10

Table 6-9 *(continued)*

Index	*Soybean Oil*	*Cotton-seed Oil*	*Soybean Meal*	*Soybeans*	*Rye*	*Wheat*
	Futures Price Series					
Interest Rate:						
Commercial paper	.09	.17	.12	.06	.16	.15
Treasury bills	.06	.17	.07	.05	.14	.14
Bankers' acceptances	.11	.15	.10	.08	.10	.14
Stock Market						
Dow Jones Industrial						
Price Index	.13	.08	.05	.13	.07	.06
Standard and Poor's "500"						
Price Index	.02	.09	.12	.14	.07	.06

only 0.11 and 0.13 for cottonseed oil and soybean oil respectively. Low coherences also appear between futures prices and the various interest rates. Of these, the higher coherences are discovered for cottonseed oil, reaching 0.17 for the rate on commercial paper, 0.17 for the three-month treasury rate, and 0.15 for bankers' acceptances.

One can conclude from the various coherence values that the influence of credit conditions cannot be easily deciphered, although a few of the coherences are sufficiently high to suggest a limited participation of commodity prices in credit cycles. Once again, the ranking of these indicators in the stepwise regression equations of Chapter 7 should offer evidence as to their relative influence on price.

Stock Market Interactions

One aspect of futures price behavior that is of some interest in the study of cyclical interactions is the relationship between futures and stock prices. Futures

Table 6-10

Economic Conditions Response: Average Coherence Between Cash Prices and Selected Economic Indicators

Monthly: First Differences
August 1957-June 1966
Observations = 107
Estimated Lags = 24

	Cash Price Series					
Index	*Soybean Oil*	*Cotton seed Oil*	*Soybean Meal*	*Soybeans*	*Rye*	*Wheat*
Business Conditions						
Industrial Production	.07	.04	.07	.10	.10	.11
Layoff Rate	.15	.12	.15	.12	.18	.21
Dow Jones Spot						
Price Index	.14	.17	.12	.11	.24	.26
Credit Conditions						
Consumer Installment Credit;						
Extended	.16	.10	.11	.08	.18	.20
Repaid	.12	.08	.10	.11	.11	.09
Net Credit	.20	.12	.12	.11	.18	.20
Federal Reserve:						
Borrowed	.12	.12	.07	.05	.10	.16
Excess	.16	.10	.06	.10	.13	.06
Net Reserves	.14	.09	.06	.07	.13	.12

Table 6-10 *(continued)*

Index	Cash Price Series *Soybean Oil*	*Cotton-seed Oil*	*Soybean Meal*	*Soybeans*	*Rye*	*Wheat*
Interest Rate:						
Commercial paper	.09	.15	.15	.09	.13	.11
Treasury bills	.07	.21	.11	.05	.13	.12
Bankers' acceptance	.13	.13	.08	.08	.09	.10
Stock Market						
Dow Jones Industrial						
Price Index	.15	.06	.10	.08	.08	.15
Standard and Poor's "500"						
Price Index	.02	.09	.06	.10	.08	.14

prices for the above commodities are compared to the Dow Jones Index of 65 Stocks and the Standard and Poor's Index of 500 Stocks. The cross-spectral results are reported in Tables 6-9 and 6-10. The coherence levels between futures prices and both stock price indexes are very low, generally below 0.10. To provide a more adequate test of this relationship as well as of that between commodity prices and the previously tested indicators, both cash and futures prices are considered in aggregate form. Cross-spectra are estimated between the Dow Jones Spot and Futures Indexes, the stock market indexes and the other business cycle indicators. The coherences appearing in Table 6-11 generally indicate that economic fluctuations do not influence commodity price aggregates any more than the prices of individual commodities. In fact, the coherence between the futures price index and either stock market price index is only 0.06. The only suggestion of a possibly significant coherence occurs between the futures price index and either the net change in credit (0.17) or borrowed reserves (0.18).

In general, the relationships between the various economic indicators are not at all clear except for a chance link between layoffs and credit, as well as for some interaction among the interest rates. The layoff rate appears to lead

Table 6-11

Average Coherence Between Price Indexes and Selected Economic Indicators

Monthly: First Differences
August 1957-June 1966
Observations = 107
Estimated Lags = 24

		Standard and Poor's "500" Price Index	Consumer Installment Credit: Extended	Consumer Installment Credit: Repaid	Consumer Installment Credit: Net Credit	Dow Jones: Spot Price Index	Dow Jones: Futures Price Index	Layoff Rate	Industrial Production	Federal Reserve: Excess	Federal Reserve: Borrowed	Federal Reserve: Net Reserves	Interest Rates: Commercial Paper	Interest Rates: Treasury Bills	Interest Rates: Bankers' Acceptances
	Dow Jones Industrial Stock Price Index	.94	.14	.14	.12	.09	.06	.20	.14	.18	.18	.15	.13	.10	.09
	Standard and Poor's "500" Price Index		.13	.13	.11	.08	.06	.20	.12	.16	.18	.14	.11	.10	.09
Consumer Installment Credit	*Extended*			.56	.90	.14	.14	.39	.20	.20	.31	.19	.16	.10	.15
	Repaid				.35	.12	.09	.25	.14	.20	.16	.16	.10	.08	.11
	Net Credit					.14	.17	.39	.18	.16	.33	.17	.17	.11	.14
Dow Jones	*Spot Price Index*						.53	.17	.09	.10	.15	.08	.14	.13	.08
	Futures Price Index							.08	.06	.09	.18	.05	.10	.09	.10
	Layoff Rate								.22	.19	.22	.23	.16	.18	.15
	Industrial Production									.17	.16	.20	.22	.23	.19
Federal Reserve	*Excess*										.17	.58	.31	.27	.31
	Borrowed											.38	.15	.16	.15
	Net Reserves												.26	.24	.24
Interest Rates	*Commercial Paper*													.61	.56
	Treasury Bills														.63

consumer credit extended, but this lead is not significant even though the accompanying coherence is 0.39. Of greater value is the dependence between the interest rates. The Treasury Bill rate displays a coherence of 0.61 with the rate on prime commercial paper and 0.63 with the bankers' acceptance rate; the former also leads both of the latter with a fixed angle lead which is approximately $\pi/10$ and significant at the 95% level.

Conclusions

The hypothesis presented at the outset of this chapter has described a number of price determinants suitable for explaining commodity price fluctuations. The individual determinants have been subsequently analyzed to learn which might be appropriate for inclusion into an actual price model. The coherence found between prices and the components of supply and demand confirm the results of the previous chapter: that in the short run only a limited relationship exists between price and quantity. When the quantity variables are transformed to measure the pressure of demand on supply, the ratios produce only an equal or marginally better explanation than the individual components.

The price influences arising from the cross-elasticity of demand or substitution in the market give the best explanation of price change. Although only moderate coherences appear, commodity prices can be related to indexes representing the prices of close substitutes. These indexes, however, suffer several limitations. They do not reflect detail such as the separate cross-elasticities of demand which could be more fully explained in a simultaneous model. Nor do they indicate whether the interaction results from demand adjustment, supply adjustment, stock adjustment, or a combination of several such adjustments.

The expansions and contractions of the economy also influence price fluctuations, but the levels of coherence achieved are lower than any of the above. A major difficulty is that the duration of even the shortest economic fluctuations such as the business cycle is much greater than the period of a futures contract. For most price determinants, however, the presence of even low coherences can help to explain some of the variation in commodity price behavior. By aggregating several of these determinants into a single equation, a much better explanation can be obtained.

A final weakness concerning the various results is that no clear evidence exists showing which of the determinants provides a relatively better explanation of price change. It is for this reason, as well as the above one of aggregating the determinants that we introduce the methods of stepwise regression.

7 Explanatory Equations and Results

Introduction

The present chapter summarizes the results of applying stepwise regression methods to the price determinants selected from a general hypothesis of price behavior. The stepwise method has been employed to construct explanatory equations for the cash and futures price-difference series of soybean oil, cottonseed oil, soybean meal, soybeans, rye, and wheat. The presentation of results from these equations is primarily statistical. A battery of statistical measures including multiple coherence, multiple correlation, the F ratio, and the Durbin-Watson statistic are applied to the stepwise equations to determine their goodness of fit. Included also are graphs of estimated versus actual price differences, multiple coherence, and the spectrum of residuals. The present chapter, therefore, specifies which variables, taken individually or together, provide the best explanation of commodity price fluctuations. Integration of the equations into a general model of price behavior is attempted in Chapter 8.

The Stepwise Approach

Chapter 2 has shown how stepwise regression methods are appropriate for explaining stationary time series, using past values of that series or stationary explanatory series (see pages 59-61). In this part of the study, the stepwise method has helped us to construct explanatory equations of price behavior, using past values of the price series as well as a number of explanatory variables. The latter include variables found useful in Chapter 6, together with hedging and speculating variables investigated in Chapter 5. The procedure for selecting explanatory variables for the individual commodity equations has been simply to enter into the initial stepwise selection procedure any variable whose average coherence value exceeds roughly 0.10.

The most crucial aspect of operating the stepwise method with the above variables has been deciding which variables to include in the explanatory equations. In each case, the classical criterion for including variables (as described in Chapter 2) has been followed; the first variable to enter the regression is that one best explaining the variance of the price series of interest where the variable is selected on the basis of its possessing the highest partial F value of the included variables. The stepwise algorithm then proceeds to select another variable and, once again, chooses from among the remaining variables that one satisfying the F criterion. No variable is included unless its partial F value meets a predetermined level of significance. At each step, the program also tests the previously entered variables to ascertain their continued significance with the addition of a new variable. This assures that all entered variables will explain prices significantly.

The classical criterion presents the difficulty of deciding how many steps to use or when to stop adding further variables. As will be explained in the Appendix to Chapter 9, it almost always involves overfitting the explanatory equations or including additional variables which are not statistically significant. Thus, the equations presented in this chapter are somewhat optimistic in terms of (1) the total number of price determinants accepted as significantly important and (2) the values reached for the coefficient of determination and average multiple coherence.

This method or philosophy of model building has been particularly useful here because it enables us to increase the degree of price explanation by introducing several rather than a single explanatory variable as well as to rank the included variables in the order of their relative price explanation. As such, the stepwise method has provided a direct, statistical basis for constructing the various commodity price equations. We have avoided any predisposition arising from economic theory which would force variables into the equation, mainly because an a priori specification of variables in the equations could lead to a less than optimum explanation. This latter view, while it should not be generally applied to the stepwise method, has worked effectively in the present circumstances.

The principal criticism which can be directed against the above method of selecting price influences is that it limits the explanation of price to merely a single set of variables, with no consideration of the interaction between the variables. Such an approach can be criticized as being pragmatic, especially when compared to more elaborate simultaneous-equation procedures, but it has certain advantages with short-run data and can emphasize influences which are often omitted in the simultaneous approach.[1]

Reporting the Equation Results

The results of the stepwise regression analysis as performed on each of the price-difference series are reported in tabular and graphical form. The accompanying tables list: (1) the independent variables which serve as inputs to the stepwise regression; (2) the estimated regression equations in steps; and (3) criteria for judging the quality of the explanation, including the overall F ratio, coefficient of determination, average multiple coherence, and the Durbin-Watson statistic. The graphs include estimated versus actual price differences, multiple coherence diagrams, and spectra of residuals.

Concerning the criteria included in the tables, both the F ratio test and the significance test of the multiple correlation coefficient included at each step evaluate the significance of the explanatory variables, except that the former tests the values of the corresponding regression coefficients against zero and the latter tests the value of the correlation coefficient (or its value squared) against zero. The advantage of including the coefficient of determination is that increases or changes in this coefficient at each step of the regression reflect the partial correlation of the newly added variable. The remaining statistics, the multiple coherence, the spectrum of residuals and the Durbin-Watson values, are reported only at the cut-off point, where the quality of the regression is judged.[a]

The cutoff points identified in the tables represent the step of maximum degree of price explanation achieved for the various equations. More particularly, they have been defined as that step beyond which the next explanatory variable to enter would cause the total explanation to become insignificant, using the F ratio at the 95% level. This procedure varies somewhat from commodity to commodity, but it generally defines the cutoff point. No further variables (with few exceptions) are accepted as adding to the price explanation once the cutoff point is reached in an attempt to avoid criticisms of "data mining." We have, however, included in the tables the next variable to enter the equation after the cutoff point is reached, mainly to afford a better understanding of the total range of possible influences for a price series.

With respect to the graphs, the first one described for each equation plots both estimated and actual price differences. The reported period is historical, extending from August 1957 to June 1966. Note also that it has not been possible to include extreme price differences in the graphs and certain price swings extend only to graph boundaries. The second graph, the multiple coherence diagram, is interpreted such that a relatively constant diagram assures that the included variables explain price equally well over all frequency ranges. The final graph, the spectrum of residuals, obtains its values as a by-product of the multiple coherence computation.[b] Since a flat spectrum of first difference residuals implies an absence of autocorrelation in the residuals, this graph is especially useful for testing autocorrelation where the Durbin-Watson statistic is no longer valid, i.e., in regressions containing lagged, endogenous variables.[2]

Several difficulties arise in interpreting the results presented in some of the tables and graphs. With regard to the stepwise regressions, the major difficulty is that a newly entered variable occasionally forms a multicollinear relationship with the previously included variables. Multicollinearity can produce variation or instability in the estimates of the regression coefficients and their respective variances, thus upsetting the correlation and F ratio measures.[3] Unless the instability caused by the entering variable is particularly high, the entered variable has not been removed from the equation.[c]

A second difficulty involves the testing of the autocorrelative properties of the regression residuals. As reported above, the spectrum of residuals is

---

[a]Significance tests for the F ratio, coefficient of determination, and multiple coherence are applied at the 95% level while the Durbin-Watson statistic is evaluated at the 99% level.

[b]An advantage of computing the multiple cross-spectrum is that the algorithm can simultaneously produce an estimate of the spectrum of residuals. See Chapter 2, cf. p. 55.

[c]Considerable change in magnitude or change in sign of the affected regression coefficient was accepted as a mark of instability.

especially useful for testing autocorrelation where the Durbin-Watson statistic is only marginally applicable, i.e., in equations containing lagged endogenous variables. The computed spectra of residuals, however, have not been free from fluctuations even where the residuals appear to be reasonably uncorrelated. In retrospect, this was found to result from having too narrow a "spectral window" or weighting function to smooth the associated spectral density function. While these fluctuations do present somewhat of a problem in interpreting the diagrams, they should not deter us from drawing conclusions with respect to the residuals. At least, where a trend in fluctuations clearly is present or absent, the autocorrelation found in the residuals can be interpreted.

A final difficulty is that the reader may find considerable differences between the values of average coherence and the coefficient of determination for a particular multiple relationship. Since differences between these values do not upset the interpretation of results, the explanation of this phenomenon has been deferred to the appendix to this chapter.

The Explanatory Equations[4]

Soybean Oil

Table 7-1 lists the variables chosen to help explain futures price fluctuations. At least five variables enter the equation significantly, but only the first four can be considered appropriate. The F values for the oil index, short hedging, foreign index, and net consumer installment credit are significant at the 95% level ($F = 101.75 > 3.94$, $15.34 > 3.09$, $3.33 > 2.70$, and $3.10 > 2.46$).[d] The next variable to come in is lagged price. This variable seems significant ($F = 3.90 > 2.30$) but it is not included since the sudden rise in the F value from 3.10 to 3.90 implies serial correlation between lagged price and the dependent price variable. The multiple correlation reached at this stage is 0.60 and the multiple coherence is 0.98. Both are significant at the 95% level

[d]The F-value comparisons identify the regression value first and the distribution or table value second, i.e., F regression $= 101.75 > F$ Table $= 3.94$ at the 95% level. This same order is followed for correlation and coherence values.

($R^2 = 0.60 > 0.08$ and $C = 0.98 > 0.63$). To test whether the average multiple coherence is significantly different from zero, only the test of simple coherence mentioned in Granger and Hatanaka is available.[5] Unfortunately, this test refers only to coherence values reported at specific frequency points and can be applied only approximately in the present situation.[e] (See p. 162.)

The accompanying Figure 7-1 suggests a close fit between the estimated and actual price differences. Accordingly, the constant multiple coherence diagram indicates that the included variables explain price differences equally well over the short-, middle-, and long-run frequencies. Both the spectrum of residuals and the Durbin-Watson statistic ($d = 2.01 > d_u = 1.63$) denote a lack of autocorrelation in the residuals.[f] (See p. 163.)

The final model reached for the cash price explanation is similar to the futures model except that a physical variable, stocks, enters the regression at the second step. Figure 7-2 reports correspondence between the estimated and actual price differences, and the coherence diagram is flat over all frequencies. This agrees with the multiple correlation ($0.59 > 0.08$) and average coherence values ($0.93 > 0.63$) reported in Table 7-2, which are significant at the 95% level. Because of the lagged dependent variable in the regression, the Durbin-Watson statistic cannot be applied to the residuals. Referring to the spectrum of residuals, one finds a slight trend indicative of a low degree of negative autocorrelation. The specification of these equations follows especially well what would be expected from economic reasoning. Hedging, a measure of futures activity, is the first variable after the oil index to enter the futures price explanation, while stocks, a measure of physical activity, is the corresponding variable for the cash price explanation. This pattern also occurs with several of the remaining equations. (See pp. 164-165.)

---

[e]For example, the equivalent measure of degrees of freedom, $n/m = 106/24 = 4.4$, lies between 4 and 6. For $n/m = 4$, a coherence value of .54 is necessary for significance at the 90% level and .63 at the 95% level. For the next step $n/m = 6$, .37 is required at the 90% level and .45 at the 95% level. Since considerable difference exists between these values, the results of this test can be accepted only roughly.

[f]The Durbin-Watson test proposes that no positive autocorrelation is present in the residuals when the estimated d statistic is greater than the upper bound d_u. If d is less than the upper bound d_u and greater than the lower bound d_l, then the test is inconclusive.

Table 7-1

Soybean Oil Futures Prices: Stepwise Explanation of Price Behavior

Monthly: First Differences
August 1957-June 1966
Observations = 107

Regression In Steps:

1. $Y = -0.00616 + 0.764X_1$
   (0.0758)
   F value = 101.75
   $R = 0.70$; $R^2 = 0.49$

2. $Y = -0.0150 + 0.717X_1 + 0.00000182X_2$
   (0.0721) (0.000000464)
   F value = 15.34
   $R = 0.75$; $R^2 = 0.56$; $\Delta R^2 = 0.07$

3. $Y = -0.0141 + 0.686X_1 + 0.00000175X_2 + 0.0162X_3$
   (0.0733) (0.000000461) (0.00890)
   F value = 3.33
   $R = 0.76$; $R^2 = 0.58$; $\Delta R^2 = 0.02$

4. $Y = -0.0131 + 0.670X_1 + 0.00000170X_2 + 0.0177X_3 - 0.000111X_4$
   (0.0731) (0.000000457) (0.00885) (0.0000631)
   F value = 3.10
   $R = 0.78$; $R^2 = 0.60$; $\Delta R^2 = 0.02$
   $\bar{C} = 0.98$; $DW = 2.01$

5. $Y = -0.120 + 0.630X_1 + 0.00000173X_2 + 0.0153X_3 - 0.000144X_4 + 0.135X_5$
   (0.0748) (0.000000451) (0.00881) (0.0000644) (.0686)
   F value = 3.90
   $R = 0.78$; $R^2 = 0.60$; $\Delta R^2 = 0$

Y = Futures prices

X_1 = Oil index

X_2 = Short hedging

X_3 = Foreign price index

X_4 = Consumer installment credit: Net

X_5 = Lagged price Y_{t-1}

X_6 = Demand

X_7 = Supply

X_8 = Consumption

X_9 = Production

X_{10} = Stocks

X_{11} = Consumption/Stocks

X_{12} = Stocks/Consumption

X_{13} = Production/Consumption

X_{14} = Production/Demand

X_{15} = Federal Reserve: Excess reserves

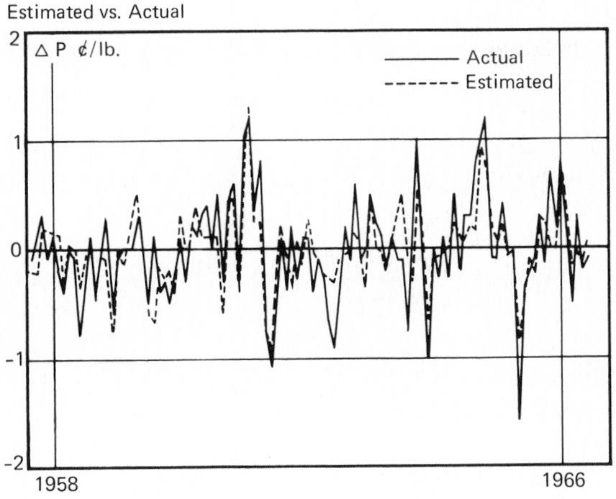

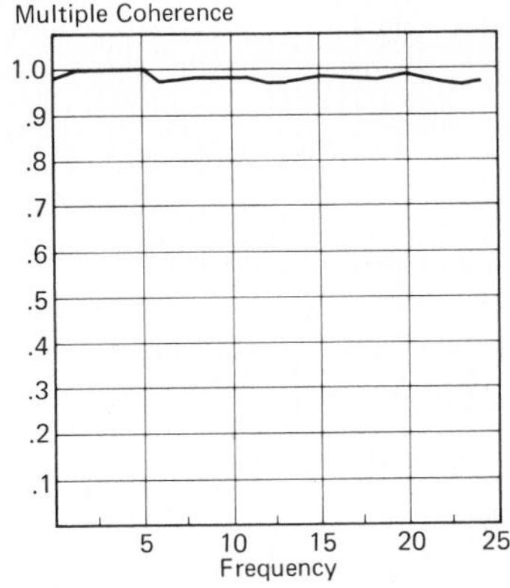

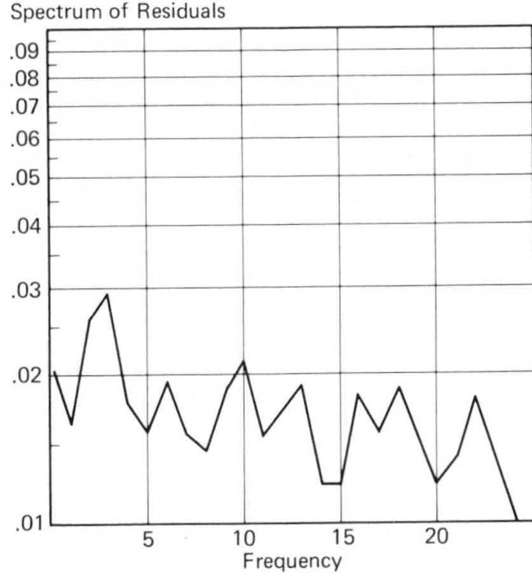

Figure 7-1 Regression of Soybean Oil Futures Price Differences.

Table 7-2

Soybean Oil Cash Prices: Stepwise Explanation of Price Behavior

Monthly: First Differences
August 1957-June 1966
Observations = 107

Regression in Steps:

1. $Y = -0.00337 + 0.785X_1$
(0.0783)
F value = 100.59
$R = 0.70$; $R^2 = 0.49$

2. $Y = -0.000956 + 0.811X_1 - 0.00175X_2$
(0.0758) (0.000572)
F value = 9.37
$R = 0.74$; $R^2 = 0.52$; $\Delta R^2 = 0.03$

3. $Y = -0.00472 + 0.780X_1 - 0.00167X_2 + 0.00000113X_3$
(0.0753) (0.000560) (0.000000482)
F value = 5.52
$R = 0.75$; $R^2 = 0.56$; $\Delta R^2 = 0.04$

4. $Y = -0.00409 + 0.739X_1 - 0.148X_2 + 0.00000109X_3 + 0.145X_4$
(0.0763) (0.000558)(0.000000474) (0.0666)
F value = 4.73
$R = 0.77$; $R^2 = 0.59$; $\Delta R^2 = 0.03$

5. $Y = -0.00298 + 0.714X_1 - 0.140X_2 + 0.00000103X_3 + 0.179X_4 - 0.000126X_5$
(0.0765) (0.000552)(0.000000469) (0.0682) (0.0000669)
F value = 3.56
$R = 0.77$; $R^2 = 0.59$; $\Delta R^2 = 0$
$\overline{C} = 0.93$; $DW = 2.06$;

6. $Y = -0.00247 + 0.699X_1 - 0.00143X_2 + 0.000000992X_3 + 0.166X_4 - 0.000130X_5 + 0.00986X_6$
(0.0778) (0.000552) (0.000000470) (0.0692) (0.0000670) (0.00924)
F value = 1.14
$R = 0.77$; $R^2 = 0.60$; $\Delta R^2 = 0.01$

Y = Cash prices
X_1 = Oil index
X_2 = Stocks
X_3 = Short hedging
X_4 = Lagged price Y_{t-1}
X_5 = Consumer installment credit: Net
X_6 = Foreign price index
X_7 = Demand
X_8 = Supply
X_9 = Consumption
X_{10} = Production
X_{11} = Consumption/Stocks
X_{12} = Stocks/Consumption
X_{13} = Production/Consumption
X_{14} = Production/Demand
X_{15} = Federal Reserve: Excess Reserves

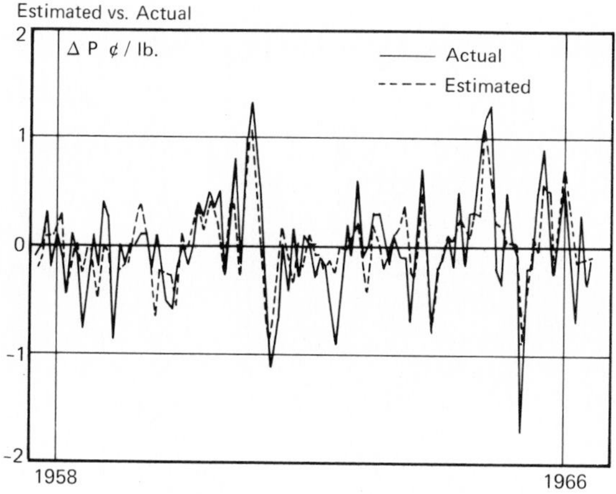

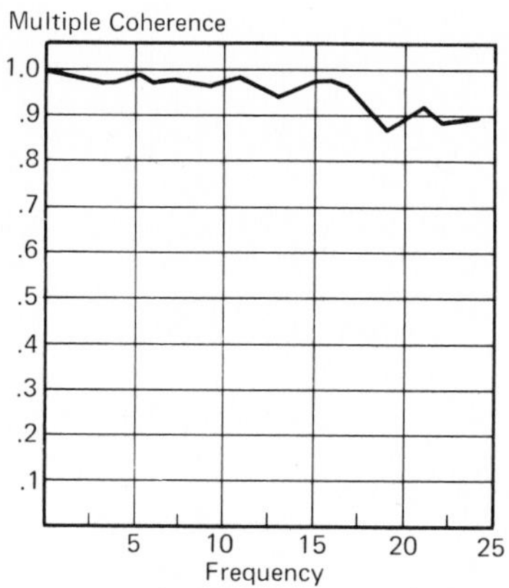

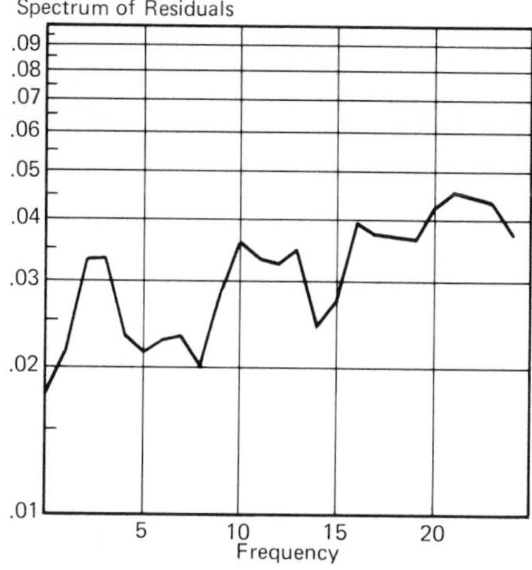

Figure 7-2 Regression of Soybean Oil Cash Price Differences.

Cottonseed Oil

From the given list of input variables in Table 7-3, the stepwise regression for futures prices enters the oils index, the consumption/stocks ratio, lagged prices, short hedging, and the interest rate on commercial paper. The first four of these variables show significant F values at the 95% level ($F = 47.80 > 3.94$, $11.11 > 4.82$, $2.96 > 2.70$, $2.93 > 2.46$). The fifth variable, the interest rate on commercial paper, is an economic influence different from the previous influences, but adds no explanation to the variance of futures prices. After the first four variables, the coefficient of determination reaches a value of 0.42 and the average multiple coherence is 0.95. Both are significant at the 95% level ($R^2 = 0.42 > 0.08$ and $\bar{C} = 0.95 > 0.63$). (See p. 168.)

The fit of estimated to actual price differences illustrated in Figure 7-3 is less perfect than that shown for soybean oil. Although the level of correlation found between prices and the explanatory variables is low, the coherence diagram is constant over all frequencies. The corresponding spectrum of residuals fluctuates widely, but there is no implication of autocorrelation. (see p. 169.)

The stepwise equation for cash price behavior differs mainly in the positioning of the lagged price variable. As shown in Table 7-4, lagged price is the first variable to enter the regression. One would not expect a high correlation between the first difference of a variable and its first lag, but a separate check of the autoregressive nature of the series revealed limited first-order serial correlation. While the inclusion of this variable results in relatively unstable estimates, the lagged dependent variable seems essential to explaining cottonseed oil price change and is included in the equation presented in Table 7-4. The remaining variables which enter the equation significantly are the oil index and the production/stocks ratio. Both the coefficient of determination and the average coherence are significant at the 95% level ($R^2 = 0.46 > 0.06$ and $\bar{C} = 0.96 > 0.63$). Figure 7-4 displays a quality of fit similar to that found in the futures price equation. The coherence diagram is constant over all frequencies, while the spectrum of residuals has a peculiar negative slope, suggesting second-order autocorrelation. (See pp. 170-171.)

Table 7-3

Cottonseed Oil Futures Prices: Stepwise Explanation of Price Behavior

Monthly: First Differences
August 1957-June 1966
Observations = 107

Regression in Steps:

1. $Y = 0.0202 + 0.662X_1$
   (0.0957)
   F value = 47.80
   $R = 0.58$; $R^2 = 0.34$

2. $Y = 0.0195 + 0.700X_1 - 1.033X_2$
   (0.0921) (0.310)
   F value = 11.11
   $R = 0.62$; $R^2 = 0.38$; $\Delta R^2 = 0.04$

3. $Y = 0.0192 + 0.667X_1 - 0.924X_2 + 0.138X_3$
   (0.0932) (0.313) (0.0796)
   F value = 2.96
   $R = 0.63$; $R^2 = 0.40$; $\Delta R^2 = 0.02$

4. $Y = 0.0198 + 0.643X_1 - 0.898X_2 + 0.157X_3 + 0.00000138X_4$
   (0.0934) (0.311) (0.0798) (0.000000807)
   F value = 2.93
   $R = 0.65$; $R^2 = 0.42$; $\Delta R^2 = 0.02$
   $\overline{C} = 0.95$; $DW = 1.92$

5. $Y = 0.0163 + 0.678X_1 - 1.028X_2 + 0.149X_3 + 0.00000133X_4 + 0.270X_5$
   (0.0970) (0.326) (0.0798) (0.000000805) (0.209)
   F value = 1.62
   $R = 0.65$; $R^2 = 0.42$; $\Delta R^2 = 0$

Y = Futures prices

X_1 = Oils index

X_2 = Consumption/Stocks

X_3 = Lagged price Y_{t-1}

X_4 = Short hedging

X_5 = Interest rate: Commercial paper

X_6 = Demand

X_7 = Consumption

X_8 = Exports

X_9 = Production

X_{10} = Demand/Stocks

X_{11} = Production/Stocks

X_{12} = Interest rate: Treasury Bills

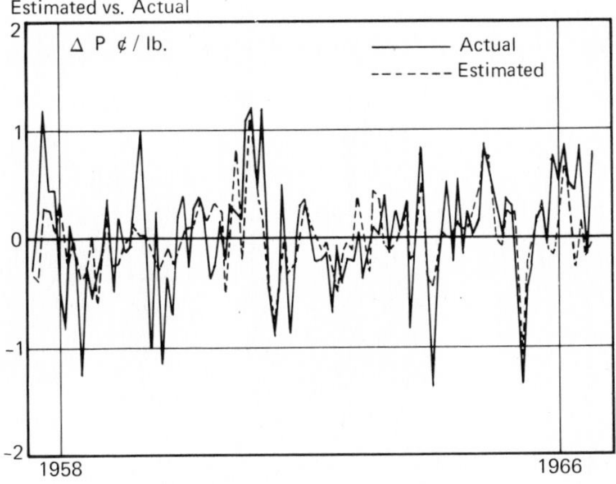

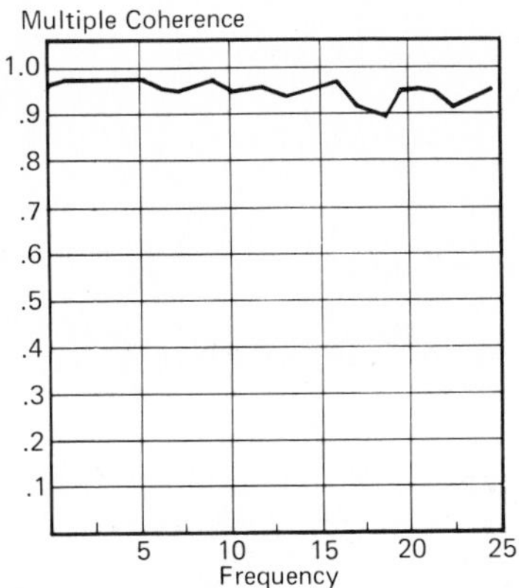

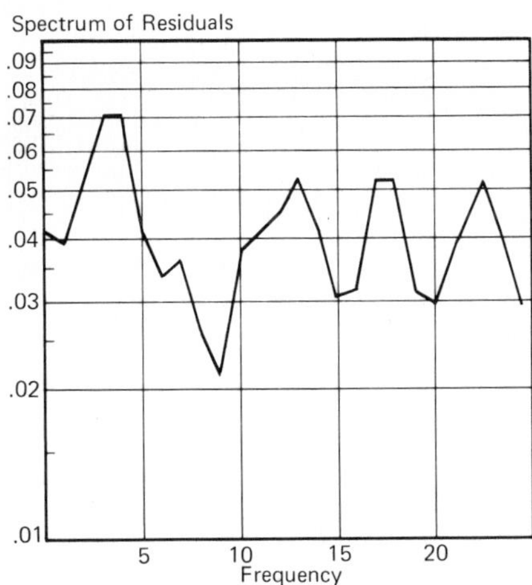

Figure 7-3 Regression of Cottonseed Oil Futures Price Differences.

Table 7-4

Cottonseed Oil Cash Prices: Stepwise Explanation of Price Behavior

Monthly: First Differences
August 1957-June 1966
Observations = 107

Regression in Steps:

1. $Y = 0.0159 + 0.464X_1$
   (0.0859)
   F value = 29.19
   $R = 0.47$; $R^2 = 0.22$

2. $Y = 0.0195 + 0.425X_1 + 0.475X_2$
   (0.0776) (0.0942)
   F value = 25.51
   $R = 0.61$; $R^2 = 0.37$; $\Delta R^2 = 0.15$

3. $Y = 0.0200 + 0.355X_1 + 0.536X_2 - 0.582X_3$
   (0.0748) (0.0895) (0.148)
   F value = 15.52
   $R = 0.68$; $R^2 = 0.46$; $\Delta R^2 = 0.09$
   $\overline{C} = 0.96$; $DW = 1.74$

4. $Y = 0.0203 + 0.375X_1 + 0.518X_2 - 0.578X_3 + 0.00000108X_4$
   (0.0760) (0.0901) (0.147) (0.000000793)
   F value = 1.86
   $R = 0.68$; $R^2 = 0.47$; $\Delta R^2 = 0.01$

Y = Cash prices

X_1 = Lagged price Y_{t-1}

X_2 = Oil index

X_3 = Production/Stocks

X_4 = Short hedging

X_5 = Demand

X_6 = Supply

X_7 = Consumption

X_8 = Exports

X_9 = Production

X_{10} = Consumption/Stocks

X_{11} = Demand/Stocks

X_{12} = Interest rate: Treasury bills

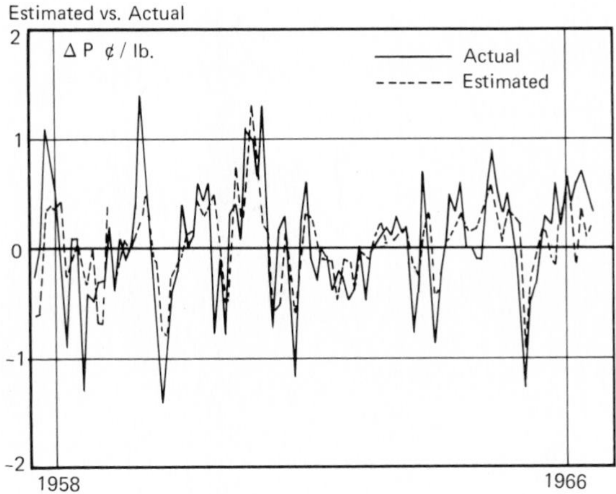

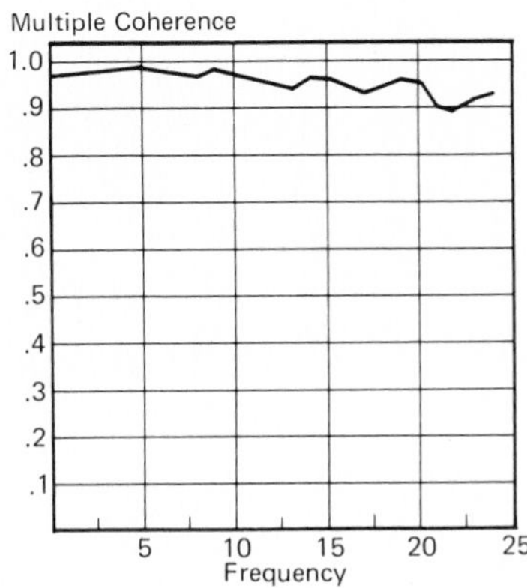

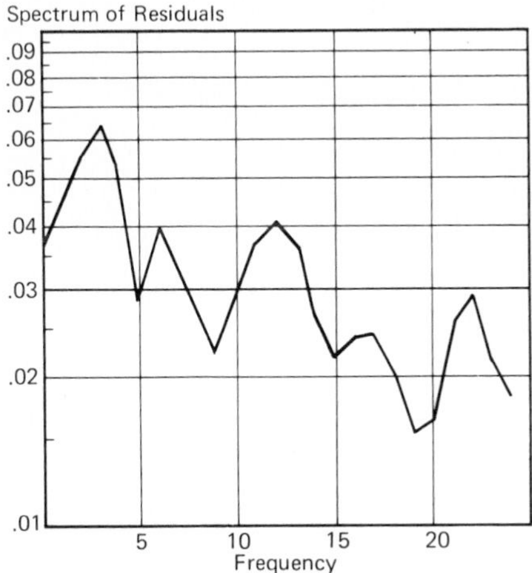

Figure 7-4 Regression of Cottonseed Oil Cash Price Differences.

Soybean Meal

The first variables to enter the stepwise regression explaining meal futures prices are the meal index, long speculating, stocks, and the stock/consumption ratio in that order. As shown in Table 7-5, the appearance of the stocks/consumption ratio immediately after stocks does suggest a multicollinear relationship. Actually, the ratio is a measure of excess stocks rather than stock level, and introducing the ratio causes the regression estimates to vary only slightly.

The next variables to be included are the interest rate on commercial paper followed by demand. The cutoff point is chosen just beyond the inclusion of the interest rate, even though the overall F value is significant at the 95% level for both the interest rate and demand. The latter has been removed because the ratio of the regression coefficient to its standard error is small (1.96 required for significance using the t test at the 95% level). The coefficient of determination and the multiple coherence reached at the cut-off point are significant at the 95% level ($R^2 = 0.34 > 0.09$ and $C = 0.67 > 0.63$). The poor fit of estimated to actual price differences described in Figure 7-5 as well as the relatively lower level of multiple correlation both agree with the excessive fluctuations in the accompanying coherence diagram. The coherence is higher in the seasonal frequencies and much lower in the shorter-run frequencies. This suggests that only annual movements in prices have been explained. While the spectrum of residuals is difficult to interpret, the Durbin-Watson statistic does not suggest autocorrelation ($d = 1.87 > d_u = 1.65$). (See pp. 174-175.)

The major change in the specification of the cash price equation is that the soybean crushing margin, defined in Chapter 6, is the first variable to enter. This suggests that the soybean meal cash prices are more related to the decision to crush soybeans than are the futures prices. One would also expect a relationship between the margin and meal prices rather than between the margin and oil prices, since beans are crushed principally for meal. The next variables to enter significantly, as reported in Table 7-6 are the meal index, demand, and long speculating. The soybean stocks variable enters before demand, but since stocks is a quantity variable similar to demand and produces instability in the regression coefficients, it is omitted. The coefficient of determination and average coherence achieved at the cutoff point are significant at the 95% level ($R^2 = 0.46 > 0.32$ and $C = 0.70 > 0.63$). While the fit of estimated to actual values as shown in Figure 7-6 corresponds to that of futures prices a more greatly exaggerated seasonal peak occurs in the coherence diagram, confirming the explanation at only seasonal frequencies. Both the spectrum of residuals and the Durbin-Watson statistic are inconclusive with respect to autocorrelation ($d_u = 1.63 > d = 1.59 > 1.46 = d_l$). (See pp. 176-177.)

Table 7-5

Soybean Meal Futures Prices: Stepwise Explanation of Price Behavior

Monthly: First Differences
August 1957-June 1966
Observations = 107

Regression in Steps:

1. $Y = 0.308 + 2.025X_1$
(0.468)
F value = 18.74
$R = 0.44$; $R^2 = 0.19$

2. $Y = 0.293 + 1.972X_1 + 0.0000211X_2$
(0.444) (0.00000595)
F value = 12.55
$R = 0.48$; $R^2 = 0.23$; $\Delta R^2 = 0.04$

3. $Y = 0.282 + 1.75X_1 + 0.0000241X_2 + 0.0291X_3$
(0.436) (0.00000584) (0.0101)
F value = 8.33
$R = 0.54$; $R^2 = 0.29$; $\Delta R^2 = 0.06$

4. $Y = 0.249 + 1.595X_1 + 0.0000243X_2 + 0.0808X_3 - 33.686X_4$
(0.432) (0.00000572) (0.0245) (14.564)
F value = 5.35
$R = 0.56$; $R^2 = 0.31$; $\Delta R^2 = 0.02$

5. $Y = 0.279 + 1.374X_1 + 0.0000252X_2 + 0.0844X_3 - 35.286X_4 - 2.139X_5$
(0.448) (0.00000570) (0.0243) (14.462) (1.261)
F value = 2.87
$R = 0.58$; $R^2 = 0.34$; $\Delta R^2 = 0.03$
$\overline{C} = 0.67$; $DW = 1.87$

6. $Y = 0.286 + 1.502X_1 + 0.0000244X_2 + 0.114X_3 - 57.618X_4 - 2.164X_5 - 0.00752X_6$
(0.451) (0.00000567) (0.0300) (19.788) (1.251) (0.00459)
F value = 2.68
$R = 0.61$; $R^2 = 0.37$; $\Delta R^2 = 0.02$

Y = Futures prices
X_1 = Meal index
X_2 = Long speculating
X_3 = Stocks
X_4 = Stocks/Consumption
X_5 = Interest rate: Commercial paper
X_6 = Demand
X_7 = Lagged price Y_{t-1}
X_8 = Supply
X_9 = Consumption
X_{10} = Production
X_{11} = Soybean consumption
X_{12} = Soybean stocks
X_{13} = Consumption/Stocks
X_{14} = Production/Stocks
X_{15} = Soybean margin
X_{16} = Consumer installment credit: Extended
X_{17} = Consumer installment credit: Net

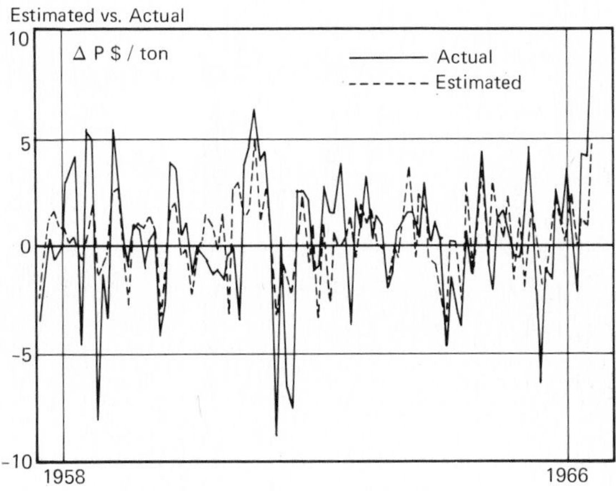

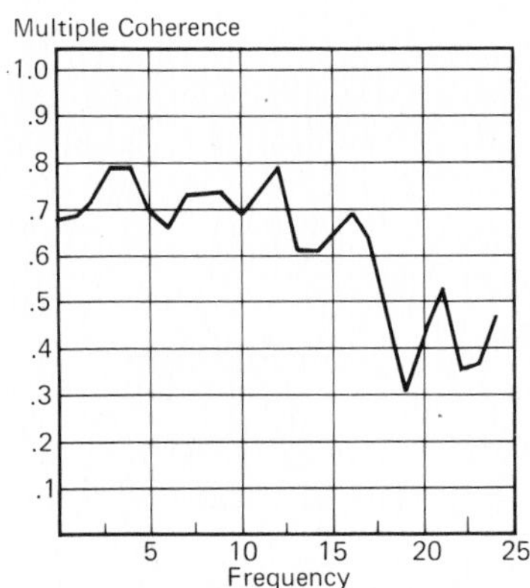

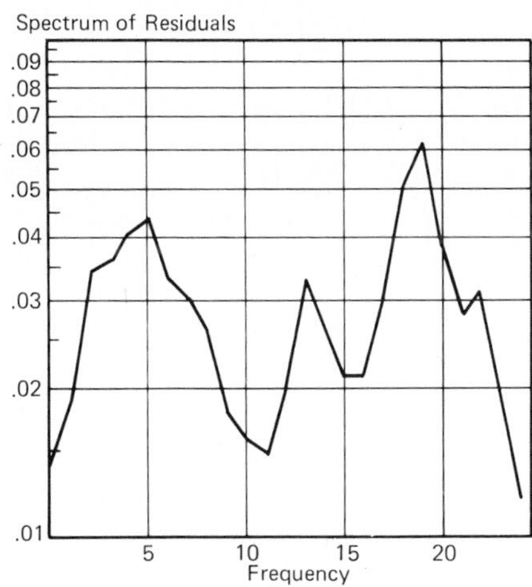

Figure 7-5 Regression of Soybean Meal Futures Price Differences.

Table 7-6

Soybean Meal Cash Prices: Stepwise Explanation of Price Behavior

Monthly: First Differences
August 1957-June 1966
Observations = 107

Regression in Steps:

1. $Y = 0.378 + 0.276X_1$
   (0.0412)
   F value = 44.70
   $R = 0.55$; $R^2 = 0.30$

2. $Y = 0.325 + 0.258X_1 + 2.138X_2$
   (0.0387) (0.530)
   F value = 16.27
   $R = 0.63$; $R^2 = 0.40$; $\Delta R^2 = 0.10$

3. $Y = 0.367 + 0.240X_1 + 2.476X_2 - 0.0120X_3$
   (0.0378) (0.523) (0.00403)
   F value = 10.09
   $R = 0.67$; $R^2 = 0.45$; $\Delta R^2 = 0.05$

4. $Y = 0.355 + 0.233X_1 + 2.442X_2 - 0.0118X_3 + 0.0000150X_4$
   (0.0372) (0.513) (0.00395) (0.00000670)
   F value = 5.03
   $R = 0.69$; $R^2 = 0.47$; $\Delta R^2 = 0.02$
   $\overline{C} = 0.70$; $DW = 1.59$

5. $Y = 0.349 + 0.238X_1 + 2.268X_2 - 0.00856X_3 + 0.0000170X_4 + 11.771X_5$
   (0.0371) (0.524) (0.00450) (0.00000679) (7.925)
   F value = 2.21
   $R = 0.69$; $R^2 = 0.48$; $\Delta R^2 = 0.01$

Y = Cash prices
X_1 = Soybean margin
X_2 = Meal index
X_3 = Demand
X_4 = Long speculating
X_5 = Stocks/Consumption
X_6 = Production
X_7 = Stocks
X_8 = Soybean consumption
X_9 = Soybean stocks
X_{10} = Consumption/Stocks
X_{11} = Production/Stocks
X_{12} = Interest rate: Commercial paper
X_{13} = Lagged price Y_{t-1}

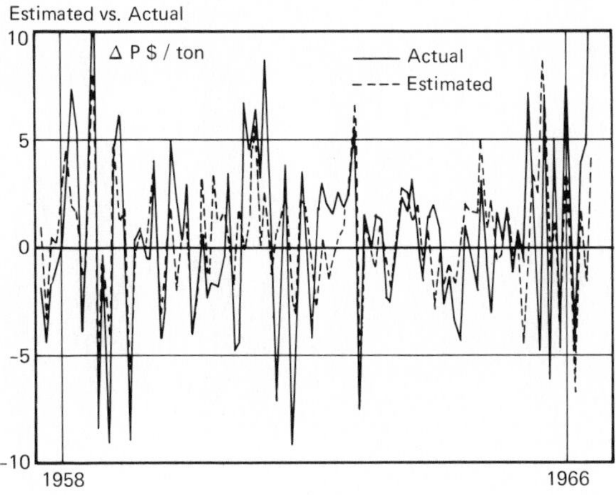

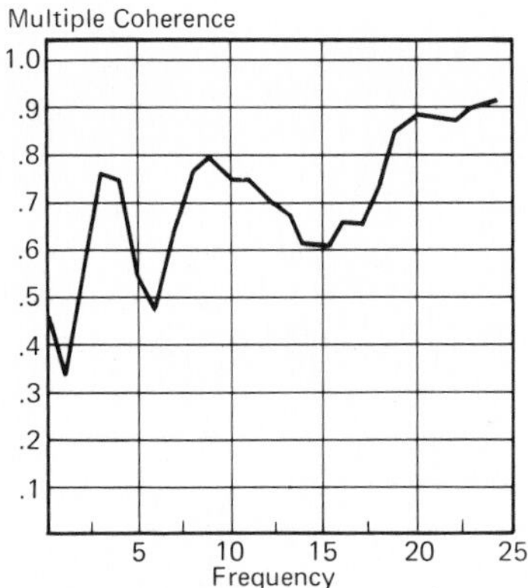

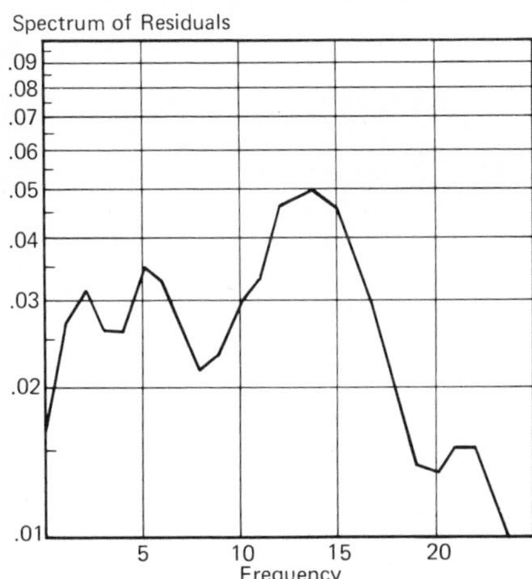

Figure 7-6 Regression of Soybean Meal Cash Price Differences.

Soybeans

Of the possible explanatory variables listed in Table 7-7, the first variable to enter the explanation of futures prices is the yield-weight price index. This conforms to the common belief that soybean prices depend on the values of oil and meal. The crushing margin enters next, but is omitted from the equation since the margin added to the yield index produces the same price series as that of the dependent variable. The next significant variables to enter are the lagged price, short hedging, and the net change in consumer installment credit. At this point, the resulting coefficient of determination and average coherence are significant at the 95% level ($R^2 = 0.61 > 0.08$ and $\bar{C} = 0.90 > 0.63$). The advantage of including the lagged dependent variable is shown in Figure 7-7, where the equation responds to the wide fluctuations in prices. The multiple coherence diagram is constant over all but the shortest-run frequencies; the spectrum of residuals is remarkably flat, indicating no autocorrelation. (See pp. 180-181.)

The yield-weight price index, lagged prices, and short hedging also are the first three variables to enter the explanation for cash prices. The stocks variable, which was the first insignificant variable to enter the futures equation, now appears significantly in the cash equation ($F = 3.36 > 2.46$). Table 7-8 further reports that the next variable to enter, the stocks/consumption ratio, is insignificant. After the inclusion of the stocks variable, the coefficient of determination and average coherence are both significant at the 95% level ($R^2 = 0.60 > 0.08$ and $\bar{C} = 0.88 > 0.63$). As disclosed in Figure 7-8, the equation responds to price swings similar to the futures equation. The coherence diagram is correspondingly flat except for the shortest-run frequencies. The spectrum of residuals is sufficiently flat to imply a lack of serious autocorrelation. (See pp. 182-183.)

Table 7-7

Soybeans Futures Prices: Stepwise Explanation of Price Behavior

Monthly: First Differences
August 1957-June 1966
Observations = 107

Regression in Steps:

1. $Y = 0.430 + 0.507X_1$
   (0.0637)
   F value = 63.29
   $R = 0.62;\ R^2 = 0.38$

2. $Y = 0.252 + 0.450X_1 + 0.405X_2$
   $(0.0568)\ (0.0714)$
   F value = 32.22
   $R = 0.73;\ R^2 = 0.53;\ \Delta R^2 = 0.15$

3. $Y = 0.203 + 0.429X_1 + 0.412X_2 + 0.000150X_3$
   $(0.0525)\ (0.0657)\ (0.0000341)$
   F value = 19.45
   $R = 0.77;\ R^2 = 0.59;\ \Delta R^2 = 0.06$

4. $Y = 0.220 + 0.413X_1 + 0.437X_2 + 0.000142X_3 - 0.00227X_4$
   $(0.0527)\ (0.0665)\ (0.0000340)\ (0.00126)$
   F value = 3.24
   $R = 0.78;\ R^2 = 0.61;\ \Delta R^2 = 0.02$
   $\overline{C} = 0.90;\ DW = 1.96$

5. $Y = 0.600 + 0.406X_1 + 0.408X_2 + 0.000133X_3 - 0.00216X_4 - 0.236X_5$
   $(0.0527)\ (0.0693)\ (0.0000346)\ (0.00125)\ (0.164)$
   F value = 2.05
   $R = 0.79;\ R^2 = 0.62;\ \Delta R^2 = 0.01$

Y = Futures prices
X_1 = Yield index
X_2 = Lagged price Y_{t-1}
X_3 = Short hedging
X_4 = Consumer installment credit: Net
X_5 = Stocks
X_6 = Demand
X_7 = Consumption
X_8 = Exports
X_9 = Consumption/Stocks
X_{10} = Demand/Stocks
X_{11} = Soybean index
X_{12} = Grain index
X_{13} = Soybean margin
X_{14} = Federal Reserve: Excess
X_{15} = Interest rate: Commercial paper

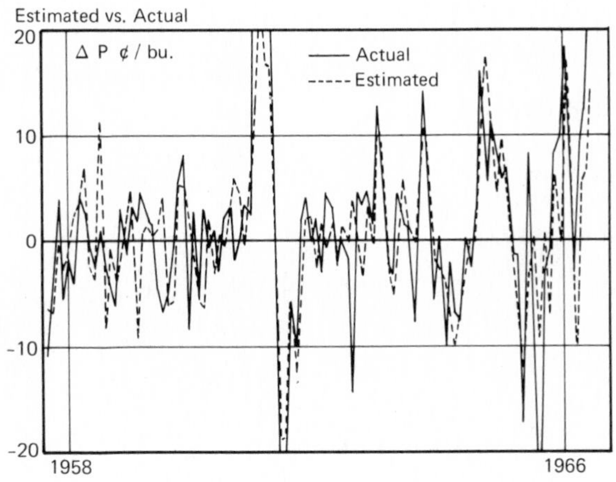

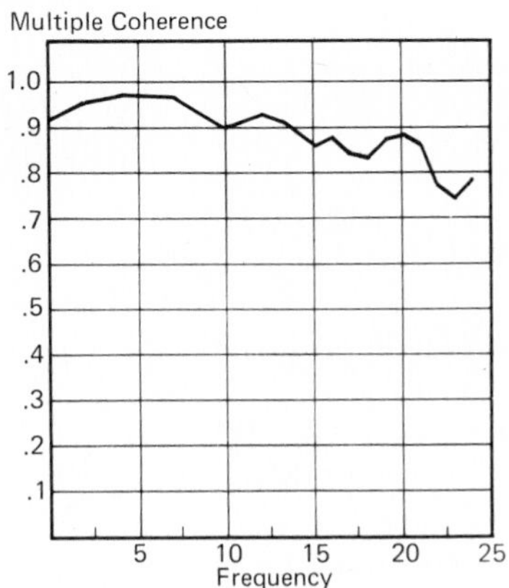

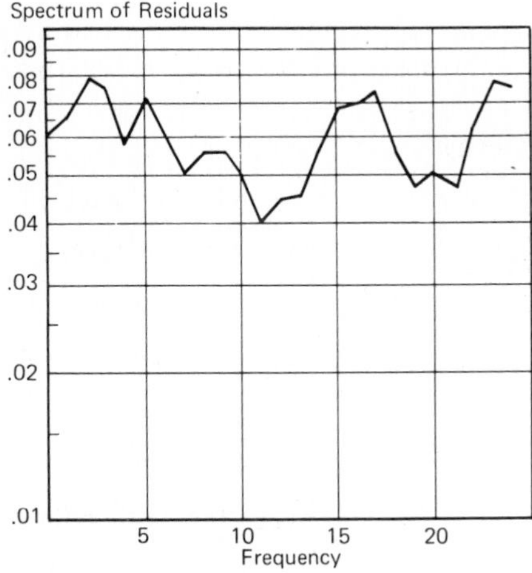

Figure 7-7 Regression of Soybeans Futures Price Differences.

Table 7-8

Soybeans Cash Prices: Stepwise Explanation of Price Behavior

Monthly: First Differences
August 1957-June 1966
Observations = 107

Regression in Steps:

1. $Y = 0.398 + 0.572X_1$
   (0.0594)
   F value = 93.01
   $R = 0.69$; $R^2 = 0.47$

2. $Y = 0.276 + 0.516X_1 + 0.310X_2$
   (0.0562) (0.0706)
   F value = 19.20
   $R = 0.75$; $R^2 = 0.56$; $\Delta R^2 = 0.09$

3. $Y = 0.238 + 0.500X_1 + 0.333X_2 + 0.0000919X_3$
   (0.0551) (0.0694) (0.0000356)
   F value = 6.64
   $R = 0.76$; $R^2 = 0.58$; $\Delta R^2 = 0.02$

4. $Y = 0.737 + 0.490X_1 + 0.299X_2 + 0.0000765X_3 - 0.310X_4$
   (0.0548) (0.0710) (0.0000362) (0.169)
   F value = 3.36
   $R = 0.77$; $R^2 = 0.60$; $\Delta R^2 = 0.02$
   $\overline{C} = 0.88$; $DW = 1.86$

5. $Y = 0.726 + 0.498X_1 + 0.300X_2 + 0.0000655X_3 - 0.306X_4 + 5.058X_5$
   (0.0552) (0.0710) (0.0000378) (0.169) (4.876)
   F value = 1.08
   $R = 0.77$; $R^2 = 0.60$; $\Delta R^2 = 0$

Y = Cash prices
X_1 = Yield index
X_2 = Lagged price Y_{t-1}
X_3 = Short hedging
X_4 = Stocks
X_5 = Consumption/Stocks
X_6 = Demand
X_7 = Consumption
X_8 = Exports
X_9 = Demand/Stocks
X_{10} = Soybean index
X_{11} = Grain index
X_{12} = Soybean margin
X_{13} = Consumer installment credit: Net
X_{14} = Interest rate: Commercial paper

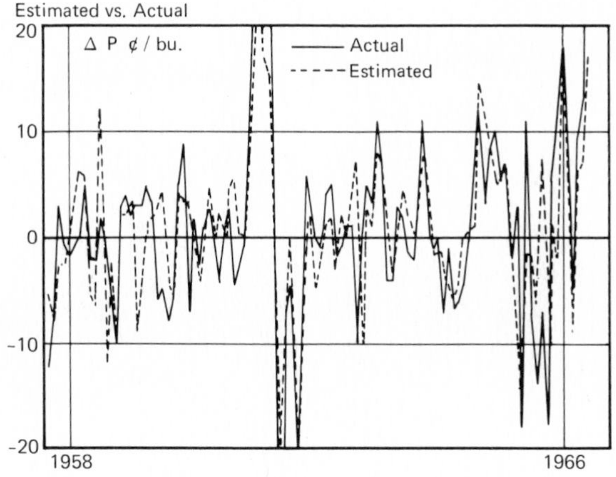

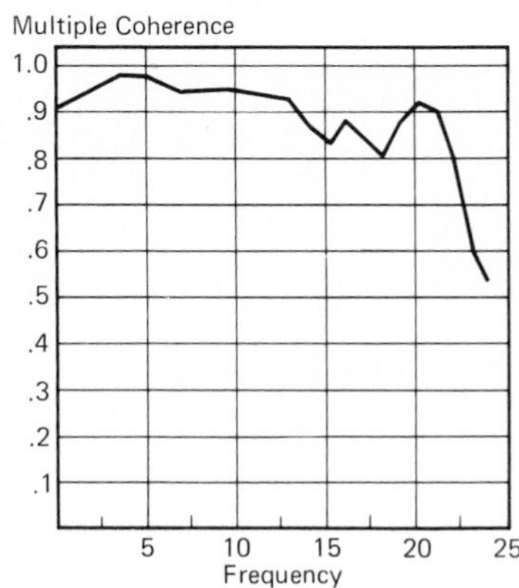

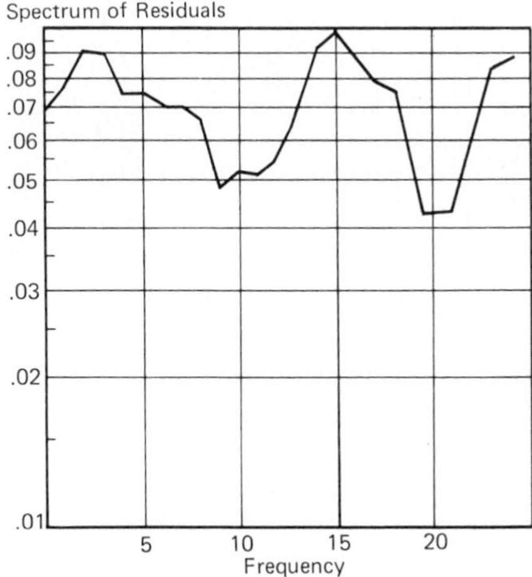

Figure 7-8 Regression of Soybeans Cash Price Differences.

Rye

The first explanatory variables to enter the rye futures price equation are the consumption/stocks ratio, the grain index, and short hedging in that order. When short hedging is added to the explanation, Table 7-9 reports a slight instability in the regression coefficients, symptomatic of a multicollinear relationship. The instability, however, is not considered sufficient to justify removing that variable. The level of explanation which could be reached at this stage or by including the next variable is low. At the cutoff point, the coefficient of determination is significant but the multiple coherence is not ($R^2 = 0.22 > 0.06$ and $\bar{C} = 0.47 < 0.63$). The low level of correlation is reflected in the poor fit of estimated to actual price differences, shown in Figure 7-9. Accordingly, the coherence diagram fluctuates widely about only moderate coherence values. While the Durbin-Watson statistic reveals no autocorrelation ($d = 1.74 > d_u = 1.60$), the spectrum of residuals is inconclusive. (See pp. 186-187.)

The explanation of cash behavior differs from the above in that stocks enters first and then is followed by the grain index, the demand/stocks ratio, and short hedging. Table 7-10 shows some multicollinearity with the addition of the grain index, but not a sufficient amount to warrant its removal. The coefficient of determination improves for the cash price explanation and is significant at the 95% level ($R^2 = 0.36 > 0.08$). The coherence value, however, remains insignificant ($C = 0.52 < 0.63$) and this result, together with the fluctuating coherence diagram shown in Figure 7-10, suggests a poor explanation for the cash price series. The Durbin-Watson statistic discloses no autocorrelation ($d = 2.10 > d_u = 1.63$), while the spectrum of residuals signifies a form of negative autocorrelation. (See pp. 188-189.)

Table 7-9

Rye Future Prices: Stepwise Explanation of Price Behavior

Monthly: First Differences
August 1957-June 1966
Observations = 107

Regression in Steps:

1. $Y = -0.112 - 99.988X_1$
   (30.664)
   F value = 10.63
   $R = 0.30$; $R^2 = 0.10$

2. $Y = -0.145 - 97.633X_1 + 0.403X_2$
   (29.655) (0.140)
   F value = 8.28
   $R = 0.40$; $R^2 = 0.16$; $\Delta R^2 = 0.06$

3. $Y = -0.133 - 99.307X_1 + 0.421X_2 + 0.00143X_3$
   (28.622) (0.135) (0.000488)
   F value = 8.62
   $R = 0.48$; $R^2 = 0.22$; $\Delta R^2 = 0.06$
   $\overline{C} = 0.47$; $DW = 2.03$

4. $Y = -0.141 - 100.777X_1 + 0.446X_2 + 0.00138X_3 - 10.469X_4$
   (28.646) (0.138) (0.000491) (10.100)
   F value = 1.07
   $R = 0.48$; $R^2 = 0.22$; $\Delta R^2 = 0$

Y = Futures prices

X_1 = Consumption/Stocks

X_2 = Grain index

X_3 = Short hedging

X_4 = Exports/Stocks

X_5 = Demand

X_6 = Stocks

X_7 = Stocks/Consumption

X_8 = Demand/Stocks

X_9 = Rye index

X_{10} = Consumer installment credit: Extended

X_{11} = Consumer installment credit: Net

X_{12} = Federal Reserve: Net reserves

X_{13} = Interest rate: Commercial paper

X_{14} = Lagged price Y_{t-1}

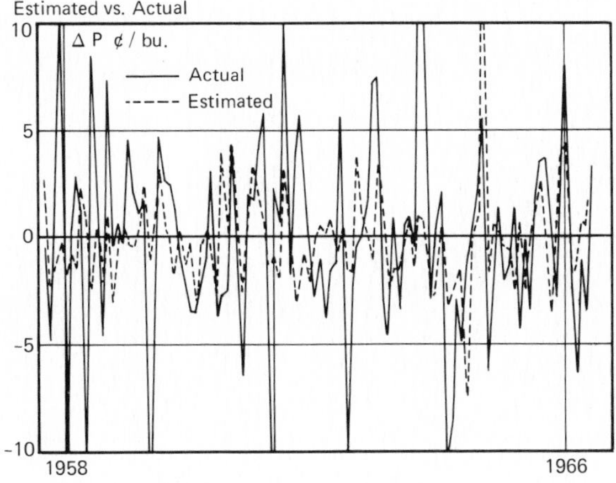

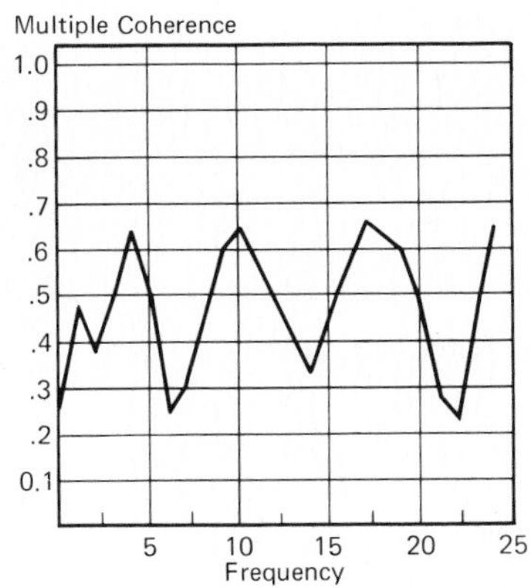

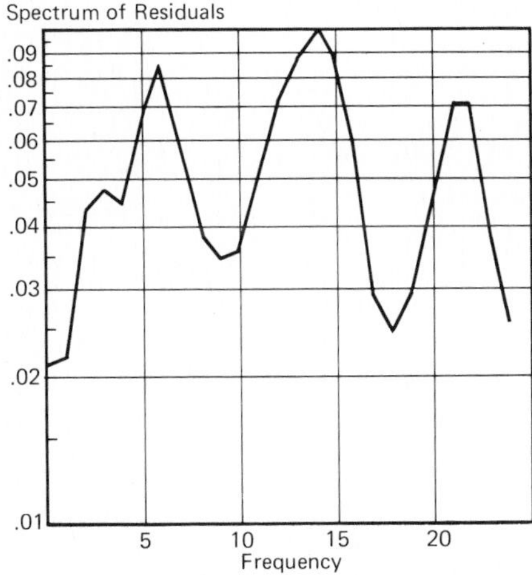

Figure 7-9 Regression of Rye Futures Price Differences.

Table 7-10

Rye Cash Prices: Stepwise Explanation of Price Behavior

Monthly: First Differences
August 1957-June 1966
Observations = 107

Regression in Steps:

1. $Y = -0.142 + 0.000339X_1$
   (0.0000773)
   F value = 19.20
   $R = 0.39$; $R^2 = 0.15$

2. $Y = -0.187 + 0.000373X_1 + 0.496X_2$
   (0.0000707) (0.104)
   F value = 22.65
   $R = 0.56$; $R^2 = 0.31$; $\Delta R^2 = 0.16$

3. $Y = -0.197 + 0.000304X_1 + 0.527X_2 - 17.581X_3$
   (0.0000761) (0.103) (7.937)
   F value = 4.91
   $R = 0.58$; $R^2 = 0.34$; $\Delta R^2 = 0.03$

4. $Y = -0.190 + 0.000305X_1 + 0.532X_2 - 16.333X_3 + 0.000614X_4$
   (0.0000754) (0.102) (7.902) (0.000365)
   F value = 2.81
   $R = 0.60$; $R^2 = 0.36$; $\Delta R^2 = 0.02$
   $\bar{C} = 0.52$; $DW = 2.10$

5. $Y = -0.196 + 0.000293X_1 + 0.532X_2 - 14.351X_3 + 0.000575X_4 + 0.00454X_5$
   (0.0000758) (0.102) (8.031) (0.000366) (0.00357)
   F value = 1.62
   $R = 0.60$; $R^2 = 0.36$; $\Delta R^2 = 0$

Y = Cash prices
X_1 = Stocks
X_2 = Grain index
X_3 = Demand/Stocks
X_4 = Short hedging
X_5 = Consumption
X_6 = Demand
X_7 = Exports
X_8 = Consumption/Stocks
X_9 = Stocks/Consumption
X_{10} = Exports/Stocks
X_{11} = Rye index
X_{12} = Consumer installment credit: Extended
X_{13} = Consumer installment credit: Net
X_{14} = Lagged price Y_{t-1}

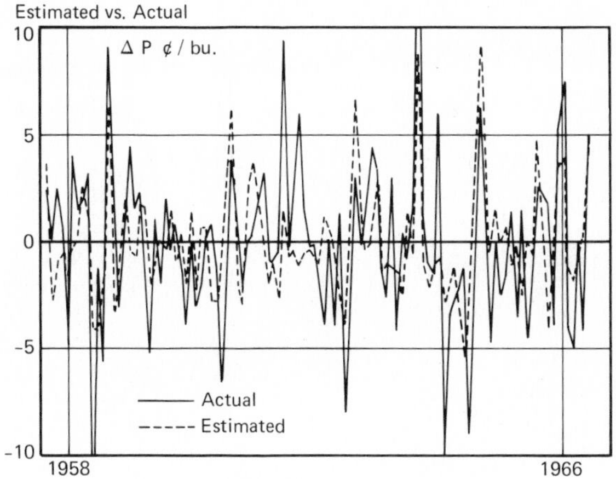

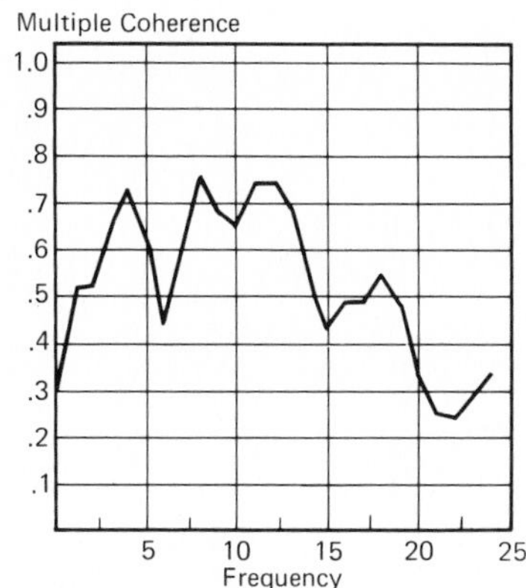

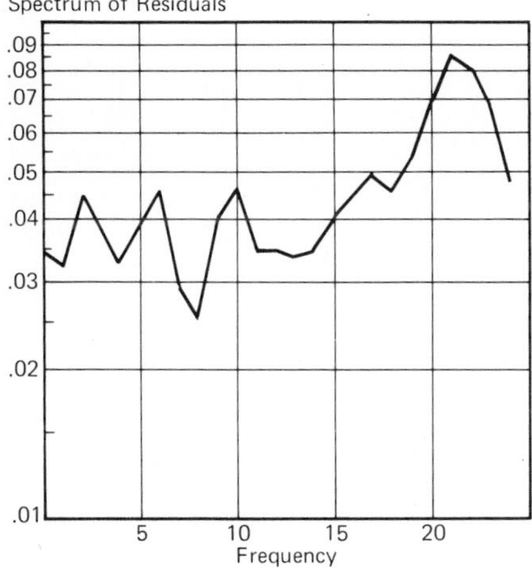

Figure 7-10 Regression of Rye Cash Price Differences.

Wheat

Wheat futures and cash price fluctuations proved to be the most difficult of the commodities to explain. First of all, wheat is not normally competitive with any other grain, and consequently wheat prices cannot be explained by the prices of the other grains. As shown in Tables 6-6 and 6-7, the coherences of wheat futures and cash prices with the grain price index are 0.12 and 0.16 respectively. An alternative approach for determining the response of wheat prices to other prices is to construct an index reflecting the general price level. One method suggested in commodity literature consists of dividing the wheat price series by the Dow Jones spot or futures price index and of subsequently using the index to explain price movements.[6] As could be expected, such an index is highly correlated with wheat prices; this is reflected in the high coherences (0.97, 0.80) in Tables 7-11 and 7-12 (pp. 192 and 194).

The equations derived for wheat prices, therefore, display high levels of correlation and coherence, but this relationship results from serial correlation between wheat prices and the index rather than between prices and the explanatory variables. As a result, both the wheat futures and cash explanations are extremely inadequate. The major difficulty encountered, however, is not that wheat prices fail to respond to prices or other economic determinants, but rather that the extensive controls placed on wheat prices by the government prevents such a response. This particular explanation has been put forth by both Gray and Hieronymus. Gray has produced empirical evidence showing that the government loan program induces the price pattern peculiar to wheat; Hieronymus has explained the seasonal pattern in terms of a buying and selling reaction pattern to the loan price.[7]

Of the explanatory variables listed in Table 7-11, the relative index, long speculating, and lagged price enter significantly into the regression for futures prices. The maintenance price level or farm parity price comes in next, but is not significant. The coefficient of determination and the average coherence produced from the first three variables are significant at the 95% level ($R^2 = 0.86 > 0.06$ and $\bar{C} = 0.96 > 0.63$). The diagrams of Figure 7-11 are rendered somewhat meaningless by the serial correlation between the dependent price series and the relative price index. The coherence diagram is flat and no autocorrelation is displayed by the spectrum of residuals. (See pp. 192-193.)

Practically the same explanation occurs for cash price fluctuations. The relative index and short hedging in that order are the only variables to enter the regression significantly. Table 7-12 reports determination and coherence values of 0.75 and 0.80, both of which are significant at the 95% level. The coherence diagram given in Figure 7-12 fluctuates sufficiently to indicate that cash prices are not satisfactorily explained by the given price influences. Finally, no autocorrelation can be detected from the residual spectrum or the Durbin-Watson statistic ($d = 1.97 > d_u = 1.58$). (See pp. 194-195.)

Table 7-11

Wheat Futures Prices: Stepwise Explanation of Price Behavior

Monthly: First Differences
August 1957-June 1966
Observations = 107

Regression in Steps:

1. $Y = -0.240 + 127.581X_1$
   (5.380)
   F value = 56.23
   $R = 0.92$; $R^2 = 0.84$

2. $Y = -0.244 + 127.318X_1 + 0.000190X_2$
   (5.290) (0.0000881)
   F value = 4.66
   $R = 0.92$; $R^2 = 0.85$; $\Delta R^2 = 0.01$

3. $Y = -0.205 + 127.161X_1 + 0.000203X_2 + 0.0789X_3$
   (5.208) (0.0000870) (0.0382)
   F value = 4.27
   $R = 0.93$; $R^2 = 0.86$; $\Delta R^2 = 0.01$
   $\bar{C} = 0.97$; $DW = 1.53$

4. $Y = -0.208 + 127.161X_1 + 0.000210X_2 + 0.0802X_3 + 0.0646X_4$
   (5.224) (0.0000879) (0.0383) (0.107)
   F value = 0.27
   $R = 0.93$; $R^2 = 0.86$; $\Delta R^2 = 0$

Y = Futures prices
X_1 = Relative index
X_2 = Long speculating
X_3 = Lagged price Y_{t-1}
X_4 = Parity price
X_5 = Demand
X_6 = Consumption
X_7 = Stocks
X_8 = Consumption/Stocks
X_9 = Stocks/Consumption
X_{10} = Demand/Stocks
X_{11} = Exports/Stocks
X_{12} = Grain index
X_{13} = Consumer installment credit: Net
X_{14} = Consumer installment credit: Extended
X_{15} = Interest rate: Commercial paper

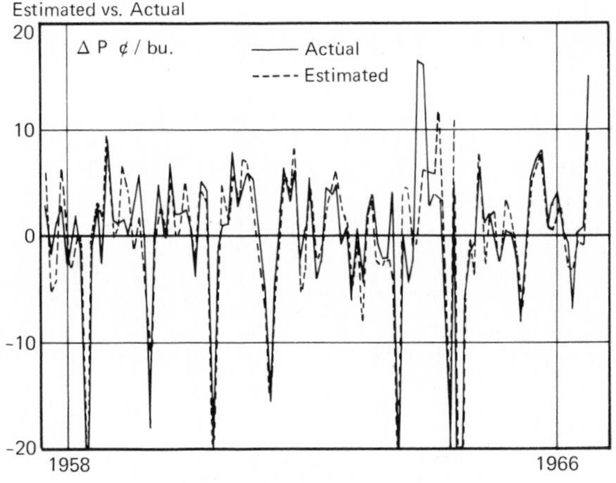

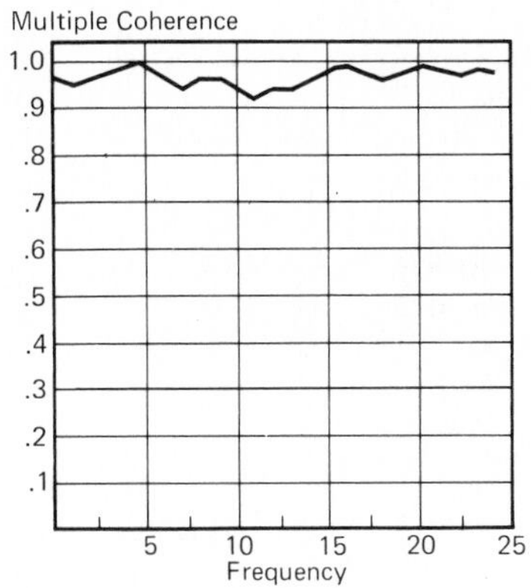

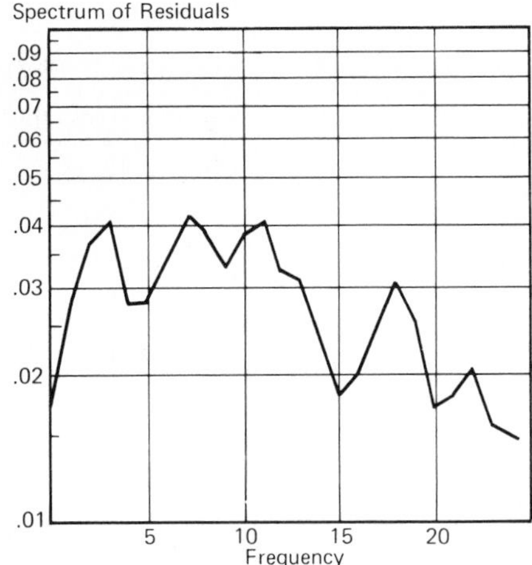

Figure 7-11 Regression of Wheat Futures Price Differences.

Table 7-12

Wheat Cash Prices: Stepwise Explanation of Price Behavior

Monthly: First Differences
August 1957-June 1966
Observations = 107

Regression in Steps:

1. $Y = -0.143 + 140.828X_1$
   (8.453)
   F value = 27.76
   $R = 0.85$; $R^2 = 0.72$

2. $Y = -0.157 + 140.358X_1 - 0.0000622X_2$
   (8.199) (0.0000226)
   F value = 7.58
   $R = 0.86$; $R^2 = 0.75$; $\Delta R^2 = 0.03$
   $\overline{C} = 0.80$; $DW = 1.97$

3. $Y = -0.147 + 140.508X_1 - 0.0000640X_2 - 0.146X_3$
   (8.190) (0.0000226) (0.131)
   F value = 1.24
   $R = 0.86$; $R^2 = 0.75$; $\Delta R^2 = 0$

Y = Cash prices

X_1 = Relative index

X_2 = Short hedging

X_3 = Parity price

X_4 = Demand

X_5 = Consumption

X_6 = Stocks

X_7 = Consumption/Stocks

X_8 = Stocks/Consumption

X_9 = Demand/Stocks

X_{10} = Exports/Stocks

X_{11} = Grain index

X_{12} = Consumer installment credit: Net

X_{13} = Consumer installment credit: Extended

X_{14} = Interest rate: Treasury bills

X_{15} = Lagged price Y_{t-1}

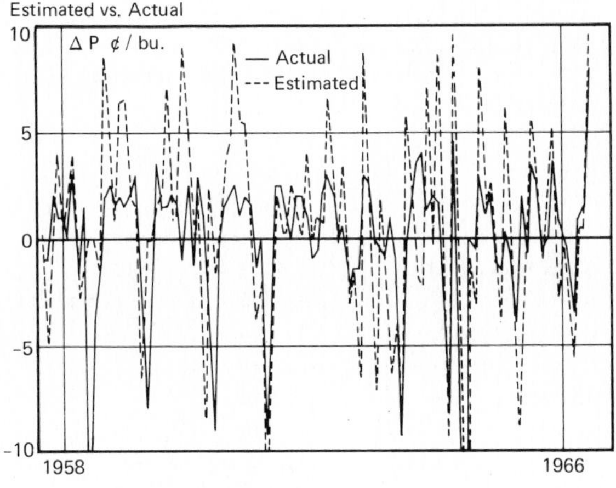

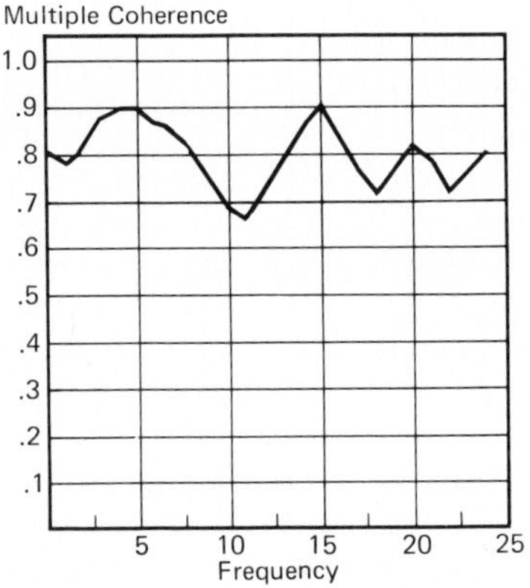

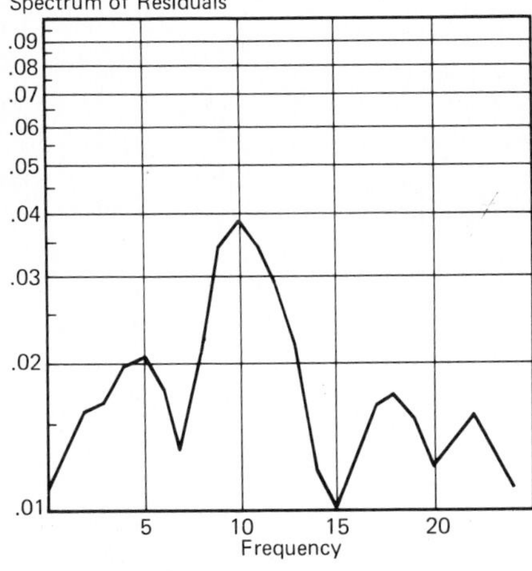

Figure 7-12 Regression of Wheat Cash Price Differences.

Conclusions

The results of the price explanations taken together will be evaluated within the framework of a general model of price behavior in the next chapter. For the present, it would be helpful to comment on the degree of explanation achieved in the individual equations. It is worthwhile to begin with the appropriateness of the stepwise method as a technique for formulating the equations. The method's appropriateness can be judged in terms of the ordering of the explanatory variables as well as in terms of their total effect in aggregate. Concerning the first of these points, one finds a rational ordering of the explanatory influences in the various equations. The specification of futures price equations tends toward speculative influences while cash price explanations favor physical influences. This favorable outcome is particularly evident for soybean oil, where short hedging and stocks are among the first variables to enter the futures and cash price equations respectively.

The stepwise method also proved effective for aggregating the various price influences. The simple coherence values between futures prices and the corresponding price indexes, for example, are 0.51, 0.36, 0.26, 0.44, and 0.21 for the soybean oil, cottonseed oil, soybean meal, soybeans, and rye price series respectively. When these indexes are aggregated with other price influences in the explanatory equations, the corresponding multiple coherence values are higher, with values of 0.98, 0.95, 0.67, 0.90, and 0.47. A similar comparison can be drawn for the cash price series. Simple coherence values between cash prices and the price indexes taken in the same commodity order are 0.51, 0.27, 0.19, 0.52, and 0.24. The corresponding explanatory equations display higher multiple coherences of 0.95, 0.96, 0.70, 0.88, and 0.52 respectively. These values all support the premise that commodity price explanation can be improved by aggregating the various influences, even where the individual price correlations are small.

Evidence as to the quality of fit achieved in aggregating the variables can be obtained from the multiple correlation coefficients and the various spectral diagrams. The coefficients of determination found for the soybean oil, cottonseed oil, soybean meal, soybeans, and rye futures equations are 0.60, 0.42, 0.31, 0.61, and 0.22. Equivalent values for the cash price equations are 0.59, 0.46, 0.47, 0.60, and 0.36 respectively. These values reflect at least a moderate degree of correlation for soybean oil, cottonseed oil, soybean meal, and soybeans and a low degree of correlation for rye. When the corresponding multiple coherence diagrams are examined, one finds constantly high coherences for soybean oil, cottonseed oil, and soybeans but not for soybean meal and rye. This suggests that for at least three of the commodities, almost all of the frequency components of the price series are moderately explicable.

The corresponding spectra of residuals have exhibited several forms of autocorrelation, although these results have not always been confirmed by the Durbin-Watson statistic. With the exception of the soybean oil and cottonseed oil cash equations, the commodity equations exhibiting moderate levels of correlation also displayed residual spectra free from autocorrelation. The relative degree of fluctuation in the spectra of residuals suggests that the equation residuals do not always have the most favorable properties, i.e., the normal distribution required to satisfy the least-squares application. These diagrams, however, could be made smoother with an improved spectral window. It should be emphasized that while the Durbin-Watson statistic best measures first-order autocorrelation, the spectrum of residuals is capable of detecting first and higher order, positive and negative autocorrelation. In conclusion, one finds a moderate fit for possibly five of the twelve price difference equations. This is not a very high score, but it is reasonable when one considers the near random character of the price fluctuations.

Appendix to Chapter 7

A Comparison of Correlation and Coherence Values

Examining the regression results of Chapter 7, one finds a discrepancy between the multiple correlation coefficients squared and the average multiple coherence values. Simple correlation coefficients squared have also been estimated. Although they are not reported in Chapter 7, these values differ from the average coherence values of Chapter 6. The purpose of this appendix, therefore, is to provide an insight into the differences between correlation and coherence values.

That coherence should represent a measure analogous to that of the correlation coefficient squared or the coefficient of determination can easily be seen from their respective definitions.

$$C(\omega) = \frac{c^2(\omega) + q^2(\omega)}{f_x(\omega) \cdot f_y(\omega)} \tag{7.A.1}$$

$$r^2 = \frac{\text{cov}(y, x)^2}{\text{var}(y) \cdot \text{var}(x)} \tag{7.A.2}$$

The numerator of $C(\omega)$, $c^2(\omega) + q^2(\omega)$ is analogous to the covariance squared in the correlation definition, and the product of individual spectra is similar to the product of the individual variances at frequency ω. The estimating procedures, however, differ for each definition, and, as will be explained below, the estimated values are similar only under certain circumstances.

To determine these circumstances, consider some of the the coherence and correlation values mentioned above. Table 7A-1 summarizes the simple correlation and average coherence values found between soybean oil futures prices and the various price influences. For the one influence (oil index) with a highly significant level of correlation ($t_r = 9.89 \gg 1.96$), the correlation squared value (0.49) approaches that of the average simple coherence (0.51).[g] This same result also occurs for several of the other commodities analyzed earlier. When the nonsignificant correlations are inspected ($t_r < 1.96$), the coherences are much greater than the correlations squared. Average coherences between prices and production, the consumption/stocks ratio, and net consumer instalment credit are 0.14, 0.12, and 0.21 as compared to the respective correlation squared values of 0.02, 0.01, and 0.03. This same result also occurs with the multiple correlation and multiple coherence values. As indicated in Table 7A-2, most of the F values are only slightly greater than the F levels at the cut-off point.[h] Accordingly the coherence values diverge sharply from the correlation values squared. Soybean oil, cottonseed oil, soybean meal, soybeans, and rye show average multiple coherence values of 0.98, 0.95, 0.67, 0.90, and 0.47 in contrast

[g]When $t = r\,(n-2)^{1/2}/(1-r^2)^{1/2}$ is compared to the critical value ($t_{0.95} = 1.96$) of the t distribution, it describes the significance of the sample correlation coefficient against zero.

[h]Rye is an exception to this pattern ($F = 8.62 > 2.46$) but the dependent and independent variables are insufficiently correlated for the coherence and correlation values to be similar.

Table 7A-1

Average Coherence Compared to the Simple Correlation Coefficient Squared: Soybean Oil Futures Prices and Explanatory Variables

Monthly: First Differences
August 1957-June 1966
Observations = 107
Estimated Lags = 24

	$\bar{C}$[a]	r^2	t_r
Consumption	.18	.04	2.08
Production	.14	.04	1.32
Consumption/Stocks	.12	.01	1.28
Stocks/Consumption	.21	.03	1.78
Oil index	.51	.49	9.89
Foreign index	.17	.09	3.31
Short hedging	.25	.14	4.10
Consumer installment credit: Net	.21	.03	1.90

[a]$\bar{C}$ = Coherence averaged over all frequencies.

to the multiple correlations squared of 0.60, 0.42, 0.35, 0.62, and 0.22 respectively.

The main reason for these observed differences is that (unlagged) correlations and average coherence are actually quite different, and alternative ways of measuring the degree to which series are related. The coherence represents the square of the correlation between corresponding frequency components and is so interpreted *at each frequency.* The average coherence is merely a convenient way of summarizing the overall level of the coherence diagram. When a

Table 7A-2

Average Multiple Coherence Compared to the Multiple Correlation Coefficient Squared: Futures Prices and Explanatory Variables

Monthly: First Differences
August 1957-June 1966
Observations = 107
Estimated Lags = 24

	$\overline{C}$ [a]	R^2	*F Value*	$F_{.95}$ *Level*
Soybean oil	.98	.60	3.10	2.46
Cottonseed oil	.95	.42	2.93	2.46
Soybean meal	.67	.35	2.87	2.30
Soybeans	.90	.62	3.24	2.46
Rye	.47	.22	8.62	2.46

[a] $\overline{C}$ = Coherence averaged over all frequencies.

coherence is formed, the use of the optimum lag structure is implied, all lag differences being taken out, as it were, into the phase diagram. The unlagged correlation coefficient, on the other hand, does not allow for any lag structure, as a lagged correlation may have a higher value. Also the unlagged correlation coefficient is an overall, summary measure and takes no account of the idea of decomposing a series into frequency components. There are, therefore, two important reasons why average coherence and squared unlagged correlation can differ: (1) the two time series being used to compute the statistic may have a lag structure, e.g., one series lags the other by k time units; and (2) the theoretical coherence diagram need not be constant, i.e., can change with frequency.

To illustrate these possibilities, first consider the simple model $X_t = Y_{t-k}$, k being some integer. Y_t, and hence X_t, is a white noise series with zero mean and unit variance. Then

$$
\begin{aligned}
r = \text{corr}\,(X_t, Y_t) &= \text{cov}\,(X_t, Y_t) \\
&= E(Y_t Y_{t-k}) \\
&= 0 \qquad (7.A.3)
\end{aligned}
$$

as Y_t is white noise. But, at the same time, X_t is fully determined by Y_t and so the coherence $C(\omega) = 1$, all ω and hence the theoretical average coherence

$$\bar{C} = \frac{1}{2\pi} \int_{-\pi}^{\pi} C(\omega)\, d\omega = 1. \tag{7.A.4}$$

This is, of course, an extreme example but does illustrate how average coherence and unlagged correlation can have quite different values due to the presence of lags.

Now consider cases where there is no lag structure. Suppose that X_t is a white noise series but that Y_t need not be. Further, suppose that both series have zero means and have cross-covariances

$$\begin{aligned} \mu_s = E(X_t Y_{t-s}) &= 0 \qquad s \neq 0 \\ &= \mu_0 \qquad s = 0 \end{aligned}$$

then the coherence will be

$$C(\omega) = \frac{\left(\dfrac{\mu_0}{2\pi}\right)^2}{f_x(\omega)(f_y(\omega)}$$

but as X_t is white noise, $f_x(\omega) = \sigma_x^2/2\pi$ and so

$$C(\omega) = \frac{\mu_0}{\sigma_x^2 \cdot \dfrac{f_y(\omega)}{2\pi\, \sigma_y^2}} = r^2 \cdot \frac{2\pi\sigma_y^2}{t_y(\omega)} \tag{7.A.5}$$

where $r^2 = \mu_x^2/\sigma_x^2\sigma_y^2$ is the square of the unlagged correlation coefficient. It follows that average coherence

$$\begin{aligned} \bar{C}(\omega) &= \frac{1}{2\pi} \int_{-\pi}^{\pi} C(\omega)\, \alpha\omega \\ &= r^2\, \sigma_y^2 \int_{-\pi}^{\pi} f_y^{-1}(\omega)\, d\omega \end{aligned} \tag{7.A.6}$$

which will not in general be equal to r^2. However, if Y_t is *also* white noise, then one gets $\bar{C}(\omega) = r^2$. Thus, in the last case, theoretically at least, average coherence and unlagged correlation squared are the same. This is not the only case. It was pointed out in Chapter 2 that if a series is filtered, then this does not alter the cross-spectrum between it and some other series. Thus, if X_t and Y_t are both white noise series with μ_0 = cov (X_t, Y_t) and if $F(X_t)$ and $F(Y_t)$ are two filtered versions of these series, then again coherence will be a constant and average coherence and squared unlagged correlation will theoretically be equal.

It is seen that a lag structure between the series will generally mean that average coherence and squared unlagged correlation should not be expected to be the same. If no lags are present then the two quantities may be identical but usually will not be so.

There is one further point that can explain a difference. Experience and simulation studies have shown that estimated coherence is often badly biased, the bias being towards 0.5. Thus, if two series are uncorrelated or only correlated to a small extent, the theoretical coherence is small, but the estimated coherence will be biased upwards. This bias alone would explain much of the differences noted in Table 7A-1.

There seems to be little point in discussing further the relative merits of the two measures of total relationships discussed above. Both are merely summary statistics, the only full measure is the whole coherence diagram. The average coherence takes greater account of any lag structure, but gives equal weight to all frequency components. If there are no lags, the squared unlagged correlation coefficient has certain advantages, essentially weighting each component by its importance, in terms of the product of the two power spectra and also having better tests available for use with it.

The comparability of multiple coherence and the coefficient of determination is essentially similar to that between simple coherences and correlations, as discussed above.

A General Model of Commodity Price Fluctuations

Introducing the Model

A general model of commodity price fluctuations is developed in the present chapter. It can be considered a model since it analyzes directly the relationship existing between prices and their determinants for a number of commodities. It can be termed general since it combines the experience of these commodities into an explanation of both futures and cash price fluctuations. The formulation of the model follows the method of spectral decomposition and integrates the empirical results of the earlier chapters to provide an explanation for (1) daily price fluctuations, (2) weekly price fluctuations, (3) monthly, futures price fluctuations and (4) monthly, cash price fluctuations. Only a simple model is offered for daily and weekly price fluctuations; random walk alone can reasonably describe these fluctuations. A more complex model is offered for the monthly futures and cash price fluctuations. Certain regularities appear in these fluctuations and the stepwise results imply that these regularities can be explained by certain forces acting in the market and in the economy. The model, therefore, attempts to integrate the findings for the daily, weekly, and monthly prices into a comprehensive explanation of price behavior in the short run.

Integration of Earlier Results

In explaining economic phenomena over time, one encounters the problem that slightly different patterns of behavior appear over short-, middle- and long-run periods. Forces accounting for economic behavior in the short run often prove irrelevant in the long run, where slower-moving forces such as the business cycle, secular trend, or even structural changes in the economy assume greater importance. In this section, we explain how a general model of price behavior can be formulated to accommodate at once the short-, middle-, and long-run fluctuations. The rationalization is based on spectral decomposition as well as results obtained in the earlier chapters.

Spectral Decomposition

A principal characteristic of commodity price fluctuations, confirmed earlier in this study, is that the pattern of these fluctuations rarely remains constant. Changes in prices, for example, may be quite irregular from one month to the next, yet when the same changes are observed twelve months apart, a strong resemblance may appear. The problem of constructing a general model of price change, therefore, is one of explaining these different price variations all at the same time. This problem is analagous to that of disentangling the seasonal, cyclical, and trend components of a time series and can be solved with spectral decomposition. As explained in Chapter 2 (pages 44,50-51), spectral decomposition permits a simultaneous interpretation of the short-, medium-, and long-run fluctuations of a price series. It has been used in Chapter 4 as well as in later chapters to separate long-run from short-run price behavior. Figure 8-1 further illustrates this principle; the spectrum of a price series has been divided into its low-, middle- and high-frequency ranges to describe its long-, medium- and short-run price fluctuations respectively.

Interpretation of these various frequency ranges can be improved by employing additional spectra which have been computed from prices complementary to those used for the basic spectra. If we consider our monthly price data as the source for the basic spectra, then weekly and daily prices can be used to further the interpretation of those spectra. For instance, long-run frequencies are best interpreted in the basic monthly spectra, but middle-run and short-run frequencies can be better explained by also examining results from weekly and daily spectra respectively.

Having computed roughly corresponding spectra for daily, weekly, and monthly price fluctuations, we are now able to construct such a decomposed model. Thus, the general model of price behavior can explain price fluctuations in the short-, medium- and long-run frequency ranges of monthly spectra, where the ranges of frequencies correspond to those of Figure 8-1. Monthly prices have been used to interpret long-run periods between 48 months and 6 months, weekly prices to interpret medium-run periods from 6 months or 24 weeks to 12 weeks, and daily prices to interpret short-run periods between 12 weeks or 84 days to about 60 days.[a]

Results to Be Included in the Model

We are able to interrelate a substantial number of the results presented in this study by integrating them into a more comprehensive model or explanation of price behavior. The first results of interest appear in Chapter 3, where the random walk model was confirmed with monthly, weekly, and daily spectra of price differences. A slight demarcation of behavior could be found in price behavior since for a number of commodities, some seasonality or regularity could be found in the long-run frequencies of the monthly spectra. These results led us to develop a more complex model, principally to explain the regularities.

A brief review shows that extension of the simple or random walk model

[a]The choice of frequency ranges corresponding to the above periods conforms to that selected for monthly price analysis in Chapters 4 and 5. The weekly data can describe periods as short as two weeks and the daily data can describe periods as short as two days.

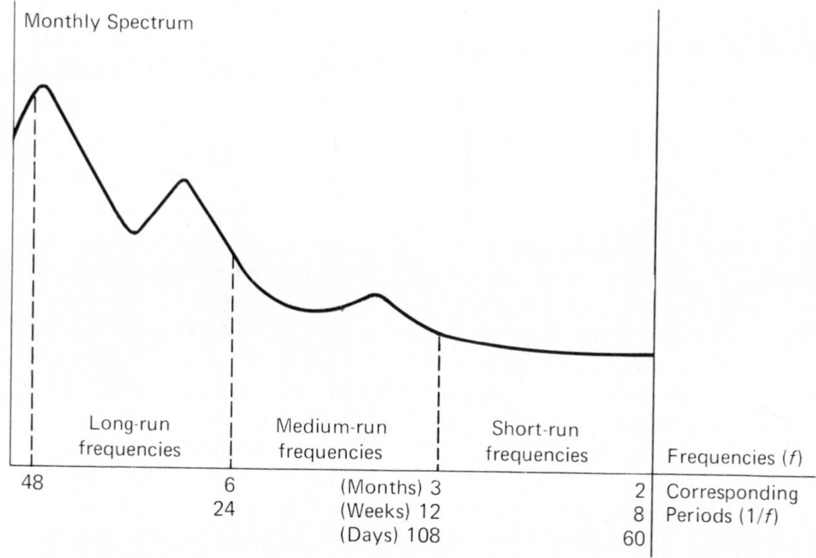

Figure 8-1 Spectral Decomposition of the Monthly Price Spectrum.

took place in Chapters 4, 5, 6, and 7. Chapter 4 extended the price explanation from past values of price to other price series, including price series of substitutable commodities. The number of possible explanatory variables was increased in Chapter 5, with analysis of simple quantity variables such as demand, supply, speculating, and hedging. That chapter also revealed that market imbalance or the excess of speculating over hedging helps indicate when the random walk model, as opposed to a more complex model, would be more appropriate for explaining price fluctuations. Other variables, both endogenous and exogenous, were studied in Chapter 6 as possible price determinants. Most of these determinants have since been ranked in terms of their relative importance and aggregated into explanatory equations of price change in Chapter 7. Generalization of these equation results provides the basis for the present model.

A General Model of Commodity Price Fluctuations

The general model of price behavior presented in the following paragraphs is not a model in a fully quantitative sense; it does, however, provide us with an explanation of price fluctuations generalized from a group of selected commodities. Its principal quality is that it not only identifies generating functions underlying the price fluctuations, it also suggests forces likely to have helped produce these fluctuations. Accordingly, the model is divided into four sections: (1) daily price fluctuations, (2) weekly price fluctuations, (3) monthly, futures price fluctuations, and (4) monthly, cash price fluctuations.

Daily Price Fluctuations

The general model of price behavior begins with daily price changes. As suggested by the spectra of monthly prices in the short-run frequency range and confirmed by the spectra of daily prices, the random walk model still provides the best explanation of daily price fluctuations. This result is confirmed for changes in both futures and cash prices and for a number of commodities from the feed-grain and textile-fibre groups. Only two commodities prove to be exceptions: cocoa futures prices and cotton futures and cash prices.

An examination of the variance of price changes overnight and over the weekend for corn, soybeans, and wheat has revealed that these variances are almost as large at these times as during the day. Taking the "speed" of the market as measured by the variance of the price change per unit time, one can conclude that the random walk model not only explains price behavior during periods of active trading; it also applies when the market is closed but operates at a slower speed. In effect, this tendency of prices to form even during periods of no trading activity indicates that daily prices are highly sensitive to expectations concerning the state of the market.

Weekly Price Fluctuations

The random walk model continues to be relevant for explaining monthly price changes in the middle-run frequencies. This result has also been substantiated by using weekly prices whose behavior covers approximately the same frequency range. Included in this list of weekly prices are lard and soybean oil as well as a number of commodities from the list of daily prices, i.e., corn, oats, rye, soybeans, and wheat. Only soybean oil price differences fail to display a random walk. The estimated power spectra for the included prices are relatively flat; but, in contrast to the daily spectra, occasional jumps appear in the weekly spectra which correspond to the systematic components found in the monthly price series. None of these jumps are significant for either the futures or the cash price series except for the seventeen week component in cash corn, which agrees with the four month component in the monthly spectrum.

An additional test performed with the weekly price series serves as a check on the stability of the model. It has been suggested that with future prices, one might expect the following patterns of behavior: negatively autocorrelated daily prices in response to technical reaction, randomly behaving weekly prices in response to normal trading activity, and positively autocorrelated monthly prices in response to short-term trends. A test of daily, weekly, and monthly spectra presented in Chapter 3, however, has shown this theory to be false: the random walk model provides the best explanation of price change over all three intervals. (It should be noted that this result does not agree with those found for the stock market. Tests with transactions data available for that market indicate the presence of regular patterns. Certain patterns are also found when the span of observations is increased to quarterly.)[1]

Monthly Fluctuations – Futures Prices

In the explanation of monthly price changes, a major transition occurs. While the accompanying spectra generally confirm the random walk model, this model ceases to be valid in the long-run frequencies, as confirmed with both the first difference and the original series spectra. Both sets of spectra suggest that in this frequency range certain systematic and seasonal components are superimposed on the basic random component. These more regular components, as discovered in Chapter 3, need not be traded away as soon as they appear. Storage of a commodity, for example, provides for the possibility of a seasonal rise in price regardless of speculative trading. Even without this possibility, however, it has been shown that trading need not remove any patterns except the more obvious ones. The original series or typical shape spectra suggest, in addition to these seasonal components, the presence of a 30-50-month business cycle component. Since coherence diagrams between prices and the more long-run economic forces display higher power in the long-run frequencies, the business cycle component appears to result from the interaction of prices with these forces. Consequently, one can best proceed to explain price fluctuations in this frequency range by interpreting the relative influence of these forces in terms of the stepwise results.[b]

Given that the present results rely on the experience of only six commodities, one can say that monthly changes in futures prices basically follow the random walk model except in the long-run frequencies, where price changes are determined by the following factors, listed according to their importance:

1. Prices of substitutable commodities or commodities related through a lesser cross-elasticity of demand.
2. Hedging and speculating activity as they reflect the composition of the market.
3. Supply and demand, either in the form of individual components or ratios which indicate market pressures.
4. Business cycles or, more specifically, expansions and contractions in the availability of credit.

[b]A shift in the form of prices from closing to averages takes place at this point. This transition will have no effect on the results presented here, except for the comments offered concerning the averaged random walk in Chapter 9.

That these particular factors in that order generally explain monthly price changes can be substantiated by examining the stepwise regression results for each of the commodities. These results are summarized in Table 8-1. The importance of each of the entering variables can be judged by comparing the R^2 values at each step of the regression. The significance of the overall explanation can be determined by relating the F and R^2 values from the regression to the F and R^2 levels given in the heading of the table.[c] The first explanatory variable to enter the stepwise regression for four of the commodities is the price index of substitutable commodities or, as in the case of soybeans, commodities substitutable in conversion. The only excluded commodity is rye, where the consumption/stocks ratio enters first. Wheat could also be considered as departing from this pattern except that it has been omitted from the discussion altogether because of the overriding influence of the government loan program. The next variable to enter for four of the commodities is the level of hedging or speculating, although the soybeans model includes the lagged variable at an intermediate step. The remaining two commodities, rye and cottonseed oil, enter both a price index and the consumption/stocks ratio before the level of hedging. When the next price influence is considered, no uniform choice can be made, except that the consumption/stocks ratio is significant in the cottonseed oil and rye equations and stocks in the soybean meal equation. Business cycle indicators are included before the cutoff point for soybeans, soybean meal, and soybean oil. Of all explanatory influences, this group is the least important.

It is evident that in these equations the explanation of price change is heavily dependent on changes in the prices of related commodities as well as in the lagged price variables. To determine the extent of this dependence, Table 8-2 shows the same stepwise regressions with the price variables removed. The coefficients of determination for each equation are much lower than before; and for cottonseed oil, the F values become insignificant. These results indicate that the price effects of cross-elasticity should be included in any attempt to explain monthly futures prices. Physical variables represent the first influence to enter the stepwise regressions for all commodities except soybean oil, where hedging comes in first. Hedging and speculating follow as the next set of explanatory variables; either enters significantly into the cottonseed oil, soybeans, and rye equations. Even though the credit indicators enter most of the stepwise regressions before the cutoff point, their inclusion produces only a small increase in the coefficients of determination. In fact, the interest rate in the soybean meal equation is the only significant credit variable. This conforms to the evidence from Table 8-1 that credit indicators add little to the explained variance.

---

[c]The classical F criterion presented for the stepwise methods results in overfitting of the equations. For an estimate of the degree of overfitting, see appendix to Chapter 9.

Table 8-1. An Explanatory Model of Futures Price Behavior

Monthly: First Differences, August 1957-June 1966; Observations = 107

Commodity		*Variables Entering in Steps*					
		1	*2*	*3*	*4*	*5*	*6*
Critical Levels	F at 95% R^2 at 95%	3.94 (0.04)	3.09 (0.05)	2.70 (0.06)	2.46 (0.08)	2.30 (0.09)	2.19 (0.11)
Soybean Oil		*Oil Index*	*Short Hedging*	*Foreign Price Index*	*Consumer Installment Credit: Net*	P_{t-1}	*Production*
	F value	101.75	15.34	3.33	3.10	3.90	0.68
	R^2	0.49	0.56	0.58	0.60	0.60	0.60
Cottonseed Oil		*Oil Index*	*Consumption/ Stocks*	P_{t-1}	*Short Hedging*	*Interest Rate: Commercial Paper*	*Consumption*
	F value	47.80	11.11	2.96	2.93	1.67	1.64
	R^2	0.32	0.38	0.40	0.42	0.42	0.43
Soybean Meal		*Meal Index*	*Long Speculating*	*Stocks*	*Stocks/ Consumption*	*Interest Rate: Commercial Paper*	*Demand*
	F value	18.74	12.55	8.33	5.35	2.87	2.68
	R^2	0.19	0.23	0.29	0.32	0.35	0.37
Soybeans		*Yield Index*	P_{t-1}	*Short Hedging*	*Consumer Installment Credit: Net*	*Stocks*	*Consumption/ Stocks*
	F value	63.29	32.22	19.45	3.24	2.05	1.79
	R^2	0.38	0.53	0.60	0.62	0.62	0.64
Rye		*Consumption/ Stocks*	*Grain Price Index*	*Short Hedging*	*Exports/ Stocks*	*Federal Reserves: Net*	*Consumer Installment Credit: Extended*
	F value	10.63	8.28	8.62	1.07	0.84	0.46
	R^2	0.10	0.16	0.22	0.22	0.22	0.22
Wheat		*Relative Price Index*	*Long Speculating*	P_{t-1}	*Parity Price*	*Interest Rate: Treasury Bills*	*Consumption*
	F value	56.23	4.66	4.27	0.37	0.44	0.27
	R^2	0.84	0.85	0.86	0.86	0.86	0.86

Table 8-2. An Explanatory Model of Futures Price Behavior: Price Indexes and Lagged Prices Removed

Monthly: First Differences, August 1957-June 1966; Observations = 107

Commodity		*Variables Entering in Steps* 1	2	3	4	5	6
Critical Levels	F at 95%	3.94	3.09	2.76	2.46	2.30	2.19
	R^2 at 95%	(.04)	(.05)	(.06)	(.08)	(.09)	(.11)
Soybean Oil		*Short Hedging*	*Consumer Installment Credit: Net*	*Stocks*	*Demand*	*Supply*	*Production/ Demand*
	F value	4.51	3.94	3.35	2.83	2.35	2.10
	R^2	0.08	0.10	0.12	0.12	0.12	0.13
Cottonseed Oil		*Consumption/ Stocks*	*Short Hedging*	*Consumption*	*Interest Rate: Commercial Paper*	*Supply*	*Demand/ Stocks*
	F value	1.87	2.49	2.14	1.72	1.43	1.22
	R^2	0.03	0.07	0.08	0.08	0.08	0.08
Soybean Meal		*Soybean Stock*	*Stocks*	*Stocks/ Consumption*	*Interest Rate: Commercial Paper*	*Demand*	*Soybean Crushings*
	F value	5.78	8.12	8.38	8.44	7.21	6.29
	R^2	0.10	0.19	0.25	0.29	0.30	0.31
Soybeans		*Stocks*	*Short Hedging*	*Federal Reserves: Excess*	*Interest Rate: Commercial Paper*	*Consumer Installment Credit: Net*	*Consumption/ Stocks*
	F value	7.59	8.00	6.59	5.40	4.58	3.96
	R^2	0.13	0.19	0.20	0.21	0.22	0.22
Rye		*Consumption*	*Short Hedging*	*Federal Reserves: Net*	*Consumer Installment Credit: Extended*	*Consumer Installment Credit: Net*	*Stocks/ Consumption*
	F value	5.32	6.16	4.86	3.96	3.49	2.98
	R^2	0.09	0.15	0.16	0.16	0.17	0.17
Wheat		*Interest Rate: Commercial Paper*	*Long Speculating*	*Demand*	*Interest Rate: Treasury Bills*	*Consumption/ Stocks*	*Consumption*
	F value	1.11	1.55	1.05	0.91	0.83	0.72
	R^2	0.02	0.03	0.04	0.04	0.05	0.04

Monthly Fluctuations – Cash Prices

The general model can be used to provide a separate explanation of cash price changes in the long-run frequencies. This follows directly from the stepwise results of Chapter 7, where cash prices exhibit a response to physical and speculative influences different from that of futures prices. Such a result had been suggested earlier. In Chapter 3, cash and futures price spectra for the same commodity were sometimes found to be shaped differently. Similarly, in Chapter 4 it was discovered that futures prices did not represent expected values of cash prices.

That physical influences better explain cash prices than do speculative influences can be seen in Table 8-3. Furthermore, the retention of speculative influences in the cash price equations suggests that futures activity is sufficiently strong to influence price formation in the cash market. The factors responsible for cash price fluctuations in the long-run frequencies, therefore, can be ordered as follows:

1. Prices of substitutable commodities or commodities related through a lesser cross-elasticity of demand.
2. Supply and demand, either in the form of individual components or ratios which indicate market pressures.
3. Hedging and speculating as they reflect the composition of the market.
4. Business cycles or, more specifically, expansions and contractions in the availability of credit.

When the individual commodity results in Table 8-3 are examined, one finds that the first set of influences to enter for all commodities except rye are the price indexes of substitutable commodities. In the case of cottonseed oil, the lagged price enters before the price index, a result already explained in Chapter 7. For soybean meal, the crushing margin enters before the price index, but this does not upset the ranking of the influences; it only indicates that soybean meal prices are more related to the decision to crush soybeans than are soybean oil prices. The physical variables become the second set of influences to enter the stepwise regression. Stocks enter for soybean oil, demand for soybean meal, and the production/stocks ratio for cottonseed oil. Even before the price index, stocks are also the first variable to enter the rye equation. The hedging and speculating variables come in next. With the inclusion of these variables, the overall F values remain significant for all commodities except cottonseed oil. For the latter, the coefficient of determination hardly rises with hedging, indicating that this variable adds no explanation to price change. Credit indicators, the final set of influences to enter the equations, cannot be considered an immediate influence on cash prices. The net consumer credit series, included in the soybean oil equation before the cutoff point is reached, is hardly significant since its addition fails to increase the coefficient of determination.

The explanation of cash prices, similar to futures prices, is greatly dependent on the price indexes of substitutable commodities. Table 8-4 shows that most

Table 8-3. An Explanatory Model of Cash Price Behavior
Monthly: First Differences, August 1957-June 1966; Observations = 107

Commodity		*Variables Entering in Steps*					
		1	*2*	*3*	*4*	*5*	*6*
Critical Levels	F at 95%	3.94	3.09	2.70	2.46	2.30	2.19
	R^2 at 95%	(0.04)	(0.05)	(0.06)	(0.08)	(0.09)	(0.11)
Soybean Oil		*Oil Index*	*Stocks*	*Short Hedging*	P_{t-1}	*Consumer Installment Credit: Net*	*Foreign Price Index*
	F value	100.59	9.37	5.52	4.73	3.56	1.14
	R^2	0.49	0.53	0.56	0.59	0.59	0.60
Cottonseed Oil		P_{t-1}	*Oil Index*	*Production/ Stocks*	*Short Hedging*	*Supply*	*Consumption*
	F value	24.19	25.51	15.52	1.86	1.13	0.10
	R^2	0.22	0.37	0.46	0.47	0.47	0.47
Soybean Meal		*Soybean Margin*	*Meal Index*	*Demand*	*Long Speculating*	*Stocks/ Consumption*	*Production*
	F value	44.70	16.27	10.09	5.03	2.21	0.50
	R^2	0.30	0.40	0.45	0.47	0.48	0.48
Soybeans		*Yield Index*	P_{t-1}	*Short Hedging*	*Stocks*	*Consumption/ Stocks*	*Exports*
	F value	93.01	19.20	6.64	3.36	1.08	0.93
	R^2	0.47	0.56	0.58	0.60	0.60	0.60
Rye		*Stocks*	*Grain Index*	*Demand/ Stocks*	*Short Hedging*	*Consumption*	*Exports/ Stocks*
	F value	19.20	22.65	4.91	2.81	1.62	2.14
	R^2	0.15	0.31	0.34	0.36	0.36	0.37
Wheat		*Relative Price Index*	*Short Hedging*	*Parity Price*	P_{t-1}	*Interest Rate: Treasury Bills*	*Consumption/ Stocks*
	F value	27.76	7.58	1.24	1.04	1.03	0.83
	R^2	0.72	0.75	0.75	0.75	0.75	0.76

Table 8-4. An Explanatory Model of Cash Price Behavior: Price Indexes and Lagged Prices Removed

Commodity		*Variables Entering in Steps*					
		1	*2*	*3*	*4*	*5*	*6*
Critical Level	*F* at 95%	3.94	3.09	2.70	2.46	2.30	2.19
	R^2 at 95%	0.04	0.05	0.06	0.08	0.09	0.11
Soybean Oil		*Short Hedging*	*Consumer Installment Credit: Net*	*Stocks*	*Demand*	*Supply*	*Production/ Demand*
	F value	4.51	3.94	3.35	2.35	1.82	1.62
	R^2	0.08	0.10	0.12	0.12	0.13	0.13
Cottonseed Oil		*Production/ Stocks*	*Short Hedging*	*Demand/ Stocks*	*Consumption*	*Consumption/ Stocks*	*Supply*
	F value	5.67	4.06	3.02	2.40	1.98	1.68
	R^2	0.10	0.10	0.10	0.11	0.11	0.11
Soybean Meal		*Production*	*Long Speculating*	*Interest Rate: Commercial Paper*	*Stocks/ Consumption*	*Consumption/ Stocks*	*Demand*
	F value	2.75	3.92	3.69	3.20	2.92	2.54
	R^2	0.05	0.10	0.12	0.14	0.15	0.15
Soybeans		*Stocks*	*Exports*	*Short Hedging*	*Interest Rate: Commercial Paper*	*Consumer Installment Credit: Net*	*Demand/ Stocks*
	F value	6.29	5.04	4.52	3.91	3.28	2.84
	R^2	0.10	0.13	0.15	0.16	0.16	0.17
Rye		*Stocks*	*Consumption*	*Consumption/ Stocks*	*Short Hedging*	*Stocks/ Consumption*	*Exports/ Stocks*
	F value	9.60	7.22	7.07	6.15	5.54	4.94
	R^2	0.16	0.17	0.22	0.23	0.25	0.26
Wheat		*Short Hedging*	*Stocks/ Consumption*	*Exports/ Stocks*	*Demand/ Stocks*	*Federal Reserve: Net*	*Interest Rate: Treasury Bills*
	F value	1.27	1.34	1.48	2.13	2.12	2.14
	R^2	0.02	0.04	0.05	0.10	0.11	0.13

coefficients of determination drop significantly when price indexes as well as lagged prices and the crushing margin are removed from the stepwise regressions. Given these conditions, physical influences are the first to enter the stepwise regressions for all commodities except soybean oil. The next variables to enter for all commodities except rye are either speculating or hedging. Since the coefficients of determination increase only negligibly with the addition of the speculative variables, it would be helpful to review the significance of their inclusion. From Table 8-4, one finds that speculating and hedging enter significantly only for soybeans, soybean meal, and soybean oil. A similar inspection of the credit indicators reveals that the interest rate on commercial paper in the soybeans equation is the only such variable to enter significantly in the above equations.

Conclusions

The quality of the model has been indicated in the discussion of individual equation results in Chapter 7. It is worth repeating at this point that the levels of multiple correlation achieved are sufficiently high to indicate that forces in the market and in the economy do help to explain long-run fluctuations in monthly commodity prices. A better criterion for assessing the model's quality is its ability to forecast. Consequently, the ensuing chapter will be devoted to a comparison of forecasts produced by the model to those produced by alternative methods.

The most important single aspect of the model is the extent to which changes in the levels of hedging and speculating are related to changes in prices. As specified in the monthly explanation of futures prices, speculating and hedging are the second set of influences to enter the stepwise equations for four out of six commodities. More importantly, these same influences also enter significantly for four out of six commodities in the cash price equations. This result substantiates the conviction held throughout this study that futures market activity influences price behavior not only in that market, but also in the cash market.

In summary, several major implications can be drawn from the model regarding commodity price behavior. These implications, however, result only from the experience of a limited number of commodities. While almost one-half of the commodities traded on American futures markets have been included in the daily and weekly explanations, only results from six commodities or twelve price series provide the basis for the monthly explanations. Furthermore, the latter explanations depend on only low to moderate correlations. Accepting these limitations, the major implications of the model can be stated as follows: (1) random walk provides an explanation of monthly price fluctuations in the short and middle-run frequencies; (2) random walk is no longer fully appropriate in the long-run frequencies; (3) more than one force is necessary for explaining price fluctuations in this frequency range; and (4) these forces can be effectively aggregated to provide a better explanation of price change.

Forecasting Commodity Prices

The results achieved from the general model of price behaviour developed in the previous chapters have shown that commodity price fluctuations can be explained, in part at least, by relating them to forces in the market and in the economy. The model developed was, of course, an explanatory model and has no direct use for forecasting. With explanatory models some of the variables used to explain a price at a particular time are also measured at the same time. For a forecasting model, values of variables occurring only at previous times can be used. In this chapter, predictive models are constructed in a manner similar to that used earlier for the explanatory model.

The success or otherwise of such models can only be judged by comparing the results obtained from the model with results from other methods of forecasting. A number of forecasts have been constructed using a variety of the currently most popular techniques. These techniques are outlined in the following section and the results obtained from them are then discussed in the later sections of the chapter.

Available Forecast Techniques

A variety of forecast techniques are available to the commodity price forecaster. These range from elaborate simultaneous equation systems to methods utilizing simple price averages. The intention in this first section is to review these techniques, principally as they have appeared in the literature. Greater attention is drawn to the techniques which are applicable to monthly price fluctuations although this invariably includes a comparison with methods more relevant for quarterly or annual fluctuations. The analysis includes the following techniques: (1) single econometric equation, (2) simultaneous econometric equations, (3) adaptive or exponential smoothing, (4) naive or mechanical, (5) Box-Jenkins models, (6) balance sheet, (7) charting, and (8) gaming.

Single Econometric Equation

An appropriate starting point is with a forecasting technique which is most relevant for the general model. The single equation technique refers to econometric forecasts or price forecasts which are based on a set of economic influences rather than solely on the past values of the price series itself. This method has been criticized as being pragmatic because it often searches for causal influences with some disregard for specification according to the reasonings of economic theory. The criticism of "data mining" has also arisen since the economist of today can often produce a variety of forecast equations just by an exhaustive search of possible models.[1] By being reasonably careful in specifying such models, however, one can produce forecasts for annual, quarterly, or monthly prices. Furthermore, the cost of developing these equations is far less than that of the more elaborate simultaneous systems.

The single equation method can be summarized briefly since it resembles the approach employed earlier for constructing the commodity price equations. The first stage in this procedure is to discover, according to the principles of economic theory, a set of influences which display a definite relationship to the commodity price series. In the present study, for example, these influences have been found to result from the interaction of supply and demand, market composition, and the cyclical activity of the economy. Once these influences are identified in the form of appropriate variables, they can be arranged into a multiple, linear regression. At this stage, the explanatory variables must not only be reasonably correlated with prices; they must also be relatively independent of one another (although the degree of independence can, in fact, be relatively low when the equation is purely of a forecasting nature). The only remaining requirement is that the explanatory variables be individually predicted one period ahead or else that the same variables be lagged one or more periods behind the price series. The coefficients necessary for prediction are estimated according to the method of least squares, and greater independence among the explanatory variables ensures that the estimates will be unbiased.

The popularity of this method in predicting variables, especially those influenced by cyclical activity, is already known. Its application to commodity price forecasting has been much more limited. Shisko has suggested the use of this method for forecasting annual sugar and cocoa prices. His published results, however, have never extended beyond a simple model employing only a pressure index, and the forecast prices have never been for a duration of less than a year.[2] Hieronymus has similarly produced a single equation model for soybean meal prices, but it also is restricted to annual data.[3] Some discussion has also appeared as to the advantages of this method over the more elaborate simultaneous equation systems. Shepherd claims that, at least for agricultural commodities, single equation methods can devote greater attention to problems of autocorrelation and also produce lower bias when small samples are encountered.[4] A similar opinion can also be found in an early study by Fox.[5]

Simultaneous Econometric Equations

The simultaneous equation approach has proven to be more useful for predicting annual and quarterly prices. It represents the only method which attempts to include all of the relevant variables in the market and in the economy. When the various market factors are highly multicollinear as, for example, in production and inventory models, the method becomes less suitable for forecasting. In addition, the expense of constructing a multi-equation system is such that, to be justified, the method must produce forecasts consistently superior to those of the single equation approach.

When one desires a more complete picture of market behaviour, however, the simultaneous equation approach is the more useful. Its principal attribute is that it can produce forecasts where the line of causation between prices and supply, demand or other factors is not unilateral.[6] In this situation the various dependent and independent variables are simultaneously or jointly determined, and this simultaneity can be removed only by formulating a separate equation for each of the variables. The specification of such a system follows that of a single equation in as far as an a priori attempt is made to identify all possible influences. Only now a wider range of influences can be included and these influences are arranged into a set of interacting equations. The principal requirement of such a system is that the identification criterion be satisfied or that certain conditions be met between the number of structural equations and the number of endogenous or jointly dependent variables. Since ordinary least squares may fail to estimate the equations properly, one can call upon alternative methods such as two-stage least squares, full-information maximum-likelihood or three-stage least squares.[7] Forecasts are produced by predicting some variables one period ahead or by adopting a lagged structure.

The simultaneous equation models which have been published to date for various commodities consider only annual prices. Probably the most elaborate of these studies is the wool model constructed by Witherell.[8] He presents a twenty-four equation model of the world wool market with dynamic multipliers which take into account the lagged effect of certain exogenous variables. His forecast of American wool prices for 1954-1955 reflects a forecast error of only 3%.[9] A modified version of a market model can be found in Weymar's study of the cocoa market.[10] Houck has constructed a six-equation model for the soybean - soybean oil - soybean meal market.[11] Oil and bean prices, however, have been substantially underestimated for the only prediction year, 1961. Slightly more elaborate models have been constructed for the same market, but they do not concentrate on price forecasting.[12]

Exponential Smoothing

The exponential smoothing approach can also be considered a single equation method, but emphasis is shifted from economic influences to a purely statistical analysis of past price behavior. The method can be applied to annual, quarterly, or monthly prices; but, as will be shown later, it is more effective in the shorter run, where prices may contain seasonal components. Its principal advantage is that under the appropriate circumstances, it can inexpensively supply a large number of routine forecasts.

The method which is followed in constructing an exponentially smoothed forecast equation is noneconomic or purely statistical. It requires some regularity in the price series, and where a graph of the prices or the spectrum fails to display cyclical or seasonal components, an equation cannot be easily constructed. When these components do appear, forecasts can be prepared from a linear equation whose independent variables are functions of time such as trends, polynomials, exponentials, or sinusoids. The term exponential smoothing arises because greater weight is given to present than to past information, the weights given to a piece of information exponentially declining the further one retreats into the past. The actual techniques for constructing the exponentially smoothed models as well as for selecting the proper discounting factors can be found in Brown.[13]

Only one paper has been published in which exponential smoothing has been directly applied to commodity price series. Jarrett has produced forecasts for six price series representing six different qualities of Australian wool.[14] Although his methods are not as sophisticated as some of those suggested by Brown or those offered in the present study, he does include the effect of shifting seasonals and discounts past information. For the period February 1961 through June 1964, he reports an average forecast error of 5% for one of the price series and 4% for the remainder. Some discussion also follows of the method's success in predicting turning points.

Naive Methods

Naive or mechanical forecasts have frequently been employed in economic analysis, especially as a standard of comparison for more elaborate forecasts. The naive method is extremely simple and normally involves nothing more than a forecast based on a simple or weighted average of the most recent observations. In some instances, the magnitude of previous forecast errors is also taken into account. While the limitations of this method are obvious, its principal advantage is that forecasts are practically cost free.

The more simple forms of naive models can be classified as "no change" and "same change."[15] The no-change model is particularly useful for price forecast comparisons since its prediction of no change in prices is that of the random walk hypothesis, $\hat{P}_{t+1} = P_t$ (see pages 63-65). The same-change model is slightly different and implies that a particular price will continue to change in the same direction and by the same magnitude as the previous change. Thus, the best predictor of next period's price change is the current price change, $\Delta\hat{P}_{t+1} = P_t - P_{t-1}$. Expressed in terms of price levels, it becomes a weighted sum, $\hat{P}_{t+1} = 2P_t - P_{t-1}$. Other naive models perform extrapolation by weighted averages. Jarrett, for example, has also forecast his six wool price series by taking a simple average of the current and most recent price, $\hat{P}_{t+1} = (P_t + P_{t-1})/2$. Surprisingly, he obtains an average forecast error similar to that of his exponentially smoothed forecasts, although the turning point error is somewhat higher.

Slightly more complex models have also been proposed for naive forecasting. A simple autoregressive model such as that suggested by Cooper and Jorgenson would not only extend prediction to the weighted sum of a greater number of past prices but would also estimate the weights in an optimal manner.[16] While these weights would be superior to those of the no-change and same-change methods, the autoregressive scheme could also include geometric or other nonlinear terms. Witherell, however, has estimated an autoregressive scheme for a set of monthly wool prices, and has found no lags significant after the first one. Thus he prefers a first-order autoregressive process including an error term which is a weighted average of the current and the previous month's stochastic error.[17]

$$\hat{P}_{t+1} = P_t + \alpha_0 e_t + \alpha_1 e_{t-1}$$

where $e_t = P_t - P_{t-1}$ and α_0, α_1 represent appropriate weights. Monthly wool forecasts have been prepared by him using a simpler version of this model. One-month-ahead forecasts produced a forecast error of approximately 3% for the period January 1965 to May 1966.

One possible model not covered in the literature is one suggested by the random walk or no-change model. The data used in this chapter are monthly averaged prices, as in most of the previous chapters. If the instantaneous price change series follows a random walk model, which the results of Chapter 3 suggested would be at least a very good approximation to the truth, then monthly averaged prices would follow what might be called the "averaged random walk model." This averaged model was examined in the Appendix to Chapter 3, where it was shown that the first differences of averaged prices would follow a simple moving average model. It follows that if X_t is a monthly averaged random walk and denoting $Y_t = \Delta X_t$ then Y_t will approximately be given by the third order autoregressive scheme

$$Y_t - 0.3Y_{t-1} + 0.09Y_{t-2} - 0.027Y_{t-3} = \eta_t$$

where η_t is white noise. It follows that the predictor of Y_{t+1} arising from this model is

$$\hat{Y}_{t+1} = 0.3Y_t - 0.09Y_{t-1} + 0.027Y_{t-2}$$

This predictor has also been used on our data.

Box-Jenkins

The naive forecasts are based on very simple models independent of the actual data. One would usually expect to produce better forecasts by considering a wider class of models and then finding the particular model of this class which apparently best fits the past data. An interesting class of models has recently been suggested by Box and Jenkins.[18] The series is first differenced a number of times to remove any local trend, then twelfth differenced to remove any seasonal factor; finally a moving average or autoregressive model is fitted to the resulting data. If a backward (or lag) operator B is defined by $Bx_t = x_{t-1}$

so that

$$B^j x_t = x_{t-j}$$

the Box-Jenkins model may be written

$$(1 - B)^p (1 - B^{12})^q A(B) x_t = C(B) \eta_t$$

where $A(B)$, $C(B)$ are polynomials in B and η_t is white noise. The usual values for p are 0, 1, or 2 and q is usually 0 or 1. The analysis involved is concerned with what values of p and q to use and then with fitting the stationary autoregressive/moving average model by choosing the parameters in $A(B)$ and $C(B)$. These parameters are essentially chosen by a criteria of minimized least squares, by considering a number of possible models and using a maximum likelihood surface. For actual details of the technique, readers are referred to the recent book by Box and Jenkins.[19]

The model used here has a certain adaptive property and can account for certain types of nonstationarity. It thus clearly provides a worthwhile class of models from which predictors can be obtained. Only experience will show whether it is of a type that will provide really useful forecasts in the field of economics.[20]

Balance Sheet Approach

The balance sheet approach is used where commodities are traded on the world market. In particular, the supply and demand for a commodity must be spread over a sufficient number of countries such that the world totals are the most important influence in price determination. Under these circumstances, only annual prices are likely to be of interest. The principal advantage of the method is that it provides a means of prediction in a situation where the lack of extensive data prevents econometric or statistical analysis. Its principal drawbacks, however, are not only its subjectivity but its high cost in terms of data collection and maintenance.

The method consists essentially of building up a picture of world demand and supply and of determining their relative effect on price.[21] One begins by collecting the necessary data for the relevant countries. A balance sheet is constructed such that supply (composed of production and imports) must equal demand (composed of consumption, exports and stock changes) for each country. The balance sheet must further be divided according to whether countries are net importers or exporters. The pressure on prices is determined first by constructing the balance sheet for the current year, which may require a few predictions, and for the forecast year, which involves entirely predictions. The most important factors are the relative levels of production and demand as defined in terms of exports and imports: (1) "export availability" implies an excess of production over demand and (2) "import requirements" implies an excess of demand over production.

Assuming the forecasts of production will not be affected by future price changes and that the forecast of demand depends on unchanging prices in the base year, one can proceed to the price forecast. The difference between the sum of export availabilities and import requirements for all countries gives the surplus or deficit out of current production that will determine the market price. Once a judgment is made as to the level of this price, consecutive corrections can be made for the effect of forecast or realized price on stock-holding. Ashby has applied the balance sheet approach to the sugar market, but gives no indication of its forecast accuracy.[22] He does, however, mention that this approach is more suitable where (1) demand is inelastic and not divided between two or more end products and (2) production occurs only once a year and among small producers. Even where these requirements are met, however, the forecast price is unlikely to be closely met, since market forces over the following year are changing sufficiently rapidly to produce a new equilibrium price.

Charting

The price following method of the chartist differs considerably from the above methods of the economist and the statistician.[23] Their only resemblance is that charting also relies on the past history of prices. Charting is more popularly known in stock market applications where it is referred to as "technical analysis." The chartist follows the attitude that any attempt to follow supply, demand, or new information leads to substantial forecast error. Market action is the best guide to forecasting prices; accordingly, the patterns which develop in price formation provide the best indication of whether prices are going to rise or fall. Furthermore, it is only these patterns which furnish a reasonable estimate of the relative strength of demand and supply. While such an approach may be irrelevant for quarterly or annual price movements, some speculators believe that it is useful for predicting shorter-run price movements.

To forecast price changes by the charting method, one must be attentive to the actual geometric patterns which prices form. These may take the form of triangles, head and shoulders, or tops and bottoms. The basic philosophy of charting is that patterns will repeat themselves. By identifying a particular pattern or trend development, one can subsequently predict the extent of price movement as well as the timing of turning points. Two different forms of charts are employed. The first plots the high, low, and closing price against time. The second disregards time and records price changes on swing or point and figure charts which recognize only the amplitude and frequency of price changes. The analysis brought to these charts can be either a subjective interpretation of recurring patterns or an objective computation of trends. These trends are normally estimated by simple moving averages; and, today, many brokers utilize computers to provide this information for their customers.

Charting has been advocated mainly by technicians who believe that the markets have a memory and, thus, base their decisions on an assumed dependence in consecutive price movements.[24] Unfortunately, few economists have analyzed this technique and none have reported on its forecast accuracy. Donchian has presented gain and loss figures that result from trading futures contracts according to this method, but does not include any analysis of forecast accuracy.[25] Since many of the trading decisions involved with this method are based on objectively forecast trends, it should prove relatively easy to determine its forecast quality.

Gaming

Although gaming has been suggested as a possible method for predicting commodity price fluctuations, we have no information regarding techniques of construction or reliability. That simulation, principally in the form of a business game, can be applied to the problem of commodity price fluctuations can be understood from some of its characteristics. Games can describe a competitive situation; include a large number of players or traders; lead to a minimax or determinate solution; and, lastly, can be constructed to provide a scenario of almost any market. Their principal advantage is that the results of each period of play are fed back into the decision process for the following period. This provides a degree of realism for commodity markets since traders are constantly evaluating opinions of others as to what the price should be. At the same time, the approximation of reality is a drawback for gaming. One must be able to abstract from the real market of commodity price fluctuations to obtain a workable set of economic relationships. If this set becomes too large, then the simulation process becomes too costly to produce efficient results. Since many random elements such as new information influence commodity markets, it is doubtful that this method could ever produce any meaningful forecasts.

Forecasts from the Transformed General Model

The various techniques of forecasting commodity prices having been reviewed, the problem at hand is to compare price-difference forecasts obtained from a transformed version of the general model to forecasts obtained from some of the alternatives: exponential smoothing, Box-Jenkins models, and various naive forecasts. The present section contains a review of the procedure by which the forecast equations have been constructed from the general model. Such a transformation has been possible because the variables of the explanatory equation appear to satisfy the single equation criteria of reasonable correlation with price and relative independence of one another. The main part of the discussion, therefore, has been devoted to the application of stepwise regression methods. While these methods can be utilized to produce the various forecast equations, the results must be carefully examined before any conclusions can be drawn concerning the model's predictive performance. The forecasts are always for one month ahead and are based on the same data as was used to construct the general model.

Transforming the General Model

The general model has demonstrated that commodity price fluctations can be explained by the following factors:

1. Prices of substitutable commodities or commodities related through a lesser cross-elasticity of demand.
2. Hedging and speculating activity as they reflect the composition of the market.
3. Supply and demand, either in the form of individual components or ratios which indicate market pressures.
4. Business cycles or, more specifically, expansions and contractions in the availability of credit.

These factors have been translated into explanatory variables and appear in the various price-difference equations. As given in Chapter 7, however, the equations define only contemporaneous relationships and are not suitable for forecasting. To produce forecasts, one must either predict the explanatory variables first or else lag the same variables behind the dependent price variable.

The lagging procedure has been adopted for the present study since the stepwise regression program provides for the lagging of both dependent and independent variables. While none of the coherence values described earlier were sufficiently high to indicate that a phase lag existed between price differences and the differences of the various explanatory variables, the stepwise results have suggested that a lagged relationship may be usefully formed for the purposes of forecasting. The correlations between price differences and the differences of the various variables lagged up to twelve months proved to be low, but certain lags were optimal or displayed higher correlations than others. Furthermore, the lags in several different situations, especially with respect to hedging and speculating, conformed to the expectations of economic theory. Earlier stepwise results have also suggested the importance of lagging the dependent variable. Thus, the forecast models are formulated according to the belief that current values of the dependent variable depend not only on past values of the explanatory variables, but also upon past values of itself.

One drawback with the stepwise approach under these conditions is that the

F test for the inclusion of variables is no longer valid. The total number of forecast models which become possible with the inclusion of twelve lags for five or more variables now makes the degrees of freedom accompanying the F test meaningless. If too many variables were to be included in the forecast model, the method could easily be accused of data mining. A cutoff point, therefore, has been established, following Kendall's suggestion of minimized residual variance.[26] Although the use of such a method is important for a discussion of the forecast equations, a critical description has been deferred to the appendix of this chapter.

Forecast Equations

The forecast equations which have been reached for the various price-difference series resemble the equations established from the general model, except that the explanatory and dependent price variables are now lagged. The method of constructing the forecast equations has been to enter into the stepwise regressions the variables which were originally selected before the cutoff point was reached. These variables have been summarized in Tables 7-1 to 7-12 of Chapter 7 (see pages 162-194). The new stepwise regression now considers a smaller number of variables than those entered into the original stepwise regressions, but, since these variables are lagged for twelve consecutive months, the total number of possible explanations increases. Occasionally, a formerly significant variable becomes insignificant in the lagged equation and is accordingly deleted. For one or two of the regressions, an additional variable is entered where it appears to contain relevant forecast information. These few adjustments, along with the second-stage stepwise results, are summarized below. It should be noted that all variables are used in first-differenced form.

The reported regression coefficients and standard errors are based on first differences of average monthly prices for the period August 1957 to June 1966. In a later section the predictive performance of the models is assessed for the period July 1966 to June 1967. Finally, the coefficients of the regression model were recalculated for the whole period August 1957 to June 1967 and the resulting small changes found in the values of these coefficients are tabulated. As before, both the dependent and independent variables are in first difference form.

Soybean Oil. Experience with soybean oil price forecasts suggests that production be included in stepwise regression for futures price differences. This variable is not included in the cash price regression since physical influences are already present in the form of the stocks variable. When the stepwise results are compared to those of Table 7-1, one finds that the net change in consumer credit is replaced by production, and the foreign index is no longer included.

The forecasting equation for futures prices that was found is:

$$\hat{P}_{F,t} = \underset{}{0.00697} - \underset{(0.689 \cdot 10^{-6})}{1.557 \cdot 10^{-6}X_{1,t-8}} + \underset{(0.00106)}{0.00319X_{2,t-3}}$$

$$+ \underset{(0.0953)}{0.271X_{3,t-1}} \qquad R^2 = 0.236$$

where X_1 = short hedging, X_2 = production, and X_3 = lagged price. The forecast equation for soybean oil cash price differences has been formed from the original set of explanatory variables with no additional variables. Hedging enters the cash price equation as does lagged price.

$$\hat{P}_{C,t} = 0.0155 + \underset{(0.0972)}{0.303X_{1,t-1}} - \underset{(0.714 \cdot 10^{-6})}{1.711 \cdot 10^{-6}X_{2,t-8}} \qquad R^2 = 0.174$$

where X_1 = lagged price and X_2 = short hedging.

Cottonseed Oil. The forecast equation for cottonseed oil futures price differences resembles the original equation, except that the order in which the variables enter the equation has changed.

$$\hat{P}_{F,t} = 0.255 + \underset{(0.370)}{0.93X_{1,t-7}} + \underset{(0.0953)}{0.251X_{2,t-1}} + \underset{(0.107)}{0.271X_{3,t-9}}$$

$$- \underset{(0.904 \cdot 10^{-6})}{1.983 \cdot 10^{-6}X_{4,t-10}} \qquad R^2 = 0.213$$

where X_1 = consumption/stocks, X_2 = lagged price, X_3 = oil index, and X_4 = short hedging. For the cash price forecast equation, the production/stocks ratio is replaced by short hedging.

$$\hat{P}_{C,t} = 0.0214 + \underset{(0.0869)}{0.484X_{1,t-1}} + \underset{(0.101)}{0.285X_{2,t-9}}$$

$$- \underset{(0.860 \cdot 10^{-6})}{2.004 \cdot 10^{-6}X_{3,t-10}} \qquad R^2 = 0.316$$

where X_1 = lagged price, X_2 = oil index, and X_3 = short hedging.

Soybean Meal. The specification of the futures forecast equation has shifted considerably from its original structure. The rate at which soybeans are crushed into meal and oil offers some predictive value as does lagged price.

$$\hat{P}_{F,t} = 0.282 + \underset{(0.0995)}{0.306X_{1,t-1}} - \underset{(0.0360)}{0.0994X_{2,t-1}} \qquad R^2 = 0.156$$

where X_1 = lagged price and X_2 = soybean crushing margin. The cash price forecast equation similarly shows the meal prices are related to the decision to crush, but demand replaces lagged price.

$$\hat{P}_{C,t} = \underset{}{0.248} - \underset{(0.0495)}{0.116X_{1,t-1}} + \underset{(0.00492)}{0.0106X_{2,t-1}} \qquad R^2 = 0.117$$

where X_1 = soybean crushing margin and X_2 = demand.

Soybeans. Both of the soybean forecast equations express dramatically the influence of levels of hedging activity on price formation. Lagged price enters both equations first, suggesting that autocorrelation is present in soybean price differences. Hedging then enters at the next two stages for both variables. Since the hedging lag is similar in both equations, this tends to discount the possibility of a spurious result. For future prices

$$\hat{P}_{F,t} = 0.845 + \underset{(0.0945)}{0.415X_{1,t-1}} - \underset{(0.0467 \cdot 10^{-3})}{0.131 \cdot 10^{-3}X_{2,t-7}}$$

$$- \underset{(0.0509 \cdot 10^{-3})}{0.136 \cdot 10^{-3}X_{2,t-10}} \qquad R^2 = 0.357$$

and cash prices

$$\hat{P}_{C,t} = 0.941 + \underset{(0.0978)}{0.316X_{1,t-1}} - \underset{(0.0514 \cdot 10^{-3})}{0.151 \cdot 10^{-3}X_{2,t-8}}$$

$$- \underset{(0.0501 \cdot 10^{-3})}{0.142 \cdot 10^{-3}X_{2,t-11}} \qquad R^2 = 0.316$$

where X_1 = lagged price and X_2 = short hedging.

Rye. The futures forecast equation, as for cottonseed oil, is similar to the original equation. The grain index, however, has entered before the consumption/stocks ratio.

$$\hat{P}_{F,t} = -0.0150 - \underset{(0.143)}{0.386X_{1,t-3}} - \underset{(2.863)}{5.858X_{2,t-12}}$$

$$+ \underset{(0.000491)}{0.000975X_{3,t-11}} \qquad R^2 = 0.189$$

where X_1 = grain index, X_2 = consumptions/stocks ratio and X_3 = short hedging. For cash prices, the lagging procedure was not as successful. Rye price changes were shown to be dependent on the prices of competitive grains but only short hedging entered next.

$$\hat{P}_{C,t} = -0.0273 - \underset{(0.118)}{0.424X_{1,t-3}} + \underset{(0.000419)}{0.000852X_{2,t-3}} \qquad R^2 = 0.146$$

where X_1 = grain index and X_2 = short hedging.

Wheat. The most extreme change in the original specification occurs with the wheat equations. The wheat relative index, the principle explanatory variable, offers little predictive value and the remaining variables do not enter the forecast equation significantly. This result is further complicated by the previous realization that fluctuations in wheat prices are determined by government loan influences. The simplest alternative to this dilemma has been to select several obvious relationships and to test their predictive value. Thus, future prices are related to lagged prices, hedging, and the next change in consumer credit; cash prices are related to lagged prices and hedging plus stock levels. The stepwise results show that for both futures and cash prices, hedging offers some predictive value as does the twelfth-difference of price, an autoregressive indicator of the seasonal induced by the loan program. For futures price differences

$$\hat{P}_{F,t} = 0.116 + \underset{(0.0914)}{0.189X_{1,t-12}} - \underset{(0.0000443)}{0.000135X_{2,t-2}} \qquad R^2 = 0.212$$

and cash price differences

$$\hat{P}_{C,t} = -0.0757 + \underset{(0.0928)}{0.187X_{1,t-10}} - \underset{(0.000042)}{0.000114X_{2,t-11}} \qquad R^2 = 0.110$$

where X_1 = lagged price and X_2 = short hedging.

Interpretation. While the above results demonstrate that it has been possible to include two or three lagged variables into each equation before the cutoff point is reached, the multiple correlations achieved and variables selected do not conform closely to those found for the original or nonlagged equations respectively. In the cottonseed oil equations, for example, the oil index is no longer the first variable to enter the futures equation and the production/stocks ratio no longer enters the cash equation. Interpreting the coefficients of determination, therefore, one finds that the explained sum of squares for the futures and cash forecast equations amounts to only 21% and 32% of the total sums of squares respectively. Coefficients of determination for the remaining equations have been summarized in Table 9-1 and range from 0.110 for the soybean meal cash equation to 0.357 for the soybeans futures model.

These various results suggest that, when lagged relationships are considered, the specification of the general model changes or becomes unstable. This is

Table 9-1

Coefficients of Determination: Commodity Futures and Cash Price Differences—Forecast Equations

	R^2: *Futures*	R^2: *Cash*
Soybean oil	.236	.174
Cottonseed oil	.213	.316
Soybean meal	.156	.117
Soybeans	.357	.316
Rye	.189	.146
Wheat	.212	.110

further implied by the slight changes occurring in some of the regression coefficients from the beginning to the end of the forecast period. Table 9-2 summarizes the values of the regression coefficients (calculated over two periods, each beginning in August 1957, the first ending June 1966 and the second ending in June 1967). Although the intercepts do vary for almost all regressions, the deviation of the explanatory coefficients is much less severe. These deviations would be much more critical, if the equations were explaining series with a substantial trend or marked seasonal. Since the model is concerned with changes in the explanatory variables as well as in prices, and since these changes tend to be highly random and not closely correlated for pairs of variables, the adjustments in the regression coefficients should not be interpreted too critically.

Forecasts from Alternative Methods

As mentioned above, the accuracy of the single equation forecasts will be evaluated by comparing them to forecasts produced by alternative methods. Exponential smoothing, Box-Jenkins, and naive methods have been selected as suitable for the alternative forecasts. Since little is known of the forecast performance of these alternatives, it is also interesting to learn how well they forecast individually as well as comparatively.

Table 9-2

Regression Coefficients from Price Difference Forecast Equations, August 1957 to June 1966, and June 1967

Commodity	*Month*	*a*	b_1	b_2	b_3	b_4
				Futures Prices		
Soybean oil	6-66	0.00697	$-1.557 \cdot 10^{-6}$	0.00319	0.271	–
	6-67	-0.00462	$-0.775 \cdot 10^{-6}$	0.00346	0.250	–
Cotton oil	6-66	0.0255	0.930	0.251	0.271	$-1.983 \cdot 10^{-6}$
	6-67	-0.0013	1.117	0.159	0.135	$-1.819 \cdot 10^{-6}$
Soy meal	6-66	0.282	0.306	-0.0994	–	–
	6-67	0.071	0.180	-0.1220	–	–
Soybeans	6-66	0.845	0.415	-0.000131	-0.000136	–
	6-67	0.485	0.430	-0.000110	-0.000137	–
Rye	6-66	-0.015	-0.386	-5.858	-0.000975	–
	6-67	-0.011	-0.248	-5.804	0.00124	–
Wheat	6-66	0.116	0.189	0.000135	–	–
	6-67	-0.233	0.172	0.000135	–	–
				Cash Prices		
Soybean Oil	6-66	0.0155	0.303	$-1.711 \cdot 10^{-6}$	–	–
	6-67	0.0061	0.248	$-1.549 \cdot 10^{-6}$	–	–
Cotton oil	6-66	0.0214	0.484	0.285	$-2.004 \cdot 10^{-6}$	–
	6-67	0.0017	0.423	0.188	$-1.882 \cdot 10^{-6}$	–
Soy meal	6-66	0.248	-0.116	0.0106	–	–
	6-67	0.431	-0.128	0.0078	–	–
Soybeans	6-66	0.941	0.316	-0.000142	-0.000151	–
	6-67	0.456	0.304	-0.000158	-0.000136	–
Rye	6-66	-0.0273	-0.424	0.000852	–	–
	6-67	-0.0016	-0.291	0.000861	–	–
Wheat	6-66	-0.076	-0.000114	0.187	–	–
	6-67	-0.152	-0.000106	0.141	–	–

Exponentially Smoothed Forecasts

The exponential smoothing method, as previously described, yields price forecasts which are based on past values of the same price series. This relationship is expressed in the form of a linear equation where each of the components represents a function of time such as a trend, cycle, or seasonal. The coefficients of the various components in the equation are estimated by a method of weighted least squares regression. The weighting of the coefficients is exponential, greater weight being given to the more recent observations. Account is taken of shifting cyclicals and seasonals because the coefficients are updated each period.

The general smoothing model as described by Brown expresses price $P(t)$ as a sum of several specified functions of time $X_1(t), X_2(t), \ldots, X_m(t)$ with parameters $a_1, a_2, \ldots, a_m$.[27]

$$P(t) = a_0 + a_1 X_1(t) + a_2 X_2(t) + \ldots + a_m X_m(t) \tag{9.1}$$

The estimates of $a_1, a_2, \ldots, a_m$ are formed by minimizing the residual sums of squares, now weighted by the exponential discounting factor β. The discounted sums of squares is given by

$$\text{D.S.S.} = \sum_{t=1}^{T} \beta^{T-t} \left[P(t) - \sum_{i=1}^{m} a_i X_i(t) \right]^2 \tag{9.2}$$

where $t = 1, \ldots, T$ and $\beta \leqslant 1$. The forecast equation resulting from this procedure can be described as follows

$$\hat{P}(T + \tau) = \sum_{i=1}^{m} a_i(T)\, X_i(\tau) \tag{9.3}$$

where $\hat{P}(\tau)$ represents prices in the forecast period τ. To specify the forecast equation for a given commodity price series, one must select the deterministic time functions as well as the discounting factor β^q (q refers to the number of functions including the constant term). Brown recommends that the value $\beta^q = 0.90$ be selected as a "general utility value."[28] Quicker discounting follows for values of $\beta^q < 0.90$ and slower discounting for $\beta^q > 0.90$. The proposed list of time components includes (1) polynomials, (2) trigonometric functions such as the sine and cosine, (3) exponentials of the form e^{at}, (4) autoregression, and (5) combinations of these components.[29]

The major objective of the type of model used in this section is to estimate the current mean or level of the series as well as possible and thus to concentrate on the deterministic, time-function components rather than on stochastic components such as autoregressive residuals. The exponential discounting ensures that more recent values of the series are given greatest weight and so any changes in level are quickly realized and followed by the predictor.

Table 9-3

Coefficients of Determination:[a] Commodity Futures and Cash Price Differences—Exponential Smoothing Forecast Equations

	R^2: *Futures*	R^2: *Cash*
Soybean oil	.091	.146
Cottonseed oil	.051	.097
Soybean meal	.299	.278
Soybeans	.295	.332
Rye	.139	.119
Wheat	.210	.155

[a]Estimated from $\frac{\text{Discounted regression sums of squares}}{\text{Discounted total sums of squares}}$

The general features of the Brown model were contained in a program made available to the authors.[b] An attempt was made to specify the forecast models as well as possible although a greater investment of time could conceivably lead to slightly better forecasts. The deterministic functions were selected on the basis of an examination of the various price graphs as well as the spectra corresponding to these graphs. From the results of Table 1-1 and Figure 1-7, for example, one can specify the wheat futures equation to contain sinusoids of 12, 6, 4, and 3 months, each of which represents the seasonal and its harmonics respectively. Weights have been chosen at $\beta^q = 0.70$ for most price series since the random behavior of these series requires a quicker discounting than that obtained for $\beta^q = 0.95$. The same time functions and weights are used for both futures and cash equations since it has proven difficult to specify the components any more closely for the separate price series. The price series cover the full time period (August 1957 to June 1966) except for the soybean series which were shortened because of the discontinuity in the pattern of price fluctuations. That the resulting forecast models represent a reasonable standard for comparison can be seen from Table 9-3. The coefficients of determination

[b]This program represents a modified version of the C.E.I.R. program for general exponential smoothing which was provided through the courtesy of George Hext. The various forecast models and price forecasts were prepared by Dr. D. Reid.

reported in that table indicate that the explained sums of squares represent from 5.1% to 33.2% of the total sums of squares, values which are roughly similar to those of the previous forecast equations. These values may also be biased downwards since the coefficients of determination could be formed only on the basis of discounted sums of squares. The equations which have been formulated for the month-ahead forecasts are reported below. As before, $P_{F,t}$ relates to futures price changes and $P_{C,t}$ to cash price changes.

Soybean Oil. $\beta^8 = 0.65$

$$\hat{P}_{F,t} = 0.2506 \sin \frac{2\pi t}{12} - 0.0115 \cos \frac{2\pi t}{12} + 0.0007t \sin \frac{2\pi t}{12}$$

$$+ 0.0038t \cos \frac{2\pi t}{12} + 0.0049 \sin \frac{2\pi t}{6} + 0.2551 \cos \frac{2\pi t}{6}$$

$$- 0.0025t \sin \frac{2\pi t}{6} + 0.0104t \cos \frac{2\pi t}{6} \qquad R^2 = 0.09$$

$$\hat{P}_{C,t} = 0.3351 \sin \frac{2\pi t}{12} + 0.2415 \cos \frac{2\pi t}{12} + 0.0028t \sin \frac{2\pi t}{12}$$

$$+ 0.009t \cos \frac{2\pi t}{12} + 0.2823 \sin \frac{2\pi t}{6} + 0.2158 \cos \frac{2\pi t}{6}$$

$$+ 0.0021t \sin \frac{2\pi t}{12} + 0.0097t \cos \frac{2\pi t}{12} \qquad R^2 = 0.146$$

Cottonseed Oil. $\beta^7 = 0.75$

$$\hat{P}_{F,t} = 0.4744 + 0.0228t + 0.0002t^2 + 0.1574 \sin \frac{2\pi t}{12}$$

$$- 0.2602 \cos \frac{2\pi t}{12} + 0.0282 \sin \frac{2\pi t}{6} + 0.043 \cos \frac{2\pi t}{6} \qquad R^2 = 0.051$$

$$\hat{P}_{C,t} = 0.4434 + 0.0208t + 0.0002t^2 - 0.0209 \sin \frac{2\pi t}{12}$$

$$- 0.2873 \cos \frac{2\pi t}{12} + 0.0372 \sin \frac{2\pi t}{6} + 0.001 \cos \frac{2\pi t}{6} \qquad R^2 = 0.097$$

Soybean Meal. $\beta^8 = 0.70$

$$\hat{P}_{F,t} = 1.4669 + 0.0315t - 3.8937 \sin\frac{2\pi t}{12} + 3.082 \cos\frac{2\pi t}{12} - 1.1592 \sin\frac{2\pi t}{6} - 3.3312 \cos\frac{2\pi t}{6} + 1.3198 \sin\frac{2\pi t}{4} - 0.0373 \cos\frac{2\pi t}{4} \qquad R^2 = 0.299$$

$$\hat{P}'_{C,t} = 1.7792 + 0.0375t - 3.6767 \sin\frac{2\pi t}{12} + 3.6266 \cos\frac{2\pi t}{12} + 0.0134 \sin\frac{2\pi t}{6} - 3.1787 \cos\frac{2\pi t}{6} + 1.2218 \sin\frac{2\pi t}{4} + 0.7644 \cos\frac{2\pi t}{4} \qquad R^2 = 0.278$$

Soybeans. $\beta^7 = 0.70$ (Data begins August, 1961.)

$$\hat{P}_{F,t} = 6.2159 - 3.6311 \sin\frac{2\pi t}{12} + 1.7473 \cos\frac{2\pi t}{12} - 0.599 \sin\frac{2\pi t}{6} - 1.7955 \cos\frac{2\pi t}{6} - 0.0433 \sin\frac{2\pi t}{8} + 0.1121 \cos\frac{2\pi t}{8} \qquad R^2 = 0.295$$

$$\hat{P}_{C,t} = 8.8736 - 4.0575 \sin\frac{2\pi t}{12} + 4.0677 \cos\frac{2\pi t}{12} - 1.6090 \sin\frac{2\pi t}{6} - 1.9394 \cos\frac{2\pi t}{6} - 0.0297 \sin\frac{2\pi t}{8} + 0.0919 \cos\frac{2\pi t}{8} \qquad R^2 = 0.332$$

Rye. $\beta^7 = 0.70$

$$\hat{P}_{F,t} = 2.7683 + 0.6629 \sin\frac{2\pi t}{12} + 2.3710 \cos\frac{2\pi t}{12} - 0.8422 \sin\frac{2\pi t}{6} - 0.1387 \cos\frac{2\pi t}{6} - 0.0169 \sin\frac{2\pi t}{8} + 0.0436 \cos\frac{2\pi t}{8} \qquad R^2 = 0.139$$

$$\hat{P}_{C,t} = 1.5096 + 0.7414 \sin \frac{2\pi t}{12} + 1.3705 \cos \frac{2\pi t}{12} - 0.4273 \sin \frac{2\pi t}{6}$$

$$+ 0.0347 \cos \frac{2\pi t}{6} - 0.0077 \sin \frac{2\pi t}{8} + 0.0373 \cos \frac{2\pi t}{8} \qquad R^2 = 0.119$$

Wheat Futures. $\beta^{10} = 0.70$

$$\hat{P}_{F,t} = 3.4920 + 0.1026t + 7.1910 \sin \frac{2\pi t}{12} + 0.8855 \cos \frac{2\pi t}{12}$$

$$- 6.0105 \sin \frac{2\pi t}{6} - 4.1755 \cos \frac{2\pi t}{6} + 0.8044 \sin \frac{2\pi t}{4}$$

$$+ 3.6719 \cos \frac{2\pi t}{4} + 7.9310 \sin \frac{2\pi t}{3} - 1.7700 \cos \frac{2\pi t}{3} \qquad R^2 = 0.210$$

Wheat Cash. $\beta^8 = 0.76$

$$\hat{P}_{C,t} = 2.9014 + 0.0911t + 6.0435 \sin \frac{2\pi t}{12} + 0.5157 \cos \frac{2\pi t}{12}$$

$$- 0.3644 \sin \frac{2\pi t}{6} + 3.0388 \cos \frac{2\pi t}{6} - 1.6079 \sin \frac{2\pi t}{4}$$

$$- 0.3272 \cos \frac{2\pi t}{4} \qquad R^2 = 0.155$$

Naive Forecasts

The naive methods which can be considered the most appropriate for commodity price comparisons are those of the no-change and same-change forecasts. The no-change hypothesis when expressed in terms of price differences or changes implies that no change will occur at all.

$$\Delta\hat{P}_{t+1} = P_{t+1} - P_t = 0$$

As mentioned earlier, this prediction is identical to that of the simple random walk model, $\hat{P}_{t+1} = P_t$. For any of the forecast models to predict price better than what could be predicted on the basis of a simple random walk, therefore,

Table 9-4

Coefficients of Determination:[a] Commodity Futures and Cash Price Differences—Averaged Random Walk Model

	R^2: *Futures*	R^2: *Cash*
Soybean oil	0.07	0.09
Cottonseed oil	0.02	0.12
Soybean meal	0.02	-0.08
Soybeans	0.18	0.14
Rye	-0.07	-0.01
Wheat	-0.04	0.04

[a]Estimated from $R^2 = 1 - \dfrac{\text{sum of squares of forecast errors}}{\text{sum of squares of price changes}}$

the model's forecasts must have a lower mean square error than that of the no-change method, i.e., the realized price change.

The same-change method states that price will continue to change in the same direction and by the same amount as the most recent price change.

$$\Delta\hat{P}_{t+1} = P_t - P_{t-1}$$

While this method does not offer as stringent a forecast alternative as the no-change method, it does furnish some evidence as to the explanation provided by the economic factors in the single equation forecasts. Since these naive models are imbedded in most of the single equation models by the use of lagged price changes, the equations containing lagged price should reflect a lower mean square error than that of the same-change model. The extent to which the former do perform better, therefore, is a measure of the forecast effectiveness of the economic factors.

As explained above, the random walk hypothesis used in conjunction with average monthly data suggests that price changes $Y_t = \Delta P_t$ can be forecast by $\hat{Y}_{t+1} = 0.3Y_t - 0.09Y_{t-1} + 0.027Y_{t-2}$. Table 9-4 shows the resulting R^2 values, i.e., the proportion of the variance of ΔP_t explained by this averaged random walk model, for the period August 1957 to June 1966.

If an averaged price series did exactly obey an averaged random walk and then one predicted it using the above predictor, the theoretical value of R^2 can be found precisely. If Y_t denotes the averaged price change series, then as proved in the appendix to Chapter 3, it will obey

$$Y_t = \eta_t + \alpha\eta_{t-1}$$

where $\alpha = 0.27$ for a price series averaged over a month and η_t is a white noise series. Thus

$$\text{var } Y_t = (1 + \alpha^2) \text{ var } \eta_t$$

$$R^2 = 1 - \frac{\text{var } \eta_t}{\text{var } Y_t}$$

$$= \frac{\alpha^2}{1 + \alpha^2}$$

$$= 0.068 \quad \text{when} \quad \alpha = 0.27$$

The values of R^2 recorded in Table 9-4 may be considered as estimates of this theoretical value if the underlying price series is accepted to be a random walk. It is worth noting that these estimates may take on a negative value, as no parameters have been estimated from the data in determining the model. The average value of the estimated R^2 is 0.05 for the cash prices, is 0.03 for the futures prices, and the overall average is 0.04.

Box-Jenkins Predictors

We are grateful to Dr. D. Reid for providing us with Box-Jenkins predictors for each of the cash price and futures series. He developed the basic program for use in connection with his Ph.D. study and was kind enough to use it on our data.[30] Considering the actual price series, one first differencing was always found to be desirable to stabilize the series, but usually no further first or twelve differences were suggested in the techniques as being necessary. We then attempted to fit to the first difference series the simplest moving average or autoregressive model which provided the best fit to past data. Values of R^2 for these models can be found in Table 9-5.

Each of these models that best fitted the data over the period August 1957 to June 1966 ($n = 107$) are described below in terms of the lag operator B such that $B^j x_t = x_{t-j}$. For each of the futures price series, a model of the form $(1 - B)x_t = (1 + \theta B)e_t$ was always specifically considered and θ found which produced the best fit to the data. We call this the simple moving average model. As the averaged random walk model is of this form with $\theta = 2 - \sqrt{3} \triangleq 0.27$, such models are of particular interest.

Table 9-5

Coefficients of Determination: Box-Jenkins Models, August 1957 - June 1966

	R^2: *Futures*	R^2: *Cash*
Soybean oil	0.08	0.06
Cottonseed oil	0.17	0.16
Soybeans meal	0.07	0.02
Soybeans	0.27	0.14
Rye	0.01	0.00
Wheat	0.33	0.20

Note: The best model, in terms of R^2, is used.

Soybean Oil. The best-fitting Box-Jenkins model for soybean oil futures was found to be

$$(1 - B)(1 - 0.277B)\hat{P}_{F,t} = e_t \qquad R^2 = 0.08$$

but the simple, moving average model

$$(1 - B)\hat{P}_{F,t} = (1 + 0.25B)e_t \qquad R^2 = 0.07$$

was almost as good.

For cash prices, the best model was

$$(1 - B)(1 - 0.284B)\hat{P}_{Ct} = e_t \qquad R^2 = 0.06$$

Cottonseed oil. The best model for futures prices was

$$(1 - B)(1 - 0.277B)\hat{P}_{F,t} = e_t \qquad R^2 = 0.17$$

which was again hardly distinguishable from the best simple moving average model

$$(1 - B)\hat{P}_{F,t} = (1 + 0.25\text{B})e_t \qquad R^2 = 0.15$$

It so happens that these equations are identical to those found for soybean oil futures but the R^2s are larger.

The model for cash prices was

$$(1 - B)(1 - 0.414B)\hat{P}_{C,t} = e_t \qquad R^2 = 0.16$$

Soybean Meal. For futures prices, two models were found to fit equally well, one being a simple moving average model

$$(1 - B)(1 - 0.216B)\hat{P}_{F,t} = e_t \qquad R^2 = 0.07$$

and

$$(1 - B)\hat{P}_{F,t} = (1 + 0.25B)e_t \qquad R^2 = 0.07$$

It is worth noting that for each of the three futures series considered so far, the Box-Jenkins model is essentially identical to the averaged random walk model, but this is not so for the other three commodities.

The model for cash prices was

$$(1 - B)(1 + 0.039B)\hat{P}_{C,t} = e_t \qquad R^2 = 0.02$$

which is seen to be very near to a pure random walk model, as was the best simple, moving average fitted.

$$(1 - B)\hat{P}_{C,t} = (1 - 0.05B)e_t \qquad R^2 = 0.01$$

Soybeans. Good fits were found for soybean futures prices by two models

$$(1 - B)(1 - 0.50B)\hat{P}_{F,t} = e_t \qquad R^2 = 0.27$$

and

$$(1 - B)\hat{P}_{F,t} = (1 + 0.45B)e_t \qquad R^2 = 0.24$$

Once more, there is little difference in goodness of fit between the two models.

The fit was less good for cash prices, the best model being

$$(1 - B)(1 - 0.38B)\hat{P}_{C,t} = e_t \qquad R^2 = 0.14$$

Rye. The best models for rye futures were indistinguishable from a simple random walk model, i.e.,

$$(1 - B)(1 + 0.006B)\hat{P}_{F,t} = e_t \qquad R^2 = 0.01$$

and the best simple moving average model had $\theta = 0$.

For cash prices two models gave the same fit

$$(1 - B)(1 + 0.026B)\hat{P}_{C,t} = e_t \qquad R^2 = 0$$

and

$$(1 - B)\hat{P}_{C,t} = (1 + 0.05B)e_t \qquad R^2 = 0$$

Both models differ only slightly from a pure random walk.

Wheat. Wheat futures prices were found in Chapter 3 to have a strong seasonal component and this was detected by the Box-Jenkins approach. The best model was

$$(1 - B)(1 - 0.392B^{12})\hat{P}_{F,t} = (1 - 0.25B^4)e_t \qquad R^2 = 0.33$$

and this model fitted the data very much better than the best simple moving average model

$$(1 - B)\hat{P}_{F,t} = (1 + 0.1B)e_t \qquad R^2 = 0.02$$

For cash prices, the best model also involved a seasonal term, i.e.,

$$(1 - B)(1 - 0.195B^{12})\hat{P}_{C,t} = e_t \qquad R^2 = 0.2$$

and this fits much better than the best simple moving average model, which is

$$(1 - B)\hat{P}_{C,t} = (1 + 0.25B)e_t \qquad R^2 = 0.04$$

Forecasting Accuracy

When selecting a predictive model, the basic stages are to first select the type of model to be used and then to utilize the data to estimate any parameters involved. This process makes it difficult to compare the goodness of fit of two alternative models as the parameters are generally chosen to optimize the goodness of fit. In ordinary regression theory the number of parameters involved in the model can be taken into account in any measure of fit, such as R^2, by considering the relevant degrees of freedom of the distribution of this quantity under a set of reasonable assumptions. However, it is not easy to do this for all of the predictors used in this chapter. The problem is inherently more difficult when dealing with intercorrelated and autocorrelated time series. The use of

Table 9-6

Comparative Coefficients of Determination

	Econometric Equation	*Exponential[a] Smoothing*	*Box-Jenkins*	*Averaged Random Walk*
		Futures		
Soybean oil	.24	.09	.08	.07
Cottonseed oil	.21	.05	.17	.02
Soybean meal	.16	.30	.07	.02
Soybeans	.36	.30	.27	.18
Rye	.19	.14	.01	-.07
Wheat	.21	.21	.33	-.04
		Cash Prices		
Soybean oil	.17	.15	.06	.09
Cottonseed oil	.32	.10	.16	.12
Soybean meal	.12	.28	.02	-.08
Soybeans	.32	.33	.14	.14
Rye	.15	.12	.00	-.06
Wheat	.11	.16	.20	.04
Average R^2	.21	.19	.12	.04

[a]Note that the R^2 for exponential smoothing is based on discounted sums of squares.

stepwise regression moves the problem into a field of even greater conceptual difficulty and no satisfactory solution has yet been found. It follows that to simply compare the goodness of fit of alternative predictors over the set of data from which their parameters have been estimated could give misleading results. However, for the sake of general interest, the R^2 measures of goodness of fit found above for various of the more important predictive models are shown in Table 9-6.

With the definition of R^2 used above, i.e., the proportion of variance of price change explained by the model, it should be noted that a model involving no parameter estimation, such as the averaged random walk, can have a negative R^2. For any model which used the data to fit parameters, the criteria used is essentially one of optimizing R^2 and so a negative value cannot occur. From the definition, the R^2 for the no-change naive model will always be zero.

From Table 9-6 it is seen that on the whole the econometric equation and the exponential smoothing technique give the highest R^2s. This is almost certainly illusionary as both effectively overfit the data due to the number of possible variables that these methods consider (see Appendix to this chapter). The Box-Jenkins models obtain relatively high R^2 values for cottonseed oil, soybeans, and wheat, the latter due to a seasonal factor, but have low R^2 for the other commodities. The averaged random walk consistently produces low R^2 values, apart from soybeans. The overall impression, with no R^2 value above 0.33 illustrates well the extreme difficulty in predicting commodity price changes.

As explained above, a measure of goodness of fit such as R^2, does not necessarily tell one anything about the actual *predictive* ability of the model. To do this the only reliable method is to see how well the models actually do predict over some set of data occurring after the set used when estimating the parameters of the models. For our price series, the models were fitted using data for the period August 1957 to June 1966. Each model was used to predict one month ahead for the period July 1966 to June 1967. Although this provides only twelve figures it should be sufficient to indicate whether or not any single model or method of prediction is fairly consistently the best of those used. The criterion used in the comparison is the mean squared predictive error, i.e.,

$$\text{M.S.E.} = \frac{1}{n} \sum_{i=1}^{n} (A_i - F_i)^2 \tag{9.4}$$

Where A_i is the actual price and F_i is the forecast price. This is, of course, a very direct measure of the forecasting ability of each method with a small mean squared error being preferable to a large value.

Table 9-7 shows the observed mean squared errors for various forecasting methods over the twelve-month period. It is seen from Table 9-7 that the same-change and exponential smoothing forecasts are consistently inferior to the others and can be immediately dismissed from further consideration. Simply taking the lowest value for the mean squared forecasting error in each row, the averaged random walk has given the best set of forecasts for seven of the thirteen cases (there being two rows for soybean cash prices), the no-change or simple random walk model has proved to be the best on four occasions and the Box-Jenkins and the econometric equation are best once each. However, such an oversimple summary hardly does justice to the relative performance of the various techniques. We examine the results in more detail in the next two sections, the first of which considers the individual commodities; the second compares the forecasting methods.

Table 9-7

Mean Square Error Comparison: Price Difference Forecasts, July 1966-June 1967

	Econometric Equation (1)	*Exponential Smoothing* (2)	*Box-Jenkins*[a] (3)	*Same Change* (4)	*No Change* (5)	*Averaged Random Walk* (6)
			Futures Prices			
Soybean oil	0.55	0.73	0.49	0.85	0.52	0.48
Cottonseed oil	1.13	1.41	1.03	2.03	0.97	1.04
Soybean meal	17.41	19.89	18.40	42.80	17.67	19.50
Soybeans	127.00	138.80	120.00	194.70	148.00	102.20
Rye	24.42	29.40	21.50	54.50	21.60	25.24
Wheat	84.76	95.93	86.20	166.67	77.53	80.43
			Cash Prices			
Soybean oil	0.93	1.08	0.84	1.43	0.84	0.78
Cottonseed oil	0.85	1.01	0.72	1.14	0.72	0.66
Soybean meal	19.59	19.20	20.69	32.13	19.91	17.22
Soybeans	326.80	314.30	322.50	539.60	346.00	304.40
Rye	13.08	9.87	7.56	15.50	7.58	7.59
Wheat	83.92	79.08	72.09	115.33	70.16	59.64
Soybeans[b]	50.70	114.30	31.60	168.30	112.40	39.00

[a]Omitting value for September 1966 which has an extremely high error term for all methods.

[b]The mean squared error is for the Box-Jenkins model with the highest R^2.

Forecasting Models for Each Commodity

In this section, each of the six commodities is considered in turn and the apparently best forecasting model discussed.

Soybean Oil

For both cash and futures prices, the averaged random walk model provides the best forecast. In each case the best Box-Jenkins model is almost identical to the averaged random walk and so performs almost as well in forecasting. The econometric models do slightly worse in predicting, both contain a lagged price term with a coefficient near 0.3 and so are again not very different from the averaged random walk model. The evidence is thus clear that the averaged random walk model is the best predictive model that has been found, suggesting that monthly closing prices follow a simple random walk, i.e., changes in monthly closing prices are not predictable from previous changes *or* from the other economic variables considered when constructing the econometric model.

Cottonseed Oil

For futures, the no-change or simple random walk model predicted fractionally better than the averaged random walk and the Box-Jenkins model. For cash prices, the averaged random walk proved to be slightly better than the no-change and Box-Jenkins model. Over the data for which models were fitted, the Box-Jenkins model was almost indistinguishable from the averaged random walk for futures prices but was slightly different for cash prices. The econometric models both predicted slightly worse than the averaged random walk and both contained lagged price changes. For cash prices, the lagged price change entered first in the stepwise regression with a coefficient of 0.484 (almost identical with that found for the equivalent Box-Jenkins model); for futures, the lagged price difference entered second with a coefficient of 0.254. The evidence is not conclusive but it strongly suggests that, at the very least, the averaged random walk model is a good approximation to the optimum model. Thus, as far as prediction is concerned, it will be very difficult to do better than an averaged random walk model for averaged monthly prices. Similarly, the monthly closing price changes will be extremely difficult to predict from earlier changes.

Soybean Meal

For soybean meal a rather confusing picture arises. The fitted Box-Jenkins model for futures is essentially the same as the averaged random walk model. The econometric model for futures also has a lagged price change entering as the first variable with a coefficient of 0.306, being the same as the averaged random walk model would suggest. However, over the forecast period the no-change or simple random walk model performs slightly better than the averaged random walk or the Box-Jenkins. The econometric model performs even better still, although only slightly, possibly suggesting that the second variable used, the soybean crushing margin, is of use in prediction.

For cash prices, the picture is again confused. The Box-Jenkins model found was essentially the same as the no-change or simple random walk model, yet both of these models performed slightly worse in predicting than did the averaged random walk model. The econometric model did not include any lagged price changes but nevertheless was the second most successful technique over the forecasting period, with the soybean crushing margin entering the equation first, followed by demand.

Overall, it seems that soybean meal prices follow a model close to either the simple or averaged random walk models but that other variables, particularly the crushing margin, do contain useful predictive information.

Soybeans

For both cash and futures prices, the averaged random walk gave the best predictive performance. However, if a month for which a particularly large cash price change occurred is excluded, the Box-Jenkins model did slightly better, although this model was almost the same as the averaged random walk. Of the two Box-Jenkins models fitted to the futures prices changes, the autoregressive model ($R^2 = 0.27$) fitted fractionally better than the moving average model ($R^2 = 0.24$), yet it was the moving average model which, in fact, predicted better (M.S.E. = 99.0 for moving average, 120.0 for autoregressive). In the econometric model, lagged price change entered first for both sets of prices, with a coefficient of 0.415 for futures and 0.316 for cash but the use of other variables in the model reduced the predictive performance.

It would again seem to be very difficult to produce better forecasts than those given by the averaged random walk model.

Rye

The simple random walk model seems to be clearly the best for both cash and future rye prices. This model had the best predictive performance (although only extremely marginally over the averaged random walk model for cash prices); the Box-Jenkins models closely approximated the simple random walk model and the econometric models did not contain lagged price changes.

At first sight this is a rather odd result as the prices provided to us by U.S. Department of Agriculture were said to be monthly averaged prices. Subsequent enquiry found that the prices we had been using were not, in fact, formed in the same way as other monthly averaged prices. For all of the other commodities, the monthly averaged prices were simply the average of the daily closing prices.

However, the monthly rye prices are formed as follows: the price of each carlot of rye, reported as sold in the Minneapolis Daily Market Record for the Minneapolis market, is used in computing a daily average price over the number of cars listed. To compute the monthly average, the daily prices are multiplied by the weights and the aggregate divided by the number of cars sold, provided at least some carlots have been sold in the month. If no cars are reported as sold, no prices are reported. It is seen that this series uses averaged daily prices rather than daily closing prices and also weights each day according to the volume of transactions for the day. If daily closing prices followed a simple random walk, the extra averaging and the weight might add sufficient extra variability for the monthly average prices to also follow a model very similar to the simple random walk, although it is difficult to see why this should be so on theoretical grounds.

The Grain Division of the Consumer and Marketing Service of the U.S. Department of Agriculture was kind enough to also supply us with monthly average prices for rye formed by simply averaging daily closing prices. However, the spectrum of the first differences of this series was very flat and was almost identical to the spectrum of the first differences of the monthly weighted average price that we have used throughout our investigation. It therefore seems that the particular way in which rye monthly average prices have been formed does not account for the fact that rye prices appear to obey a simple random walk rather than the averaged random walk found for the other commodities we considered.

The results seem to be quite clear, with monthly averaged rye prices following a simple random walk. The reason for this seems to be less clear. As has been stated before, the simple random walk and the averaged random walk are actually quite similar models and it is not always easy to distinguish between them given a hundred or so observations. It is thus possible that the wrong model of the two has been obtained due to sampling errors and lack of significance in our methods for differentiating between the models. Nevertheless, the weight of evidence is all in favor of the monthly average prices following a simple random walk. If this were strictly so, one might expect daily or weekly closing price series to follow some model other than a simple random walk, but this was not found to be so in our investigations reported in Chapter 3. Thus, although the empirical results are clear, as are the implications for forecasting, it must be admitted that in this single instance the results are not completely consistent.

Wheat

In our earlier spectral studies, wheat was found to have an important seasonal component. The Box-Jenkins models for both cash and futures prices had a seasonal factor and achieved relatively very high R^2 values. The econometric models also contained price changes lagged by twelve months or thereabouts. One would thus expect either of these models to produce the best forecasting performance. Yet, in fact, the averaged random walk clearly produced the best forecasts of cash prices and for futures prices forecasts based on the no-change, simple random walk model proved to be the best, slightly better than those from the averaged random walk.

The reason why the seasonal component was found to have no predictive value was clear from a plot of the data. Whereas over the first half of the period there was a clear seasonal, this term seemed to decline in importance in later years until over the final year, which we attempted to predict, no seasonal movement at all was observable. Whether or not the seasonal factor will reappear in subsequent years cannot, of course, be determined from the data.

One must again conclude that one or other of the random walk models will provide the best predictor, unless the seasonal factor again becomes important. The evidence is insufficient to choose between them although it slightly favours the averaged random walk model.

Summary

Using only twelve pieces of data it is obviously difficult to differentiate between two very similar models. The models we have called the simple and averaged random walks do, in fact, differ only slightly when producing forecasts. For all of the six commodities considered in this chapter, one or the other of these random walk models seems to provide the best forecast. The weight of evidence suggests that the averaged random walk, when using averaged monthly data, provides almost the best available forecast for five of our six commodities. This suggests that the simple random walk will prove to be, at worst, an excellent approximation to the truth when using end-of-month closing prices. The only commodity which seemed to be clearly different from the others was rye, for which the simple random walk model proved to be the best.

The fact that we have not been able to find a consistently better forecasting model than random walk is surprising. It is true that in other speculative markets, particularly the stock market, the random walk model has not been improved upon when using monthly data. However, commodity markets are less active than a stock market, involve fewer participants, in some cases have prices exhibiting seasonal components, can feature real supply and demand pressures. All of these factors suggest that one could predict price changes. The results unfortunately do not confirm that belief. It seems that information on supply and demand pressures, for instance, is largely in the public domain and so is already reflected in the price. Any new, unexpected piece of information then causes an unpredictable change in price. Such a hypothesis has not been directly tested for the commodity market but a similar result, concerning earnings and dividends, has been found for the stock market.[31] If true, then it seems that the efforts made by some companies to determine the current supply or crop situation before it is generally known may be worthwhile if it can be shown that the market reacts strongly to news about supply. Unfortunately, the results in

Chapters 5 and 7 do not show this clearly. It is quite possible that price changes due to speculative activity swamp those due to demand and supply information.

Note on the Forecasting Techniques

Suppose one accepts that one or other of the random walk models provides the best forecast for each commodity, one can ask how well the three forecasting techniques involving estimation and analysis have performed. The three methods involved are the single equation econometric model using stepwise regression, the Box-Jenkins models and the exponentially smoothing models.

A critical discussion of the stepwise regression technique is given in the appendix to this chapter. The econometric forecasting equations have on the whole performed well, although apparently extraneous variables have occasionally been included. In the cases of soybean oil, cottonseed oil, soybean meal (futures only), and soybeans, the predictive equations have all included a lagged price change (lagged by one time unit), and on five occasions this lagged change entered the model in the first step. The coefficients averaged 0.334 which is close to what one would expect if the averaged random walk model were the true model. For rye, no lagged price change was included, as other techniques showed to be correct. For wheat, the seasonal factor was evident in the fitted model but, as explained above, this proved to provide a poor prediction due to the reduction of importance of this factor in recent years. The goodness of fit, measured by R^2, was consistently optimistic but given the complexity of the technique and the sample size used the overall performance of the method was satisfactory. On the evidence available, one could have a certain amount of confidence in using multivariate models estimated by stepwise regression programs.

The Box-Jenkins models have also consistently produced a model very near to that found to be the best. Of course, if explanatory variables other than previous price changes had been found to contain useful predictive information, the Box-Jenkins models would need to be generalized to include these variables. The model for wheat included the seasonal which subsequently was found to be misleading, but if a method had been used which continually updated the model, this factor would probably not have been included in the final model from which predictions were made. The Box-Jenkins models included in our analysis assumed that the parameters of the model were time-invariate. The evidence thus again suggests that when attempting to predict a time series from its past, the Box-Jenkins method will perform satisfactory. However, it must be emphasized that the Box-Jenkins method considers a particular class of models and that this class includes the random walk models considered and found to be optimal.

The exponential smoothing method did not perform very well. The reason is because this method concentrates on any deterministic components in the series and these components were found to be of no importance in commodity price change series.

It has recently been suggested[32] that one can frequently produce a better forecast by combining two or more forecasts produced by alternative techniques. This will not be true, of course, if one of the forecasts combined is, in fact, the optimum forecast. We made a small study of the possibility of using this idea by combining the forecast produced by the econometric model and the average random walk. However, as the latter was generally found to be the optimum forecast, or nearly so, it is not surprising that it was found that the combined forecast was generally worse than that produced by the average random walk model.

Forecast Error and the Price Level

It is of interest to ask whether or not there is any relationship between the variance of the forecast errors and the general price level of the series. Table 9-8 shows the mean price and σ, the square root of the mean squared forecasting error from the averaged random walk model for each commodity over the period July 1966 to June 1967. This was, of course, the period over which the relative quality of our forecasts was judged. The errors from the averaged random walk model were used for consistency and because this model seemed to be nearly the best available model in all cases. (As the table also shows, if errors from the simple random walk model are used for rye, there is little change.) The coefficient of stability, defined as σ/mean, is seen to be remarkably stable, lying about an average value of 0.05. This strongly suggests that σ and the mean are closely related, series having a high average price and a high forecast error variance. If this result can be extrapolated to other commodities, it means that it will be difficult to obtain a forecast which has a lower square root of mean square error than 5% of the price level. If one cares to assume normality of forecast errors, a further implication would be that the majority of forecasts should lie in the range $(1 \pm 0.1)P$, where P is the current price level. These results are consistent with similar ones found for the stock market and also with the suggestion made frequently in economics and marketing that attitudes towards price changes can be best characterized in terms of changes in log prices rather than changes in absolute prices.

If one accepts from the table that σ/mean is approximately a constant, it thus follows that

$$\sigma = 0.05 \text{ mean}$$

However, a plot of σ against mean does not fully support such a linear model, indicating rather a nonlinear relationship. Plotting the logs of both quantities suggests the relationship

$$10\sigma = (\text{mean})^{0.84}$$

i.e.,

$$\frac{\sigma}{\text{mean}} = 0.1(\text{mean})^{-0.16}$$

Table 9-8

Coefficient of Stability, July 1966-June 1967

	Mean	σ^a	$\frac{\sigma}{mean}$
		Futures Prices	
Soybean oil	10.7	0.69	0.065
Cottonseed oil	14.9	1.02	0.068
Soybean meal	77.4	4.44	0.057
Soybeans	300.7	10.11	0.034
Rye[c]	125.3	5.03	0.040
Wheat	175.6	8.97	0.052
		Cash Prices	
Soybean oil	11.0	0.87	0.079
Cottonseed oil	13.2	0.81	0.062
Soybean meal	82.8	4.14	0.020
Soybeans	307.4	17.40	0.057
Rye[c]	119.2	2.78	0.023
Wheat	178.3	7.71	0.043

Average $\frac{\sigma}{\text{mean}} = 0.051$

[a] σ = square root of the mean squared error from the average random walk model.

[b] The definition of the coefficient of stability used here is not the conventional one; rather it represents the standard deviation of the forecast errors (essentially price changes) divided by the mean.

[c] If σ had been based on the simple random walk model, for futures one has $\sigma = 4.65$ and $\sigma/\text{mean} = 0.037$, the cash the same as shown. The differences are seen to be of little importance.

so that σ/mean decreases as mean increases. As these relations are based on only twelve points, they are extremely tentative. Nevertheless, there does seem to be a strong relationship between σ and the mean price level.

Stepwise Regression Methods

The single equation, econometric model used in this and the previous two chapters have been constructed using a time-series stepwise regression technique. The object of this appendix is to examine critically the performance of this technique, which is being used increasingly with economic data. It has been pointed out in Chapter 2 and elsewhere that the major problem with the technique is knowing when to stop, that is, when to add no further variables. What we have done is to treat the method like classical regression, and, consequently, have applied the classical criterion to the significance and worth of the variable last added to the equation. It has been realized throughout that this criterion will almost inevitably include variables that have no significance and should not have been included. However, it was thought that overfitting was less dangerous than underfitting, that is, stopping too soon. Until proper tests are available specifically for stepwise regression, and there seems to be little prospect of completely suitable tests being available soon, the method we have used seems reasonably sensible. It is realized of course that the resulting coefficient of determination, R^2, will be optimistic, and this has certainly been proven by the results presented earlier in this chapter.

The classical coefficient of determination, however, can be corrected for such a bias by taking into account the number of variables that have been included in the equation. This corrected version of R^2 is defined as

$$R_c^2(k) = 1 - \left[1 - \left(R^2(k)\frac{n-1}{n-k-1}\right)\right] \qquad (9A.1)$$

where

n = number of observations for each of k variables

k = number of explanatory variables, and

$$R^2(k) = 1 - \frac{\text{variance of residual}}{\text{variance of variable being explained}}$$

The major assumption necessary for making this correction is that the most recently added variable has been chosen at random from the set of possible variables for inclusion. If this last variable, and all others, do not improve the explanation then, theoretically at least, $R_c^2(k)$ should be constant for all $k > k_0$, where k_0 represents the number of significant explanatory variables included in the model. For example, consider the simple regression equation

$$Y_t = a_0 + a_1X_t + \epsilon_t \qquad (9A.2)$$

where Y_t is the variable being explained, X_t is an explanatory variable and ϵ_t is a white noise series uncorrelated with all other possible explanatory variables. In this case $k_0 = 1$ since X_t is the first and only variable suitable for explaining Y_t. That any explanatory variables further added to this equation do not significantly increase R^2 can be seen from the following expression which shows the change in R^2 to be a fixed constant.

$$R^2(k + 1) - R^2(k) = \frac{1 - R_c^2(k_0)}{n - 1}$$

for any $k > k_0$.

When using stepwise regression or similarly programmed equation-solving techniques, even the above corrected R^2 will lead to an improper fit of variables. In stepwise regression, for example, the program selects the best or more relevant explanatory variables from the set of all possible such variables which will *most* increase R^2, even though the increase may not be significantly nonzero. Thus, one needs to test not the change in R^2 against zero but the maximum of the possible changes in R^2 against zero. In these circumstances, one would not necessarily expect $R^2(k + 1) - R^2(k)$ to be constant with increasing k even for $k > k_0$. Rather, the change in R^2 would be a function of n, k, k_0, and m, the number of explanatory variables considered.

We are able to examine this possibility by using some of the stepwise results obtained in this study. When the forecasting equations were constructed with the stepwise regression program, no constraint was applied to the number of explanatory variables which could be included in the equation. The above results, nevertheless, were obtained by applying a judgmental rule to the program output. Altogether, twelve steps were permitted for each commodity price equation, clearly overfitting the equation. The results from other forecasting methods suggest in fact that usually only the first step was significant, although the second variable entering might also be occasionally relevant. Table 9A-1 shows the changes in $R^2(k)$ at each step for each price equation. The actual variables involved at each step have not been shown as they are almost certainly not important. The final column of the table shows the average change in $R^2(k)$ over the commodities. The average is seen to decrease smoothly as k increases, as shown in Figure 9A-1. If we assume that $k_0 = 1$ on every occasion, the averages might represent estimates of the expected change in R^2 when the entering variable is not significant. Under this assumption, we see that in going from step one to step two, a change in R^2 of 0.05 would be by no means unusual. Although such a result might be useful in interpreting the particular set of data with which we are concerned, the result may not have any general applicability, since changes in R^2 generally will depend both on the sample size and also the total number of explanatory variables under consideration. If Figure 9A-1 is extrapolated backwards, it suggests that R^2 for the first step needs to be greater than at least 0.08 for the entering variable to be of significance. However, we have little confidence in the method by which this number has been obtained.

If the forecasting model had only contained variables which contributed a change in R^2 clearly above the averages shown in Table 9A-1 then the number of variables that would have been used, with associated R^2 values are shown in Table 9A-2. The variables that would have been included can be deduced from

Table 9A-1

Percentage in Change in R^2 in Stepwise Regression Forecasting Models

	Rye		Wheat		Soybean Oil		Cottonseed Oil		Soybean Meal		Soybeans		Average % Change
Step	*C*[a]	*F*[b]	*C*	*F*	*C*	*F*	*C*	*F*	*C*	*F*	*C*	*F*	
1	11	10	7	18	12	11	23	7	7	8	19	24	13.2
2	4	5	4	4	5	6	4	6	5	8	7	6	5.35
3	3	4	2	3	5	7	5	4	3	3	6	6	4.25
4	4	2	2	1	2	4	3	4	5	4	2	3	3.00
5	4	4	2	1	2	4	4	4	2	4	3	3	3.08
6	2	3	1	1	3	2	2	4	3	3	3	3	2.50
7	3	2	2	1	2	3	1	3	3	3	1	5	2.42
8	3	2	1	1	3	3	2	2	2	3	1	3	2.16
9	3	3	1	1	3	2	2	2	2	4	1	2	2.16
10	3	2	1	1	3	2	0	3	3	2	2	1	1.92
11	2	3	1	1	2	2	2	3	2	3	1	3	2.08
12	5	2	1	2	1	1	0	2	2	3	1	1	1.75

[a]C = Cash Prices.
[b]F = Futures Prices.

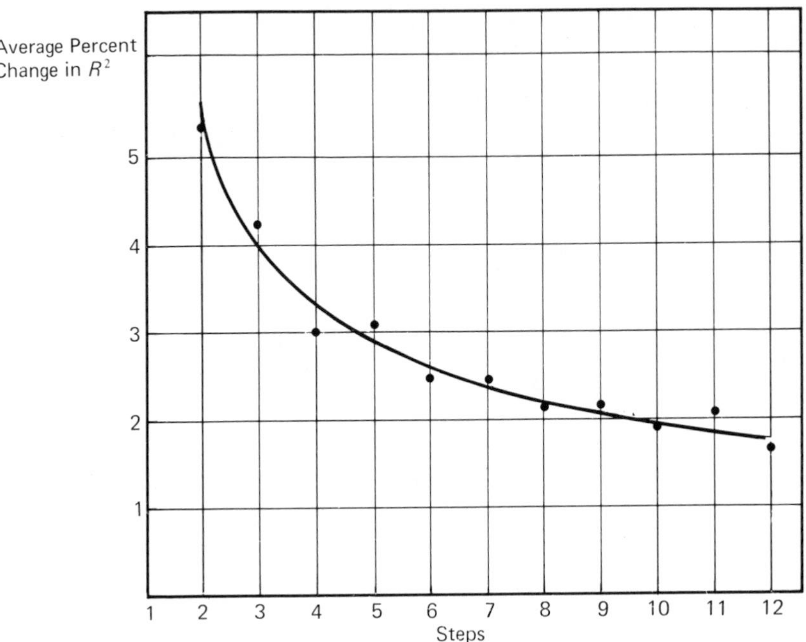

Figure 9A-1 Average Percentage Change in R^2 with Successive Steps in Regression.

the equations presented in the discussion of the transformed general model earlier in this chapter, where the variables are shown in order of appearance in the model. Cases marked with an asterisk are such that even the first entering variable is of doubtful significance.

In general, it is seen that as suggested above, the cutoff point would have been earlier in most cases and the resulting model would have been closer to the models suggested by other forecasting techniques as being nearly optimal. It must again be emphasized that this is an extremely tentative analysis, being based on a single set of calculations rather than any wider experience or a proper theoretical analysis.

A similar analysis could be performed on the explanatory equations obtained by stepwise regression in Chapter 7, assuming the figures in Table 9A-1 to be applicable. As before, cutoff would generally have occurred earlier, resulting in a reduction in R^2. Details are shown in Table 9A-3.

The actual decline in R^2 by making the cutoff earlier is generally not particularly important as by far the biggest contribution to R^2 is always made by the variable entering at the first step.

Although the problem of properly selecting the cutoff point is still a difficult one, we must repeat the conclusion made earlier that in our opinion the stepwise regression procedure performs very well compared to alternative methods and is a useful addition to the tools available to econometricians and model builders who do not have to specify the form of their model too closely.

Table 9A-2

Variables Entered in the Forecasting Equations

	Number of Variables Actually Used	R^2	*Number of Variables Probably Significant*	R^2
			Futures	
Soybean oil	3	.24	3	.24
Cottonseed oil	4	.21	1	.07*
Soybean meal	2	.16	2	.16
Soybeans	3	.36	1	.24
Rye	3	.19	1	.10
Wheat	2	.21	1	.18
			Cash	
Soybean oil	2	.17	1	.12
Cottonseed oil	3	.32	1	.23
Soybean meal	2	.12	1	.07*
Soybeans	3	.32	2	.26
Rye	2	.15	1	.11
Wheat	2	.11	1	.07*

Table 9A-3

Variables Entered in the Explanatory Equations

	Number of Variables Actually Used	R^2	*Number of Variables Probably Significant*	R^2
		Futures		
Soybean Oil	4	.60	2	.56
Cottonseed oil	4	.42	2	.38
Soybean meal	5	.35	1	.19
Soybeans	4	.62	3	.60
Rye	3	.22	3	.22
Wheat	3	.86	1	.84
		Cash		
Soybean oil	4	.59	1	.53
Cottonseed oil	3	.46	3	.46
Soybean meal	4	.47	2	.40
Soybeans	4	.60	2	.56
Rye	4	.36	2	.31
Wheat	2	.75	1	.72

10 Conclusions

In Review

This final chapter draws together and focusses upon some of the more important aspects of commodity price behavior emanating from this study. First of all, the results achieved are compared to goals originally formulated. This serves as a general summary for the chapter results, as well as draws attention to results having possible further implications. These implications are next discussed in terms of their points of impact: (1) on commodity producers and consumers, (2) on commodity price theory, and (3) on statistical methods. Since the similarity of futures price behavior to stock price behavior helped to provide incentive for this study, the commodity price results are compared to those found recently for stock markets. Finally, as in any attempt to explain a phenomenon, one inevitably encounters new problems to be solved and new results to be deciphered; the chapter thus concludes with a discussion of problems warranting further research.

The Results

The principal aim of this study has been to test various theories of commodity price behavior, and to construct a more general explanatory and predictive model of price fluctuations. It has, of course, been necessary to keep separate the explanatory and predictive aspects. One can use unlagged values of appropriate variables to *explain* prices but one must use lagged values of the same variables to *predict* prices. We have considered four types of hypotheses from which conclusions are drawn for the explanatory aspects of the model.

The random walk hypothesis. Futures and cash price changes are uncorrelated with earlier price changes. This hypothesis was largely confirmed, despite some evidence of seasonal components for monthly series. The random walk hypothesis is concerned only with prices measured at specific moments of time. If one uses averaged monthly prices, for instance, then the hypothesis must be amended. (Refer to Chapter 3.)

The expectations hypothesis. Futures prices represent an expectation of the cash price at the time of the maturity of the futures contract. This hypothesis can be tested only by relating it to the predictability of cash price fluctuations. Results of Chapter 9 strongly suggest that, for the commodities used in our study, cash price changes are not predictable. It thus follows that the best predictor of a future cash price is the current cash price. This being the case, the expectations hypothesis would lead one to expect a high degree of relatedness between current cash and current futures prices. Such a relationship was found, with cash and futures prices being highly correlated and unlagged to each other. Near futures prices were found to be more highly related to current cash prices than were more distant futures. They were also found to be more highly related in the long run than in the short run. Although these results by no means refute the expectations hypothesis, neither do they necessarily prove it. Other explanations for these results are possible; for example, both futures and cash price series could be influenced simultaneously by the same flow of unpredictable pieces of information reaching the market. What the results do imply, however, is that futures traders seem unable to predict future or cash price changes, thereby anticipating the results of Chapter 9. (Refer to Chapter 4.)

The simple demand hypothesis. Prices are determined by quantity relatives such as supply, demand, or volume of trading. Little direct relationship was found between price changes and changes in variables such as volume, open interest, supply, and demand. But some evidence of a relationship was found between price changes and the levels of speculation and hedging. Stock market studies have already indicated that classical demand analysis is inappropriate for strongly speculative markets, this fact being further confirmed with the consideration of commodity markets. In short, present results show that the simple demand model cannot be considered valid for explaining short-run price fluctuations. (Refer to Chapter 5.)

The general hypothesis of price behavior. Prices are determined by a wider range of influences considered as acting not only through demand and supply but also through economic and speculative conditions. When constructing explanatory and predictive models, one must be extremely careful in selecting possible variables to be included in the model. The formulations of the three hypotheses given above can be seen as a move to selecting such variables. In the first hypothesis prices were explained or predicted only by past prices. Then, the set of possible explanatory variables was widened in the second and third hypotheses to include other prices as well as several quantity-related variables. Finally, with the general hypothesis, the range of explanatory variables is expanded to include various endogenous and exogenous influences. Results of testing the hypothesis shows that the levels of coherence achieved between prices and demand and supply arranged as pressure ratios are only marginally greater than those achieved between prices and the individual variables. The best explanation of price changes has arisen from the cross-elasticity of demand or commodity substitution. That is, price fluctuations tend to be related to indexes reflecting the price movements of substitute commodities. The influence of the business cycle, either in the form of general business conditions or more specific credit conditions, gives only marginal results. It appears, therefore, that only a few variables exert a reasonable influence on short-run price fluctuations, and that the strength of the relationship varies from stronger in the long-run to weaker in the short-run frequencies. (Refer to Chapter 6.)

The obvious next step to forming the general explanatory model was to combine the variables considered appropriate into individual equations explaining price change. Such equations, constructed using stepwise regression techniques, are reported on in Chapter 7. The separate equation results were then aggregated and generalized in Chapter 8 to obtain the general model of price behavior. As would be expected, several limitations were met. The influences affecting price changes varied sufficiently from commodity to commodity to prevent the generalization from applying to all commodities. In addition, the availability of data for only a small group of commodities seriously restricted this aspect of the study. Limitations aside, the model has helped improve our understanding of price behavior. Considering first the individual equations which compose the model, the levels of multiple correlation achieved indicate that several of the above influences could be aggregated to produce a better explanation of price change. Secondly, the order in which the variables entered the equation confirmed our reasoning; futures prices are better explained by speculative influences and cash prices are better explained by physical influences.

We finally proceeded from the explanatory aspects to the predictive aspects of the model. The explanatory results cannot be used directly for prediction since they involve explaining future prices in terms of future values of some of the variables where these values are generally unknown. To permit the individual explanatory equations to be used as predictive equations, stepwise regression techniques were applied to lagged values of variables which proved important in the former. It has been shown that stepwise regression techniques, employing presently available methods of determining cutoff points, give optimistic levels of degrees of goodness of fit; consequently, the equations were fitted over part of the available data and their ability to predict one month ahead was then tested over an additional year of data. To provide comparison and to help interpret the results from the models, a number of other methods of forecasting were also considered. These ranged from various naive and smoothing methods to that recently introduced by Box and Jenkins. The results from the forecast analysis presented in Chapter 9 are quite clear. In general, future price changes of both futures prices and cash prices are not predictable or, at most, are only slightly predictable. When considering different forms of the data, this conclusion holds for instantaneously recorded data, but must be rephased slightly for averaged data.

Implications of the Results

Some of these results have implications over and above those directly connected with the theories and hypotheses which have been tested. These range from revisions in methods of forecasting prices to increased use of spectral methods in model building. Three possible areas of impact are suggested in the present discussion: (1) commodity producers and consumers, (2) commodity price theory, and (3) statistical methods. The first of these areas, in addition to being divided into implications for producers and consumers, also considers the combined effect of these groups on market equilibrium. The order of presentation of these areas is the same.

Implications for Commodity Consumers and Producers

Commodity Consumers. Of major concern in this study is the manufacturer or processor who must purchase commodities for resale after conversion. The fact that he is forced to buy at least some of his raw material on a speculative market which produces irregular and unpredictable price fluctuations introduces even greater difficulties into his purchasing policy. His best mode of action is not clear. If the commodity is bought on a market which is not highly speculative, then it may be possible to make useful predictions of futures prices, at least in the long run. There may be a seasonal component in the prices, which would be worth taking into account, provided his storage costs can be kept sufficiently low. By sufficient research, he may be able to obtain an idea of future supply of the commodity, such as a crop size, before this is ascertained by the rest of the market. Our explanatory model suggests that such information could be of predictive value. A large buyer, of course, does have one piece of demand information not available to the rest of the market and which may be of consequence, that is, the size and timing of his own purchases. The buyer would have to make a decision whether or not to be an active participant in the market. He might use his purchases and inventories in an attempt to profit from trading in the market; or he might decide to be a passive buyer, either accepting the inevitability of price fluctuations or counteracting them by a hedge. The extent to which he will practice the former depends on his monopoly position in the market.

Commodity Producers. The major problem also facing producers is their in ability to forecast prices. Although limited commodity price forecasting may be possible, the degree to which random walk dominates short-term price fluctuations emphasizes the problems which producers encounter. In the United States, for example, they cannot predict when to place crops on the market or when to move them into storage, nor can they insure themselves against risk by using elemental hedging.

In many of the developing countries, these same problems exist and are even magnified. Most often, random walk in price fluctuations leads to monthly and annual instability in earnings from exports, although some experts believe this problem to be exaggerated. Nonetheless, fluctuations in export earnings do have an impact on economic planning and growth. Some examples of this impact are interruptions in planned investment programs leading to cutbacks in educational and medical facilities, scarcities of foreign replacement equipment resulting in excess capacity for secondary industries, and injuries to a country's credit-worthiness, reducing incentives of lenders to continue development finance.[1] Not many forecasting suggestions can be offered producers different from consumers except that the random walk finding should encourage commodity agreements between suppliers, as will be emphasized in the next section.

Market Equilibrium. The most obvious implication of random walk in commodity prices is that demand and supply are seldom in equilibrium at a given point in time. This is a known fact of commodity price behavior: demand tends to be inelastic with prices constantly adjusting to fluctuations in supply. Whereas markets which are in equilibrium lead to stable prices over time, commodity markets clearly produce unstable prices over time. Certain of the results reached in this study can help us to explain the disequilibrium and the resulting price instability; they can also help us to control equilibrium to improve price stability. Implications are discussed for both domestic and international markets.

Two questions which have recently met renewed attention in *domestic* commodity markets are the following: (1) Can "excessive" speculation be defined and measured? (2) Can "excessive" speculation be associated with the irregular price fluctuations found in these markets?[2] These questions are similar to ones asked earlier in this study, specifically on pages 123-130. At this point we need only note that it has been possible to measure excess speculation by means of the speculative index, which measures the excess of speculation present over that necessary to balance hedging in the market. In addition, excess speculation can be related to the patterns found in price fluctuations; the results supporting this conclusion have been summarized in Table 10-1. Referring to that table, commodities which experience substantial excess speculation display almost a pure random walk in first differences (index values of 1.26 and 1.25 associated with Group I); commodities having moderate excess speculation show slight regularity in price differences (index values of 1.22, 1.18, and 1.19 associated with Group II); and commodities showing the least excess speculation tend to have the highest price regularity of the included commodities (index values of 1.16, 1.19, and 1.12 associated with Group III).

The implications which exist for *international* commodity markets relate to the problems of implementing price agreements. Our results can be brought to bear on these agreements in two ways: (1) the evidence gathered regarding excess speculation can lead to conclusions concerning the instability of price fluctuations, and (2) the realization that price fluctuations follow a random walk can lead to a better technical basis for quantitative control of these fluctuations.

With respect to the first of these results, one difficulty encountered in encouraging commodity price agreements has been the lack of a method which would link the speculative activity in the market to instability in the resulting prices. As mentioned in Chapter 1, various theories exist, but no one has been able to prove whether speculation stabilizes or destabilizes prices in the market. While the present authors do not pretend to have such evidence in hand, the

Table 10-1[a]

Speculation and Instability in Monthly Futures Prices, January 1950-June 1965

	Speculative Index	*Seasonal Groups*	$\overline{X}$	σ_x	*Stability Ratio*
Potatoes ($/cwt.)	1.26	I	2.48	0.81	.34
Cottonseed oil (¢/lb.)	1.25	I	14.79	2.84	.19
Soybean meal ($/ton)	1.22	II	61.87	10.50	.17
Corn (¢/bu.)	1.19	II	135.13	22.60	.17
Soybean oil (¢/lb.)	1.18	II	11.23	2.53	.22
Rye (¢/bu.)	1.16	III	138.09	28.40	.21
Soybeans (¢/bu.)	1.31	III	263.59	37.20	.14
Wheat (¢/bu.)	1.19	III	207.96	24.90	.12
Oats (¢/bu.)	1.12	III	73.34	10.70	.15

[a]The results shown in this table are not directly comparable to those shown in Table 9-8. Here we use closing prices and σ_x is the standard deviation of these prices. In the previous chapter averaged closing prices were used and σ was the standard deviation of the forecast errors (essentially of price changes). It was noted in Table 9-8 that σ/mean was fairly stable from commodity to commodity. The same appears to be true here, even with a longer time span and a different definition of σ (apart from potatoes). Comparing the results with Table 9-8, it is worth noting that the highest value for σ/ mean was found for cottonseed oil and the lowest value was found for soybeans. This confirms the relationship between speculation and instability found in the above figures.

results in Table 10-1 regarding excess speculation can also be related to a measure of price stability reported in that table, the ratio of the standard deviation of a commodity price series to its mean. Excepting the speculative index for soybeans and the stability ratio for soybean oil, the index and ratio values found for the other seven commodities tend to follow a general pattern. Commodities such as potatoes, cottonseed oil, and soybean meal with high speculative indexes (1.26, 1.25, 1.22) also exhibit the highest instability in the ratios (0.34, 0.19, 0.17). Oats and wheat at the bottom of the list display lower speculative indexes (1.12, 1.19) and lower stability ratios (0.15, 0.12). This pattern becomes more apparent when the seasonal groupings are included. Random price series are associated with the highest instability values (Group I with 0.34, 0.19), less random series coincide with moderate instability values (Group II with 0.17, 0.17, 0.22), and the seasonal price series with the lowest instability values (Group III with 0.15, 0.14, 0.12). The result of this analysis, therefore, is that excess speculation can be linked not only to commodity price fluctuations which are relatively more random but also to fluctuations which are also relatively more unstable. In a recent study evidence was presented suggesting that speculators' transactions often moderate rather than accentuate price volatility, both for cash and futures prices.[3] It is also stated that for an extended period in 1947-1948, high initial margin requirements probably did help curtail very short-term price fluctuations. However, "given the present state of market data collection and analysis, the Commodity Exchange Authority would find it difficult to determine whether, when, and how to apply margin controls to limit price volatility."

The second result which can be considered of importance for price agreements is the discovery that commodity price fluctuations follow a known model – that of random walk. The result can be of help for selecting among alternative stabilization schemes or for deciding on the nature of a specific price stabilization mechanism such as buffer stocks. For example, planners may have the following alternatives available: (1) an "automatic" scheme which sets prices free to vary between maximum and minimum price levels; (2) an "arbitrary" scheme in which prices are fixed by adjusting them to corresponding production levels and export quotas; or (3) a "compromise" scheme which may be a blend of the two.[4] Here, the realization that price changes follow a random walk and do not react strongly to changes in production might lead to the following conclusions: (1) an "automatic" scheme should be preferred to one relating price to quantity, and (2) the actual "range" to be set for prices in the scheme can be derived from the properties of the random walk model.

Implications for Commodity Price Theory

The statistical results reported in this study have confirmed the difficulty of applying traditional or classical market theory to the explanation of commodity price behavior in the short run. We now proceed one step further to demonstrate that this theory is in fact inappropriate for commodity markets. To begin with, such markets, at least those featuring futures trading, resemble "bid" or "auction" markets. The only previous record of an attempt to incorporate the price-making activity found on auction markets into the mainstream of price theory can be found in the writings of the Austrian economists. Much of their work, especially on the role of demand or utility in explaining prices, has since become integrated into classical price theory. Their explanation of auction markets has not. Marshall, who was responsible for that integration, thought of market prices as reflecting intentions to buy and sell over the course of the day rather than as adjusting to constantly changing bids and offers. What he failed to emphasize was that markets to which price theory might be applicable differ considerably in character. Commodity markets resemble an immediate rather than a planned adjustment market and feature price fluctuations which are almost instantaneous rather than temporal. In addition, they lack a clear definition of buyers and sellers. Buyers and sellers may be found in the form of manufacturers or producers, but to this must be added participants such as speculators, operators, or stockholders – all of whom are constantly reversing their position in the market.

These facts all suggest that classical theory must be rejected as a model for explaining short-run price behavior, especially as found in commodity cash and futures markets. A number of economists such as Taussig and Working have already taken steps in this direction. Taussig modified classical theory with his notion of the "penumbra" and Working replaced it with his theory of "anticipatory prices." Our results also indicate that a new theory should be devised – one which conforms to our findings concerning price behavior. This behavior can be explained to some extent by the general model presented in Chapter 8, but the low correlations reached between prices and their determinants reflect its inadequacies. It appears, therefore, that commodity price fluctuations are explicable by several different models and that we are incapable of distinguishing among them.

Three causes, in particular, can be cited as being responsible for this dilemma. As explained above, the first relates to the lack of a clear definition between buyers and sellers in the markets. If the actual list of market participants is examined, one finds: (1) producers who are primarily sellers, (2) manufacturers and processors who are buyers before conversion and sellers afterwards, (3) hedgers who buy and sell for insurance or gain, (4) speculators who buy and sell for gain, and (5) stockholders or merchants who also buy and sell for gain. A second cause is the susceptibility of the participants to market expectations or new information. In addition to their interpreting this information with different trading motives in mind, the information itself is often dubious or irrelevant. Coincidental with this problem is the lack of a key actor in the market whose functioning might help explain price fluctuations. In the stock market, the specialist who controls the exchange of bids and offers can be seen as helping to generate the random price fluctuations which develop there. No counterpart for this phenomenon exists in commodity markets, except perhaps when the occasional malpractice of directing all transactions through a single broker takes place.[5]

In conclusion, the authors believe that a more realistic model of short-run price behavior should enlarge upon our present results to encompass the following:

1. *Market structure:* the appropriate deterministic forces in the market as suggested by the endogenous and exogenous variables found important in this study.
2. *Market composition:* the relative numbers and effects of market participants, including producers, manufacturers, processors, hedgers, speculators, stockholders, and merchants.
3. *Market psychology:* the response of these participants to market information where response varies according to trading motives, and information ranges from relevant to irrelevant.

Implications for Statistical Methods

Although our primary aim in this study has been to investigate commodity prices, a secondary aim has been to determine the quality of a number of theoretical methods when applied to a wide range of data. The use of spectral methods with single or pairs of series is now commonplace, but the use of methods designed to accommodate more than two series has been limited. Especially the techniques of partial and multiple spectra and stepwise regression have seldom been applied to economic data. The greatest gap in earlier studies has been in the too few attempts to combine the spectral and model-building approaches. The present findings suggest that these multiple series methods perform very well, providing consistent and clearly interpretable results. The lack of proper statistical tests associated with some of the methods has on occasion limited the depth of interpretation, but presumably such tests will become available as the techniques gain in popularity.

The basic idea underlying spectral methods, the decomposition of a variable into frequency components, has proved useful when interpreting the results, not only of the spectral analysis but also of model-building. For the latter, spectral decomposition has enabled us to specify the general model over specific frequency ranges as well as to use the multiple coherence diagram to see if a model was fitting all frequency components equally well.

Stepwise regression does seem to have admirable theoretical properties as an explanatory technique for constructing explanatory or predictive models when many explanatory variables are involved and when one has less a priori knowledge than is usually assumed when constructing an econometric model. The method has worked very well in practice, despite the lack of a completely satisfactory method for stopping the addition of variables to the model. The methods used for determining the cutoff point produced models with optimistic goodness of fit, without encountering serious overfitting. This problem was considered in detail in the appendix to Chapter 9.

As one might expect, the spectral and model-building approaches proved to be complementary rather than competitive. Specific hypotheses involving one or two series, such as those listed at the outset of this chapter, were best tackled by spectral methods. Since such methods are inappropriate when one attempts to predict future values of a variable, one also has to employ regression or model-building methods. Only on one occasion were the two approaches competitive – in the consideration of the importance of supply and demand. We feel that in that part of the study, the use of both methods, i.e., a direct spectral approach and the use of supply and demand variables in the explanatory and predictive models, led to a greater understanding of the basic mechanism of the market than if only one approach had been used.

Stock Markets and Commodity Markets

The recent appearance of a study on stock markets, which is partly based on spectral methods, permits us to draw certain comparisons between those markets and the markets for commodities.[6] The empirical results reached for the two markets are noticeably similar, although several interesting differences do appear. Similarities in price behavior between these markets are considered first.

1. For both sets of prices the random walk model fits very well in general, and, for *predictive* purposes no clearly superior model has yet been found. Slight variations from this model have been found for both markets: a trend and long-run oscillations (periods of two years or more) for stock prices; and greater evidence of a seasonal component in some commodity prices. The random walk model was not found to hold when considering price changes in transactions data on the New York Stock Exchange, but this exception could not be confirmed for commodity price changes because of a lack of comparable data.

2. When attempting to *explain*, rather than predict, price changes, unlagged explanatory variables can be found: e.g., dividends and earnings for stock prices and various supply and demand variables in commodity markets. However, for both markets, the introduction of lagged values of these variables does not give improved forecasts over those provided by a random walk model.

3. Both markets seem to be almost as "active" when closed as when they are open, so that the variance of overnight (close minus open) price changes is similar in size to the variance of overday (open minus close) price changes. It could be argued that an important component in the price-determining mechanism is the flow of unexpected information, which continues throughout both day and night.

4. Prices move together. It has been found that monthly price changes of stocks of companies in the same or related industries are clearly positively correlated. A similar result has been found for interrelated commodities, such as edible oils.

5. The prices for neither market seem to be significantly related to the general economy, except possibly in the very long run. (See Table 6-6, for instance.)

The majority of the foregoing similarities can be attributed to speculative elements in the markets. Thus any clearly predictable component, of a profitable size, in either set of prices might quickly be removed by speculative activity. Similarly, movements in the price of one variable (stock or commodity) might be taken as relevant "information" by speculators, causing prices of related stocks or commodities to move in the same direction. It is debatable whether the amount of speculation, with all the associated effort involved, is a worthwhile use of a nation's resources. It can certainly be argued that a certain amount of speculation is of value; but beyond a limit, speculation can be said to be excessive. While a rough measure of excess speculation is possible for commodity markets, a corresponding measure is practically impossible for stock markets.

Some other ways in which the markets have been found to differ are as follows:

1. For commodity markets, there are real forces of supply and demand. Producers supply a real product to the market, consumers buy this product. In the latter case, some consumers use it immediately, while others convert it to products, such as margarine or bread, for sale to the general public. Without speculation, prices would be determined by ordinary supply and demand theory; however, the introduction of speculation makes this theory much less appropriate. Stock markets differ in as far as the supply of shares to the market represents only a small proportion of the total volume of trading. What trading does take place consists mostly of the supply of and demand for existing shares, and these shares constantly alternate between buyer and seller.

2. Whereas a clear relationship between the volume of transactions and the square of price changes was found for stock markets, no such relationship has been found for commodity markets.

3. There are a number of institutional differences between the markets. First, the commodity market is almost a perfect auction, while the stock market is less than a perfect auction. The latter fact results from the presence of floor specialists who alter the nature of the mechanism that generates prices.[7] Second, the commodity market features trade in cash or physical contracts as well as in futures contracts, the former being influenced by the latter. In contrast, the stock market has trade primarily in stock certificates, with futures trading relatively unimportant.[8] Finally, differences exist in the descriptive data

available for analyzing the markets. As an example, transactions data is available for stock markets but not for commodity markets; conversely, speculative and hedging data describing market balance is available for commodity markets but not for stock markets.

Future Research

Many different problems arising from this study warrant further investigation. The main prospect is for developing a more complete model of price behavior along the lines suggested earlier. Several other possibilities for further research are evident; for example, results pertaining to hedging and speculating. Changes in long speculating and short hedging have displayed not only a limited correlation with changes in commodity prices but the former also exert a fixed-angle lead over the latter. Two points appear to be crucial in explaining this phenomenon. First of all, one might investigate whether a more formal structural relationship exists between hedging, speculating, and prices. Secondly, one might establish a clearer interpretation of the fixed-angle lead found between these variables. One difficulty in performing this investigation would be that the available statistics describing hedging and speculative commitments do not accurately reflect risk transfer. This could be corrected only if the researcher has access to a more accurate breakdown of these commitments or if the Commodity Exchange Authority revises its present method of classification.

Some additional possibilities include refining the stated interrelationships between the different commodity price series, as well as applying the present results to longer-run price fluctuations. Concerning the first of these prospects, the aggregate price indexes constructed in Chapter 6 only approximate the complex cross-relationships which exist between prices, supply, and demand for the commodities involved. Since the understanding of these cross-relationships is necessary to producing better price explanation and forecasts, there is need to construct a refined model which not only considers the relative substitution of commodities over certain price ranges but which also considers the impact of competitive synthetics.

Results from the general model could also be extended to long-run models for quarterly or annual prices, since the causality underlying long-run behavior often begins in the short run. A limited amount of research has continued in this direction, and results have shown that, while the speculative influences decline in importance, the business-cycle influences become more relevant. Most long-run price models involve simultaneous equation methods, but it would be helpful to learn whether the single equation method forecasts better than the elaborate methods. Long-run price forecasts produced by this method should also be compared to forecasts obtained from the proposed statistical forecast methods, especially since the latter can lead to inexpensive, routine forecasts.

Lastly, the findings regarding the discovery of a random walk in prices can be used to improve research in areas where the known behavior of prices is only the input to performing a particular function. For example, the present results could help solve the basic problem of devising an optimum purchasing pattern for the manufacturer who buys his raw materials on a speculative market. Or, as mentioned earlier, the results could help to construct a better price stabilization mechanism for future commodity agreements. The extent to which our results really are used in applications such as these will determine the contribution of our work.

Appendixes

A Data

The data examined in this study were published by competent sources and can be accepted as being of a relatively high quality. A few series, however, did require adjustment or estimation and contain certain limitations which should be reported. In addition to a discussion of these adjustments, a table has been included which summarizes the various data sources.

Price Series

Near Futures

For all the futures price series the data has been compiled in the form of near futures prices. Where more distant futures contract prices have been introduced, a similar procedure was followed. This arrangement has been preferred to using the futures price series for a single contract month throughout the year. A comparison was made between the two methods and the near series arrangement offered a better presentation of seasonality, as was suggested by Cootner.[1]

Cash Wheat

The cash wheat series appearing in the spectrum of Figure 3.8 was compiled by Working and later tested by Kendall. Only the period 1887-1916 has been included in the present test. Working has adjusted the series by a weighting scheme such that the prices represent that grade of wheat most heavily traded on the market.[2]

Corn, Oats, Rye, and Wheat Futures

In the comparison between wheat, corn, oats, and rye near futures prices for the period 1921-1951, a simple linear interpolation was used to produce data for the missing war years.

Volume and Open Contract Series

Near Futures Volume

The near futures volume data for all commodities had to be estimated for the first six months (January 1950 to June 1965). This data was derived from the total volume of trading reported during that period where a proportion of volume was chosen equivalent to the near futures proportion of total volume in the first six months of the following year.

Open Interest

A shift in open interest classifications from total to particular markets occurred in 1960; e.g., wheat figures after 1960 represent trading on the Chicago market rather than the total for all markets combined. Little distortion of the earlier estimates has resulted from this adjustment, since trading at the markets cited already accounted for most of the trading activity. In 1964-1965 Chicago comprised 90% of the total trading in wheat, 95% in corn and rye, and 99% in soybeans. Discrepancies for other commodities were all below 1%.

Potatoes

A low level of trading activity in potatoes from January 1950 to February 1952 resulted in gaps in the open contract positions. The total loss of data was not substantial. Over the total period January 1950 to June 1965 only 10% of the data was missing from the long speculation series and 5% or less from the remaining series.

Physical Quantities

Exports

Exports of soybean oil and cottonseed oil beginning April 1961 include estimates of foreign donations; and, commencing June 1965, they cover shipments. These totals were sufficiently low prior to 1961 to prevent any serious errors in the data.

Stocks

Since only annual supply data was available for soybeans, rye, and wheat, the monthly stock figures were reached by subtracting monthly demand successively from the annual supply. The Consumer Marketing Service also reported that the given demand figures were estimates rather than actual values.

Wheat stocks = (annual) carryover + production + imports - seeds - feed - residual - (monthly) disappearance - exports

Rye stocks = (annual) carryover + production - seed - feed - residual + (monthly) imports - disappearance - exports

Soybean stocks = (annual) carryover + production - seed - feed - residual - (monthly) disappearance - exports

The seasonal pattern in stocks resulting from this technique was rather strong, but coherence comparisons showed that prices were more responsive to stocks which were estimated by this method than by an adjusted series. Only for soybeans did the pattern seem exceptional and it was removed by a seasonal adjustment procedure.

Crushing Margin

The crushing margin for soybeans which was introduced in the explanatory models was calculated from the crushing yields as follows:

Crushing margin = (oil price x oil yield) + (meal price x meal yield) - soybean price

Table A

Data Sources

Commodity	*Description*	*Time Period*	*Source*
		Monthly Prices	
Corn, cotton, cottonseed oil, eggs, lard, oats, potatoes, rye, soybean meal, soybean oil, soybeans, wheat	Monthly series of futures closing prices recorded on the final trading day of each month	January 1950 to July 1965. Lard from January 1948 to December 1962	*Commodity Futures Statistics*, Commodity Exchange Authority
Cocoa	Monthly series of cash and futures prices recorded on the final trading day of each month	January 1950 to July 1965	*Cocoa Market Report*, Gill & Duffus, Ltd., London
Corn, oats, rye, wheat	Monthly series of futures closing prices recorded on the final trading day of each month	January 1921 to December 1951	*Grain Futures Statistics 1921-1951*, Statistical Bulletin no. 131, U.S.D.A.
Corn, oats, soybeans, wheat	Monthly series of cash prices recorded on the final trading day of each month	January 1950 to July 1965	*Correspondence*, Consumer and Marketing Service, U.S.D.A.
Lard	Monthly series of cash closing prices recorded on the final trading day of each month	January 1948 to December 1962	*Yearbook*, Chicago Board of Trade
Flax, oats (Winnipeg)	Monthly series of futures prices recorded on the final trading day of each month	January 1950 to July 1963	*Grain Trade Yearbook*, Winnipeg
Cottonseed oil, rye, soybean meal, soybean oil, soybeans, wheat	Monthly series of cash prices representing an average of daily closing prices	August 1957 to June 1967	*Correspondence*, Consumer and Marketing Service, U.S.D.A.
Cottonseed oil, rye, soybean meal, soybean oil, soybeans, wheat	Monthly series of futures prices representing an average of daily closing prices	August 1957 to June 1967	*Correspondence*, Consumer and Marketing Service, U.S.D.A.
		Weekly Prices	
Corn	Weekly series of cash and futures closing prices recorded on Friday	August 1950 to September 1965	*Yearbook*, Chicago Board of Trade

Table A (*continued*)

Commodity	*Description*	*Time Period*	*Source*
		Weekly Prices	
Lard	Weekly series of cash and futures closing prices recorded on Friday	January 1959 to December 1962	*Yearbook*, Chicago Board of Trade
Oats, rye, soybean oil, soybeans, wheat	Weekly series of futures closing prices recorded on Friday	August 1961 to July 1965	*Yearbook*, Chicago Board of Trade
Soybeans	Weekly series of cash closing prices recorded on Friday	August 1961 to July 1965	*Yearbook*, Chicago Board of Trade
Wheat	Weekly series of cash prices	January 1887 to December 1916	*Wheat Studies of the Food Research Institute*, November 1934
		Daily Prices	
Cocoa	Daily series of cash and futures closing prices	August 1964 to July 1965	*Cocoa Market Report*, Gill & Duffus, Ltd., London
Coffee, cotton, rubber, sugar	Daily series of futures closing prices; cash closing prices for cotton	August 1964 to July 1965	*The Public Ledger*, London
Coffee, rubber, sugar	Daily series of cash closing prices	August 1964 to July 1965	*Daily Spot Market Price Indexes and Prices*, U.S.D.L.
Corn, oats, rye, soybeans, wheat	Daily series of futures closing prices	August 1964 to July 1965	*Yearbook*, Chicago Board of Trade
Dow Jones Indexes	Daily cash and futures indexes	August 1964 to July 1965	*Financial Times*, London
		Volume and Open Contracts	
Cotton, cotton-seed oil, corn, eggs, oats, potatoes, rye, soybean meal, soybean oil, soybeans, wheat	Monthly volume of futures transactions	January 1950 to June 1965	*Commodity Futures Statistics*, Commodity Exchange Authority
Cottonseed oil, corn, oats, potatoes, rye, soybean meal, soybean oil, soybeans, wheat	Monthly open interest by hedging and speculating categories	January 1950 to June 1967	*Commodity Futures Statistics*, Commodity Exchange Authority

(*continued*)

Table A (*continued*)

Commodity	*Description*	*Time Period*	*Source*
		Physical Quantities	
Cocoa	Monthly physical stocks, supply	January 1951 to June 1966	*Cocoa Market Report*, Gill & Duffus, Ltd., London
Cottonseed oil, soybean meal, soybean oil	Monthly physical stocks, supply, demand	January 1950 to June 1965	*Fats and Oils Statistics*, no. 376 and no. 147, U.S.D.A.
Rye, soybeans, wheat	Monthly estimates of demand	January 1950 to June 1965. Rye from July 1950	*Correspondence*, Consumer and Marketing Service, U.S.D.A.
Cottonseed oil, soybean meal, soybean oil, soybeans	Monthly stocks, production exports, and domestic consumption	August 1957 June 1967	*Fats and Oils Statistics*, No. 376, U.S.D.A. Update: *Fats and Oils Situation*, U.S.D.A.
Rye, wheat, soybeans	Monthly exports and domestic consumptions yearly supply	August 1957 to June 1967	*Correspondence*, Consumer and Marketing Service, U.S.D.A., Current issues of *Grain and Feed Statistics* as well as *Supplement for 1964*
		Business Cycle Indicators	
Selected business cycle indicators except spot and futures indexes	Monthly series unadjusted	August 1957 to June 1967	*Survey of Current Business and Biennial Supplements*, 1961-1963
Dow Jones Spot and Futures Indexes	Monthly series of closing prices reported on the final trading day of each month	August 1957 to June 1966	*Wall Street Journal*, New York

B Computations

The computations for this study have been performed through the courtesy of the computer centers at both Nottingham and Manchester Universities. The programs for the power spectrum, cross-spectrum and stepwise regression were designed in Algol for the KDF9 at the Cripps Computing Center, Nottingham University. The programs for the partial and multiple cross-spectrum were written in Atlas Autocode and required the facilities of the Atlas Computing Service, Manchester University. Programs other than the above were designed by the present author for use at Nottingham.

The spectral and cross-spectral computations were combined into a single program by Tony Hughes. This program constitutes a remodeled version of the basic spectral program using Parzen weights and normalized mean and variance. The user can specify the number of truncation points as well as the number of frequency points to be printed. The output includes the power spectra for all of the input series and the coherence and phase values for all combinations of these series.

The partial and multiple cross-spectral programs were devised by Hedley Rees. Once again, Parzen weights are used and the number of truncations and frequency points can be specified. Contrary to the basic spectral program, both of these programs compute spectral estimates by considering coherence as a generalization of partial and multiple correlation. The partial program supplies the partial spectrum for all of the input series plus the partial coherence and phase values for all combinations of these series. The multiple program produces the multiple coherence values as well as the spectrum of residuals from the generalized multiple regression. No multiple phase values are estimated, as the interpretation of these values remains questionable.

The stepwise regression program has been designed specifically for time series analysis and is built around the Bimed BMD02R program. The present program, as developed by John Payne, permits any number of lagged dependent and lagged independent variables to enter the regression. The characteristics of the regression can be determined by selecting the maximum possible number of lags for the dependent and independent variables, the F level for variables to both enter and leave the regression, as well as the tolerance level for rounding error. At each step, the program prints the coefficient of determination, the overall F value, the partial F values, the partial correlations, the regression coefficients, and the standard errors. The final output stage can also produce the Durbin-Watson statistic, regression estimates, regression residuals, and a plot of estimated versus actual values.

Last of all, the exponential smoothing forecast program was designed by David Reid who also operated the program for many of our commodity price series. The program has been constructed to forecast from a smoothed linear equation whose independent variables are a function of time such as trends, polynomials, exponentials, or sinusoids. The smoothing takes place by exponentially weighting the coefficients in the equation through a weighted least squares procedure. The discounting of past observations can take place more quickly or slowly, depending on the value chosen for the weighting or discounting factor, β. Program output consists of various equation parameters plus forecasts, actuals, and forecast errors up to a number of periods ahead.

Notes

Notes

Chapter 1
Introduction

1. Other examples and a more extensive explanation can be found in J. W. F. Rowe, *Primary Commodities in International Trade* (Cambridge: University Press, 1965), pp. 66-76.

2. W. Arthur Lewis, *Economic Survey, 1919-1939* (London: George Allen and Unwin, 1963), pp. 56, 57.

3. John W. Mellor, *The Economics of Agricultural Development* (Ithaca, N.Y.: Cornell University Press, 1966), p. 336.

4. Lord Cole and F. J. Tempel, *Raw Materials and Pricing* (Paper delivered at the Annual General Meeting of Unilever, London, 27 April 1966), pp. 10-12.

5. M. M. Postan, E. E. Rich, and E. Miller, eds., *The Economic History of Europe,* vol. 3, *Economic Organization and Policy in the Middle Ages* (Cambridge: University Press, 1963), p. 132.

6. Robert L. Reynolds, *Europe Emerges* (Madison: University of Wisconsin Press, 1961), p. 203.

7. For a more thorough discussion of the origin of these institutions see Julius B. Baer and Olin G. Saxon, *Commodity Exchanges and Futures Trading* (New York; Harper & Brothers, 1949), pp. 3-26.

8. Postan et al., op cit., p. 137.

9. Baer and Saxon, op. cit., p. 9.

10. Portions of the following discussion of the evolution of markets in London have been taken from a special edition of *The Public Ledger.* See L. G. Pine, "London: A Commercial City Since the Roman Occupation," *The Public Ledger,* suppl. (12 January 1960): 10.

11. Further discussion of the risk coverage provided by the commodity dealer can be found in Baer and Saxon, op. cit., pp. 14-19.

12. Pine, op. cit., p. 11.

13. Baer and Saxon, op. cit., p. 10.

14. *The Market Place,* booklet published by the Department of Public Information and Education, Chicago Board of Trade, p. 4.

15. A fuller discussion of the development of the futures contract can be found in Baer and Saxon, op. cit., pp. 130-142.

16. Gerald Gold, *Modern Commodity Futures Trading* (New York: Commodity Research Bureau, 1966), p. 8.

17. See, for example, R. J. Teweles, C. V. Harlow, and H. L. Stone, *The Commodity Futures Trading Guide* (New York: McGraw-Hill, 1969).

18. H. S. Houthakker, "Scope and Limits of Futures Trading," *Allocation of Economic Resources: Essays in Honor of B. F. Haley,* ed. Moses Abromovitz et al. (Stanford: Stanford University Press, 1959), p. 157.

19. L. S. Venkataramanan, *The Theory of Futures Trading* (London: Asia Publishing House, 1965), pp. 7-20.

20. Ibid., p. 11.

21. For an elaboration of this discussion see Houthakker, op. cit., pp. 141-144.

22. A summary of the various arguments can be found in Venkataramanan, op. cit., pp. 21-50.

23. Holbrook Working, "Futures Trading and Hedging," *American Economic Review* 43 (June 1953): 325.

24. Paul H. Cootner, "Speculation and Hedging," Proceedings of a Symposium on Price Effects of Speculation in Organized Commodity Markets, *Food Research Institute Studies* 7, suppl. (1967): 65-105.

25. Holbrook Working, "Speculation on Hedging Markets," *Food Research Insitiute Studies,* 1 (May 1960): 187.

26. T. A. Hieronymus, *Uses of Grain Futures Markets in the Farm Business,* Agricultural Experiment Station Bulletin 696 (Urbana: University of Illinois, September 1963), p. 8.

27. Commodity Exchange Authority, *Commodity Futures Statistics, 1965-1966,* no. 382 (Washington, D.C.: Government Printing Office, 1966), p. 5.

28. Hieronymus, op. cit., pp. 16-18.

29. See. C. W. J. Granger and O. Morgenstern, *Predictability of Stock Market Prices* (Lexington, Mass.: D. C. Heath, 1970).

30. See Rowe, *Primary Commodities,* pp. 66-69.

31. This argument has been proposed by Rowe, ibid., pp. 69-71.

32. Holbrook Working, "A Theory of Anticipatory Prices," *American Economic Review* 48 (May 1958).

33. Arnold B. Larson, "Measurement of a Random Process in Futures Prices," *Food Research Institute Studies* 1 (November 1960); C. S. Brinegar, "Statistical Analysis of Speculative Price Behavior," (Ph.D. dissertation to be published in *Food Research Institute Studies*).

34. Seymour Smidt, "A Test of the Serial Independence of Price Changes in Soybean Futures," *Food Research Institute Studies* 5 (1965); H. Houthakker, "Systematic and Random Elements in Short Term Price Movements," *American Economic Review* 51 (1961).

35. F. W. Taussig, "Is Market Price Determinate?" *Quarterly Journal of Economics* 35 (May 1929); Henry Schultz, *The Theory and Measurement of Demand* (Chicago: University of Chicago Press, 1938); H. Wold and L. Jureen, *Demand Analysis* (New York: Wiley, 1953).

36. F. H. Weymar, *The Dynamics of the World Cocoa Market* (Cambridge: MIT Press, 1968).

37. For a summary of the various arguments see Venkataramanan, op. cit., pp. 51-74.

38. Granger and Morgenstern, loc. cit.

Chapter 2
Statistical Background

1. Examples of both the spectra and cross-spectra have been taken from "Spectral Analysis of the Term Structure of Interest Rates," By C. W. J. Granger and H. J. B. Rees, *Review of Economic Studies,* Vol. 35 (1968), pp. 67-76.

Chapter 3
The Random Behavior of Commodity Prices

1. For further discussion of this problem see C. W. J. Granger and O. Morgenstern, *Predictability of Stock Market Prices* (Lexington, Mass.: D. C. Heath, 1970), ch. 3.

2. Louis Bachelier, "Theory of Speculation," in *The Random Character of Stock Market Prices,* ed. P. H. Cootner (Cambridge: MIT Press, 1964), pp. 17-78.

3. Holbrook Working, "A Random Difference Series for Use in the Analysis of Time Series," *Journal of the American Statistical Association* 29 (1934): 11-24.

4. See Granger and Morgenstern, op. cit., chs. 3, 4.

5. Holbrook Working, "New Ideas and Methods for Price Research," *Journal of Farm Economics* 38 (December 1956): 1433.

6. Holbrook Working, "Price Effects of Future Trading," *Food Research Institute Studies* (February 1960): 648; idem, "New Concepts Concerning Futures Markets and Prices," *American Economic Review* 52 (June 1962): 445-449.

7. Arnold B. Larson, "Measurement of a Random Process in Future Prices," *Food Research Institute Studies* 1 (1960): 313-324 (reprinted in Cootner, ed., see fn. 2).

8. Houthakker, "Systematic and Random Elements in Short Term Price Movements," *American Economic Review* 51 (1961); Seymour Smidt, "A Test of the Serial Independence of Price Changes in Soybean Futures," *Food Research Institute Studies* 5 (1965): 127.

9. Sidney S. Alexander, "Price Movements in Speculative Markets: Trends or Random Walks," *Industrial Management Review* 2 (1961), pp. 7-26.

10. *The Random Character of Stock Market Prices,* ed. P. H. Cootner (Cambridge: MIT Press, 1964).

11. E. F. Fama and M. E. Blume, "Filter Rules and Stock Market Trading," *Journal of Business* 39, suppl. (1966): 226-241.

12. C. W. J. Granger, "The Typical Spectral Shape of an Economic Variable," *Econometrica* 34 (January 1966): 150-161.

13. Limit values of 1.94 and 0.34 at the 95% level with $m = 48$ are reported in C. W. J. Granger and M. Hatanaka, *Spectral Analysis of Economic Time Series* (Princeton: Princeton University Press, 1965), p. 63.

14. Paul H. Cootner, "Speculation and Hedging," Proceedings of a Symposium on Price Effects of Speculation in Organized Commodity Markets, *Food Research Institute Studies* 7, suppl. (1967): ; T. A. Hieronymus, *Uses of Grain Futures Markets in the Farm Business,* Agricultural Experimental Station Bulletin 696 (Urbana: University of Illinois, 1963), p. 47; Roger W. Gray, "The Seasonal Pattern in Wheat Futures Prices Under the Loan Program," *Food Research Institute Studies* 3 (February 1962): 23-24.

15. Granger, "The Typical Shape of an Economic Variable," op. cit., p. 156.

16. Holbrook Working, "Note on the Correlation of First Differences of Averages in a Random Chain," *Econometrica* 28 (1960): 916-918; Alfred Cowles and H. E. Jones, "Some A Posteriori Probabilities in Stock Market Action,"

Econometrica 5 (1937): 280-294; Alfred Cowles, "A Revision of Previous Conclusions Regarding Stock Price Behavior," *Econometrica* 28 (1960): 909-915.

17. M. G. Kendall, "The Analysis of Economic Time Series. Part I: Prices," *Journal of the Royal Statistical Society* 96 (1953): 11-25.

18. M. D. Godfrey, C. W. J. Granger, and O. Morgenstern, "The Random Walk Hypothesis of Stock Market Behavior," *Kyklos* 17 (1964): 13-17.

19. Houthakker, loc. cit.

20.Most of these results were first pointed out by Holbrook Working in "Note on the Correlation of First Differences of Averages in a Random Chain," *Econometrica* 28 (1960): 916-918.

Chapter 4
An Expectations Theory of Cash and Futures Prices

1. H. Houthakker, "The Scope and Limits of Futures Trading," *Allocation of Economic Resources: Essays in Honor of B. B. Haley,* ed. M. Ambromovitz (Stanford: Stanford University Press, 1959).

2. See, for example, T. A. Hieronymus, *Uses of Grain Futures Markets in the Farm Business,* Agricultural Experimental Station Bulletin 696 (Urbana: University of Illinois, 1963), p. 29.

3. Holbrook Working, "Quotations on Commodity Futures as Price Forecasts," *Econometrica* 10 (1942): 29.

4. Ibid., pp. 49-50.

5. Holbrook Working, "Theory of the Inverse Carrying Charge in Futures Markets," *Journal of Farm Economics* 30 (February 1948): 15.

6. Paul A. Samuelson, "Proof that Properly Anticipated Prices Fluctuate Randomly," *Industrial Management Review* 6 (Spring 1965): 41-49.

7. For a discussion of the term structure of interest rates using such a model see Burton G. Malkiel, "Expectations, Bond Prices, and the Term Structure of Interest Rates," *Quarterly Journal of Economics* 76 (1962): 197-218.

8. See C. W. J. Granger and H. B. Rees, "Spectral Analysis of the Term Structure of Interest Rates," *Review of Economic Studies* 35 (January 1968).

9. P. H. Cootner, "Common Elements in Futures Markets for Commodities and Bonds," *Proceedings of the American Economic Association* 51 (May 1961): 176.

10. Samuelson, loc. cit.

11. C. W. J. Granger and O. Morgenstern, *Predictability of Stock Market Prices* (Lexington, Mass.: D. C. Heath, 1970).

12. A. O. Hughes, "A Study of the Distribution of Spectral Estimates" (M.Sc. thesis, University of Nottingham, 1965), pp. 74-77.

13. Granger and Rees, loc. cit.

14. For a theoretical discussion of this difficult problem see C. W. J. Granger, "Investigating Causal Relationships by Econometric Models and Cross-Spectral Methods," *Econometrica* 37 (July 1969): 424-438.

Chapter 5
The Nature of Demand

1. F. W. Taussig, "Is Market Price Determinate?" *Quarterly Journal of Economics* 35 (May 1929): 394-411.

2. See L. A. Bernstein, "How Commodity Price Charts Disclose Supply-Demand Shifts," *Commodity Yearbook* (1958): 33-42.

3. For a long-run confirmation of the functional relationship between price and demand in commodity markets see Henry Schultz, *The Theory and Measurement of Demand* (Chicago: University of Chicago Press, 1938), pp. 175-521.

4. Holbrook Working, "A Theory of Anticipatory Prices," *American Economic Review Proceedings* 48, (May 1958): 190.

5. Ibid., p. 191.

6. A recent study involving the test of a direct relationship in the stock market is that of E. F. Fama et al., "The Adjustment of Stock Prices to New Information," *International Economic Review* 10 (1969): 1-21.

7. M. D. Godfrey, C. W. J. Granger, and O. Morgenstern, "The Random Walk Hypothesis of Stock Market Behavior," *Kyklos* 17 (1964): 1-30.

8. For a discussion of some of the difficulties encountered in measuring the relationship between price and quantity see Schultz, loc. cit.; and H. Wold and L. Jureen, *Demand Analysis: A Study in Econometrics* (New York: Wiley, 1953).

9. Holbrook Working, "Speculation on Hedging Markets," *Food Research Institute Studies* 1 (May 1960): 187.

10. Gerald Gold, *Modern Commodity Futures Trading* (New York: Commodity Research Bureau, 1966), pp. 215-217.

11. Moderate levels of correlation between V and $(\Delta P)^2$ for a number of securities are reported in C. W. J. Granger and O. Morgenstern, *Predictability of Stock Market Prices* (Lexington, Mass.: D. C. Heath, 1970).

12. See R. J. Teweles, C. V. Harlow and H. L. Stone, *The Commodity Futures Trading Guide* (New York: McGraw-Hill, 1969), pp. 108-111. See also Harry Jiler, "Volume and Open Interest Analysis as an Aid to Price Forecasting," *Guide to Commodity Price Forecasting* (New York: Commodity Research Bureau, 1965).

13. For a fuller discussion of the problems of classification see Charles S. Rockwell, "Profits, Normal Backwardation and Forecasting in Commodity Futures" (Ph.D. dissertation, University of California at Berkeley, 1964), pp. 11-21.

14. Ibid., p. 17.

15. For a further discussion of how hedging and speculating determine futures prices within the supply-demand framework see J. R. Hicks, *Value and Capital* (Oxford: Clarendon Press, 1957), pp. 137-138.

16. R. D. Smith, "Short Interest and Stock Market Prices," *Financial Analysts Journal* (1968), pp. 151-154.

17. Working, op. cit., pp. 185-220.

18. Rockwell, op. cit., p.. 21; H. Houthakker, "Can Speculators Forecast Prices?" *Review of Economics and Statistics* 39 (May 1957): 144.

19. Working, op. cit., p. 197.

20. Ibid., p. 194.

21. For a test of the relationship between speculation and price behavior where the speculative index is compared to the weekly price range, see "Margins, Speculation and Prices in Grains Futures Markets," Economic Research Service (Washington, D.C.: U.S. Department of Agriculture, December 1967).

Chapter 6
Endogenous and Exogenous Influences

1. Richard P. Donchian, "Trend Following Methods in Commodity Price Analysis," *Guide to Commodity Price Forecasting*, ed. H. Jiler (New York: Commodity Research Bureau, 1965), pp. 57-59.

2. Gerald Gold, *Modern Commodity Futures Trading* (New York: Commodity Research Bureau, 1966), pp. 54-55.

3. Frederick C. Mills, *Price-Quantity Interactions in Business Cycles*, Special volume of the National Bureau of Economic Research (Princeton: Princeton University Press, 1946), p. 105.

4. See C. W. J. Granger and M. Hatanaka, *Spectral Analysis of Economic Time Series* (Princeton: Princeton University Press, 1965), ch. 12, pp. 207-262.

5. See T. G. Moore, "Stock Market Margin Requirements," *Journal of Political Economy* 74 (April 1966): 158-167, for a discussion of the relation of credit to stock market prices.

Chapter 7
Explanatory Equations and Results

1. For a discussion of reasons for using single rather than simultaneous equation procedures for explaining short-run movements, see W. J. Witherell, *Dynamics of the International Wool Market: An Econometric Analysis*, Economic Research Program Memorandum No. 91 (Princeton: Princeton University, September 1967), p. 213: and Geoffrey S. Shepherd, *Agricultural Price Analysis* (Ames: Iowa State University Press, 1963), pp. 164-169.

2. See J. Durbin and G. Watson, "Testing for Serial Correlation in Least Squares Regression: Part II," *Biometrika* 38 (June 1951): 159-178.

3. For a further explanation of the effect of multicollinearity on the results achieved see J. Johnston, *Econometric Methods* (New York: McGraw-Hill, 1963), pp. 201-207.

4. The significance levels reported for the different statistics are taken from George W. Snedecor, *Statistical Methods* (Ames: Iowa State University Press, 1956), p. 249; D. B. Owen, *Handbook of Statistical Tables* (Reading Mass.: Addison-Wesley, 1962), p. 514; C. W. J. Granger and M. Hatanaka, *Spectral*

Analysis of Economic Time Series (Princeton: Princeton University Press, 1964), p. 79; and Durbin and Watson, op. cit., pp. 173-175.

5. Granger and Hatanaka, op. cit., pp. 78-79.

6. Richard P. Donchian, "Trend Following Methods in Commodity Price Analysis," *Guide to Commodity Price Forecasting*, ed. H. Jiler (New York: Commodity Research Bureau, 1965), pp. 57-59.

7. T. A. Hieronymus, *Uses of Grain Futures Markets in the Farm Business*, Agricultural Experimental Station Bulletin 696 (Urbana: University of Illinois, 1963), pp. 47-48; Roger W. Gray, "The Seasonal Pattern in Wheat Futures Prices Under the Loan Program," *Food Research Institute Studies* 3 (February 1962): 23-24.

Chapter 8
A General Model of Commodity Price Equations

1. See C. W. J. Granger and O. Morgenstern. *Predictability of Stock Market Prices* (Lexington, Mass.: D. C. Heath, 1970).

Chapter 9
Forecasting Commodity Prices

1. D. W. Jorgenson, J. Hunter, and M. I. Nadiri, "The Predictive Performance of Econometric Models of Quarterly Investment Behavior," *Econometrica* 38 (1970), pp. 213-224.

2. Irwin Shisko, "Forecasting Sugar Prices," *Guide to Commodity Price Forecasting*, ed. H. Jiler (New York: Commodity Research Bureau, 1965), pp. 175-182; idem, "Techniques of Forecasting Commodity Prices, *Commodity Year Book* (New York: Commodity Research Bureau, 1965), pp. 30-41.

3. T. A. Hieronymus, "Forecasting Soybean and Soybean Product Prices," *Guide to Commodity Price Forecasting*, ed. H. Jiler (New York: Commodity Research Bureau, 1965), p. 166.

4. Geoffrey S. Shepherd, *Agricultural Price Analysis* (Ames: Iowa State University Press, 1963), pp. 165-166.

5. K. A. Fox, *Econometric Analysis and Public Policy* (Ames: Iowa State University Press, 1958).

6. Shepherd, op. cit., pp. 154-164.

7. For a summary of the effectives of various estimating procedures see J. Johnston, *Econometric Methods* (New York: McGraw-Hill, 1963), pp. 152-169.

8. William H. Witherell, *Dynamics of the International Wool Market: An Econometric Analysis,* Economic Research Program Memorandum No. 91 (Princeton: Princeton University, September 1967), pp. 1-212.

9. Ibid., p. 208.

10. F. Helmut Weymar, *The Dynamics of the World Cocoa Market* (Cambridge: MIT Press, 1968).

11. James P. Houck, "A Statistical Model of the Demand for Soybeans," *Journal of Farm Economics* 46 (May 1964): 366-374.

12. Roger J. Vandenborre, "Demand Analysis of the Markets for Soybean Oil and Soybean Meal," *Journal of Farm Economics* 48 (November 1966): 220-234.

13. Robert G. Brown, *Smoothing, Forecasting and Prediction of Discrete Time Series* (Englewood Cliffs: Prentice-Hall, 1963). For an application of exponential smoothing to other areas of forecasting see "Seminar of Time Series Analysis," *Statistician* 17, No. 3 (1967): 233-305.

14. F. G. Jarrett, "Short-Term Forecasting of Australian Wool Prices," *Australian Economic Papers* 4 (June-December 1965), pp. 93-102.

15. For a discussion of these methods as standards of forecast comparison see Ronald L. Cooper and Dale W. Jorgenson, *The Predictive Performance of Quarterly Econometric Models of the United States*, Institute of Business and Economic Research Working Paper No. 113 (Berkeley: University of California, Revised 1969), pp. 19-24.

16. Ibid.

17. Witherell, op. cit., pp. 255-257.

18. See G. E. Box and G. M. Jenkins, "Some Statistical Aspects of Adaptive Optimization and Control," *Journal of the Royal Statistical Society*, ser. B, vol. 24 (1962); idem, "Some Recent Advances in Forecasting and Control," *Applied Statistics* 17 (1968); idem, *Time Series Forecasting and Control* (San Francisco: Holden Day, 1970).

19. Box and Jenkins, *Time Series Forecasting and Control.*

20. See, for example, David J. Reid, "A Comparative Study of Time Series Prediction Techniques on Economic Data" (Ph.D. dissertation, University of Nottingham, 1969).

21. Much of this analysis has been taken directly from Andrew W. Ashby, "On Forecasting Commodity Prices by the Balance Sheet Approach," *Journal of Farm Economics* 46 (August 1964): 633-643.

22. Ibid., p. 637.

23. Many of these comments have been taken from Irwin Shisko, "Techniques of Forecasting Commodity Prices," op. cit., pp. 36-41.

24. See R. J. Teweles, C. V. Harlow, and H. L. Stone, The Technical Approach, *Commodity Futures Trading Guide* (New York: McGraw-Hill, 1969). ch. 7, pp. 91-112.

25. Richard P. Donchian, "Trend Following Methods in Commodity Price Analysis," *Guide to Commodity Price Forecasting*, ed. H. Jiler (New York: Commodity Research Bureau, 1965), pp. 51-56.

26. M. G. Kendall and A. Stuart, *The Advanced Theory of Statistics: Design and Analysis, and Time-Series* (London: Charles Griffin, 1966), vol. 3, pp. 476-478.

27. Brown, op. cit., p. 174.

28. Ibid., p. 179.

29. E. F. Fama et al., "The Adjustment of Stock Prices to New Information," *International Economic Review* 10 (1969): 1-21.

30. Reid, op. cit.

31. C. W. J. Granger and O. Morgenstern, *Predictability of Stock Market Prices* (Lexington, Mass.: D. C. Heath, 1970.

32. John Bates and C. W. J. Granger, "The Combination of Forecasts," *Operations Research Quarterly* 20 (1969): 451-468.

Chapter 10
Conclusions

1. For further discussion, see *Commodity Problems and Policies,* Second Session, United Nations Conference on Trade and Development, TD/8 (New Delhi: February, 1968).

2. Economic Research Service, *Margins, Speculation and Prices in Grains Futures Markets* (Washington, D.C.: U.S. Department of Agriculture, December 1967).

3. Ibid.

4. For a discussion of the history of and problems surrounding price stabilization schemes, see J. W. F. Rowe, *Primary Commodities in International Trade* (Cambridge: University Press, 1965). This example was taken from pp. 195-196 of that work.

5. See Commodity Exchange Authority, *Trading in the September 1961 Rye Future on the Chicago Board of Trade* (Washington, D.C.: U.S. Department of Agriculture, 20 September 1961).

6. C. W. J. Granger and O. Morgenstern, *Predictability of Stock Market Prices* (Lexington, Mass.: D. C. Heath, 1970).

7. For a detailed discussion of the specialist's role, see Granger and Morgenstern, ibid., ch. 11.

8. However, it was recently announced that the Chicago Board of Trade was considering setting up a central futures market in stocks (*Wall Street Journal,* 5 December, 1969).

Appendix A
Data

1. Paul H. Cootner, "Returns to Speculators, Telser versus Keynes," *Journal of Political Economy* 68 (August 1960): 416.

2. Holbrook Working, "Prices of Cash Wheat and Futures at Chicago Since 1883," *Wheat Studies of the Food Research Institute* (November 1934): 103-117.

Bibliography

Bibliography

Price Behavior[a]

*Alexander, Sydney S. "Price Movements in Speculative Markets: Trends or Random Walks." *Industrial Management Review.* 2 (May 1961): 7-26.

Armore, S. J. *The Demand and Price Structure for Food Fats and Oils.* U.S. Department of Agriculture, Technical Bulletin no. 1068. Washington, D.C.: Government Printing Office, June 1953.

*Bachelier, Louis. "Theory of Speculation." In *The Random Character of Stock Market Prices,* edited by P. Cootner. Cambridge: MIT Press, 1964.

Beckmann, M. J. "On the Determination of Prices in Futures Markets." In *Patterns of Market Behavior,* edited by M. J. Brennan. Providence: 1965.

Breimyer, Harold F. *Demand and Prices for Meat.* U.S. Department of Agriculture, Technical Bulletin no. 253, Washington, D.C.: Government Printing Office, 1961.

Brennan, M. J. "The Supply of Storage." *American Economic Review* 40 (March 1958): 50-72.

*Brinegar, C. S. *A Statistical Analysis of Speculative Price Behavior.* Ph.D. dissertation, Stanford University, 1954.

Caine, Sir Sydney. *Prices for Primary Producers.* London: Institute of Economic Affairs, 1966.

Cootner, P. H. "Stock Prices: Random vs. Systematic Changes." *Industrial Management Review* 3 (1962).

*Cootner, P. H., ed. *The Random Character of Stock Market Prices.* Cambridge: MIT Press, 1964.

*Cowles, A. "A Revision of Previous Conclusions Regarding Stock Price Behaviour." *Econometrica* 28 (October 1960): 909-915.

*Cowles, A., and Jones, H. E. "Some a Posteriori Probabilities in Stock Market Action." *Econometrica* 5 (July 1937): 280-294.

Ehrich, R. L. "Cash-Futures Price Relationships for Live Beef Cattle." *American Journal of Agricultural Economics* 51 (February 1969): 26-39.

Fama, E. F. "The Behaviour of Stock Market Prices." *Journal of Business* 38 (1965).

*Fama, E. F.; Fisher, L.; Jensen, M. C.; and Roll, R. "The Adjustment of Stock Prices to New Information." *International Economic Review* 10 (February 1969): 1-21.

Foote, R. J. *Analytical Tools for Studying Demand and Price Structure.* U.S. Department of Agriculture, Agricultural Handbook 146, Washington: Government Printing Office, 1958.

Foote, Richard J.; Klein, J. W.; and Clough, M. *The Demand and Price Structure for Corn and Total Feed Concentrates.* U.S. Department of Agriculture, Technical Bulletin no. 1061. Washington, D.C.: Government Printing Office, October 1965.

*Godfrey, M. D.; Granger, C. W. J.; and Morgenstern, O. "The Random Walk Hypothesis of Stock Market Behaviour." *Kyklos* 17 (1964): 1-30.

*Granger, C. W. J. "Some Aspects of the Random Walk Model of Stock Prices." *International Economic Review* 9 (1968): 283-287.

*Granger, C. W. J., and Morgenstern, O. *Predictability of Stock Market Prices.* Lexington, Mass.: D. C. Heath, 1970.

[a]Items marked with asterisks have been quoted in the present study.

*Granger, C. W. J., and Morgenstern, O. "Spectral Analysis of New York Stock Market Prices." *Kyklos* 16 (1963): 1-27.

Gray, Roger W. "Fundamental Price Behavior Characteristics in Commodity Futures." *Futures Trading Seminar,* II (Madison: Mimir Publishers, 1963).

Gray, Roger W. "The Search for a Risk Premium." *Journal of Political Economy* 69 (June 1961): 250-260.

Hawtrey, R. G. "A Symposium on the Theory of the Forward Market: III. Mr. Kaldor on the Forward Market." *Review of Economic Studies* 7 (June 1940): 196-205.

*Hicks, J. R. *Value and Capital.* 2d ed. Oxford: Clarendon Press, 1946, 135-142.

Hoos, Sidney, and Working, Holbrook. "Price Relations of Liverpool Wheat Futures with Special Reference to the December-March Spread." *Wheat Studies of the Food Research Institute* 16 (November 1940): 101-143.

Houck, James P. *Demand and Price Analysis of the U.S. Soybean Market.* Minnesota: Agricultural Experiment Station Bulletin no. 244, 1963.

Houck, James P. "The Relationship of Direct Price Flexibilities to Direct Price Elasticities." *Journal of Farm Economics* 46, (August 1964): 789-792.

*Houck, James P. "A Statistical Model of the Demand for Soybeans." *Journal of Farm Economics* 46 (May 1964): 366-374.

Houthakker, H. S. *Commodity Futures IV: An Empirical Test of the Theory of Normal Backwardation.* Cowles Commission Discussion Paper, Economics No. 2124, (22 June 1955).

Houthakker, H. S. "Restatement of the Theory of Normal Backwardation." *Cowles Foundation Discussion Paper,* No. 44 (18 December 1957).

*Houthakker, H. S. "Systematic and Random Elements in Short Term Price Movements." *Proceedings of the American Economic Association* 51 (May 1961): 164-172.

*Irwin, H. S. "Seasonal Cycles in Aggregates of Wheat Futures Contracts." *Journal of Political Economy* 43 (1935): 278-288.

Johnson, D. Gale. *Forward Prices for Agriculture.* Chicago: University of Chicago Press, 1947.

Kaldor, Nicholas. "A Note on the Theory of the Forward Market." *Review of Economic Studies* 7 (October 1939): 196-201.

Kaldor, Nicholas. "Speculation and Economic Stability." *Review of Economic Studies* 7 (October 1939): 1-27.

Kapur, G. P. "Prices and Production in Agriculture." *Indian Economic Journal* 11 (April-June 1964).

Kassouf, S. T. "Stock Price Random Walks: Some Supporting Evidence." *Review of Economic Statistics* (May, 1968).

*Kendall, M. G. "The Analyses of Economic Time Series Part I: Prices." *Journal of the Royal Statistical Society,* ser. A,96 (1953): 11-25.

King, G. A. *The Demand and Price Structure for By-Product Feeds.* U.S. Department of Agriculture, technical bulletin no. 1183. Washington, D.C.: Government Printing Office, August 1958.

Kogiku, K. C. "A Model of the Raw Materials Market." *International Economic Review* 8 (February 1967).

Labys, Walter C. *Commodity Price Fluctuations: A Short-Term Explanation for Selected Commodities on the American Market.* Ph.D. dissertation, University of Nottingham, 1968.

Labys, Walter C.; Rees, H. J. B.; and Elliott, C. M. "Copper Price Behaviour and the London Metal Exchange." Unpublished paper, University of Nottingham, 1968.

Langemeier, L.; and Thompson, R. G. "Study of Demand, Supply, and Price Relationships on the Beef Sector, Post World War II Period." *Journal of Farm Economics* 49 (February 1967): 169-183.

*Larson, Arnold. *Evidence on the Temporal Dispersion of Price Effects of New Market Information.* Ph.D. dissertation, Stanford University, 1960.

Larson, Arnold. "Measurement of a Random Process in Futures Prices." *Food Research Institute Studies* 1 (November 1960): 313-324.

Mandelbrot, B. "Forecasts of Future Prices, Unbiased Markets and 'Martingale' Models." *Journal of Business Security Prices* 39, Suppl. (January 1966): 242-255.

Mandelbrot, B. "The Variation of Certain Speculative Series." *Journal of Business* 36 (October 1963): 394-491.

**Margins, Speculation and Prices in Grains Futures Markets.* Economic Research Service, Washington, D.C.: U.S. Department of Agriculture, December 1967.

McCain, Wesley G. *Price Effects of Margin Changes in Commodity Futures Markets.* Ph.D. thesis, Stanford University, 1969.

Meinken, K. W. *The Demand and Price Structure for Wheat.* U.S. Department of Agriculture, Technical Bulletin no. 1136. Washington, D.C.: Government Printing Office, November 1955.

Meinken, K. W. et. al. "Measurement of Substitution in Demand for Time Series Data: Synthesis of Three Approaches." *Journal of Farm Economics* 38 (August 1956): 711-735.

*Mills, Frederick C. *Price-Quantity Interactions in Business Cycles.* National Bureau of Economic Research, Princeton: Princeton University Press, 1946.

Muth, J. F. "Rational Expectations and the Theory of Price Movements." *Econometrica* 29 (July 1961): 313-315.

Nerlove, Marc. "Adaptive Expectations and Cobweb Phenomena." *Quarterly Journal of Economics* 73 (May 1958): 227-240.

Nerlove, Marc. *Distributed Lags and Demand Analysis for Agricultural and Other Commodities.* U.S. Department of Agriculture, Agricultural Handbook no. 141. Washington, D.C.: U.S. Government Printing Office, 1958.

Nerlove, Marc. *The Dynamics of Supply: Estimation of Farmers' Response to Price.* Baltimore: Johns Hopkins Press, 1958.

Nerlove, Marc. "On the Nerlove Estimate of Supply Elasticity." *Journal of Farm Economics* 40 (August 1958): 723-728.

Nerlove, Marc. "Time Series Analysis of the Supply of Agricultural Proucts." In *Agricultural Supply Functions,* edited by Earl O. Heady et. al. Ames: Iowa State University Press, 1961.

Nerlove, Marc, and Addison, William. "Statistical Estimation of Long-Run Elasticities of Supply and Demand." *Journal of Farm Economics* 40 (November 1958): 861-880.

Peston, M. H., and Yamey, B. S. "Inter-Temporal Price Relationships with Forward Markets: A Method of Analysis." *Economica* n.s. 27 (November 1960): 355-367.

Philpott, R. P. *Fluctuations in Wool Prices,* 1870-1963. Agricultural Economics Research Unit, Publication no. 13. Lincoln College, University of Canterbury, New Zealand, 1965.

Rockwell, Charles S. "Normal Backwardation, Forecasting and the Returns to Commodity Futures Traders." *Food Research Institute Studies* 7, suppl. (1967): 107-130.

*Rockwell, Charles S. *Profits, Normal Backwardation, and Forecasting in Commodity Futures.* Ph.D. thesis, University of California at Berkeley, 1964.

Samuelson, Paul A. "Intertemporal Price Equilibrium: A Prologue to the Theory of Speculation." *Weltwirtschaftliches,* 79 (1957): 181-221.

*Samuelson, Paul A. "A Random Theory of Futures Prices." *Industrial Management Review* 6 (June, 1965).

*Schultz, H. *The Theory of Measurement of Demand.* Chicago: University of Chicago Press, 1938. Reprinted 1957.

*Shepherd, Geoffrey S. *Agricultural Price Analysis.* Ames: Iowa State University Press, 1966.

Smidt, Seymour. "A New Look at the Random Walk Hypothesis. *Journal of Financial and Quantitative Analysis* (September 1968).

*Smidt, Seymour. "A test of the Serial Independence of Price Changes in Soybean Futures." *Food Research Institute Studies* 5 (1965): 117-136.

Snape, R. H. "Price Relationships on the Sydney Wool Futures Market." *Economica* 35 (May 1968).

Stein, J. L. "The Simultaneous Determination of Spot and Futures Prices." *American Economic Review* 51 (December 1961): pp 1012-1025.

Telser, Lester G. "Futures Trading and the Storage of Cotton and Wheat." *Journal of Farm Economics* 40 (June 1958): 235-255. "Rejoinder" (August 1960): 404-415.

Telser, Lester G. "The Supply of Stocks: Cotton and Wheat." Ph.D. thesis, University of Chicago, 1956.

Thomsen, F. L., and Foote, R. J. *Agricultural Prices,* New York: McGraw-Hill, 1952.

**Trading in the September 1961 Rye Future on the Chicago Board of Trade.* Commodity Exchange Authority. Washington: U.S. Department of Agriculture, September 1961.

Turnovsky, Stephen J. "Stochastic Stability of Short-Run Market Equilibrium." *Quarterly Journal of Economics* 82 (November 1968): 666-681.

Vaile, Roland. "Cash and Futures Price of Corn." *Journal of Marketing* 9 (July 1944).

Vaile, Roland. "Inverse Carrying Charges in Futures Markets." *Journal of Farm Economics* 30 (August 1948): 574-575.

Vance, Lawrence. "Grain Market Forces in the Light of Inverse Carrying Charges." *Journal of Farm Economics* 28 (November 1946): 1036-1040.

*Vandenborre, Roger J. "Demand Analysis of the Markets for Soybean Oil Soybean Meal." *Journal of Farm Economics* 28 (November 1946): 920-934.

*Venkateramanan, L. S. *The Theory of Futures Trading.* London: Asia Publishing House, 1965.

*Waite, Warren C., and Trelogan, Harry C. *Agricultural Market Prices.* New York: Wiley, 1951.

*Weymar, F. Helmut. *The Dynamics of the World Cocoa Market.* Cambridge: MIT Press, 1968.

Weymar, F. Helmut. "The Supply of Storage Revisited." *American Economic Review* 56 (December 1966): 1226-1234.

Williamson, Oliver E., and Philips, Almorin. *Prices: Issues in Theory, Practice, and Public Policy.* Philadelphia: University of Pennsylvania Press, 1964.

*Witherall, W. H. *Dynamics of the International Wool Market: An Econometric Analysis.* Econometric Research Program Memorandum no. 91. Princeton: Princeton University Press, September 1967.

*Wold, H., and Jureen, L. *Demand Analysis: A Study in Econometrics.* New York: Wiley, 1953.

Working, Holbrook. "Cycles in Wheat Prices." *Wheat Studies of the Food Research Institute* 8 (November 1931).

*Working, Holbrook. "Futures Trading and Hedging." *American Economic Review* 43 (June 1953): 314-343.

Working, Holbrook. "Hedging Reconsidered." *Journal of Farm Economics* 35 (November 1953): 544-561.

Working, Holbrook. *Memorandum on Measurement of Cycles in Speculative Prices.* Food Research Institute, Stanford University, 1949.

*Working, Holbrook. "New Concepts Concerning Futures Markets and Prices." *American Economic Review* 52 (June 1962): 431-457.

*Working, Holbrook. "New Ideas and Methods for Price Research." *Journal of Farm Economics* 38 (December 1956): 1427-1436.

*Working, Holbrook. "Note on the Correlation of First Differences of Averages in a Random Chain." *Econometrica* 28 (October 1960): 916-918.

Working, Holbrook. "The Post Harvest Depression of Wheat Prices." *Wheat Studies of the Food Research Institute* 5 (November 1929).

Working, Holbrook. "Price Relations Between July and September Wheat Futures at Chicago since 1855." *Wheat Studies of the Food Research Institute* 9 (March 1933): 187-238.

Working, Holbrook. "Price Relations Between May and New Crop Wheat Futures at Chicago Since 1885. *Wheat Studies of the Food Research Institute* 10 (February 1934).

*Working, Holbrook. "Prices of Cash Wheat and Futures at Chicago since 1883." *Wheat Studies of the Food Research Institute* 10 (November 1934): 103-117.

Working, Holbrook. "Professor Vaile and the Theory of Inverse Carrying Charges." *Journal of Farm Economics* 31 (1949): 168-172.

*Working, Holbrook. "A Random Difference Series for Use in the Analysis of Time Series." *Journal of the American Statistical Association* 29 (1934): 11-24.

Working, Holbrook. "Tests of a Theory Concerning Floor Trading on Commodity Exchanges." *Food Research Institute Studies* 7 suppl. (1967): 5-38.

*Working, Holbrook. "A Theory of Anticipatory Prices." *American Economic Review* 48 (May 1958): 188-199.

*Working, Holbrook. "Theory of the Inverse Carrying Charge in Futures Markets." *Journal of Farm Economics,* 30 (February 1948): pp. 1-28.

Working, Holbrook. "The Theory of Price of Storage." *American Economic Review* 39 (December 1949): 1254-1262.

Working, Holbrook, and Hoos, Sidney. "Wheat Futures Prices and Trading at Liverpool since 1886." *Wheat Studies of the Food Research Institute* 15 (November 1938).

Price Forecasting

*Ashby, Andrew W. "On Forecasting Commodity Prices by the Balance Sheet Approach." *Journal of Farm Economics* 46 (August, 1964): 633-643.

*Bates, J., and Granger, C. W. J. "Combining Forecasts." *Operations Research Quarterly* 20 (1969): 451-467.

*Bernstein. L. A. "How Commodity Price Charts Disclose Supply-Demand Shifts." *Commodity Year Book* (1958): 33-42.

*Brown, Robert G. *Smoothing, Forecasting and Prediction of Discrete Time Series.* Englewood Cliffs: Prentice-Hall, 1963.

Cooper, Ronald L., Jorgenson, Dale W., *The Predictive Performance of Quarterly Econometric Models of the United States,* Institute of Business and Economic Research Working Paper, No. 113 Berkeley: University of California, Revised 1970.

*Donchian, Richard P. "Trend Following Methods in Commodity Price Analysis." In *Guide to Commodity Price Forecasting,* edited by H. Jiler, pp. 48-60. New York: Commodity Research Bureau, 1965.

Food and Agricultural Organization of the U.N. *Agricultural Commodities: Projections for 1975 and 1985,* I, Rome. (CCP67/3 *Rev.*), 1966.

Gordon, T. J., and Helmer, Olaf. "Report on a Long-Range Forecasting Study." RAND Corporation Report P-2982, Santa Monica, California, September, 1964.

Gruen, F. H. et. al. *Long-Term Projections of Agricultural Supply and*

Demand: Australia 1965 to 1980. Department of Economics, Monash University, Victoria, 1967.

*Hieronymus, T. A. "Forecasting Soybean and Soybean Product Prices." *In Guide to Commodity Price Forecasting,* edited by H. Jiler. New York: Commodity Research Bureau, 1965.

Hingorani, G. G. "Forecasting Economic Time Series Generated by Random Processes." *Proceedings* of the Business and Economic Statistics Section of the Annual Meetings of the American Statistical Association, 1966.

*Houthakker, H. S. "Can Speculators Forecast Prices?" *Review of Economics and Statistics* 39 (1957): 143-151.

*Jarrett, F. G. "Short Term Forecasting of Australian Wool Prices." *Australian Economic Papers* 4 (June-December 1965): 93-102.

*Jiler, H., ed. *Guide to Commodity Price Forecasting.* New York: Commodity Research Bureau, 1965.

*Jorgenson, D. I., Hunter J., and Nadiri, M. I. "The Predictive Performance of Economic Models of Quarterly Investment Behavior," *Econometrica* 38 (1970), pp. 213-224.

Larson, Arnold B. "Price Prediction on the Egg Futures Market." *Food Research Institute Studies* 7 suppl. (1967): 49-64.

Parkany, John. "Price Forecasting of Wood Products." Speech presented to the National Industrial Conference Board, 17 October 1968.

*Reid, David J. *A Comparative Study of Time-Series Prediction Techniques onEconomic Data.* Ph.D. dissertation, University of Nottingham, 1969.

*Seminar on Time Series Analysis. *Statistician* 17 (1967): 233-305.

*Shisko, Irwin. "Forecasting Sugar Prices." In *Guide to Commodity Price Forecasting,* edited by H. Jiler. New York: Commodity Research Bureau, 1965.

*Shisko, Irwin. "Techniques of Forecasting Commodity Prices." *Commodity Year Book* 7 (1965): 30-36.

*Theil, H. *Economic Forecasts and Policy.* Amsterdam: North-Holland Publishing, 1965.

Winters, P. R. "Forecasting Sales by Exponentially Weighted Moving Averages." *In Mathematical Models and Methods of Marketing,* edited by F.M. Bass et al. Homewood, Ill.: Irwin, 1961.

Zarnowitz, Victor. *An Appraisal of Short-Term Economic Forecasts.* National Bureau of Economic Research Occasional Paper 104. 1967.

Price Effects of Speculation

Aliber, Robert Z. "Speculation and Price Stability Once Again." *Journal of Political Economy* 72 (1964): 607-609.

Baumol, W. J. "Speculation, Profitability and Stability." *Review of Economics and Statistics,* 39 (August, 1957): 263-271.

Commodity Exchange Authority. *Speculation in Onion Futures, January-March 1957.* U.S. Department of Agriculture, Washington, D.C.: U.S. Government Printing Office, March 1957.

*Commodity Exchange Authority. *Trading in the September 1961 Rye Future on the Chicago Board of Trade.* Washington: U.S. Department of Agriculture, 20 September 1961.

*Cootner, Paul H. "Returns to Speculators: Telser versus Keynes." *Journal of Political Economy* 68 (August 1960): 397-418; reply by L. G. Telser, *ibid.*, pp. 404-415; rejoinder by P. H. Cootner, *ibid.*, pp. 415-418.

*Cootner, Paul H. "Speculation and Hedging." *Food Research Institute Studies* 7, suppl. (1967): 65-106.

Cootner, Paul H. "Speculation and the Stability of Futures Markets." Unpublished paper delivered at Summer Meeting of the Econometric Society, 1960.

*Economic Research Service. *Margins, Speculation and Prices in Grain Futures Markets.* Special Report. Washington: United States Department of Agriculture, December 1967.

Friedman, Milton. "In Defense of Destabilizing Speculation." In *Essays in Economics and Econometrics,* edited by R. W. Prouts. Chapel Hill: University of North Carolina Press, 1960.

Graf, T. F. "Hedging – How Effective Is It?" *Journal of Farm Economics* 35 (August 1953): 398-413.

Gray, Roger W. "The Attack upon Potato Futures Trading in the United States." *Food Research Institute Studies* 4 (1964): 97-121.

Gray, Roger W. "The Characteristic Bias on Some Thin Futures Markets." *Food Research Institute Studies* 1 (November 1960): 296-312 .

Gray, Roger W. "The Importance of Hedging in Futures Trading; and the Effectiveness of Futures Trading for Hedging." *Futures Trading Seminar, I,* Madison, Wis.: 1960.

Gray, Roger W. "Price Effects of a Lack of Speculation." *Food Research Institute Studies* 7, suppl. (1967): 177-193.

Gray, Roger W. "The Relationship Among Three Futures Markets: An Example of the Importance of Speculation." *Food Research Institute Studies* 2 (February 1961).

Houthakker, H. S. "Free and Stable Commodity Markets." Statement to the National Advisory Committee on Food and Fibre. September 1966.

Houthakker, H. S., and Telser, L. G. *Commodity Futures II: Gains and Losses of Hedgers and Futures Speculators.* Cowles Commission Discussion Paper: Economics no. 2090 (7 December 1952).

Howell, L. D. "Analysis of Hedging and Other Operations in Grain Futures." U.S. Department of Agriculture Technical Bulletin no. 971. Washington, D.C.: U.S. Government Printing Office, August 1948.

Howell, L. D. "Price Risks for Cotton and Cotton Products and Means of Reducing Them." U.S. Department of Agriculture Bulletin no. 1119. Washington, D.C.: U.S. Government Printing Office, July 1955.

Johnson, Leland L. "Price Instability, Hedging and Trade Volume in the Coffee Market." *Journal of Political Economy* 45 (August 1957).

Johnson, Leland L., "The Theory of Hedging and Speculation in Commodity Futures." *Review of Economic Studies* 27 (June 1960): 139-151.

Kemp, Murray C. "Speculation, Profitability and Price Stability." *Review of Economics and Statistics* 45 (May 1963). 185-189.

Larson, Arnold B. "Estimation of Hedging and Speculative Positions in Futures Markets." *Food Research Institute Studies 2* (November 1961):203-212.

Meade, J. "Degrees of Competitive Speculation." *Review of Economic Studies* 17 (1949-1950).

Snape, R. H., and Yamey, B. S. "Test of the Effectiveness of Hedging." *Journal of Political Economy* 73 (October, 1965): 540-544.

Stein, J. L. "Destabilizing Speculative Activity Can Be Profitable." *Review of Economics and Statistics* 43 (August 1961): 301-302.

Stewart, Blair. *An Analysis of Speculative Trading in Grain Futures.* U.S. Department of Agriculture Technical Bulletin no. 10001. Washington, D.C.: U.S. Government Printing Office, October 1949.

Telser, Lester G. "Safety First and Hedging." *Review of Economic Studies* 23 (1955-1956).

Telser, Lester G. "The Supply of Speculative Services in Wheat, Corn and Soybeans." *Food Research Institute Studies* 7, suppl. (1967): 131-176.

Telser, Lester G. "A Theory of Speculation Relating Profitability and Stability." *Review of Economic Studies* 41 (August 1959): 295-301.

Williams, J. B. "Speculation and the Carry Over." *Quarterly Journal of Economics* 51 (May 1936).

Working, Holbrook. "Financial Results of Speculative Holdings in Wheat." *Wheat Studies of the Food Research Institute* 7 (July 1931).

Working, Holbrook. "Futures Markets Under Renewed Attack." *Food Research Institute Studies* 5 (February 1963): 13-24.

Working, Holbrook. "Price Effects of Futures Trading." *Food Research Institute Studies* 1 (February 1960): pp. 3-31.

Working, Holbrook. "Price Effects of Scalping and Day Trading." *Proceedings of the Seventh Annual Symposium: Commodity Markets and the Public Interest.* Chicago, 1954.

*Working, Holbrook. "Speculation on Hedging Markets." *Food Research Institute Studies* 1 (May 1960): 185-220.

Working, Holbrook. "Whose Markets? Evidence on Some Aspects of Futures Trading." *Journal of Marketing* 19 (July 1954).

Yamey, Basil S. "An Investigation of Hedging on an Organized Produce Exchange." *The Manchester School* 19 (September 1951).

Yamey, Basil S. "Speculation and Price Stability: A Note." Aliber, Robert Z. "Speculation and Price Stability: A Reply." *Journal of Political Economy* 74 (April 1966): 206-208.

Futures Trading

Anderson, Matthew A. *Fundamentals and Technicalities of Commodity Futures Trading.* New York: Hutton, 1949.

*Baer, Julius B., and Saxon, Olin G. *Commodity Exchanges and Futures Trading.* New York: Harper & Brothers, 1949.

Belveal, L. Dee. *Commodity Speculation: With Profits in Mind.* Wilmette, Ill.: Commodities Press, 1967.

Blau, Gerda. "Some Aspects of the Theory of Futures Trading." *Review of Economic Studies* 12 (1944).

Campbell, Donald A. "Trading in Futures Under the Commodity Exchange Act." Symposium on the Regulatory Functions of the Department of Agriculture. *The George Washington Law Review* 26 (January 1958).

Dow. J. C. R. "A Theoretical Account of Futures Markets." *Review of Economic Studies* 7 (1939-1940): 185-195.

Gardner, Robert L. *How to Make Money on the Commodity Market,* Englewood Cliffs, N.J.: Prentice-Hall, 1962.

Gaumnitz, Edwin A., ed. *A Commodity Marketing Forum for College Teachers of Economics.* Madison: Mimir Publishers, 1966.

Glick, Ira O. *A Social Psychological Study of Futures Trading.* Ph.D. dissertation, University of Chicago, 1957.

*Gold, Gerald. *Modern Commodity Futures Trading.* New York: Commodity Research Bureau, 1966.

*Hieronymus, T. A. *Uses of Grain Futures Markets in the Farm Business.* Agricultural Experiment Station Bulletin 696. Urbana: University of Illinois, 1963.

Hoffman, G. W. "Past and Present Theory Regarding Futures Trading." *Journal of Farm Economics* 19 (February 1937): 300-308.

*Houthakker, H. "The Scope and Limits of Futures Trading." In *Allocation of Economic Resources: Essays in Honor of B. F. Haley,* edited by M. Abromovitz. Stanford: Stanford University Press, 1959.

**How to Buy and Sell Commodities.* A Booklet Published by Merrill Lynch, Pierce, Fenner and Smith, New York, 1970.

Irwin, Harold S. "Legal Status of Trading in Futures." *Illinois Law Review of Northeastern University* 32 (1937-1938).

Johnson, Leland L. *Hedging, Speculation and Futures Trading in the Coffee Market since World War II.* Ph.D. dissertation, Yale University, 1957.

Kambibayash, M. "Differences Between Security Exchange and Commodity Exchange." *Kokumin-Keizai Zasski* (November 1968), pp. 18-34.

Lermer, G. "Futures Market and Farm Programs." *Canadian Journal of Agricultural Economics* (June 1968).

The Market Place. A Booklet Published by the Department of Public Information and Education, Chicago Board of Trade.

Miller, Norman C. *The Great Salad Oil Swindle.* New York: Coward-McCann, 1965.

Phillips, J. "The Theory and Practice of Futures Trading." *Review of Marketing and Agricultural Economics* (June 1966).

Powers, Mark James. *An Economic Analysis of the Futures Market for Pork Bellies.* Ph.D. dissertation, University of Wisconsin, 1966.

Seligman, Daniel. "The Mystique of Point and Figure." *Fortune,* March 1962.

Stewart, Blair, *Trading in Wool Top Futures.* U.S. Department of Agriculture Circular no. 604. Washington, D.C.: U.S. Government Printing Office, August 1941.

*Teweles, R. J.; Harlow, C.V.; and Stone, H. L. *The Commodity Futures Trading Guide,* New York: McGraw-Hill, 1969.

U.S. Department of Agriculture. Commodity Exchange Authority, Comptroller General of the United States. *Need to Strengthen Regulartory Practices and Study Certain Trading Activities Related to Commodity Futures Markets.* Report to the Congress of the United States, July 1955.

Expectations

*Cootner, Paul H. "Common Elements in Futures Markets for Commodities and Bonds." *Proceedings of the American Economic Association* 51 (May 1961): 173-183.

Dow, J. C. R. "The Inaccuracy of Expectations." *Economica* 8 (May 1941).

Fishman, G. S. "Price Behavior Under Alternative Forms of Price Expectations." *Quarterly Journal of Economics* 78 (May 1964): 281-298.

*Granger, C. W. J., and Rees, H. J. B. "Spectral Analysis of the Term Structure of Interest Rates." *Review of Economic Studies* 25 (January 1968).

*Malkiel, Burton G. "Expectations, Bond Prices, and the Term Structure of Interest Rates." *Quarterly Journal of Economics* 76 (1962): 197-218.

Meiselman, David. *The Term Structure of Interest Rates.* Englewood Cliffs, N.J.: Prentice Hall, 1962.

Mills, E.S. *Price Output and Inventory Policy.* New York: Wiley, 1962.

Mills, E.S. "The Use of Adaptive Expectations in Stability Analysis"; and Nerlove, M. "The Use of Adaptive Expectations in Stability Analysis – Reply." *Quarterly Journal of Economics* 75 (May 1961): 330-338.

Muth, J. F. "Rational Expectations and the Theory of Price Movements." *Econometrica* 29 (July 1961): 315-335.

*Samuelson, Paul A. "Proof that Properly Anticipated Prices Fluctuate Randomly." *Industrial Management Review* 6 (Spring 1965): 41-49.

Sargent, Thomas J. "Commodity Price Expectations and the Interest Rate." *Quarterly Journal of Economics* 83 (February 1969): 126-140.

Schultz, Theodore W. "Spot and Futures Prices as Production Guides." *American Economic Review* 39 (May 1949).

Tobin, J. "Liquidity Preference as Behavior Toward Risk." *Review of Economic Studies* 25 (February 1948).

Working, Holbrook. "The Investigation of Economic Expectations."

Proceedings of the American Economic Association AER/S (May 1949).

*Working, Holbrook. "Quotations on Commodity Futures as Price Forecasts." *Econometrica* 10 (1942): 30-52.

Price Agreements

Abbot, J. C. "Marketing Institutions and Agricultural Prices as Factors Influencing Agricultural Development." In *Agriculture in Economic Development,* edited by Bruce F. Johnston and Herman Southworth. Ithaca: Cornell University Press, 1966.

Bennett, Merrill K., et al. *International Commodity Stockpiling as an Economic Stabilizer.* Stanford: Stanford University Press, 1949.

Blau, Gerda. *International Commodity Arrangements and Policies.* Commodity Policy Studies no. 16. Rome: Food and Agricultural Organization of the UN, 1964.

Brodie, Henry. *Commodity Agreements: A Partial Answer to the Problems of Developing Countries.* (Reprinted from Department of State Bulletin of 19 July 1965). Washington, D.C.: Department of State, 1965.

Cohen, B. I. "The Less Developed Countries' Exports of Primary Products." *Economic Journal* 14 (June 1968).

*Cole, Lord, and Tempel, F. J., "Raw Materials and Pricing." Paper delivered at the Annual General Meeting of Unilever, 27 April 1966. London: Unilever Ltd., 1966.

Coppock, Joseph D. *International Economic Instability.* New York: McGraw-Hill, (1962).

Davidson, Thomas L., ed. *The Problem of Free Markets and the Role of the Commodity Exchanges in the American Economy.* New York: Educational Committee of the New York Commodity Exchange.

Dulay, H. "On the Variance Effects of a Buffer-Stock Scheme: A Simulation Study of a Floor Price Plan for Wood." 4 *Australian Economic Papers* (June-December 1965): 79-92.

Erb, Guy F., and Schiavo-Camp, S. "Export Instability, Level of Development and Economic Size of Less Developed Countries." *Bulletin of the Oxford University Institute of Economics and Statistics* 31 (November 1969): 263-284.

Haviland, William E. *International Commodity Agreements.* Sponsored by the Canada Trade Committee. Montreal: Private Planning Association of Canada, 1963.

Hincle, Charles L. "The Strategy of Price Deals," Reprinted from Harvard Business Review, *Baylor (Texas) Business Studies, No. 65.*

International Monetary Fund, *The Problem of Stabilization of Prices of Primary Products.* A joint IMF-IBRB staff study. Washington: International Monetary Fund, 1968.

Kravis, Irving B. "International Commodity Agreements to Promote Aid and Efficiency: The Cost of Coffee." *Canadian Journal of Economics* 1 (May 1968).

Lamartine Yates, Paul. *Commodity Control.* London: J. Cape, 1943.

Law, Alton Dennis. *Aspects of the Theory and Practices of International*

Commodity Agreements. Ph.D. dissertation, Rutgers University, 1968.

McBean, Alasdair I. *Export Instability and Economic Development.* Cambridge: Harvard University Press, 1966.

McKinnon, Ronald I. "Futures Markets, Buffer Stocks, and Income Stability for Primary Producers." *Journal of Political Economy* 75 (December 1967): 844-861.

Maizels, Alfred. *Exports and Economic Growth of Developing Countries.* Cambridge: University Press, 1968.

Meade, James. "International Commodity Agreements." *Lloyds Bank Review* (July 1964).

Mellor, John W. *The Economics of Agricultural Development.* Ithaca: Cornell University Press, 1966.

Mund, Vernon A. *Open Markets: An Essential of Free Enterprise.* New York: Harper & Brothers, 1948.

Natu, W. R. *Regulation of Forward Markets.* Bombay: Asia Publishing House, 1962.

Pincus, John A. *International Commodity Agreements: Bonanza or Illusion?* Rand corporation Report P-3457. Santa Monica, California, 1966.

Smith, John G. *International Trade and Economic Development: A Study of Alternative Stabilization Procedures with Particular Reference to Compensatory Finance.* Ph.D. dissertation, Ohio State University, 1965.

Stalder, Andrew. *Some Aspects of International and National Primary Product Stabilization Schemes.* Paper submitted to Columbia University and Foreign Service Institute. Washington, D.C.: Department of State, 1960.

Swerling, Boris C. *Current Issues in Commodity Policy.* Essays in International Finance no. 38. Princeton University Department of Economics and Sociology. 1962.

*United Nations Conference on Trade and Development, Secretariat. *Commodity Problems and Policies: The Development of an International Commodity Policy* TD/8 Geneva: United Nations, 1967.

Individual Commodity Studies

Al-Zand, Osaka. *Olive Oil Trade and Trade Policies in the Mediterranean Region.* Ph.D. dissertation, University of Minnesota, 1969.

Andreas, D. "Commodity Markets and the Processor." *Proceedings, Eighth Annual Symposium.* Chicago: Board of Trade, 1955.

Bakken, Henry H. *Theory of Markets and Marketing.* Madison: Mimir Publishers, 1953.

Barker, R. "The Response of Production to a Change in Rice Price." *Philippine Economic Journal* (1966): 512.

Blau, Gerda. "Wool in the World Economy." *Journal of the Royal Statistical Society* 109 (1946): 179-235.

Brands, Simons. "The Decline in the Cotton Futures Market." *Food Research Institute Studies* 4 (1964).

Britton, Denis K. *Cereals in the United Kingdom.* A Report prepared for the

Home-Grown Cereals Authority. Oxford: Pergamum Press, 1969.

Brown, M. S., and Butler, J. *The Production, Marketing and Consumption of Copper and Aluminum.* London: Economist Intelligence Unit, Ltd., 1968.

Desai, Meghnad. *An Econometric Model of the World Tin Economy, 1948-1961.* Ph.D. dissertation, University of Pennsylvania, 1963.

Dholakia, H. L. *Futures Trading and Futures Market in Cotton with Special References to India.* Bombay: New Book Co., 1949.

Dominick, Jr., B. A., and Williams, F. W. *Futures Trading and the Florida Orange Industry.* Agricultural Economics Mimeo Report EC66-6. Florida Agricultural Experiment Stations, December 1965.

Drake, A. F., and West, V. I. "Econometric Analysis of the Edible Fats and Oils Economy." Agricultural Experiment Station Bulletin 695. Urbana: University of Illinois, 1963.

Ehrich, Rollo L. "The Impact of Government Programs on Wheat-Futures Markets, 1953-63." *Food Research Institute Studies* 6 (1966): 313-338.

Ertek, Tumay. *World Demand for Copper, 1948-1963: An Econometric Study.* Ph.D. dissertation, University of Wisconsin, 1967.

FAO Cocoa Study Group. *The Cocoa Situation: Recent Developments and the Outlook for Production and Demand.* Rome: UN Food and Agricultural Organization, 1961.

*Gray, Roger W. "The Seasonal Pattern in Wheat Futures Prices under the Loan Program." *Food Research Institute Studies* 3 (February 1962): 23-24.

Herfindahl, Orris C. *Copper Costs and Prices.* A Resources for the Future Study. Baltimore: Johns Hopkins Press, 1959.

Hoffman, G. W., and Duvel, J. W. T. *Grain Prices and the Futures Market: A 15 Year Survey, 1923-38.* U.S. Department of Agriculture Technical Bulletin no. 747. Washington, D.C.: U.S. Government Printing Office, January 1941.

Houck, J. P., and Mann, J. S. *Domestic and Foreign Demand for U.S. Soybeans and Soybean Products.* Agricultural Experiment Station, Technical Bulletin 256, Minneapolis: University of Minnesota, 1968.

Hunt, Hamilton, "What A Citrus Futures Market Might Mean to Citrus Growers." *The Citrus Industry* 44 (October 1965).

Isard, Walter. "Regional Commodity Balances and Inter-regional Commodity Flows." *American Economic Review* 43 (May 1953): 167-180.

Keynes, J.M. "Some Aspects of Commodity Markets." Manchester Guardian Commercial: European Reconstruction Series, Section 13, 29 March, 1923.

Kilby, Peter. "The Nigerian Palm Oil Industry." *Food Research Institute Studies* 7 (1967): 177-203.

La-Ayanne, Seth. *The Oil Palm Industry of Western Tropical Africa.* Ph. D. dissertation, Stanford University, 1969.

Lele, V. J. "Market Integration: A Study of Sorghum Prices in Western India." *Journal of Farm Economics* 49 (February 1967): 147-159.

McCalla, A. F. "Pricing in the World Feed Grain Market." *Agricultural Economic Research* 19 (October 1967).

Recto, Aida, V.W. Ruttan and M. Mangahas. "Price and Market Relationships for Rice and Corn in the Philippines." *Journal of Farm Economics* 48 (August 1966): 685-695.

Marsh, A. R. "The Relation of Futures Contracts on the Cotton Exchanges to the American Cotton Industry." In *Readings in Risk and Risk-Bearing,* edited by C. O. Hardy. Chicago: 1923.

Merrill, W. C. "Setting the Price of Peruvian Rice." *Journal of Farm Economics* 49 (May 1967): 389-402.

Mubyarto, S. *The Elasticity of the Marketable Surplus of Rice in Indonesia: A Study in Java-Modura.* Ph.D. dissertation, Iowa State University of Science and Technology, 1965.

Murti, Vedula N. *An Econometric Study of the World Tea Economy.* Ph.D. dissertation, University of Pennsylvania, 1966.

Nyberg, Albert John. *The Philippine Coconut Industry.* Ph.D. dissertation, Cornell University, 1968.

Paarlberg. Donald. *Prices of Soybeans and Soybean Products.* Agricultural Experimental Station Bulletin 538. Lafayette, Ind.; Purdue University, September 1949.

Pulino, Leonardo A. *A Recursive Model of the U.S. Domestic Soybean Market.* Ph.D. dissertation, Michigan State University, 1966.

Rourke, Blair E. *Causes and Predictability of Annual Changes in Supplies and Prices of Coffee.* Ph.D. dissertation, Stanford University 1969.

Rogers, G. B. "The Egg Pricing Problem." U.S. Department of Agriculture Agricultural Marketing Service. Washington, D.C.: U.S. Government Printing Office, 1961 (mimeographed).

*Rowe, J. W. F. *Primary Commodities in International Trade.* Cambridge: University Press ,1965.

Sharma, Vidya Vinod. *An Econometric Analysis of the Indian Oilseeds Economy and International Trade in Fats and Oils.* Ph.D. dissertation, University of Illinois, 1968.

Wesson, William T. *The Economic Importance of Futures Trading in Potatoes.* A.M.S. Marketing Research Report no. 241, U.S. Department of Agriculture. Washington, D.C.: U.S. Government Printing Office, June 1958.

Wesson, William T. *Possibilities for Futures Trading in Florida Citrus Fruit and Products.* A.M.S. Marketing Research Report no. 156, U.S. Department of Agriculture. Washington, D.C.: U.S. Government Printing Office, February 1957.

Williams, F. W. *Futures Trading: An Industry Decision.* Unpublished paper, Florida Agricultural Experiment Stations. Gainsville: University of Florida.

Unacek, Edward, Jr. *An Econometric Analysis and Forecasting Model for Pork Bellies.* Ph.D. dissertation, Texas A. and M., 1967.

Market History

Cowing, Cedric B. *Populists, Plungers and Progressives: A Social History of Stock and Commodity Speculation, 1860-1936.* Princeton: Princeton University Press, 1965.

Irwin, Harold Speer. *Evolution of Futures Trading.* Madison: Mimir Publishers, 1954.

*Lewis, W. Arthur. *Economic Survey 1919-1939.* London: George Allen and Unwin, 1963.

*Pine, L. G. "London: A Commercial History Since the Roman Occupation." Supplement to *The Public Ledger.* London, 12 January 1960.

*Postan, M. M.; Rich, E. E.; and Millar, E., eds. *The Economic History of Europe.* vol. 3: *Economic Organization and Policy in the Middle Ages.* Cambridge: University Press, 1963.

*Reynolds, Robert L. *Europe Emerges.* Madison: University of Wisconsin Press, 1961.

Taylor, C. H. *History of the Board of Trade of the City of Chicago.* Chicago: Board of Trade, 1917.

Time Series Methods

Adleman, Irma. "Long Cycles – Fact or Artifact?" *American Economic Review* 55 (June 1965). 444-463.

*Anscombe, F. J. "Topics in the Investigation of Linear Relations Fitted by the Method of Least Squares." *Journal of the Royal Statistical Society,* ser. B, vol. 29 (1967), pp. 1-52.

Bendat, Julius S., and Piersol, Allan G. *Measurement and Analysis of Random Data.* New York: Wiley, 1966.

Bendat, Julius S., and Piersol, Allan G. *Principles and Applications of Random Noise Theory.* New York: Wiley, 1968.

Blackman, R. B., and Tukey, J. W. *The Measurement of Power Spectra.* New York: Dover Publications, 1958.

*Box, G. E., and Jenkins, G. M. "Some Statistical Aspects of Adaptive Optimization and Control." *Journal of the Royal Statistical Society,* ser. B, vol. 24 (1962).

Cox, D. R., and Miller, H. D. *The Theory of Stochastic Processes.* London: Methuen, 1965.

Cunnyngham, Jon. *The Spectral Analysis of Economic Time Series.* Bureau of the Census Working Paper no. 14. Washington, D.C.: U.S. Department of Commerce, 1963.

Draper, N. R., and Smith, H. *Applied Regression Analysis.* New York: Wiley, 1966.

*Durbin, J., and Watson, G. "Testing for Serial Correlation in Least Squares Regression: Part II." *Biometrika* 38 (June 1951): 159-178.

Fishman, G. S. *Spectral Methods in Econometrics.* Cambridge: Harvard University Press, 1969.

*Fox, K. A. *Econometric Analysis and Public Policy.* Ames: Iowa State University Press, 1958.

*Granger, C. W. J. "The Typical Spectral Shape of an Economic Variable." *Econometrica* 34 (January 1966): 150-161.

*Granger, C. W. J., and Hatanaka, M. *Spectral Analysis of Economic Time Series.* Princeton: Princeton University Press, 1964.

*Granger, C. W. J., and Hughes, A. O. "Spectral Analysis of Short Series – a Simulation Study." *Journal of the Royal Statistical Society,* ser. A, vol. 131, pt. 1 (1968), pp. 83-99.

Hannan, E. J. *Time Series Analysis.* London: Methuen, 1960.

Harris, B., ed. *Spectral Analysis of Time Series.* New York: Wiley, 1967.

Hatanaka, M. "A Spectral Analysis of Business Cycle Indicators: Lead-Lag in Terms of All Time Points." Econometric Research Program, Princeton Research Memorandum no. 53. Princeton, 1963.

*Hughes, A. O. "A Study of the Distribution of Spectral Estimates." M.Sc. thesis, University of Nottingham, 1965.

*Jenkins, G. M., and Watts, D. G. *Spectral Analysis and Its Applications.* San Francisco: Holden Day, 1968.

*Johnston, J. *Econometric Methods.* New York: McGraw-Hill, 1963.

*Kendall, M. G., and Stuart, A. *The Advanced Theory of Statistics.* vol. 3: *Design and Analysis, and Time Series.* (London: Charles, Griffin, 1966), pp. 476-478.

*Nerlove, M. "Spectral Analysis of Seasonal Adjustment Procedures," *Econometrica* 32 (1964): 241-286.

Parzen, E. *Stochastic Processes.* San Francisco: Holden Day, 1962, p. 23.

*Parzen, E. *Time Series Analysis Papers.* San Francisco: Holden Day, 1968.

Rosenblatt, Murray, ed. *Proceedings of the Symposium on Time-Series Analysis.* New York: Wiley, 1963.

*Smillie, W. K. *An Introduction to Regression and Correlation.* New York: Academic Press, 1966.

Price and Related Data

Agricultural Marketing Administration. *Cotton Futures Statistics.* Washington: U.S. Department of Agriculture, 1936-1945.

Broomhall, George. "Corn Trade News." Liverpool: Northern Publishing, weekly issues 1955-1965.

*Bureau of Labor Statistics. *Daily Spot Market Price Indexes and Prices.* Washington: United States Department of Labor, weekly summary 62-65.

*Commodity Exchange Authority. *Commodity Futures Statistics.* Various yearly statistical bulletins covering the years 1947-1966. Washington: U.S. Department of Agriculture.

*Commodity Exchange Authority. *Grain Futures Statistics 1921-51.* Statistical Bulletin no. 131. Washington: U.S. Department of Agriculture, 1952.

Commodity Research Bureau. *Commodity Year Book.* New York: Commodity Research Bureau.

Consumer and Marketing Service. Cotton Division. *Cotton Price Statistics.* Washington: U.S. Department of Agriculture, volumes for various years.

*Consumer and Marketing Service. *Fats and Oils Situation.* Washington: U.S. Department of Agriculture.

*Consumer and Marketing Service. *Grain and Feeds Statistics.* Washington: U.S. Department of Agriculture.

Economic Research Service. *Statistics on Cotton and Related Data, 1925-62.* Statistical Bulletin 329. Washington: U.S. Department of Agriculture (also supplement to 1965).

*Fats and Oils Statistics, nos. 147 and 376. Washington, D.C.: U.S. Department of Agriculture.

*Gill and Duffus, Ltd. *Cocoa Market Report,* nos. 36-185. London: Howard, Jones, et. al. Ltd., 1950-1965.

Potter, Neal, and Christy, Jr., F. T. *Trends in Natural Resource Commodities.* A Resources for the Future Study. Baltimore: Johns Hopkins Press, 1962.

Index

Index

About the Authors

Walter C. Labys serves as a consultant in econometrics to the Commodities Division of the United Nations Conference on Trade and Development in Geneva. He also is a visiting lecturer at the Graduate Institute of International Studies, located in Geneva.

His present research interests include applying the results of this study to problems of econometric model-building and price stabilization in national and international markets. He is actively engaged with the lauric oils stabilization agreement being devised among countries of the Economic Commission for Asia and the Far East and the Asian Coconut Community. Other research and consulting activities have involved forecasting, gaming, growth, and urban economics including work with firms such as Unilever, New England Life, and Westinghouse as well as Abt Associates. He was a member of the Department of Economics at the University of Nottingham from 1966 through 1968.

Dr. Labys completed his Ph.D. in Economics at the University of Nottingham in 1968. A recipient of several academic awards, he earned an M.A. in Economics from the Graduate School of Arts and Sciences – Harvard University, an M.B.A. in Economics and Operations Research from Duquesne University, and a B.S. in Electrical Engineering from Carnegie-Mellon University. He is the author of several papers and a member of the American Economic Association. He was born in 1937 and is married with one child.

Clive W. J. Granger is Professor of Applied Statistics and Econometrics at the University of Nottingham, England. He obtained a First Class Honours Degree in Mathematics in 1955 and a Ph.D. on a statistical topic in 1959, both at Nottingham, where he has spent his whole career, apart from trips to the United States. He visited the Econometric Research Program at Princeton as a Commonwealth Fellow of the Harkness Fund for the session 1959-60 and revisited Princeton in the summers of 1961, 1962, 1963 and 1967. The research undertaken on the earlier visits resulted in the book *Spectral Analysis of Economic Time Series,* written with M. Hatanaka and published in 1964. He has also taught at Stanford University in 1963 and the University of California, San Diego in 1969-70.

His present research interests are in the fields of statistical forecasting, the attitudes of consumers to prices and the application of statistical techniques in economics, marketing, geography and psychology. He has published over 35 research articles, and is the joint author of three books, including *Predictability of Stock Market Prices* (with Oskar Morgenstern) published by Heath Lexington Books earlier this year.

Born 1934, he is married and has two children.